To Govern a Nation

Presidential Power and Politics

To Govern a Nation
Presidential Power and Politics

Byron W. Daynes
Brigham Young University

Raymond Tatalovich
Loyola University of Chicago

Dennis L. Soden
University of Texas, El Paso

St. Martin's Press   New York

Sponsoring editor: Beth A. Gillett
Associate editor: Jayme Heffler
Manager, Publishing services: Emily Berleth
Assistant editor, Publishing services: Meryl Gross
Project management: York Production Services
Cover design: Evelyn Horovicz
Cover art: Blake Hampton/Creative Freelancers Management, Inc.

Library of Congress Catalog Card Number: 97-65177

Manufactured in the United States of America.

3 2 1 0 9 8
f e d c b a

For information, write:
St. Martin's Press, Inc.
175 Fifth Avenue
New York, NY 10010

ISBN: 0-312-15413-5

Acknowledgments

Table 3-3: From Warren E. Miller, *Without Consent: Mass-Elite Linkages in Presidential Politics.* Copyright © 1988 by The University Press of Kentucky. Reprinted with the permission of the publisher.

Table 3-4: From Ronald B. Rapoport, Alan I. Abramowitz, and John McGlennon, eds., *The Life of the Parties: Activists in Presidential Politics.* Copyright © 1988 by The University Press of Kentucky. Reprinted with the permission of the publisher.

Acknowledgments and copyrights are continued at the back of the book on page 356, which constitutes an extension of the copyright page.

To Kathy from Bill
To Anne from Ray
To Jan from Dennis

Contents

Preface

The amount of literature on the American presidency can be staggering, particularly to the student of politics who is trying to understand how each individual president has helped to shape the office and contribute to the political system.[1] Although there are many ways to present the study of the presidency to students, we have found that by using presidential roles as an integrating framework, students can more easily understand the topics covered and relate them directly to presidential power. By examing these roles along with historical background, case studies, and the question of value, our hope is that students will come away from this course with a better understanding of the office of president.

ROLES MATTER

Political power is our concern as defined by presidential roles. Each of the five presidential roles we discuss—opinion/party leader, legislative leader, chief executive, chief diplomat, and commander in chief—varies in power and resources, regardless of who is president. We have analyzed presidential roles by focusing on five variables of presidential power. For example, whereas a president acting as commander in chief enjoys substantial legal authority to pursue his ends, this same authority appears meager when we examine the president as opinion/party leader. Our five variables (legal authority, decision-maker, public inputs, expertise, and crisis) inventory the major political and legal resources that political scientists usually cite when trying to account for the power potential of the modern president. They also allow students to make their own comparisons among the presidential roles, determining for themselves where the power is.

HISTORY MATTERS

Equally important, we feel, is a recognition of the strong historical foundation of the modern presidency. Few other books on the presidency

[1] NOTE TO THE READERS: Because all presidents up to the present have been men, the masculine pronoun is used throughout the book. In addition, references to the presidency and presidents in general also use the masculine pronoun. This usage in no way excludes the possibility or anticipation—as we acknowledge in chapter 1—that in the future women may well occupy this position.

give sustained coverage to any presidents other than the modern ones—
Franklin D. Roosevelt to Bill Clinton. These contemporary presidents
must remain a primary consideration, but we cannot ignore the fact that
great presidents of the past set important precedents for their successors,
and most contemporary presidents have been less significant political figures than George Washington, Thomas Jefferson, Woodrow Wilson, or
Abraham Lincoln. We must remember that history can and has repeated
itself in the Oval Office.

CASE STUDIES MATTER

For students of government and politics to fully understand what past
and contemporary presidents have contributed to the office, we offer multiple examples and substantial case studies (the Insight chapters) to illustrate the prospects and limits of presidential power. Students need a sense
of the evolution of this very important office and a mechanism to help them
make reasonable comparisons of the presidents' individual performances.

VALUES MATTER

It is essential for students to examine the overarching normative issue
of our time, namely whether the modern presidents have done too little to
nurture democratic governance and too much to enhance presidential
power. *To Govern a Nation: Presidential Power and Politics* thus addresses
both normative and empirical considerations, examines the contemporary
president in light of historical trends, and synthesizes the legal and political factors that underlie presidential power. Although the use of role analysis is not new to the literature, we hope this interpretation will stimulate
students seeking a general knowledge of the presidency and challenge
upper-level political science and/or history majors and graduate students.

We wish to thank the following people without whose help the book
would not have been published. First, the reviewers whose comments have
guided the project: Ryan J. Barilleaux, Miami University; John P. Burke,
University of Vermont; William Lammers, University of Southern California; William Leiter, California State University–Long Beach; Albert Nelson,
University of Wisconsin–LaCrosse; David Nice, University of Washington;
William Pederson, Louisiana State University, Shreveport; Brian J. Posler,
Millikin University; Daniel Shea, Lafayette College; Mary E. Stuckey, Uni-
versity of Mississippi; and Shirley Anne Warshaw, Gettysburg College.

Thanks to Tiffany Price, who first brought this manuscript to St. Mar-
tin's attention; the staff at St. Martin's, including sponsoring editor Beth
Gillett, assistant editor Jayme Heffler, manager of publishing services
Emily Berleth, and Susan Free of York Production Services.

About the Authors

Byron W. Daynes is professor of Political Science at Brigham Young University, Provo, Utah. Prior to his appointment at Brigham Young University, he taught at DePauw University (Greencastle, Indiana) for nineteen years and was department chair for nine of those years. His more than fifty articles and book reviews in the field of political science have appeared in *Congress & the Presidency, Political Communication, Women & Politics,* and *Presidential Studies Quarterly.* He is also coauthor and/or coeditor of four books, including *Social Regulatory Policy: Recent Moral Controversies in American Politics* (Westview, 1988), coedited with Raymond Tatalovich. Dr. Daynes holds B.S. and M.S. degrees from Brigham Young University and a Ph.D. from the University of Chicago. His areas of specialty include the American presidency as well as social policy politics.

Raymond Tatalovich received his Ph.D. from The University of Chicago, where he studied under Theodore J. Lowi. He is professor of Political Science at Loyola University of Chicago. His institutional area of specialization is the presidency and his policy focus is moral conflicts, notably the abortion controversy. Recently Professor Tatalovich coauthored *The Modern Presidency and Economic Policy* (Peacock, 1994). a comprehensive analysis of macroeconomic policymaking by the executive branch and the effects of economic conditions on presidential leadership. In addition he recently authored *Nativism Reborn? The Official English Movement and the American States* (Kentucky, 1995) and *The Politics of Abortion in the United States and Canada* (Sharpe, 1997).

Dennis L. Soden is Western Hemispheric Trade Professor of Policy Studies at the University of Texas at El Paso and directs the Public Policy Research Center there. He holds a doctorate in political science from Washington State University, a master's degree in international relations from the University of Southern California, and a bachelor's in Natural Resource Economics from the University of California at Riverside. Professor Soden is editor of a forthcoming book, *The Environmental Presidency,* and of *Global Environmental Policy and Administration.* His work has appeared in numerous journals, book chapters, and reports.

1

Presidential Roles, Power, and Policy

On January 20, 1993, William Jefferson Clinton was inaugurated as the forty-second president of the United States, and he will leave office as we enter the twenty-first century. Occupants of the White House span a period from the late eighteenth century, when the Constitution had just been established, to the present. Is it really possible to comprehend an office that has witnessed such tremendous political, economic, social, and technological changes? Are we reduced to simply studying each individual on his own terms, by reading the biographies or autobiographies of George Washington, our first president, and Abraham Lincoln, who saved the union, and Warren Harding, considered to be one president who failed, and John Kennedy, the first president to be assassinated since William McKinley?

To make this task manageable we could sample the presidents by their party affiliations, but there are more parties than you might suspect: Federalists, Jeffersonian Republicans, Whigs, Democrats, Republicans. Narrowing our analysis to only the "modern" presidents, those since Franklin D. Roosevelt, would yield an even smaller sample: only eleven men have served as president during the past six decades. Besides, looking at only the modern presidents would prevent us from understanding how the "great" presidents of the eighteenth and nineteenth centuries helped develop the office and powers that were inherited by Bill Clinton.

We need a historical perspective because George Washington and Abraham Lincoln were much more important to developing presidential power than most of the modern presidents. What criteria should guide this analysis of the presidency so that presidents, irrespective of party or time, can be appreciated solely in terms of their *contribution* to establishing the office and powers of the modern presidency?

PRESIDENTIAL ROLES

Our approach will be to study the presidential roles of those who have resided in the White House. Using roles to explain the scope of executive leadership was not uncommon in past studies of the presidency;[1]

scholars who used this approach treated roles as types of presidential responsibility so that the legislative leader role, for example, would refer to a president's responsibility for processing the executive's program through Congress. While there is no precise job description for the highest official in the land, the body politic has come to expect that presidents will seek to exert their leadership in certain policy areas. For this text, our working definition of a presidential role is *the set of expectations by political elites and the citizenry that define the scope of presidential responsibilities within a given policy area.*

What are the most important presidential roles? If you observed George Washington, Thomas Jefferson, Woodrow Wilson, or Dwight Eisenhower, or any other president, you would see that they devoted most of their leadership skills to these five presidential roles:

1. *Commander in Chief*—the only role named in Article II of the Constitution—is the nation's highest military leader.
2. *Chief Diplomat* is the role that allows presidents to define our nation's relationship to other countries.
3. The role of *Chief Executive* involves the complex and ongoing relations of the president with his staff, the federal bureaucracy, and domestic policymaking.
4. The role of *Legislative Leader* implies that the president has a policy relationship with Congress.
5. *Opinion/Party Leader* is a composite role suggesting that the president tries to build support among Americans for (a) the office of the president, (b) the incumbent, (c) the policies advocated by the president, and (d) the president's political party.

The above listing of these five presidential roles implies that the roles are not equally important. Surely a commander in chief who leads the nation into war is a more significant figure than a legislative leader who asks Congress to approve an annual budget. We suggest viewing the five presidential roles along a continuum based on their potential for presidential power:

COMMANDER - - - CHIEF - - - - - - - CHIEF - - - - - LEGISLATIVE - - - OPINION/PARTY
  IN CHIEF   DIPLOMAT   EXECUTIVE   LEADER   LEADER
   (most   (least
powerful)   powerful)

But what factors operate to make the commander in chief slightly more powerful than the chief diplomat but immensely more powerful than the opinion/party leader? Does this mean that the legislative leader is always a weaker role than the chief executive? Yes, we would say, because each presidential role is affected differently by five factors that influence presidential leadership and presidential power. To quickly grasp what those factors are, think about these five questions:

- How much *legal authority* is available to the president in this role?

- How many other *decision-makers* participate with the president in this role?

- Are *public inputs*—popular opinion and organized interests—deferential to presidential leadership or mobilized against him in this role?

- Can the president monopolize policy *expertise* and prevent outsiders from getting access to that information in this role?

- What is the likelihood that *crisis* will rally the nation around presidential leadership in this role?

ORGANIZING OUR ARGUMENT

Presidential roles are the heart of this book and we devote one chapter to the opinion/party leader (chapter 5), legislative leader (chapter 7), chief executive (chapter 9), chief diplomat (chapter 11), and commander in chief (chapter 13). Within each of these chapters we discuss how legal authority, decision-makers, public inputs, expertise, and crisis affect presidential leadership and presidential power. These chapters are highly descriptive so we need to explain how the five factors interact within each role. For that purpose a "case study" (or "Insight" chapter) comes after each of the chapters on presidential roles.

Chapter 6, Insight on Opinion/Party Leader: Clinton's Popularity and the Economy, describes how, despite a prosperous economy, President Clinton did not enjoy high popularity because forces beyond his control influenced how Americans viewed his leadership. Chapter 8, Insight on Legislative Leader: Clinton and Health Care Reform, explains why President Clinton was unable to keep his second most important campaign pledge of 1992, namely, to guarantee health care coverage for every American. Chapter 10, Insight on the Chief Executive: Clinton's "Don't Ask, Don't Tell" Policy on Gays in the Military, describes how the best presidential intentions are not enough to bring about the integration of homosexuals into the armed forces. Chapter 12, Insight on Chief Diplomat: Jimmy Carter and the Quest for Peace in the Middle East, tells us how and why President Carter was able to negotiate personally a lasting peace treaty between Egypt and Israel. Chapter 14, Insight on Commander in Chief: George Bush and the Persian Gulf War, explains how President Bush led allied forces in a successful 100-day war to force Iraq to withdraw its occupation of Kuwait. These Insights indicate whether legal authority, decision making, public inputs, expertise, and crisis work to strengthen or weaken presidential power and leadership. Now let us turn to explaining what each factor means.

LEGAL AUTHORITY

How much legal authority is available to the president in any role? We can define legal authority where specific powers have been granted to the president by (1) constitutional mandate, (2) statutory delegations by Congress, (3) rulings of the Supreme Court, and (4) the development of customs that became firmly entrenched practices of behavior. Some scholars look at laws affecting executive-legislative relationships[2] and how presidential power has been expanded or contracted by Supreme Court rulings.[3] Legal authority is "routinized" because specific powers can be passed from president to president unless, that is, the Congress rescinds its prior delegations of authority or the Supreme Court denies the president a power because of its reinterpretation of statutes or the Constitution.

A clue to the importance of legal authority can be sensed by the subtitle we chose for chapter 13 on the strongest presidential role—the commander in chief. The subtitle "Can the Constitutional Dictator Be Checked?" means that it is virtually impossible to stop a president who is determined to commit U.S. troops abroad. This lesson is confirmed by the Insight on the Persian Gulf War (chapter 14). President Bush asserted his constitutional authority under the commander in chief clause to send U.S. troops into Iraq early in 1991, but he also cited as legal justification resolutions approved by the United Nations that condemned the Iraqi invasion of Kuwait. Ultimately, the Congress yielded to President Bush by passing resolutions supporting his military intervention. When certain members of Congress appealed to the federal courts, the judiciary refused to get involved with this "political question" as to whether the president can commit armed forces despite Congress's "power" to declare war.

On the other hand, consider the subtitle to the chapter on the chief executive—"The Struggle against Congressional Government" (chapter 9). Its thesis is that Congress holds enough authority over the executive branch to challenge the president, and this story is told in the Insight on Clinton and gays in the military (chapter 10). Many observers made references to President Truman, who used an "executive order" to desegregate the armed forces, arguing that Clinton should have acted similarly to integrate gays into the military services. But Clinton chose to proceed slowly, which gave his opponents time to mobilize their forces.

Had Clinton issued an executive order, Congress could have—and probably would have—reversed the order by passing a law to reinstate the ban on homosexuals. The Constitution delegates to Congress the authority to raise a standing army and to formulate regulations for the armed forces. Senator Sam Nunn (D–Ga.), then chairman of the Armed Services Committee, argued that military personnel policy was under the jurisdiction of Congress, not the president. Nunn opposed Clinton, and members of the Senate likely would have backed him in any confrontation with the president. In the end Clinton capitulated to Nunn, to the distress of his gay supporters. This Insight illustrates that there was a legitimate disagreement between President Clinton and a key senator over which branch had final authority over military personnel.

DECISION-MAKERS

No president can act alone in discharging his responsibilities, so he must be able to order or persuade other decision-makers to follow his lead. If others balk at his leadership, the president is not likely to achieve his policy objectives. Presidential leadership is strengthened when there are relatively few decision-makers involved, but the array of decision-makers who participate varies according to each presidential role.[4] We conceptualize this factor as a series of concentric rings moving outward from the president in the center (Figure 1–1). The types of decision-makers change as we proceed along our continuum from the commander in chief role to the opinion/party leader role.

Figure 1-1. Decision-Makers in Each Presidential Role

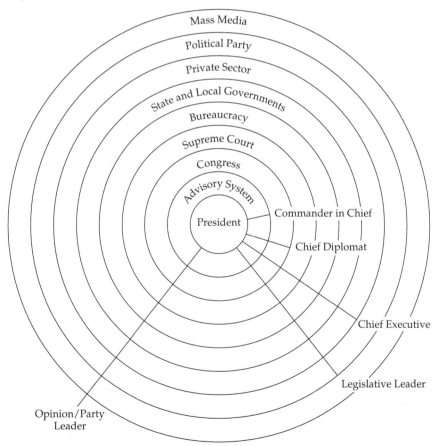

In war-making, history informs us that only the commander in chief and his closest advisors are relevant decision-makers, and not Congress, because Congress has "declared" only five wars whereas presidents have waged "undeclared" wars more than 250 times. As chief diplomat, the president consults with his advisors but must also contend with the Congress, since the Senate "ratifies" treaties, and policies like foreign aid must be approved by both houses of Congress. One reason the chief executive role is weaker is that other decision-makers participate in policymaking in addition to the president, his advisors, and Congress: the Supreme Court, the bureaucracy (which issues rules), state and local government officials, and private sector contractors (who build highways, for example).

These same decision-makers may participate in the role of legislative leader, but now an important new one is added: political parties. The congressional parties are very influential in shaping legislation, and presidential success in Congress is linked to the size of his party's majority in the House and Senate. Finally, in the opinion/party leader role every decision-maker thus far named can be a participant, since any or all of them may try to influence public opinion as to whether the president is worthy of our support.

But there is one additional type of decision-maker that many presidents come to view as an adversary—the mass media, which both transmits and interprets White House news stories for public consumption. To appreciate the positive and negative impact of the mass media on presidential leadership, juxtapose our Insight on Carter's Middle East Peace Accord (chapter 12) with the Insight on Clinton's popularity and the economy (chapter 6).

The Middle East Peace Accord was a diplomatic success that is directly attributed to Jimmy Carter. While Secretary of State Cyrus Vance made some preparatory diplomatic forays, the Congress played no role. These delicate negotiations were kept secret, and "leaks" to the press were minimized, so the American people got news reports only when public pronouncements were issued by the principals involved. Only afterward did we learn that President Carter committed billions of dollars in U.S. aid to both nations as a further inducement for them to come to an agreement. When the breakthrough in negotiations yielded a peace treaty, President Carter was received as a hero by a press that heretofore had characterized him as inept. This achievement was arguably the high point of Carter's years in office.

A different media impact is shown in chapter 6, the Insight on Clinton's popularity and the economy. His historically low approval ratings during 1993 brings into question whether decision-makers outside the White House undercut Clinton's ability to take advantage of the economic revival. The answer is Yes, because the economy was deemphasized by the media at a time when the public was subjected to an unending barrage of public criticism about the managerial missteps and blunders of the Clinton administration. Clinton withdrew two nominations for attorney general after newspapers reported that both hired illegal immigrants as domestic help. His choice of a militant civil rights advocate for another Justice Department position was labeled a "quota queen" by conservatives in Congress because she advocated racial preferences. It was highly publicized when Clinton backed away from his campaign promise to allow homosexuals in the military. Senate Republicans, who blocked his economic program, won the propaganda war with their pronouncements that wasteful spending and rising deficits would result. In domestic affairs, news reports hammered away at Clinton as being indecisive and unprincipled. In foreign affairs, friction between the Clinton administration and our European allies with regard to the Bosnian civil war became front-page news, as journalists berated Clinton's advisors, notably the secretary of state, as lacking foresight. With all this adverse publicity reported daily on the evening news and in newspaper headlines, the mass media produced news at the expense of Bill Clinton's popularity.

PUBLIC INPUTS

Democracy inherently means that public opinion and organized interests must be allowed to influence the governing process. For presidential leadership, what is relevant is (1) whether public opinion or interest groups are politically mobilized or politically passive and (2) if mobilized, whether they support or oppose the president. The president gains political leverage when the populace is behind his efforts but is disadvantaged when public opinion and/or organized interests are arrayed against him. Consider the very different consequences of such "public inputs" with respect to the Insight on Clinton's attempt to integrate homosexuals into the military forces (chapter 10) as well as the Insight on Clinton's popularity and the economy (chapter 6).

In dealing with the gays in the military issue, public opinion, as such, was probably less relevant than were organized interests, notably veterans' groups. Indeed, opinion polls showed that Americans were split on the issue, although the public seemed more supportive of nondiscrimination against gays in the workplace. When veterans were polled, however, a lopsided majority were against bringing gays into the armed services. Former members of the armed services were aligned with the Joint Chiefs of Staff and key members of Congress as the core opposition. On the other hand, traditional civil rights groups were not outspoken, fearing that gay advocacy might jeopardize their own policy agenda with the Congress. The controversy that surrounded the gay issue eroded Clinton's popularity at a time when he should have enjoyed a "honeymoon" with the electorate.

Adverse public opinion was more directly involved in the case of Clinton's popularity and the economy. The twin pillars of presidential approval are "peace and prosperity," and the first Clinton term recorded one of the best economic records since World War II. President Clinton should have enjoyed record high "approval ratings" but, in fact, his popularity during his first three years was arguably the worst of any modern president. Why? Because polls showed that Americans did not credit Clinton directly with bringing about an improved economy, that some people still had economic worries from corporate downsizing, and that personal incomes stagnated despite the general economic improvement since the 1990–1991 recession. Moreover, unlike Reagan, who publicly praised the improving economy, President Clinton did not try to convince Americans that economic prosperity was back. As a consequence, polls showed that a majority of people did not approve of his "handling of the economy" until the end of August 1996 (just two months prior to election day).

EXPERTISE

Presidential leadership is strengthened (1) when policymaking requires technical or specialized knowledge and (2) when the confidentiality and secrecy of information is ensured. By monopolizing vital information, the White House can prevent critics from scrutinizing its policy options. No president is an expert on every policy question, but he can rely on advisors, consultants, and government bureaucrats as sources of expertise. How expertise facilitates or frustrates presidential power is illustrated in the Insight on Carter and the Middle East Peace Accord (chapter 12) and the Insight on Clinton's proposal for health care reform (chapter 8).

Being the governor of Georgia hardly prepared Carter for his distinctive role in helping negotiate the Middle East Peace Accord, and surely he was no expert on Egyptian-Israeli relations. By training, however, Carter was an engineer, having to pay great attention to details; as president he was equally detail oriented. Most observers agree that his personal work habits prevented Carter from setting domestic policy priorities, but this Insight shows that here his attention to detail paid handsome rewards. For information about the adversarial relationship between Egypt and Israel, Carter turned to National Security Advisor Zbigniew Brzezinski and Secretary of State Cyrus Vance; for technical knowledge about Middle Eastern politics, he consulted area specialists in the State Department. However, a great deal of credit goes to Carter, who read documents and reports to become knowledgeable about the obstacles to peace. He invited Israeli Prime Minister Begin and Egyptian President Sadat to conduct their negotiations in the United States at Camp David, the presidential retreat, and Carter made personal overtures when the talks appeared deadlocked.

Clinton's proposal for health care reform was a debacle in policy formation. He appointed his wife, Hillary Rodham Clinton, and Ira Magaziner to cochair a Task Force to formulate a legislative proposal for Congress. The Task Force did not include key constituencies in the health care sector that had political clout and substantive expertise—organized medicine, insurance companies, the hospital sector, and the pharmaceutical industry. When the Task Force finally issued its report, those excluded interests came out against the Task Force report.

Once the Task Force reported its very ambitious (and controversial) plan, the critics, including Democrats in Congress, prepared their own versions of health care "reform" legislation. At least four different plans were publicized in the press—the Task Force proposal, one modeled after the Canadian health system, an option developed by southern conservative Democrats, and a Republican alternative. Thus, its decision to deliberate in secret backfired, and the Task Force failed to monopolize the expertise regarding the highly complex problem of health care reform. The logic of its "reforms" crumbled as opponents inside and outside government attacked its recommendations for costing too much, denying patients their choice of doctors, adding more burdensome government regulations, and lowering the quality of health care for middle-class Americans.

CRISIS

Will the nation rally behind presidential leadership during a crisis? Where other countries have constitutional provisions enabling their chief executives to declare a state of national emergency and assume dictatorial powers during grave crises, the U.S. Constitution does not grant the president the authority to suspend the separation of powers. Nonetheless, our political system has the flexibility to allow extraordinary presidential powers during crisis periods. Presidents, keenly aware of this potential, thus have an incentive to yell "crisis" in order to gain political advantage.

Crisis undermines the normal power relationships among the three branches of government when a political consensus emerges acknowledging that an emergency requires decisive action and because the president is uniquely equipped to act quickly in these situations. This factor is unpredictable, however, since the likelihood of a crisis varies depending on the presidential role. The beginning of war and international crises obviously qualify, but a "crisis" should be viewed in its broadest sense—a situation characterized by sudden, intense, and sometimes unexpected danger. Crisis conditions range widely, and include depressions, urban riots, labor strikes, domestic violence, natural disasters, disease epidemics, and political assassinations.

Our Insight on President Bush and the Persian Gulf War (chapter 14) shows that the Iraqi invasion of neighboring Kuwait precipitated a serious international crisis, which justified Bush's sending in U.S. troops. Yet, simply calling a problem a "crisis" is no assurance that the public and Congress will rally behind presidential leadership, as illustrated by the so-called health care crisis that prompted Clinton's pledge to guarantee health insurance coverage for all Americans. Comparing these Insights reveals how unreliable the crisis variable can be.

The decision by Iraqi leader Saddam Hussein to occupy the northern reaches of Kuwait, over his disputed claim to Kuwaiti oil reserves, posed a threat to Middle East stability and to the flow of crude petroleum to the United States and our European allies. The Israelis were concerned, as was our oil-rich ally, Saudi Arabia. At first public opinion was divided over whether an embargo against Iraq would dislodge Hussein or whether military force should be used. The same point was debated in Congress, though Bush and most of his advisors believed that war was inevitable or U.S. prestige in the region would suffer. Once war began, with the bombardment of Iraq and then the deployment of U.S. troops, public opinion rallied behind the commander in chief. The war distracted the public from an economy in near-recession, and approval ratings for Bush skyrocketed to an all-time high of 89 percent during the Persian Gulf War. Once the war ended and the troops came home, Bush's popularity began a steady decline that ended in his defeat by Bill Clinton.

Although it was primarily the recession that defeated Bush in 1992, the biggest domestic issue to emerge from that presidential campaign was health care reform, and Bill Clinton pledged fundamental changes to guarantee all Americans health care coverage. The mass media focused on the number of uninsured Americans, the fast-growing costs of health care, and forecasts of health care costing $1.6 trillion of the gross national product by the year 2000. Polls showed that health care was a salient issue, and the American Medical Association, the U.S. Chamber of Commerce, organized labor, and political conservatives as well as liberals supported "reforming" the health care system. Yet nothing was enacted by the Democratically controlled 103rd Congress, and by August 1994 polls showed that 39 percent of Americans favored but 48 percent opposed the Clinton health care reforms. Indeed, during 1994, a midterm election year, the public's concern about crime surpassed its worries over health care. When the Republicans won majorities in both the House and Senate in November, the health care "crisis" was over in terms of any fundamental restructuring of the health care industry.

SUMMARY

The commander in chief and chief diplomat roles are nearly equal in power, given the resources available to modern presidents; the chief executive is a distant third overall, followed closely by the legislative leader role. With so few resources available to a president as opinion/party leader, presidential power in this role would seem to be illusory, and largely a function of the incumbent's personality, political skills, policy agenda, the nature of the times, and luck.

While some very popular presidents have been elected to office, they were unable to pass that attribute on to their successors. The easygoing style of Ronald Reagan did not soften the more formal manner of George Bush. To a lesser degree, the same applies to the legislative leader and chief executive roles. Again, policy leadership must be reestablished on each incumbent's terms, since a president can rely on few antecedents established by his predecessors. No president begins his tenure as commander in chief or chief diplomat with such a power vacuum.

We show that authority, decision-making, public inputs, expertise, and crisis interact to constrain or facilitate presidential activism depending on the role(s) involved in trying to achieve a policy objective. Yet those factors alone do not explain why presidents who governed during the same historical periods—Buchanan and Lincoln, Hoover and Roosevelt, Carter and Reagan—showed such disparities in their leadership abilities.

Though we cannot separate the person from the office, persuasive skills depend on the experience and personality of the incumbent. The man (or woman, someday) who lives in the White House brings an individualized collection of talents, political experiences, and personal traits that affect whether he can make the best of a bad situation (Could Herbert Hoover ever be as charismatic as Franklin Roosevelt?) or take full advantage of the office's greatest potential (Buchanan's lack of resolve fueled secessionism, while Lincoln's use of force reunified the nation?). Presidential leadership across the five roles is not guaranteed by the office but depends on the person. The "missing link" of personality is the topic of our next chapter.

NOTES

1. Edward Corwin studied presidential authority using the roles of commander in chief, organ of foreign relations, administrative head, chief executive, and legislative leader. See Edward S. Corwin, *The President: Office and Powers*, 4th ed. (New York: New York University Press, 1957). Among the others who used this approach were Clinton Rossiter, *The American Presidency*, 2nd ed. (New York: Harcourt, Brace and World, 1960); Louis W. Koenig, *The Chief Executive*, 4th ed. (New York: Harcourt Brace Jovanovich, 1981); and Thomas A. Bailey, *Presidential Greatness: The Image and the Man from George Washington to the Present* (New York: Appleton-Century-Crofts, 1966).

2. For example, see these works by Louis Fisher: *The Politics of Shared Power: Congress and the Executive* (Washington, DC: Congressional Quarterly Press, 1981); *Constitutional Conflicts Between Congress and the President* (Princeton, NJ: Princeton University Press, 1985); *Presidential War Power* (Lawrence: University Press of Kansas, 1995).

3. A summary of the leading Supreme Court cases is provided by: David H. Rosenbloom, "Presidential Power and the Courts," in Harry A. Bailey, Jr., and Jay M. Shafritz, eds. *The American Presidency: Historical and Contemporary Perspectives* (Chicago: Dorsey Press, 1988), pp. 376–389. A classic is the work by Glendon A. Shubert, Jr., *The Presidency in the Courts* (Minneapolis: University of Minnesota Press, 1957). Also see Arthur S. Miller, *Presidential Power in a Nutshell* (St. Paul: West, 1977).

4. This decision-making factor is based on the important concept of "scope" of conflict as originally developed by E.E. Schattschneider, *The Semi-Sovereign People* (New York: Holt, Rinehart and Winston, 1960), chap. 1.

2

Incumbent or Office?
Personality as the Missing
Link to Presidential
Leadership

Of the five factors we discussed in chapter 1 that influence presidential power and leadership, the most important is legal authority. Its presence or absence is a very important consideration in how a president goes about trying to achieve his policy objectives. Two esteemed presidency scholars, Richard E. Neustadt and the late Edward S. Corwin, disagreed about the importance of the *office* versus the *incumbent* for presidential leadership. This book revisits their debate and essentially integrates the Corwin and Neustadt interpretations into a more complete explanation of presidential power.

CORWIN AND NEUSTADT REVISITED

In *Presidential Power,* Neustadt's seminal book first published in 1960, his original thesis was straightforward.[1] He argued that presidential power is not legal authority derived from the office of the presidency but rather depends on a president's ability to *persuade* based on the effective manipulation of his reputation, his prestige, and his bargaining position. It is the Washington insiders such as members of Congress and the Washington press corps who are impressed by a president's reputation, whereas outsiders are more influenced by a president's prestige or popularity. *Bargaining* involves the use of a president's office to negotiate with members of Congress or administrators, but Neustadt doubts that authority—as a direct order or command—is sufficient to assure presidential leadership.

Because presidential leadership depends on having the skill to bargain with the power brokers in Washington and to cultivate an effective image with the general public, Neustadt claimed that the *person* who occupies the White House is perhaps the most important variable in explaining policy success. Thus Neustadt favored activist presidents in the White House such as Franklin D. Roosevelt rather than so-called amateurs such as Dwight D. Eisenhower. In the 1960s Neustadt fostered the belief that Eisenhower, who had been Supreme Allied Commander during World War II, was too passive a president because he was not a professional politician and had never held prior elective office. That view of Eisenhower has undergone change in revisionist scholarship, which argues that the Eisenhower behind-the-scenes "hidden hand" leadership style yielded significant policy achievements.[2]

The earlier view of presidential power by Corwin was based on the *office,* from which the incumbent derives legal authority.[3] We share Corwin's understanding of legal authority as powers flowing from the Constitution, statutory delegations by Congress, interpretations of presidential power by the Supreme Court, and customary practice. The best example of custom "routinizing" authority was the creation of a "cabinet" by George Washington, which every president since has established. For Corwin, therefore, presidential powers rest on the law, not on the personality of the incumbent, and any president seeking to expand his personal influence beyond the legal parameters of the office may, in fact, pose a threat to the U.S. constitutional system.

In this book our approach converts this Neustadt-Corwin dichotomy into a continuum, suggesting that both authority and influence are important, depending on presidential *roles.* We believe Neustadt was correct to focus on the incumbent, not the office, because having political influence is a highly personalized attribute. But he overstated his case when he rejected legal authority as a resource available to any president by virtue of his office. Thus the Corwin-Neustadt argument over authority or persuasion is coupled with their concern about the office or incumbent. Corwin's institutional approach is compatible with the original design of the presidential office by the Framers of the Constitution. Neustadt was not the first observer who worried about what type of person would inhabit the White House.

Certain times have tested both the incumbent and the office—the Founding, the trauma of the Civil War, World War I, the Great Depression, and World War II—whereas in other eras the relative quietude of American politics did little to transform the highest office of the land. Along the way, scholars have imprinted each presidential era with a distinctive normative standard, most of which prescribed how the president ought to behave rather than how the office might be reformed. We identify six eras spanning the history of the country (see Table 2-1). The normative standards of judgment have greatly fluctuated, depending on time and circumstance, to the point where today presidential observers have come full circle to regain an appreciation for the original design of the presidency by the constitutional Framers.

Table 2-1. Normative Eras in the Presidency

Theme	Books
Intended Presidency	—Charles C. Thach, Jr., *The Creation of the Presidency 1775–1789*. Baltimore, MD: Johns Hopkins Press, 1923, 1969.
	—Leonard D. White, *The Federalists: A Study in Administrative History*. New York: Macmillan, 1948.
Imperiled Presidency	—Woodrow Wilson, *Congressional Government*. New York: Houghton Mifflin, 1985. First published in 1885.
	—James Bryce, *The American Commonwealth*. London: Macmillan, 1888. See his classic essay "Why Great Men Are Not Chosen President."
	—Woodrow Wilson, *Constitutional Government in the United States*. New York: Columbia University Press, 1908.
Idealized Presidency	—Harold J. Laski, *The American Presidency*. New York: Harper and Brothers, 1940.
	—Richard Neustadt, *Presidential Power*. New York: Free Press, 1990. First published in 1960.
	—James MacGregor Burns, *Presidential Government: The Crucible of Leadership*. Boston: Houghton Mifflin, 1966, 1973.
Imperial Presidency	—James David Barber, *The Presidential Character*. Englewood Cliffs, NJ: Prentice-Hall, 1972, 1977, 1985.
	—Arthur M. Schlesinger, Jr., *The Imperial Presidency*. Boston: Houghton Mifflin, 1974.
Impotent Presidency	—Thomas M. Franck, ed., *The Tethered Presidency* (New York: New York University Press, 1981.
	—Hugh Heclo and Lester M. Salamon, eds., *The Illusion of Presidential Government*. Boulder, CO: Westview Press, 1981.
	—Erwin C. Hargrove, *Jimmy Carter as President: Leadership and the Politics of the Public Good*. Baton Rouge: Louisiana State University Press, 1988.
	—Charles Jones, *The Trusteeship Presidency: Jimmy Carter and the United States Congress*. Baton Rouge: Louisiana State University Press, 1988.
Inflated Presidency	—Theodore J. Lowi, *The Personal President: Power Invested, Promise Unfulfilled*. Ithaca, NY: Cornell University Press, 1985.
	—Jeffrey K. Tulis, *The Rhetorical Presidency*. Princeton, NJ: Princeton University Press, 1987.
	—David R. Mayhew, *Divided We Govern: Party Control, Lawmaking, and Investigations, 1946–1990*. New Haven, CT: Yale University Press, 1991.
	—Stephen Skowronek, *The Politics Presidents Make: Leadership from John Adams to George Bush*. Cambridge, MA: Harvard University Press, 1993.
	—Charles O. Jones, *The Presidency in a Separated System*. Washington, DC: The Brookings Institution, 1994.

THE INTENDED PRESIDENCY

Although the Framers were acutely aware that George Washington would be America's first president, they did not create the office to fit that man. Knowing Washington was a committed "republican" certainly helped allay any fears that the first president might harbor promonarchy sentiments, but the Framers looked beyond Washington to craft an office within a separation of powers system of government. Their main objective was to protect individual liberties from government, so they did not imbue the presidential office with much authority. The first three articles of the Constitution outline the separation of powers system and, by lodging the legislative authority in Article I, the Framers designated Congress to be both the principal lawmaking and the representative branch of the national government.

Although many observers of the liberal persuasion bemoan the U.S. separation of powers system and look longingly at the parliamentary systems of Great Britain and Europe, the definitive study by Charles Thach[4] of how the Framers crafted Article II—the presidency article—argues that the system of separated institutions sharing powers was designed to gain independence for the president *from* Congress. In other words, Article II demarcated a sphere reserved for the executive and whose language—unlike the specific enumerated powers given to Congress in Article I—was vague enough to allow expansive interpretations by incumbents. Section 1 of Article II simply reads, "The executive Power shall be vested in a President of the United States of America."

Similar concerns motivated the Framers ultimately to reject proposals for the Congress or the people to elect the president. To allow the first would make the president a captive of legislative cabals and intrigue. To allow the second might encourage presidents to make demagogic appeals for popular support. In his definitive work on this subject, Tulis concluded, "[F]or most federalists, 'demagogue' and 'popular leader' were synonyms, and nearly all references to popular leaders in their writings are pejorative. Demagoguery, combined with majority tyranny, was regarded as the peculiar vice to which democracies were susceptible."[5] Thus the Framers opted in favor of the electoral college method by which the majority of electors (who then were chosen by state legislatures, not the people) were given the authority to choose the highest officer in the land.

To even imply that the Framers opened the door to presidential leadership does not mean that many nineteenth-century presidents availed themselves of the opportunity to assert themselves. The great and near great presidents during that era were few but did include George Washington, John Adams, Thomas Jefferson, Andrew Jackson, and Abraham Lincoln. This situation led Richard Rose to aptly describe the "traditional" presidency (prior to Franklin Roosevelt) as a "do-nothing" office.[6]

THE IMPERILED PRESIDENCY

So weak and uninspiring was the typical nineteenth-century president that two astute observers of American politics feared that presidential leadership was hopeless. One who subscribed to this dim viewpoint was Woodrow Wilson, then a young political scientist at Princeton University, who authored a classic study entitled *Congressional Government*, devoting only thirty pages to the office of president and comparing the U.S. presidential system unfavorably to the system of cabinet government in Great Britain. Wilson argued that the real power in American politics rested with Congress, and more precisely with congressional committees.[7]

He lamented the separation of powers because "it is impossible to deny that this division of authority and concealment of responsibility are calculated to subject the government to a very distressing paralysis in moments of emergency. There are few, if any, important steps that can be taken by any one branch of the government without the consent or cooperation of some other branch."[8] As for the executive, much of Wilson's discussion focused on the haphazard manner by which America recruits presidents. Unlike the situation in England, in which the recruitment process yields a prime minister with "[a] long career in Parliament [which] is at least a long contact with practical statesmanship," the American system ill prepares its presidents to gain the experience needed to manage a government. But then again, there was not very much for a president to do, according to Wilson:

> The business of the President, occasionally great, is usually not much above routine. Most of the time it is *mere* administration, mere obedience of directions from the masters of policy, the Standing Committees [of Congress]. Except in so far as his power of veto constitutes him a part of the legislature, the President might, not inconveniently, be a permanent officer; the first official of a carefully graded and impartially regulated civil service system, through whose sure series of merit-promotions the youngest clerk might rise even to the chief magistracy. He is part of the official rather than of the political machinery of the government, and his duties call rather for training than for constructive genius.[9]

Wilson's book was published in 1885, and three years later James Bryce, who became British ambassador to the United States from 1907 to 1913 and also was a student of American government, wrote another classic in the annals of presidential scholarship. In his well-known essay "Why Great Men Are Not Chosen President," Bryce described the men who served as president in these words:

> [S]ince the heroes of the Revolution died out with Jefferson and Adams and Madison some sixty years ago, no person except General Grant has reached the chair whose name would have been remembered had he not been President, and no President except Abraham Lincoln has displayed rare or striking qualities in the chair. Who now knows or cares to know anything about the personality of James K. Polk or Franklin Pierce? The only thing remark-

able about them is that being so commonplace they should have climbed so high.[10]

Although Bryce misjudged the importance of Grant, he captured the primary feeling about the ineptness of the traditional presidency. Indeed, as late as 1924 President Coolidge could still boast that he slept 11 hours for every 24 he served in the White House.[11]

The reason ("Great Men Are Not Chosen President") Bryce attributed to the American party system, which monopolized the nomination process and tended to recruit candidates who were safe rather than brilliant or charismatic. By looking for candidates who were not outspoken on the issues of the day, who had not offended any crucial voter bloc, and who showed quiet loyalty to the party organization, both Republicans and Democrats succeeded in recruiting a collection of mediocrities to serve in the highest office of the land. It was especially troubling to Bryce given that the British parliamentary system was able to recruit such luminaries as Benjamin Disraeli and William Gladstone to be prime minister during roughly the same era.

The imperiled presidency was not the image of presidential greatness that intrigued scholars, but the turn of this century caused some presidential watchers to rebound from the pessimism of earlier years. One of those was Woodrow Wilson, who was impressed enough with the energy exhibited by presidents Grover Cleveland (a Democrat) and Theodore Roosevelt (a "progressive" Republican) that he reassessed the presidential role in a book entitled *Constitutional Government in the United States*.[12] That work, published four years before Wilson himself assumed the presidency, presaged how this academic turned politician would transform the office in fundamental ways. Believing that only the president was truly a national leader, because he alone was nominated by a major political party and was chosen by a nationwide electorate, Wilson rejected the Framers' view that Congress was the legitimate representative of the people. Wilson believed his national election endowed him with a mandate to lead the country in new directions and to push his legislative agenda through Congress.

But Wilson's dream of presidential greatness did not survive the 1920 election. Victorious Warren G. Harding promised the country a "return to normalcy," and two more Republicans succeeded him in the White House: Calvin Coolidge and Herbert Hoover. Harding has been ranked a failure, Coolidge as below average, and Hoover as average (see Table 2-2 on page 25 for further discussion on presidential rankings) because President Hoover unfortunately held office when the stock market crash of 1929 ushered in the beginning of the Great Depression. Thus presidential watchers rejected the do-nothing executive of the past and sought out the exceptional leaders among the first thirty-one traditional presidents—Washington, Jefferson, Jackson, Lincoln, T. Roosevelt, and now Wilson—to endorse. These few presidents who exerted leadership in a variety of roles would join the modern presidents, beginning with Franklin D. Roosevelt, as models for an idealized conception of the presidency—also called the "heroic" presidency by Erwin Hargrove[13] and the "textbook presidency" by Thomas Cronin.[14]

THE IDEALIZED PRESIDENCY

The idealized president was a romanticized view promoted by liberal academics, notably historian Arthur Schlesinger, Jr., and political scientists Clinton Rossiter, Richard Neustadt, and James MacGregor Burns, although the first glimpse of this new interpretation can be found in a 1940 book by British political scientist Harold Laski.[15] Laski, as a member of the socialist wing of the Labour Party, was especially impressed with FDR who, he believed, would fight for the working classes. The legacy of weak executives in America only served to protect the "forces of privilege," according to his assessment:

> America needs strong government; it needs strong leadership to attain strong government; only the president . . . can provide it with the leadership it requires. But against these needs must be set all the traditional impetus of the system. The Constitution makes against it partly by its separation of powers and partly by the way in which it has distributed functions between the states and the federation. It has now become of pivotal interest to the forces of privilege in the United States to maintain for their benefit both that separation and that distribution.

To overcome the status quo, Laski believed there must be a "realignment" in the party system that develops when "[t]he interests, above all that of labor, which will be forced by them [the opposing parties] into political consciousness, will, in their turn, compel a realignment of parties into conservative and progressive." Coupled with a partisan realignment (which presumably would give rise to the dominance of a working-class-based liberal party) will be centralized leadership because

> [P]olitical parties will be compelled to centralize their leadership far more than they have before been willing to do. Centralization of leadership means, inevitably, a greater concentration of power in the president's hands simply because there is no other plane upon which it can be secured. He is likely, this is to say, to bear to his party a relationship far more like that of the British prime minister to his party than at any previous time.[16]

These themes are commonplace in the orthodoxy of liberalism: a strong president at the helm of government, holding power by leading the majority party—of a two-party system—in which the "liberals" dominate the "conservatives." This vision of class-based party competition always has been at odds with America's tradition of pragmatic, weakly organized, local, and patronage-based political parties, yet Laski's ideal—known as the "responsible party doctrine"—was endorsed by a committee of the American Political Science Association in 1950.[17]

Because the Democrats and Republicans never evolved into so-called responsible parties akin to the Labour and Conservative parties in Great Britain, liberal academics focused more energy on popularizing the idealized concept of presidential leadership. That ideal was promoted in American government textbooks, which glorified the office and especially the person who occupied it. Americans grew up expecting the president to be a storehouse of power, wisdom, and goodness, who could win wars as well as cure the nation's socioeconomic ills. The heroic president was depicted by advocate scholars as being the most important and indispensable official in the country, and his powers were expected to grow commensurate with the expanding scope of the federal government.

In line with Laski's disdain for the separation of powers, these scholars viewed Congress as a bastion of localism, conservatism, and parochialism that should be checked by a strong president who rallies the country behind national causes, progressive government, and bold leadership of the free world. Because a president has access to experts and superior knowledge, he knows what is best for the nation and its citizenry. Some even went so far as to argue (what today sounds terribly naive given the Watergate scandals) that the advisors surrounding the president—and *not* the separation of powers—would be Americans' best protection from any excessive abuse of presidential power.

In a highly celebrated 1973 book entitled *Presidential Government,* James MacGregor Burns wrote, "The only protection possible [from excessive presidential power] is the one the White House already affords: a group of men closely related to the president who can restrain him if need be. If power and decision making in the White House are collective, prudence is collective too."[18] This argument was buttressed by those advocates who viewed the president as a moral leader, one who would boldly confront the nation's problems and concerns while at the same time inspiring public confidence. Ultimately this concept of the heroic presidency implied all would be well if only the right (liberal Democratic!) person was chosen president.

THE IMPERIAL PRESIDENCY

It was also liberal Democratic academics who turned against their own president—Lyndon B. Johnson—because LBJ involved the United States in the Vietnam War, giving birth to a revisionist interpretation of presidential power. There had been voices who urged caution in America's rush to embrace the heroic model, but they were largely ignored. One was Edward Corwin who warned about the "cult of personality" and a "long-term trend at work in the world that consolidates power in the executive departments of all governments" with this result:

> [P]residential power has been at times dangerously *personalized,* and this in two senses: first, that the leadership that it affords was dependent altogether on the accident of personality, against which our haphazard method of selecting Presidents offers no guarantee; and, secondly, that there is no governmental body that could be relied on to give the President independent advice and that he was nevertheless bound to consult.[19]

Johnson's tragic blunder in Vietnam coupled with the Watergate scandals and Nixon's abuses of executive authority provoked a strong negative reaction within the scholarly community. In 1974 Arthur

Schlesinger, Jr., characterized the president as an "imperial" elected monarch, and a new rationale was developed to curb executive power.[20] The 1960s turnabout in academic opinion was reflected in the admission by well-known presidency scholar Erwin Hargrove. Noting his own willingness—shared by most other political scientists—to excuse the misuse of power by strong presidents because they presumably did so much good for the nation, Hargrove explained that his common rationalization was based on this misguided assumption:

> Presidents were guided by moral purpose and it was frankly biased in the direction of the liberal, power-maximizing Presidents . . . the argument was made that such power-striving, if rooted in personal needs, could lead to self-defeating eruptions of personality such as Theodore Roosevelt's in 1912, Wilson's rigidity in the League [of Nations] fight, and FDR's plan to pack the Supreme Court. However, it was assumed that institutional checks and balances were sufficient to control such behavior. The price was worth paying because strong political leadership was required.[21]

Those academics who opposed U.S. involvement in Southeast Asia learned a sad lesson: it is nearly impossible for public opinion, the Supreme Court, or even Congress to stop a president who is determined to wage war. As Philippa Strum, writing in 1972, declared," the American presence in Vietnam and Cambodia should lead even the most diehard proponents of increased presidential power to question their assumption that expansion of power is always a good thing."[22] Presidential abuses and deceptions surrounding the Vietnam War did bring unchecked war-making under greater (not necessarily more effective) congressional scrutiny.

Watergate became a code word for a multitude of political sins committed by Richard Nixon and his associates. Watergate—the burglary and attempted wiretap of the headquarters of the Democratic National Committee—was part of a widespread effort by the Nixon White House to harass the president's political opponents. Worse yet was the way in which Richard Nixon abused his powers of office by compiling a list of political enemies to be investigated by the Internal Revenue Service, granting favors to milk producers and favorably settling an antitrust suit involving International Telephone and Telegraph Company (ITT) in exchange for campaign contributions, and creating a secret unit (the "Plumbers") to engage in domestic surveillance and to prevent leaks of information to the press. President Nixon also impounded billions of dollars appropriated by Congress for public works programs, actions later declared illegal by the courts. These incidents led the House Judiciary Committee to consider Nixon's impeachment, charging him with interfering with the Watergate investigation and with violating his oath of office.

Revisionism stressed the need to restrain presidential power, to reassert the constitutional role of Congress, and to question the assumption that executive leadership inevitably encourages morally justifiable causes. In vogue now was a picture of the president as a mortal, with all the insecurities, needs, and fears common to any ordinary person. Watergate had a major impact on how scholars viewed the highest office. In his 1975 edition of *The Chief Executive,* Louis Koenig took account of the disturbing instances of power abuses while trying to preserve the positive aspects of the textbook presidency. He drew a distinction between "high-democracy" presidents and "low-democracy" presidents, the former reflecting the values of the "heroic" president and the latter representing presidents such as Nixon who encouraged divisiveness, were manipulative and secretive, indifferent to civil liberties, and willing to encroach on the authority of the other branches of government.[23]

Aaron Wildavsky in 1978 devised four presidential models to explain the noble and ignoble sides of presidential behavior. His prophylactic president was someone who would heed warnings of emergency conditions so the administration could plan for preventative action. Wildavsky's reactive president, in contrast, responded to problems only after the fact. His third model was the pluralist president, willing to share powers and forge policy with other institutions within the constitutional framework. But the predominant president attempts to overcome any barriers put in his way by the other institutions through the authority of his election mandate.[24] The best known effort to isolate Johnson and Nixon intellectually from the ranks of the idealized presidents was a lengthy analysis of presidential "character" by James David Barber (see later). Johnson and Nixon were categorized along with Herbert Hoover and Woodrow Wilson as "active negatives" because their psychological insecurity prevented them from admitting defeat and abandoning a policy considered by others to be a failure.

THE IMPOTENT PRESIDENCY

Americans' critical instincts had matured since the time when such questions were resolved in favor of the heroic president, but how long would the revisionist arguments be persuasive? Gerald Ford and Jimmy Carter represented a repudiation of the imperial presidency thesis because they were largely perceived (certainly by the media) as ineffective. Ford was not elected, having succeeded from vice president to president when Nixon resigned, and he faced the daunting prospect of trying to resurrect the stature of the White House, move on past the national nightmare of Watergate, and cope with a Congress solidly controlled by the Democrats. So Carter bears more responsibility for that sorry state of affairs because the advent of unified government in 1977, when the White House, the House of Representatives, and the Senate were in Democratic hands, raised public expectations that President Carter could deliver on his campaign promises. But that was not to be, as Crabb and Mulcahy recount the Carter failures in foreign affairs:

> Faced with threats to American interests abroad such as the Soviet invasion of Afghanistan, the collapse of the Iranian monarchy, and the ensuing hostage crisis, Carter (whether fairly or not) came to exemplify the "impotent presidency"—a chief executive who apparently lacked the power or the will

(or both) to respond to events decisively and in ways that effectively protected America's vital interests abroad.[25]

A 1979 article by James Fallows, former Carter speechwriter, labeled the Carter White House as "the passionless presidency," and his caricature stuck.[26] Some revisionist literature has tried to salvage Carter's reputation by arguing that events undermined him and Congress was determined to exert its authority in the aftermath of Vietnam and Watergate.[27] The present generation of political scientists seems unconvinced, mainly because Carter has been compared so unfavorably with Reagan in many ways. Books written after Carter's presidency that referred to "the tethered presidency" and the "illusion of presidential government"[28] were telling indications of how scholars viewed the office. Looking back on that era, Phillip Henderson chides the revisionists for having failed to "build a convincing case that concepts like bargaining, accommodation and persuasion are any less meaningful norms of analysis or understanding presidential politics during and after Carter's presidency than they were before he assumed office."[29]

THE INFLATED PRESIDENCY

The latest reason for apprehension is the suspicion that Americans are entering an era of one-term presidents and a crisis of governance. More and more journalists talk about deadlock, paralysis, stalemate, and gridlock in government, and some political scientists even put the blame on the separation of powers system that allows voters to elect presidents of one party while continuing the opposing party's control of Congress. That explanation, however, is too simplistic. An emerging new consensus among presidency scholars claims that no one person can control the U.S. political system; an "expectations gap" exists because the power possessed by any president has limits, whereas the responsibilities of the president are limitless.[30] This gap between public expectations and political reality, moreover, has been fueled largely by inflated presidential rhetoric[31] and the inability of "postmodern" presidents to control events in an increasingly interdependent world.[32]

The first scholar to observe this tendency in American politics was Theodore J. Lowi, who indicated how serious the problem was because

> The legal powers and responsibilities focused so directly upon the presidency have contributed to myths about the ability of presidents to meet those responsibilities. And since the rhetoric that flows from the office so magnifies the personal responsibility and so surrounds the power with mystique, it is only natural that the American people would produce or embrace myths about presidential government.[33]

The modern dilemma of the "personal president," suggests Lowi, is that presidents have been unable to achieve world peace and ensure economic prosperity. As he further argues,

The scale of presidential power and of mass expectation about presidential power is so great that presidents must, as in Watergate, attempt to control their environment to the maximum, especially those aspects of it that might tend to be barriers in the way of meeting presidential responsibilities. Those responsibilities are so pressing and so close to unmeetable that presidents must have vast contingency plans to make up the difference between expectations and realities.[34]

Other well-known scholars who have promoted the inflated presidency thesis (see Table 2-1) are Jeffrey Tulis, Stephen Skowronek, David Mayhew, and Charles Jones, although each brings a unique reading of that development. Tulis attributes the cause of rising public expectations to the "rhetorical" presidency.[35] It was Woodrow Wilson who first legitimized the modern practice of presidents seeking public approval for their programmatic agenda. Ever since that time, presidents increasingly "go public"[36] in efforts to have public opinion exert pressure on the Congress. Skowronek rejects the distinction between the historical and modern periods by offering a cyclical interpretation of political history.[37] According to his argument, presidential leadership depends as much or more on the historical era in which a president governs as the particular mix of political traits and talents he may possess. According to this explanation, Jimmy Carter did poorly because he tried to govern as a Democrat at a time when liberalism was falling into disrepute, whereas Ronald Reagan was more successful because he represented the advent of a new era of conservatism.

Because divided government seems to have become the rule rather than the exception in American politics since the late 1960s, David Mayhew took issue with a core argument of the idealized presidency school of thought that presidential leadership is more effective when unified government exists (that is, when the same political party controls both the executive and legislative branches). Mayhew found that Congress is equally as efficient in lawmaking during periods of divided party rule as when the president's party also controls Congress.[38]

In support of Mayhew, Charles Jones examined the relationships between the executive and legislative branches to determine which decision-maker (the House of Representatives, the Senate, or the president) had a decisive role in shaping the major legislation of the modern era. Like Mayhew, Jones calls for a reeducation of the American people (and the media) to appreciate the original separation of powers design of the Framers. As Jones states, "The American presidency carries a burden of lofty expectations that are simply not warranted by the political or constitutional basis of the office."[39] Instead, he advocates "an alternative perspective to that of the advocates of responsible party, presidency-centered, unified government: a perspective of a separated system that I judge to be consistent with the constitutional order and historical practice."[40]

In summation, there has been a shifting back and forth in the normative criteria that observers have applied to the person who occupies the White House. Lyn Ragsdale recalls that presidents have been called everything from "impressive" to "imperial."[41] Scholars have venerated strong and weak presidents on different occasions; they have been shocked at the misuse of powers by some presidents but also frustrated at the inability of other presidents to assert their constitutional powers more effectively.

PERSONALITY AND PRESIDENTS

We have argued that presidential leadership is affected by five factors, but some incumbents have taken greater advantage of legal authority, decision making, public inputs, expertise, and crisis than have others to shape the presidency. To argue that the relative position of the five roles we discussed in chapter 1 is more or less the same in 1990 as in 1890, however, is not to deny a larger political truth: all five roles have been greatly expanded over time.

Today the strongest and the weakest presidential roles—commander in chief and opinion/party leader—are qualitatively more powerful than they were intended to be at the time of the Founding.[42] Thus political scientists commonly distinguish between "modern," or contemporary, presidents and their "historical" predecessors.[43] The presidency has been fundamentally transformed, and relatively few premodern presidents had significant impact on that historical development. Those who did are the incumbents ranked as "great" or "near great," and there was substantial agreement among scholars, even before the first Schlesinger poll of academics was taken in 1948 (Table 2-2).

Five surveys of presidential scholars from 1948 through 1996 (Table 2-2) agree that Lincoln was the greatest of the greats, followed by Washington or Franklin Roosevelt. Jefferson and Wilson were considered greats until the 1996 Schlesinger (Jr.) poll reclassified them as near greats. Heretofore the near greats have generally included John Adams (who was dropped to high average in 1996), Jackson, Polk, Theodore Roosevelt, and Truman. Because the majority of presidents have had less visible impact on the office and the nation's destiny, what this suggests is that policy leadership must depend on *personality* as well as power resources. It is the personality and temperament of the incumbent that facilitates or frustrates his ability to mobilize authority, decision making, public opinion, expertise, and crisis through policy leadership.

At the high end of the rankings scholars have agreed that greatness or near greatness in the presidency requires exceptional leadership, particularly during times of crisis. The Schlesinger (Sr.) polls of 1948 and 1962, however, reflected the normative era of the idealized president, which continues to be manifested in the 1996 Schlesinger (Jr.) rankings.

It seems hard to imagine how Clinton would score higher than any

Table 2-2. How Scholars Have Ranked the Presidents

	Schlesinger Poll[a] (1948) Ratings[f]	Schlesinger Poll[b] (1962) Ratings[f]	Maranell-Dodder Poll[c] (1970) Prestige	Murray-Blessing Poll[d] (1982) Ratings[f]	Schlesinger Poll[e] (1996) Ratings[g]
1	Lincoln (G)	Lincoln (G)	Lincoln	Lincoln (G)	Lincoln (G)
2	Washington (G)	Washington (G)	Washington	F. Roosevelt (G)	F. Roosevelt (G)
3	F. Roosevelt (G)	F. Roosevelt (G)	F. Roosevelt	Washington (G)	Washington (G)
4	Wilson (G)	Wilson (G)	Jefferson	Jefferson (G)	Jefferson (NG)
5	Jefferson (G)	Jefferson (G)	T. Roosevelt	T. Roosevelt (NG)	Wilson/Jackson (NG)
6	Jackson (G)	Jackson (NG)	Wilson	Wilson (NG)	T. Roosevelt (NG)
7	T. Roosevelt (NG)	T. Roosevelt (NG)	Truman	Jackson (NG)	Truman (NG)
8	Cleveland (NG)	Polk (NG) and Truman (NG)	Jackson	Truman (NG)	Polk (NG)
9	J. Adams (NG)	J. Adams (NG)	Kennedy	J. Adams (AA)	Eisenhower (HA)
10	Polk (NG)	Cleveland (NG)	J. Adams	L. Johnson (AA)	J. Adams (HA)
11	J.Q. Adams (A)	Madison (A)	Polk	Eisenhower (AA)	Kennedy (HA)
12	Monroe (A)	J.Q. Adams (A)	Cleveland	Polk (AA)	L. Johnson (HA)
13	Hayes (A)	Hayes (A)	Madison	Kennedy (AA)	Cleveland (HA)
14	Madison (A)	McKinley (A)	Monroe	Madison (AA)	McKinley (HA)
15	Van Buren (A)	Taft (A)	J.Q. Adams	Monroe (AA)	Monroe (HA)
16	Taft (A)	Van Buren (A)	L. Johnson	J.Q. Adams (AA)	Madison (LA)

Table 2-2. How Scholars Have Ranked the Presidents *(continued)*

	Schlesinger Poll[a] (1948) *Ratings[f]*	Schlesinger Poll[b] (1962) *Ratings[f]*	Maranell-Dodder Poll[c] (1970) *Prestige*	Murray-Blessing Poll[d] (1982) *Ratings[f]*	Schlesinger Poll[e] (1996) *Ratings[g]*
17	Arthur (A)	Monroe (A)	Taft	Cleveland (AA)	J.Q. Adams (LA)
18	McKinley (A)	Hoover (A)	Hoover	McKinley (A)	Clinton (LA)
19	A. Johnson (A)	B. Harrison (A)	Eisenhower	Taft (A)	Reagan (LA)
20	Hoover (A)	Arthur (A) and Eisenhower (A)	A. Johnson	Van Buren (A)	B. Harrison (LA)
21	B. Harrison (A)	A. Johnson (A)	Van Buren	Hoover (A)	Van Buren (LA)
22	Tyler (BA)	Taylor (BA)	McKinley	Hayes (A)	Taft (LA)
23	Coolidge (BA)	Tyler (BA)	Arthur	Arthur (A)	Hayes (LA)
24	Fillmore (BA)	Fillmore (BA)	Hayes	Ford (A)	Bush (LA)
25	Taylor (BA)	Coolidge (BA)	Tyler	Carter (A)	Carter (LA)
26	Buchanan (BA)	Pierce (BA)	B. Harrison	B. Harrison (A)	Arthur (LA)
27	Pierce (BA)	Buchanan (BA)	Taylor	Taylor (BA)	Ford (LA)
28	Grant (F)	Grant (F)	Coolidge	Tyler (BA)	Coolidge (BA)
29	Harding (F)	Harding (F)	Fillmore	Fillmore (BA)	Taylor (BA)
30		Buchanan	Coolidge (BA)	Tyler (BA)	
31		Pierce	Pierce (BA)	Fillmore (BA)	
32		Grant	A. Johnson (F)	Hoover (F)	
33		Harding	Buchanan (F)	Nixon (F)	
34			Nixon (F)	Pierce (F)	

Table 2-2. How Scholars Have Ranked the Presidents (*continued*)

	Schlesinger Poll[a] (1948) Ratings[f]	Schlesinger Poll[b] (1962) Ratings[f]	Maranell-Dodder Poll[c] (1970) Prestige	Murray-Blessing Poll[d] (1982) Ratings[f]	Schlesinger Poll[e] (1996) Ratings[g]
35			Grant (F)	A. Johnson (F)	
36			Harding (F)	Grant (F)	
37				Buchanan (F)	
38				Harding (F)	

[a] Arthur Schlesinger, Sr., "The U.S. Presidents," *Life* (Nov. 1, 1948), p. 65.

[b] Arthur Schlesinger, Sr., "Our Presidents: A Rating by 75 Historians," *New York Times Magazine* (July 29, 1962), pp. 12 ff.

[c] Gary Maranell and Richard Dodder, "Political Orientation and Evaluation of Presidential Prestige: A Study of American Historians," *Social Science Quarterly* 51 (Sept. 1970), p. 418.

[d] Robert Murray and Tim Blessing, "The Presidential Performance Study: A Progress Report," *Journal of American History* (Dec. 1982), pp. 540–541.

[e] Arthur M. Schlesinger, Jr., "The Ultimate Approval Rating," *New York Times Magazine* (Dec. 15, 1996), pp. 46–51.

[f] William Henry Harrison and James Garfield are not included in these surveys. Legend: G = Great; NG = Near Great; AA = Above Average; A = Average; BA = Below Average; F = Failure.

[g] William Henry Harrison and James Garfield are not included in this survey. Legend: G = Great; NG = Near Great; HA = High Average; LA = Low Average; BA = Below Average; F = Failure. Within each of these six categories, Schlesinger simply listed the presidents in chronological order rather than provide an exact ranked "score" for each. However Schlesinger provides the frequency of rankings for each president so this numerical ordering reflects our calculations based on assigning a value to each rank as follows: G = 4, NG = 3, HA or LA = 2, BA = 1, and F = 0. For example, Jefferson was ranked great by 12 scholars (48 points), near great by 16 scholars (48 points), and average by 1 scholar (2 points), for a total of 98 points. The total was divided by the number of scholars ranking each president; for Jefferson 29 of the 32 scholars did so, to derive an average score (3.3793 for Jefferson), which ranks him behind Lincoln (4.00), FDR (3.9688), and Washington (3.9677). Using this method we ordered the presidents within the categories derived by Schlesinger, but one discrepancy was found. Hoover (with 1.0333) was ranked a failure, whereas Fillmore (with 1.000) was ranked below average. Our composite score would reverse their positions, making Hoover the lowest ranked among the below average presidents and Fillmore the highest ranked among the failures.

of his immediate predecessors including Reagan[a] because scholarly assessments of the first two years of the Clinton administration were harshly critical.[44] The 1962 Schlesinger poll rushed to judgment in ranking Eisenhower twenty-second (average) based on one year in office, but since then he has steadily risen in the polls. Republicans cluster at the lower end of the 1996 rankings, as they did in the 1948 and 1962 standings. If we exclude Theodore Roosevelt, Wilson, Franklin Roosevelt, and Truman as exceptional among the twentieth-century presidents, and score the other thirteen presidents since 1900, the 1996 Schlesinger poll shows the remaining Democrats on average to be better presidents than the Republicans.[b]

Although the five factors we have listed that affect presidential leadership are available to any incumbent, naturally there is no guarantee that all presidents will make use of them. Looking back over U.S. history, for example, different individuals, although they were president during roughly the same era, held sharply contrasting views of the office and styles of leadership. This phenomenon has impressed presidency watchers, who commonly differentiate between "active" and "passive" types of presidents (Table 2-3).

So unique were the leadership styles of the first three U.S. presidents that James MacGregor Burns classified them as Hamiltonian, Madisonian, and Jeffersonian.[45] The Hamiltonian type (named after George Washington's secretary of the treasury) represents an heroic leader who uses personal skills to increase executive power. The less activist Madisonian model, typified by President John Adams, accepts a literal view of the separation of powers argument that Congress should be the dominant branch of government. The preferred model is named for Thomas Jefferson, who imposed his policy agenda on both the executive and legislative branches through a disciplined party organization.

James Buchanan, who showed almost no leadership ability, was followed by Abraham Lincoln, the greatest of the greats, and the Lincoln-Buchanan contradiction illustrated for Sidney Hyman the active and passive extremes of presidential leadership.[46] Hyman also believed that President Grover Cleveland represented a middle position, in which presidents were not bold innovators but, instead, were defensively oriented and reacted against Congress by using their veto power often.

The colorful Theodore Roosevelt, rated near great in two Schlesinger polls, was succeeded by William Howard Taft, who has been ranked no better than average. The Roosevelt-Taft dichotomy is well known among students of the presidency because both incumbents articulated well-reasoned arguments for their contradictory views of presidential power.

[a]Our composite score for Clinton is 1.7308 based on the ratings of him by twenty-six scholars in the Schlesinger, which is higher than the score for Bush, Reagan, Carter, and Ford. For our methodology, see Table 2.2, footnote g.
[b]After averaging the composite scores for nine Republicans (1.2501) and four Democrats (1.9347), these results based on the Schlesinger distribution would classify the Republicans as a group as "below average" and the Democrats as a group as "low average."

Table 2-3. Personality and Leadership

President	Barber Classification	Burns Typology	Hargrove Dichotomy	Hyman Typology
Washington	passive-negative	Hamiltonian		
Adams	active-negative	Madisonian		Cleveland
Jefferson	active-positive	Jeffersonian		Lincoln
Madison	passive-positive			
Monroe				
J.Q. Adams				Cleveland
Jackson		Jeffersonian		Lincoln
Van Buren				Cleveland
W. Harrison				Buchanan
Tyler				
Polk				Lincoln
Taylor				
Fillmore				Buchanan
Pierce				Buchanan
Buchanan				Buchanan
Lincoln		Hamiltonian		Lincoln
Johnson				
Grant				Buchanan
Hayes				Cleveland
Garfield				Buchanan
Arthur				Buchanan
Cleveland				Cleveland
B. Harrison				
McKinley				Buchanan
T. Roosevelt		Hamiltonian	action	Lincoln
Taft	passive-positive	Madisonian	restraint	Buchanan
Wilson	active-negative	Jeffersonian	action	Lincoln
Harding	passive-positive			Buchanan
Coolidge	passive-negative			Buchanan
Hoover	active-negative		restraint	Buchanan
F. Roosevelt	active-positive	Hamiltonian	action	Lincoln
Truman	active-positive		action	Lincoln
Eisenhower	passive-negative			Buchanan (1st term) Cleveland (2nd term)
Kennedy	active-positive		action	
L. Johnson	active-negative		action	
Nixon	active-negative			
Ford	active-positive			
Carter	active-positive			
Reagan	passive-positive			
Bush	active-positive			
Clinton	active-positive			

Sources: James David Barber, *The Presidential Character* (Englewood Cliffs, NJ: Prentice Hall, 1993) and "Predicting Hope with Clinton at Helm," *Raleigh News Observer* (Jan. 17, 1993); James MacGregor Burns, *Presidential Government* (Boston: Houghton Mifflin, 1973); Erwin C. Hargrove, *Presidential Leadership: Personality and Political System* (New York: Macmillan, 1966); Sidney Hyman, "What Is the President's True Role?" *New York Times Magazine* (Sept. 7, 1958).

President Taft drew a highly legalistic interpretation that portrays the chief executive as a "magistrate" sworn to uphold the constitutional separation of powers system. Taft described his opinion as follows:

> The true view of the Executive function is, as I conceive it, that the President can exercise no power which cannot be fairly and reasonably traced to some specific grant of power or justly implied and indicated within such express grant as proper and necessary to its exercise. Such specific grant must be either in the Federal Constitution or in an act of Congress passed in pursuance thereof. There is no undefined residuum of power which he can exercise because it seems to him to be in the public interest. . . . The grants of Executive power are necessarily in general terms in order not to embarrass the Executive within the field of action plainly marked for him, but his jurisdiction must be justified and vindicated by affirmative constitutional or statutory provision, or it does not exist.[47]

Taft believed the president could do no more than what was specifically granted to him by the Constitution and statutes. In contrast, an open-ended doctrine was advocated by Theodore Roosevelt: the president could do anything unless explicitly denied to him by the Constitution or the laws of Congress. According to Roosevelt, the president is supposed to act as a "steward" to safeguard the welfare of ordinary people. As he wrote,

> The most important factor in getting the right spirit in my Administration, next to the insistence upon courage, honesty, and a genuine democracy of desire to serve the plain people, was my insistence upon the theory that the executive power was limited only by specific restrictions and prohibitions appearing in the Constitution or imposed by the Congress under its Constitutional powers. My view was that every executive officer . . . was a steward of the people bound actively and affirmatively to do all he could for the people, and not to content himself with the negative merit of keeping his talents undamaged in a napkin. I declined to adopt the view that what was imperatively necessary for the Nation could not be done by the president unless he could find some specific authorization to do it. My belief was that it was not only his right but his duty to do anything that the needs of the Nation demanded unless such action was forbidden by the Constitution or the laws.[48]

So accurately did those autobiographical statements by Taft and Roosevelt reflect on the force of personality in shaping presidential roles and power that Erwin Hargrove proposed another dichotomy.[49] The presidents of action like Theodore Roosevelt were each a "political artist whose deepest needs and talents were served by a political career" in sharp contrast with presidents of restraint in the image of Taft who generally "did not put a high value on personal or presidential power, and in the course of their careers they did not develop political skills."

As we already noted, the imperial presidency thesis led to James David Barber proposing the most elaborate classification of presidential personality.[50] Barber not only differentiated among presidents according to the degree of activity (active or passive) but also according to the degree of self-satisfaction (positive or negative). The "active-positive" type (Jefferson) was self-confident and actively pursued important policy goals, as did

Franklin D. Roosevelt, Harry Truman, and John F. Kennedy. But "active-negative" presidents, such as Woodrow Wilson, Herbert Hoover, Lyndon Johnson, and Richard Nixon, become overly rigid and too committed to a failing policy, which led Barber to conclude that active-negative types are dangerous personalities. Unlike other scholars in this tradition, Barber paid closer attention to the deviant personality attributes that ought to be avoided when Americans nominate and elect someone to the highest office. A different kind of political danger results from passivity.

Both passive-positives who crave affection (Taft, Harding, Reagan) and passive-negatives (Washington, Coolidge, Eisenhower) for whom duty calls allowed the nation to drift without presidential leadership; they simply ignored pressing social problems. The Barber typology has led some scholars to analyze certain behavioral aspects of presidential leadership. William Pederson shows that active-positives are more likely to grant amnesty[51] and are less likely to have been lawyers (lawyer-presidents have worse civil liberties records than presidents who were not lawyers[52]), whereas active-negatives (LBJ and Nixon) are more security conscious (in their use of the Secret Service) than presidents with healthier personalities.[53]

At base, however, the Barber typology is not without controversy because only Dwight D. Eisenhower and Ronald Reagan, among the modern presidents, were judged as passive presidents. As we noted earlier, a flourishing revisionist scholarship now bolsters Eisenhower's style of behind-the-scenes leadership,[54] and other contemporary observers have drawn sharp contrasts between the enormous policy impact of President Ronald Reagan and the generally lackluster performance of his predecessor, Jimmy Carter. Although Barber includes Carter in his active-positive category, according to some polls Carter is already being designated as one of the ten worst presidents.[55] Moreover, America's greatest president, Abraham Lincoln, is curiously omitted from Barber's analysis, and one persuasive essay alleges that, in fact, Lincoln most likely would be an active-negative, which would have effectively destroyed the argument that Barber was trying to make.[56]

The earlier typologies by Sidney Hyman, Ervin Hargrove, and James MacGregor Burns point to one enduring relationship between personality and power. Hargrove's presidents of action are mostly considered to be Lincoln-type presidents by Hyman, and most presidents in the Lincoln category Burns called Jeffersonians or Hamiltonians. All the presidents in these four categories are rated among the top ten: Washington, Jefferson, Jackson, Polk, Lincoln, Teddy Roosevelt, Wilson, FDR, and Truman. (The exception, John Adams, was highly rated but not portrayed as having the strongest leadership style.) As a group these activist presidents pushed these roles to their creative potential, even the weaker roles. Jefferson was the strongest legislative leader among the presidents, while Lincoln achieved a power that few others had by combining the commander in chief role with the chief executive role, while Franklin Roosevelt showed unusual strength as a commander in chief. The development of these roles under these presidents added resources that underlie presidential power and created a political legacy for their successors in the White House. They, in essence, defined the parameters of presidential power, which extends into the modern era.

PERSONALITY, POWER, AND STYLE

Barber's typology of presidential "characters" would seem to fall short of an adequate analysis of most of the contemporary presidents (especially Ford, Carter, Bush, and Clinton) given their domestic records, since Barber labeled each of them active-positives. Yet none of these presidents had significant policy achievements; none of them approached those of Franklin Roosevelt. Ford's domestic agenda focused on restraining Democratic spending, while Bush neglected domestic policy, preferring to direct his energies to international concerns. Carter's domestic achievements were also limited, while Clinton's primary emphasis in his first term—health care—failed to gain Congressional support.

Bill Clinton is seemingly an active-positive, but his character may be tinged with active-negativism as well. He works hard and dedicates himself to achieving goals, but analyst Stanley Renshon believes that Clinton's compulsive behavior is "closer to the driven investments of energy of active-negative Lyndon Johnson" rather than Kennedy or Truman. Moreover, Clinton is too thin-skinned for an active-positive when he is publicly criticized. Says Renshon, "Most people wish to think well of themselves but Bill Clinton appears to have come to believe the *best* of himself and to have discounted evidence from his own behavior that all is not as he believes it to be."[57]

There is no better illustration of this self-delusion than how Clinton reacted to the daily barrage of negative news reports in early 1997 that the White House entertained contributors who gave "soft" money (for party activities) to the Democratic National Committee and that some guests were convicted felons and others who made illegal contributions were foreign citizens and corporations. Rather than admit to ethical lapses or illegalities, Clinton blamed the system of campaign finances and, at one point, even justified those practices by alleging his reelection was crucial to protect America in the future from the excesses of Republican legislators.

Perhaps we should be more concerned with the impact of personality on war-making and diplomacy. Even there, however, Kellerman and Barilleaux point out that the relationship between personality and presidential power is tenuous: "Drawing a straight line between presidential personality (cause) and a particular political outcome (effect) is difficult if not impossible to do."[58] Some have tried, however, and Kellerman and Barilleaux point to the research by Doris Kearns on LBJ, Bruch Mazlish on Nixon, and Betty Glad's works on Carter and Reagan.

Kearns found a connection between LBJ's personality and Vietnam, concluding, "The influence of Johnson's personality on the decision making in Vietnam is [easy] to observe in his conduct of the war—[particularly] in the decision to conceal its nature and extent from the American people. . . . This decision was Lyndon Johnson's decision."[59]

Mazlish rejected the notion that anti-Communist fighter Richard Nixon flip-flopped when he pursued a policy of détente with the Soviet Union. Nixon's religious upbringing was Quaker, and Mazlish argued that "he also sincerely believes in working for peace. . . . The roots of this conviction lie deep in the Nixon family. . . . I am prepared to believe Nixon when he says he has 'an obsession on this point.'"[60]

Betty Glad alleged that Jimmy Carter's highly idealized self-image affected his handling of the Iran hostage crisis and the Soviet invasion of Afghanistan,[61] whereas she believed that Ronald Reagan had psychological reasons for viewing the conflict between the United States and the Soviet Union in stark good versus evil terms. Glad claimed that stereotyping a "culturally approved out-group, the communists, as well as his manifest tendencies to show aggression in fantasy and verbal attack upon them, suggests he has projected [uncontrollable anger] outward to a safe target."[62]

Barber makes a plausible argument about the impact of personality on behavior in his discussion of presidential "style," which has three aspects: "Style is the President's habitual way of performing his three political roles: rhetoric, personal relations, and homework."[63] Individuals act, in other words, based on their personal strengths and thus develop a style of behavior. Rhetoric involves speechmaking; personal relations involves one-on-one dealings with other people; and homework involves intellectual curiosity and concern for details.

A man of few words and not comfortable dealing with other people, Herbert Hoover's "main weapon . . . was neither oratory nor interpersonal persuasion, but his mastery of information." The same can be said regarding Jimmy Carter, whom Barber characterizes as "a rabid empiricist, a data-hound, an information freak in the White House" who was "a speed-reader and map-scanner, a list-making blueprint planner and memorandum annotator."[64]

Richard Nixon had difficulty operating with other political leaders in close quarters, which is why he chose strong-willed individuals to protect him from interpersonal conflicts. He emphasized rhetoric and was known as a forceful debater who used oratory as a political weapon. Lyndon Johnson, however, was no spell-binding speechmaker, nor was he very concerned about details, a reason that may explain the many administrative problems which befell his Great Society domestic programs. He excelled at cutting deals with other influential decision-makers as he had when he was Senate Majority Leader. He was a tall and impressive figure who resorted to the so-called "Johnson treatment" to intimidate his own legislative partisans, and this style continued during his presidency. Barber contended that "Johnson exemplifies as no other President in history an emphasis on personal relations. He was in a constant whirl of conversation, face to face and on the telephone; much of the drama and entertainment biographers find in him traces to his perennial palaver. Johnson

talking was a performer, nearly always interesting even to those who de-
tested him."[65]

Time magazine portrayed Ronald Reagan's management style as
"mellow," but detached and very dependent on his staff.[66] Barber adds
that this passive-positive president had a management style that rejected
homework in exchange for an extraordinary emphasis on rhetoric. The
president liked to play "host" to members of Congress, charming them,
but he left the "wheeler-dealer" negotiations up to his staffers.[67] Reagan's
ability to speak, Barber contends, was his real strength; it was rhetoric
that formed the "experiential base" for Reagan's "real politics."[68]

SUMMARY

Logic dictates that personality must make a difference in presidential
leadership, but analysts have not had an easy time validating that relationship empirically. The old active versus passive distinction made intuitive sense because the facts show Lincoln was more assertive than
Buchanan, Theodore Roosevelt expressed a fundamentally different view
of presidential power than Taft, and Reagan put to rest the notion that
Carter would be typical of our late twentieth-century presidents.

This concern about finding the right kind of person for the White
House has occurred during four normative eras in presidential scholarship—imperiled, idealized, imperial, and impotent. Only the intended
president of the Framers and the contemporary focus on an inflated president emphasize the office within the U.S. separation of powers system.
Today scholars would like to reeducate public opinion and scale down the
public's expectations about presidential leadership, encouraging incumbents to stop making promises they know they cannot keep.

The seminal work by James David Barber reflected collective worries
about an imperial president who may be dangerous to America's constitutional system. Not many scholars have tried to verify Barber's personality typology, and the few existing studies suggest the relationship between character and performance is complex and elusive. That a linkage
between personality and style of leadership exists is one aspect of Barber's analysis that seems entirely plausible and comports with reality.
Thus personality matters, but the search goes on to explain how and
when character affects the prospects for presidential leadership and
power.

NOTES

    1. Richard E. Neustadt, *Presidential Power and the Modern Presidents: The Politics of
Leadership from Roosevelt to Reagan* (New York: Free Press, 1989). The first edition was pub-
lished in 1960.
    2. The volume that initiated the revisionist movement on Eisenhower was Fred I.
Greenstein, *The Hidden-Hand Presidency, Eisenhower as Leader* (New York: Basic Books, 1982).

3. Edward S. Corwin, *The President: Office and Powers, 1787–1957*, 4th ed. (New York: New York University Press, 1957). This first edition was published in 1940; for an update done posthumously, see Edward S. Corwin, *The President: Office and Powers, 1787–1984*, 5th rev. ed., by Randall W. Bland, Theodore T. Hindson, and Jack W. Peltason (New York: New York University Press, 1984).

4. Charles C. Thach, Jr., *The Creation of the Presidency 1775–1789* (Baltimore: Johns Hopkins Press, 1969).

5. Jeffrey K. Tulis, *The Rhetorical Presidency* (Princeton, NJ: Princeton University Press, 1987), p. 28.

6. Richard Rose, *The Postmodern President: George Bush Meets the Postmodern World*, 2nd ed. (Chatham, NJ: Chatham House, 1991), p. 22.

7. Woodrow Wilson, *Congressional Government* (New York: Houghton Mifflin, 1985).

8. Ibid., p. 186.

9. Ibid., p. 170.

10. James Bryce, *The American Commonwealth*, vol.1 (New York: G.P. Putnam's Sons, 1959), p. 27.

11. Irvin H. Hoover, *Forty-two Years in the White House* (Boston: Houghton Mifflin, 1934), pp. 266, 268, in Rose, *The Postmodern President*, p. 22.

12. Woodrow Wilson, *Constitutional Government in the United States* (New York: Columbia University Press, 1908).

13. Erwin C. Hargrove, *The Power of the Modern Presidency* (New York: Knopf, 1974), p. 21.

14. Thomas E. Cronin, *The State of the Presidency* (Boston: Little, Brown, 1980), chap. 3. Cronin developed this thesis of the "textbook" presidency as early as 1970 in a paper delivered to the American Political Science Association.

15. Harold J. Laski, *The American Presidency* (New York: Harper and Brothers, 1940).

16. Ibid., pp. 243–244, 251.

17. "Toward a More Responsible Two-Party System," *American Political Science Review* 44 (Sept. 1950), Supplement.

18. James MacGregor Burns, *Presidential Government: The Crucible of Leadership* (Boston: Houghton Mifflin, 1973), p. 308.

19. Edward S. Corwin, *The President: Office and Powers*, 4th ed. (New York: New York University Press, 1957), p. 312.

20. See Arthur M. Schlesinger, Jr., *The Imperial Presidency* (Boston: Houghton Mifflin, 1974).

21. Erwin C. Hargrove, "The Crisis of the Contemporary Presidency," in James David Barber, ed., *Choosing the President* (Englewood Cliffs, NJ: Prentice-Hall, 1974), p. 17.

22. Philippa Strum, *Presidential Power and American Democracy* (Pacific Palisades, CA: Goodyear, 1972), p. 29.

23. Louis W. Koenig, *The Chief Executive*, 3rd ed. (New York: Harcourt Brace Jovanovich, 1975), pp. 336–339.

24. Aaron Wildavsky and Sanford Weiner, "The Prophylactic Presidency," *The Public Interest* 52 (Summer 1978), p. 9.

25 Cecil V. Crabb, Jr., and Kevin V. Mulcahy, "The Elitist Presidency: George Bush and the Management of Operation Desert Storm," in Richard W. Waterman, ed., *The Presidency Reconsidered* (Itasca, IL: F.E. Peacock, 1993), p. 276.

26. James Fallows, "The Passionless Presidency: The Trouble with Jimmy Carter's Administration," *The Atlantic Monthly* (May 1979), pp. 33–48.

27. See Erwin C. Hargrove, *Jimmy Carter as President: Leadership and the Politics of the Public Good* (Baton Rouge: Louisiana State University Press, 1988); Charles Jones, *The Trusteeship Presidency: Jimmy Carter and the United States Congress* (Baton Rouge: Louisiana State University Press, 1988).

28. Thomas M. Franck, ed., *The Tethered Presidency* (New York: New York University Press, 1981); Hugh Heclo and Lester M. Salamon, eds., *The Illusion of Presidential Government* (Boulder, CO: Westview Press, 1981).

29. Phillip G. Henderson, "Carter Revisionism: The Flight from Politics," *Political Science Reviewer*. [forthcoming].

30. See Richard W. Waterman, ed., *The Presidency Reconsidered* (Itasca, IL: F.E. Peacock, 1993).

31. See Jeffrey K. Tulis's inventive argument making the case for the consequences of rhetoric on the modern presidency in his *The Rhetorical Presidency* (Princeton, NJ: Princeton University Press, 1987).

32. Richard Rose argues that the postmodern president today is faced with a situation in which he possesses insufficient resources to meet international challenges and is forced to deal as more of an equal partner with other nations. See *The Postmodern President: George Bush Meets the World*, 2nd ed. (Chatham, NJ: Chatham House, 1991), p. 306; Ryan J. Barilleaux defines a postmodern president as one whose role is different from modern presidents in the political order and who operates from a changed political agenda. See his *The Postmodern Presidency: The Office after Ronald Reagan* (New York: Praeger, 1988).

33. Theodore J. Lowi, *The Personal President: Power Invested, Promise Unfulfilled* (Ithaca, NY: Cornell University Press, 1985),p. 151.

34. Ibid., p. 178.

35. Jeffrey K. Tulis, *The Rhetorical Presidency* (Princeton, NJ: Princeton University Press, 1987).

36. Also see Samuel Kernell, *Going Public: New Strategies of Presidential Leadership*, 2nd ed. (Washington, DC: CQ Press, 1993).

37. Stephen Skowronek, *The Politics Presidents Make: Leadership from John Adams to George Bush* (Cambridge, MA: Harvard University Press, 1993).

38. David R. Mayhew, *Divided We Govern: Party Control, Lawmaking, and Investigations 1946–1990* (New Haven, CT: Yale University Press, 1991).

39. Charles O. Jones, *The Presidency in a Separated System* (Washington, DC: The Brookings Institution, 1994), p. 281.

40. Ibid., p. 285.

41. Lyn Ragsdale, *Presidential Politics* (Boston: Houghton Mifflin, 1993), p. 469.

42. On this subject the seminal work is Charles C. Thach, Jr., *The Creation of the Presidency, 1775–1789* (Baltimore: Johns Hopkins Press, 1969). The original publication date was 1923. Also see Thomas E. Cronin, ed., *Inventing the American Presidency* (Lawrence: University Press of Kansas, 1989).

43. Case studies of presidents in the premodern era are found in Sidney M. Milkis and Michael Nelson, *American Presidency: Origins and Development, 1776–1990* (Washington, DC: CQ Press, 1990).

44. See Colin Campbell and Bert A. Rockman, *The Clinton Presidency: First Appraisals* (Chatham, NJ: Chatham House, 1996).

45. James MacGregor Burns, *Presidential Government* (Boston: Houghton Mifflin, 1973).

46. Sidney Hyman, "What Is the President's True Role?" *New York Times Magazine* (Sept. 7, 1958).

47. William Howard Taft, *Our Chief Magistrate and His Powers* (New York: Columbia University Press, 1916), pp. 139–140.

48. Theodore Roosevelt, *An Autobiography* (New York: Charles Scribner's Sons, 1929), p. 357.

49. Erwin C. Hargrove, *Presidential Leadership: Personality and Political System* (New York: Macmillan, 1966).

50. James David Barber, *The Presidential Character* (Englewood Cliffs, NJ: Prentice-Hall, 1985). The first edition of this work was published in 1972.

51. William David Pederson, "Amnesty and Presidential Behavior: A 'Barberian' Test," in William David Pederson, ed., *The "Barberian" Presidency* (New York: Peter Lang, 1989), pp. 113–127.

52. Thomas Meredith Green and William David Pederson, "The Behavior of Lawyer-Presidents: A 'Barberian' Link," in Pederson, *The "Barberian" Presidency*, pp. 153–167.

53. Dwight L. Tays, "Presidential Reaction to Security: A Longitudinal Study," in Pederson, *The "Barberian" Presidency*, pp. 169–188.

54. His military background made Eisenhower particularly suited to directing national security affairs, as argued by Phillip G. Henderson, *Managing the Presidency: The Eisenhower Legacy—From Kennedy to Reagan* (Boulder, CO: Westview Press, 1988).

55. Steve Neal, "Our Best and Worst Presidents," *Chicago Tribune Magazine* (Jan. 10, 1982), pp. 9–18.

56. Jeffrey Tulis, "On Presidential Character," in Joseph M. Bessette and Jeffrey Tulis, eds., *The Presidency in the Constitutional Order* (Baton Rouge: Louisiana State University Press, 1981), pp. 283–313.

57. Stanley A. Renshon, "A Preliminary Assessment of the Clinton Presidency: Character, Leadership and Performance," *Political Psychology* 15 (1994), pp. 382, 380. Also see Stanley A. Renshon, *The Clinton Presidency: Campaigning, Governing, and the Psychology of Leadership* (Boulder, CO: Westview Press, 1995), pp. 57–87.

58. Barbara J. Kellerman and Ryan J. Barilleaux, *The President as World Leader* (New York: St. Martin's Press, 1991), p. 69.

59. Doris Kearns, *Lyndon Johnson and the American Dream* (New York: Harper & Row, 1976), p. 393.

60. Bruce Mazlish, *In Search of Nixon: A Psychohistorical Inquiry* (New York: Basic Books, 1972), pp. 138–139.

61. Betty Glad, *Jimmy Carter: In Search of the Great White House* (New York: Norton, 1980), p. 505.

62. Betty Glad, "Black and White Thinking: Ronald Reagan's Approach to Foreign Policy," *Political Psychology* (March 1983), p. 68.

63. Barber, *The Presidential Character*, 3rd ed., p. 5.

64. Ibid., p. 448.

65. Ibid., pp. 66–67.

66. *Time*, (Feb. 6, 1994), p. 23.

67. James David Barber, *The Presidential Character: Predicting Performance in the White House*, 4th ed. (Englewood Cliffs, NJ: Prentice Hall, 1992), p. 228.

68. Ibid., p. 255.

3

The Political Connection: Recruiting and Nominating a President

The Constitution includes only three formal requirements to be president: "No person except a natural born citizen, or a citizen of the United States at the time of the adoption of this Constitution, shall be eligible to the office of the President; neither shall any person be eligible to that office who shall not have attained to the age of thirty-five years, and been fourteen years a resident within the United States." By these criteria alone, millions of Americans would be eligible to run for president, but these formal requirements are augmented by informal ones, which we call *availability standards*. Nearly four decades ago a famous presidency scholar, Clinton Rossiter, offered this characterization of what qualities a presidential candidate ought to have:

> [The candidate] must be, according to unwritten law: a man, white, a Christian. . . . He almost certainly must be: a Northerner or Westerner, less than sixty-five years old, of Northern European stock, experienced in politics and public service, healthy. . . . He ought to be: from a state larger than Kentucky, more than forty-five years old, a family man, of British stock, a veteran, a Protestant, a lawyer, a state governor, a Mason, Legionnaire, or Rotarian— preferably all three, a small-town boy, a self-made man, especially if a Republican, experienced in international affairs, a cultural middle-brow who likes baseball, detective stories, fishing, pop concerts, picnics, and seascapes.[1]

His observation suggested that, because winning presidential candidates must be supported by more voters than not, they tend to be representative sociologically of the demographic groups and social values that predominate in our political culture. But four decades have passed, bringing about social and technological changes, a revolution in civil rights, and greater tolerance of diversity. With the election of John F. Kennedy those old standards began to crumble. Since 1960 presidents have been southerners, one has been a Catholic, one lived in a small state, several have been neither a governor nor a lawyer, one was divorced and our most recent incumbent had no military experience and acknowledged marital infidelity.

CHANGING AVAILABLITY STANDARDS

What kinds of people are elected president (Table 3-1)? William Jefferson Clinton is the 41st person to be inaugurated president of the United States (but he is officially the 42nd president because Grover Cleveland served two nonconsecutive terms). He, like those who preceded him, is white, male, and Protestant. In 1960 John F. Kennedy was the first Catholic to win the highest office. Thus ended the political legacy of 1928 when Republican Herbert Hoover soundly defeated his Democratic rival, Alfred E. Smith, an Irish Catholic political boss from New York City, affirming the conventional wisdom that no Catholic could win the presidency. Kennedy's nomination generated more support from Catholic voters, but his religion hurt him in the South among fundamentalist Protestants.

John F. Kennedy also lowered the age threshold by becoming the youngest (at forty-three) president-elect. (Kennedy was not the youngest president, however, because forty-two-year-old Vice President Theodore Roosevelt succeeded to the office after William McKinley was assassinated.) Yet the age factor did not handicap Ronald Reagan who was elected in 1980 at age sixty-nine. Clinton represented the passing of a generation, a fact he noted during the 1992 campaign and reinforced by choosing a youthful Al Gore as his running mate. Whereas past presidents could recollect the Great Depression, World War II, and the Cold War of the 1950s, Clinton was a student during the 1960s and thus had a special rapport with youthful voters.

The bias against southern candidates also has passed. The trauma of the Civil War encouraged Republican candidates to wave the "bloody shirt" in their anti-Democratic rhetoric, which made it risky for the Democrats, although until recently they dominated what they perceived as the solid South, to put forward a presidential nominee from Dixie. Woodrow Wilson was born in Virginia, but his political credentials were established in New Jersey; Truman lived in Missouri, and Lyndon Johnson was a Texan who assumed the office after the tragedy of Kennedy's assassination. Not until 1976 did Jimmy Carter overcome this obstacle, which made it easier for the Democrats to nominate Clinton, who was then governor of Arkansas.

Studies of political recruitment find that elites are more homogeneous socially as one proceeds from the local to the state to the national level of government. So it is not surprising that American presidents are more alike than are members of the House of Representatives or even the Senate. Except for Kennedy, whose antecedents were Irish, all presidents trace their ethnic origins to the United Kingdom or another northern European country. Most presidents attained higher levels of education and prestigious occupations—most typically lawyers—than the population, and they came from more affluent class backgrounds based on their fathers' occupations. Clinton was a Rhodes Scholar, although his roots (briefly) in Hope, Arkansas, were quite humble (Clinton does not own a home in Arkansas and is clearly the least affluent president of modern times).

Table 3-1. Demographic Attributes of Presidents, 1789–1996*

Attribute	N	Attribute	N
Sex		20,000–99,000	5
Male	41	100,000–515,547	3
Race		*Prior Office Held*	
Caucasian	41	State legislature	1
		Governor	9
Religion		Federal administration	8
Catholic	1	House of Representatives	1
Jewish	0	Senate	4
Protestant	40	Vice president	14
Episcopalian	11	No public office	4
Presbyterian	6		
Unitarian	4	*Father's Occupation*	
Methodist	4	Statesman/Politician	4
Disciples of Christ	3	Business/Finance	17
Baptist	4	Skilled Tradesman	6
Dutch Reformed	2	Military Career	3
Quaker	2	Learned Profession	7
Congregationalist	1	Farmer/Planter	3
Not specified	3	Salesman	1
Education Level		*State of Residence*	
College degree	28	South (Confederacy)	13
Some college	5	Virginia	5
No college	8	Tennessee	3
		Louisiana	1
Age (At Inauguration)		Texas	2
35–45	2	Georgia	1
46–55	21	Arkansas	1
56–65	16	Non-South	28
66+	2	Massachusetts	4
		New York	8
Party Affiliation		Indiana	1
Republican	17	New Hampshire	1
Democrat	14	Illinois	2
Democratic-Republican	4	Pennsylvania	1
Whig	3	Ohio	6
Federalist	2	New Jersey	1
Union/Republican	1	California	2
		Missouri	1
Ethnic Origins		Michigan	1
English	18		
Other Anglo-Saxon	17	*Mobility*	
Dutch	3	Resided in state of birth	22
Swiss-German	2	Resided in state not of birth	19
Irish	1		
		Occupation	
Size of Birthplace		Law	20
Under 5,000	16	Military	7
5,000–19,000	17		

Table 3-1. Demographic Attributes of Presidents, 1789–1996* *(continued)*

Attribute	N	Attribute	N
Tailor	1	Haberdasher	1
Educator/Teacher	2	Newspaper editor	1
Engineer	1	Writer	1
Farmer/Planter	3	Oil Business	1
Actor	1	Public service/Politics	2

*(N = 41) Grover Cleveland is counted once in these distributions.

Being wealthy is not a liability in American politics (both Franklin Roosevelt and John F. Kennedy were born to extremely wealthy families) unless a lifetime of affluence gives a candidate the image of being too aristocratic. Senator Tom Harkin (D–Iowa), an early contender for the 1992 Democratic nomination, continually made mocking references to the incumbent as George Herbert Walker Bush, to imply that the Bush Ivy League pedigree caused him to lose touch with ordinary people. But Harkin's ridicule seemed to have backfired as being too strident. So, looking back, apparently education, occupation, and class origins were less relevant to presidential electability because they are less visible to the public, whereas other factors, such as religion, gender, or race, were obstacles to recruiting non-Christians, women, or minorities as president. But opinion polls show that Americans, more than ever before, are willing to consider candidates regardless of their religion, gender, or race (Figure 3-1). A survey taken in the late 1980s found that upward of 80 percent would be willing to elect a woman, a Jew, an African American, or a Catholic as president. Not all barriers have fallen, however; a Gallup Poll in 1983 found that 42 percent would vote for an atheist and only 29 percent would elect a homosexual to America's highest office.[2]

In 1984 Democratic presidential candidate Walter Mondale chose Geraldine Ferraro to be the first woman vice presidential candidate, and 1992 was portrayed as the "Year of the Woman" given the unprecedented numbers running and elected to Congress. Women have been elected prime minister in such nations as Israel, India, and Great Britain, and polls show that more and more Americans do not perceive gender as a disqualification for the highest office. Yet no woman has emerged in either party as a leading candidate for the presidency.

Signs also indicate that racial considerations may be less important today. Civil rights leader Jesse Jackson was the close runner-up behind Michael Dukakis in the 1988 contest for the Democratic presidential nomination. Jackson had great name recognition, perhaps too much. His effort to forge a "rainbow" coalition was confined mainly to the black community because whites held strongly negative evaluations of his candidacy. During the 1996 pre-primary campaign, however, an African American surfaced as the only Republican who could defeat President Clinton in the

Figure 3-1. Changes over Time in Willingness of Public to Elect Qualified Member of Particular Groups to Presidency

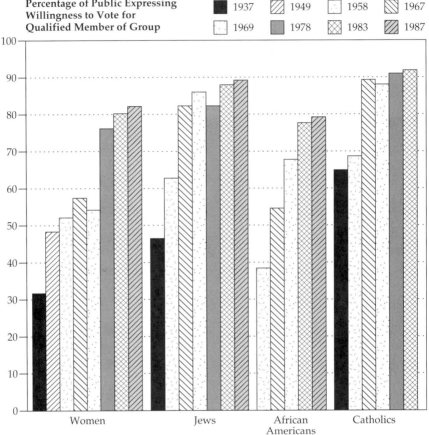

early polls. He was General Colin Powell, who served in the Reagan administration but was elevated to chairman of the Joint Chiefs of Staff by President Bush. There was tremendous press speculation—and apprehension inside the Clinton White House—that Powell would declare his candidacy, but ultimately he cited personal reasons and dropped out.

With the notable exception of Dwight D. Eisenhower, who was the Supreme Allied Commander during World War II and never held elective office, presidents are politicians. Unless the prospective candidate is a military hero, like Eisenhower or Colin Powell, holding public office is essential to giving a candidate name recognition and political connections with party leaders. According to one study, "The route to presidential prominence is overwhelmingly political—90 percent of the persons surfacing in the polls between 1936 and 1972 were public officeholders."[3] Thirty-seven presidents held public office prior to their election. Carter, Reagan, and Clinton were governors before campaigning for the presidency.

One-third of U.S. vice presidents have succeeded to the highest office, mainly upon the death (or resignation in Nixon's case) of the incumbent. Rarely are vice presidents able to win the White House outright, despite their closeness to the Oval Office. George Bush made history by being the first person since Martin Van Buren, in 1837, to succeed directly by election to the presidency from the vice presidency. Since the 1930s U.S. senators have had a better chance of becoming vice president than governors, House members, or members of the Cabinet, and two recent senators were chosen as vice presidential running mates: George Bush picked Senator Dan Quayle (R–Ind.) in 1988 and Bill Clinton chose Senator Albert Gore (D–Tenn.) in 1992. Quayle's political chances ended with Bush's defeat in 1992, whereas Clinton's reelection in 1996 virtually assures that Gore will be a serious presidential contender in the year 2000.

Before the modern era of mass communications, an important political consideration was that presidential candidates come from states with large populations. Before radio and television were widespread, the public relied on newspapers for its political information and it was more difficult for candidates to achieve national recognition. Also, the electoral college method of electing presidents (chapter 4) is a winner-take-all system that gives the presidential candidate who wins the plurality of popular votes in a state its entire allocation of electoral votes. So it made sense for presidential candidates to begin their national campaign with a large base of electoral votes from their home states, particularly because research has determined that presidential candidates (as well as their running mates[4]) get more voter support in their "home state" than elsewhere.[5]

Since 1789 more than three-fifths of U.S. presidents have resided in California, Illinois, Massachusetts, Michigan, New York, Pennsylvania, and Ohio. Today, with the heavy reliance on television to reach voters throughout the country, it is not such a liability for candidates to be recruited from small states. Since the 1960s more Democratic than Republican candidates have had their residence in small states—Hubert Humphrey in 1968 (Minnesota), George McGovern in 1972 (South Dakota), Jimmy Carter in 1976 (Georgia), and Bill Clinton (Arkansas). Although Barry Goldwater, senator from Arizona, was nominated by the GOP in 1964, Nixon and Reagan (both from California) plus Bush (Texas) all had roots in very large states. Although successful presidential candidates no longer need to live in the largest states, it does remain true that both parties' candidates must focus their energies on winning the electoral votes in the key states if they are to have any chance of victory.

NOMINATING CONVENTIONS

An index to the importance of political parties in any regime is the degree to which they monopolize the nominating process. When they do, aspirants for public office must establish their commitment to the party organization and to its principles or they will find it difficult or nearly impossible to secure elective office. The presidential nominating process has undergone three fundamental changes, beginning with (1) the legislative *caucus*, which lasted until 1824, (2) then the *nominating convention* when the political parties really monopolized the presidential selection process, and (3) since 1972 with the *ratifying convention* where the successful presidential contender arrives at the national party convention with enough support to guarantee his nomination.

In 1789 and 1792 there were no organized parties in the United States and a political consensus supported the election of George Washington. But the policies President Washington adopted caused the emergence of factions: the Federalists rallied behind the leadership of Treasury Secretary Alexander Hamilton and the Democratic-Republicans coalesced around Secretary of State Thomas Jefferson (who resigned his position in 1793) and Congressman James Madison. In 1796 the Federalist leadership chose Washington's vice president, John Adams, as their presidential candidate, and the Jeffersonian-Republican members of Congress "caucused" to nominate Thomas Jefferson for president. In 1800 both the Federalists and the Democratic-Republicans relied on the legislative caucus to nominate their national tickets, giving birth to "King Caucus," which survived until 1824.

King Caucus was replaced by the nominating convention. The Anti-Masons, a minor party, held the first convention in 1831, but when the Democratic Party convened its first national convention in Baltimore later that year to nominate Andrew Jackson,[6] it established the model by which major U.S. political parties have nominated candidates ever since. The convention does more than nominate presidential and vice presidential candidates; it writes the party platform, establishes party rules of procedure, and unites the party factions behind the presidential campaign.

Delegates to the party conventions are selected according to party rules and state law. Historically, the states have allowed differing methods for selecting delegates: by state conventions, appointment, state caucuses (as in Iowa today), or by primary election. The presidential primary has become the predominant method of choosing convention delegates since 1968. Before then, delegates chosen by primary election comprised the majority in only one Democratic convention (1916) and two Republican conventions (1916 and 1920).[7] More typically delegates were recruited from the ranks of elected leaders affiliated with that party—mayors, governors, members of Congress, state and local officials, and party activists.

The nomination process and the deliberations of the party convention can define the ideological tone of a campaign and commit the presidential candidate to very specific policies, which explains why ideological factionalism has affected past campaigns. During the 1940s and 1950s, for example, two warring factions debated Republican strategy at its conventions: the conservative "Taft wing" and the moderate "Eastern wing."[8] The nomination of Dwight D. Eisenhower in 1952 was a victory for the moderates, but the conservatives fought back and captured the party nomination in 1964 with Barry Goldwater. Being a more diverse party, the battle for the Democratic presidential and vice presidential nominations involved the entire political spectrum during that period. When Franklin D. Roosevelt chose Harry Truman to be his running mate in 1948, for example, it represented a center-right political coalition. In 1960 the decision by John F. Kennedy to pick Lyndon Baines Johnson as the vice presidential candidate reflected the politics of a left-center coalition within the Democratic convention.[9]

The factionalism in both parties following the Great Depression of the 1930s and World War II of the 1940s was based on economic issues, but the policy agenda changes with the times. The 1960s were a turbulent period in American politics, with the nation torn by anti–Vietnam War protests, civil rights demonstrations, student activism, and lawlessness. Although far apart in their personal ideologies, the nominations of Richard Nixon and Hubert Humphrey in 1968 both represented control by their party's establishment. Nixon was more moderate than outspoken GOP liberals like Governor Nelson Rockefeller of New York, and Humphrey—although a very liberal senator (D–Minn.) before he became vice president—was attacked by the political left and the political right within the Democratic Party. Humphrey was challenged for the presidential nomination by Senators Eugene McCarthy (D–Minn.) and Robert Kennedy (D–N.Y.) because he was identified with the unpopular Vietnam War policies of President Lyndon Johnson. At the same time segregationist governor George Wallace of Alabama bolted the Democratic Party to organize his own American-Independent Party in an effort to win the presidency.

Factionalism means that a party cannot present a unified image to the country, particularly a problem for the out-party because the president symbolizes the goals and ideology of the in-party. For this reason it is virtually impossible for a party to repudiate its president. Few incumbents have been denied renomination by their party—only Tyler, Andrew Johnson, Pierce, Fillmore, Buchanan, and Chester Arthur—and it has never happened in the twentieth century. Certain presidents have declined to seek renomination, however, including Theodore Roosevelt, Calvin Coolidge, Harry Truman, and Lyndon Johnson. For Truman and Johnson the decision to retire from public life was prompted by a steep decline in their popularity. If renominated, however, a president is not easily defeated. Only four incumbents have been defeated for reelection in this century, three of them quite recently: Taft in 1912, Ford in 1976, Carter in 1980, and Bush in 1992.

It is unlikely that the political parties today can nominate an unknown person for the highest office, although such "dark horse" presidential candidates were not infrequently nominated before the 1920s. Usually they would emerge as the nominee after the front-runners for the party nomination deadlocked. The last time conventions turned to a dark horse candidate was in 1920 for the Republicans (Warren G. Harding, who was elected) and in 1924 when the Democrats required 103 ballots to nominate John W. Davis. Nowadays the parties are compelled to turn to celebrity candidates given the influence of the mass media and public opinion polling as well as the impact of the presidential primaries.[10]

Conventions usually can establish a degree of unity behind their candidate because the convention choice typically is also the party membership's choice. During the 1936 to 1972 period, one study found that in 19 of those 20 campaigns the final preconvention leader in the opinion polls, if he actively sought it, was in fact nominated by the party.[11] Only once was the pre-primary leader in the polls defeated in key presidential primaries and then denied the nomination: in 1972 Senator Edmund Muskie (D–Maine) faltered and Senator George McGovern (D–S.D.) was nominated instead. McGovern was the first candidate in modern times to overcome his weak support among party leaders as well as his low standing in the opinion polls to capture the nomination. His maneuver would have been impossible before the widespread use of presidential primaries.

In 1972 three-fifths of the delegates to the Democratic national convention were chosen in primaries. In the past a contender for the nomination had the option of considering an "insider" or "outsider" strategy. Insider candidates worked through the party organization and developed political contacts with important officials in the various states; outsider candidates who lacked those contacts entered the primaries to prove their superior vote-getting ability. John F. Kennedy in 1960 used an outsider strategy against the odds-on favorite, Senator Hubert H. Humphrey (D–Minn.), whose insider strategy relied on the party professionals. By doing well in a state with heavy Protestant concentrations (West Virginia), Kennedy showed he was more electable and laid to rest the concerns about his Catholicism. Today, with the widespread use of primaries, no serious contender for the presidency can ignore them and hope to be drafted by the convention for the nation's highest office.

PRIMARIES AND CAUCUSES

The year 1968 was not a good one for the Democrats. The party was seriously divided after primary challenges against President Lyndon Johnson were mounted by Senator Eugene McCarthy (D–Minn.) and Senator Robert Kennedy (D–N.Y.), brother of President Kennedy (Robert was assassinated after his victory in the 1968 California primary). When the Democratic convention was held in Chicago to nominate Vice President Hubert H. Humphrey, the American people witnessed via television a traumatic political event. Inside the convention dissidents were charging "boss rule" and outside anti-Vietnam demonstrators and student radicals were confronting the Chicago police in what one report termed a "police riot." Because Humphrey was nominated without winning any delegates in the primaries, dissidents charged that the convention was ignoring the views of the rank-and-file Democrats and was controlled by party bosses, notably Mayor Richard J. Daley of Chicago.

Humphrey was nominated anyway, but to address that grievance the delegates to the 1968 convention adopted a resolution requiring the state party organizations to give "all Democrats a full, meaningful, and timely opportunity to participate" in the selection of delegates to future conventions. As a result, the Democratic National Committee chairman appointed a Commission on Party Structure and Delegate Selection to be cochaired first by Senator George McGovern (D–S.D.) and later by Representative Donald Fraser (D–Minn.). The McGovern-Fraser Commission recommended far-reaching reforms to make the 1972 convention more representative of membership opinion.

The immediate beneficiary of those reforms was McGovern, who exploited the new system to capture the nomination in 1972, but many specific recommendations were short lived because later party commissions further revised its rules. Perhaps the most controversial proposal by the commission was a so-called quota system that required the representation of "minorities, women, and young people in reasonable relationship to their presence in the population of the state." Between 1968 and 1972 the number of women delegates increased from 13 to 40 percent, black participation increased from 5.5 to 15 percent, and participation by delegates aged thirty or under rose from 4 to 21 percent.[12]

The changes proposed by the McGovern-Fraser Commission for selecting delegates is the fundamental reason why presidential primaries have become so important today for both Democrats and Republicans. Given the complexity of its reforms, it was very difficult for state party organizations to comply at every stage of the nomination process if they wanted to retain the use of state caucuses and state conventions for selecting delegates. As a consequence many states turned to the primary election as the easiest method of reforming their delegate selection process.

Before 1972 many states allowed voters to cast ballots in preferential primaries to express their support for the various individuals seeking their party's nomination. This device, called the beauty contest because it measured rank-and-file party opinion toward the various presidential hopefuls, was entirely separate from the laws and party rules that governed how each state chose its delegates to the national conventions. The 1972 reforms gave the party rank and file a real voice in presidential nominations mainly through the extensive use of binding primaries, although a few states retained the caucus system of choosing delegates. In this kind of primary, voters are able to choose among slates of delegates who are committed, or pledged, to one specific presidential contender. If the delegates pledged to support that candidate, say Bill Clinton in 1992, win the plurality of votes cast, then they are entitled to attend the Democratic national convention. Once there, however, the rules bind them to vote only for Bill Clinton on the first ballot, unless Clinton releases his delegates from that obligation. Sometimes the losing presidential contender will release his or her delegates from that first ballot commitment, allowing them to support the winner in order to foster party unity.

A more complicated alternative to the primary election is the party caucus in which the rank and file actively participate in choosing the delegates to the national conventions. Nearly one in six delegates are chosen through caucus systems, and best known among this group is Iowa, which holds the first state caucus. In February, Iowans meet face to face in precinct caucuses to choose delegates to attend county conventions in March. They in turn select delegates to congressional district conventions in May. These district conventions choose district delegates to the national convention, and in June a state party convention picks at-large delegates to attend the national party convention. Because the caucus system is so cumbersome and time consuming, its use is limited to sparsely populated and rural states.

Many disputes arose over the implementation of the 1972 reform recommendations by state party organizations, and one eventually reached the Supreme Court. It involved the makeup of the Illinois delegation. One group of delegates were the so-called regular Democrats under Chicago mayor Richard J. Daley, but a rival group was organized by a reform coalition that included the Reverend Jesse Jackson. The 1972 convention refused to seat Daley and his allies, which caused the litigation, but eventually the Supreme Court in *Cousins v. Wigoda* (1975) ruled that the regulations of the national political parties take precedence over state laws regarding the qualifications and eligibility of delegates to the party conventions.

McGovern's defeat forced the Democratic Party to reevaluate its party rules and find ways to reduce internal factionalism and guarantee a larger say by party professionals and elected officials. A wave of new study commissions followed. The Mikulski Commission replaced the strict quotas with affirmative action guidelines for the 1976 convention. In 1976 the Democratic convention mandated a Winograd Commission, which offered an array of new rules for 1980 including that proportional representation of delegates be adopted in each state and the old winner-take-all system be eliminated. Yet another attempt was made by the Hunt Commission to redefine the party rules for the 1984 party convention. Its major recommendation was the addition of several hundred superdelegates to the convention, comprised of party professionals and elected officials who would not be selected through the caucuses or primaries and who ideally would remain uncommitted to any prospective nominee. The hope was that these superdelegates would act as a moderating force and facilitate compromise should no candidate emerge from the preconvention primary/caucus battles with a majority of the convention delegates. The superdelegates represented almost 20 percent of the membership of recent Democratic conventions (superdelegates are not a special category of delegates to Republican conventions).

THE NOMINATION CAMPAIGN

As political scientist Austin Ranney once put it, the nomination process is more important than the general election for "deciding the kind of person who [will] occupy the White House."[13] If so, then who are the voters in primary elections and how do they choose from among the presidential contenders? Because voting turnout is lower in primaries than in general elections, those who participate have a disproportionate say in the selection process. There is research on who they are—generally primary voters have more education, income, and occupational status than nonvoters[14]—but fewer studies have been done on how they make choices.

Party affiliation (a key determinant of voting in general elections) is not operative in primary elections so voters have to rely more heavily on candidate image and ideology. A study by Wattier of the 1980 GOP primaries in Florida, Illinois, Massachusetts, and New Hampshire found that "primary voters usually support the candidate [Bush or Reagan] closer to their ideological identification."[15] Wattier extended his analysis to the 1980 Democratic primaries of ten states and found that "[Ted] Kennedy received a larger percentage of the liberal vote (62%); Carter, a larger percentage of the conservative vote (60%). The votes of moderates were more evenly divided. Kennedy received 48%; Carter, 52%."[16] Thus the preconvention strategies that prospective nominees contrive are aimed at appealing to the party rank and file by ideology and issue positions or the candidate's personal attributes and character. In the modern era of weakened party organizations, preconvention campaigns are highly personalized insofar as candidates create their own organizational apparatus, engage in fund-raising to garner a federal subsidy, and develop an issue agenda to attract a personal following among distinct voter groups in the primaries.

Like Clinton in 1996, Reagan in 1984, and Nixon in 1972, popular incumbents do not face nomination challenges, but presidents who seem vulnerable do. Ideological-based candidates challenged Ford in 1976, Carter in 1980, and Bush in 1992. Ever since Ronald Reagan appeared at the 1964 GOP convention that nominated Barry Goldwater, he had cultivated strong conservative credentials, and his high-profile position of California's governor gave him instant recognition. He announced his bid for the nomination in November 1975 and "his manner of doing so showed the strength of the challenge he was to make. The night before, he answered questions in New Hampshire, then flew to Washington's National Press Club for the announcement itself, then went on to press conferences in Florida, North Carolina and California."[17] For his part, President Ford tried to placate his party's conservative wing, by signaling that Vice President Nelson Rockefeller (the liberal former governor of New York) would be dropped from the 1976 ticket, but ultimately Ford chose a classic incumbency strategy of getting the GOP organizations in Ohio, New York, Pennsylvania, and Michigan to endorse his reelection. In the end he barely survived the Reagan challenge, but then lost to Jimmy Carter.

President Carter had to confront Senator Ted Kennedy (D–Mass.) whose 1980 candidacy represented the liberal wing of the party (organized labor and civil rights groups) that had become totally alienated with Carter's policies. Unlike Ford, who did not believe his nomination would be threatened, the Carter team made preparations in advance. One of their tactics was to change the rules of the game to favor the incumbent. According to the delegate selection rules formulated by the Winograd Commission, delegates chosen in primaries would not be allocated according to each candidate by "proportional representation" unless that candidate received 15 percent or more of the vote (which was designed to discourage splintering the delegates among too many contenders). Also, Carter's supporters altered the primary dates for Alabama and Georgia, moving them ahead to March 11, 1976, to coincide with the Florida primary, so Carter could win that entire bloc of southern delegates.[18]

As the primary season unfolded, knowing he could not defeat Kennedy on the issues that appealed to rank and file Democrats, Carter instead raised the character issue by recalling Chappaquiddick (where a car driven by Kennedy plunged into a canal and killed a young woman aide) and Kennedy's marital problems. Kennedy's political challenge quickly faltered, although he vowed to continue his fight with Carter for policy concessions on the convention floor.

Whereas Ford reverted to incumbency to fend off Reagan and Carter, and manipulated the party rules to solidify his early primary victories, President Bush when confronted with the insurgency of Patrick Buchanan tried to coopt the latter's conservative agenda. Gerald Pomper explains Bush's dilemma this way:

> George Bush consistently misread the nature of the challenge from Patrick Buchanan or, perhaps, read the challenge very well but chose not to heed its implications. Buchanan's attack on George Bush from the political right evoked in the president a desperate political fear—that one of the core groups of Republican voters he had inherited from Ronald Reagan and that had served as a foundation of his 1988 victory might be lost. This segment of the electorate is variously referred to as "social conservatives" or "moralists"—voters whose support of Republican candidates derives from their opposition to abortion, gun control, and gay rights and their support for school prayer and strict controls on immigration.[19]

Buchanan leveled a devastating attack by using close-up TV shots of George Bush in 1988 uttering what became those infamous words—"Read my lips: no new taxes"—in political advertisements across New Hampshire, and in the primary Buchanan lost 37 percent to Bush's 53 percent. Moreover, exit polls showed that the protest vote for Buchanan was based on economic grievances—not his social agenda—and after New Hampshire Buchanan's support began to falter. But this experience influenced President Bush, who "openly capitulated to his party's right wing and came closer than any incumbent president to finding himself on the threshold of the general election in the position of a factional candidate. By allowing the conservatives to showcase such issues as 'family values' at the convention, Bush allowed the moralistic tenor of the party to degenerate into fanaticism and meanness of spirit, repelling the middle-of-the-road voter."[20]

The first presidential primary is in New Hampshire and the first caucus state is Iowa, and winning or losing those contests may depend more on the interpretation by media elites and the public relations spin control it gets from the candidate's staff than the actual number of votes cast. In 1972 Senator Ed Muskie (D–Maine) won 46.4 percent of the primary vote in New Hampshire, against George McGovern's 37.2 percent, but Muskie was deemed the loser because he was expected to do much better in a state neighboring his own. Worse than that, at a press conference in New Hampshire front-runner Muskie shed tears in an emotional defense of his wife, who was accused by conservative publisher William Loeb of the *Manchester Union Leader* of having a drinking problem. As a comparison, in 1992 the Democratic primary contenders held a debate and, taking an assertive approach, Bill Clinton angrily reacted when former California governor Jerry Brown publicly accused Hillary Rodham Clinton of channeling state business to her Little Rock law firm.

New Hampshire and Iowa are crucially important, not because of their size, but their "temporal primacy: Iowa results, plus media spin, structure the alternatives for the New Hampshire primary. These two events together plus media spin structure alternatives for everything that follows."[21] To reduce the political impact of those two small states, several southern states scheduled their primaries on the same day in March—"Super Tuesday"—in hopes that candidates forced to compete simultaneously in Alabama, Florida, Georgia, Kentucky, Louisiana, Mississippi, Missouri, North Carolina, Oklahoma, Tennessee, and Texas (also the Maryland, Massachusetts, and Rhode Island primaries were scheduled the same day) would have to moderate their views in order to win over more conservative southern voters. This development of moving ahead the dates of so many caucuses and primaries is called front-loading the campaign: future presidential contenders have to begin their organizing and fund-raising efforts a year or more before the actual election year.

The front-loading process obviously offers advantages to established, well-known figures in both parties and works against outsiders like Jimmy Carter, whose 1976 primary campaign was a textbook example of how someone without name recognition organizes a run for the White House. That Jimmy Carter, a one-term governor of Georgia, could win the presidential contest suggests that under the right political conditions, and with luck and good timing, relative unknowns can achieve celebrity status by effective use of the mass media. The fact that Carter was a political unknown (on the popular quiz show "What's My Line?" the panelists could not identify Carter as the governor of Georgia) benefited him during the period after Watergate when Washington insiders were suspect.

But an effective primary campaign requires organization and plannning. Carter decided to run for president in the fall of 1972; he began making contacts within the party including a meeting with Democratic national chairman Robert Strauss in March 1973, which resulted in Carter's appointment to chairman of the 1974 Democratic campaign. During most of 1974 Carter traveled around the country, making more contacts, and planning to spend a lot of time in the key states of New Hampshire, Iowa, and Florida during 1975. Still Carter was no political celebrity until a straw poll of Democratic activists attending a dinner in Ames, Iowa on October 5, 1975, was publicized. Carter's aides anticipated that a straw poll would be taken and encouraged his supporters to attend the gathering, so when the *Des Moines Register* took the survey, Jimmy Carter emerged with 23 percent, which led a respected columnist for the *New York Times* to headline his front-page story "Carter Appears to Hold a Solid Lead in Iowa."[22] No more was Carter an unknown quantity.

More than once a highly publicized scandal has derailed presidential ambitions. It happened to Senator Gary Hart (D–Colo.), the runner-up in the 1984 Democratic primary competition, who was the 1988 favorite among party rank and file. Hart, a married man, was photographed by a Miami reporter with an attractive model, Donna Rice, who was alleged to have been sexually involved with Hart. Recollects Gerald Pomper: "Comedians literally transformed his campaign into a joke. Among the more printable quips was Johnny Carson's suggestion that Hart's campaign slogan was, 'He's back in the saddle again.' Hounded by reporters, and despite some public support, Hart withdrew from the race."[23]

Scandalous behavior did not end Clinton's 1992 presidential bid, however, which perhaps holds the record as the best recent example of spin control by campaign handlers. Clinton declared victory in New Hampshire by claiming he was the "comeback kid," and the press widely accepted the idea of a resurgent Clinton even though he finished second (25 percent) to former senator Paul Tsongas (D–Mass.), who won 33 percent of the vote. Although Clinton was considered the front-runner, commentators had expected Massachusetts-bred Tsongas to have done even better, whereas Clinton's second-place finish was judged in terms of all the press revelations about his infidelity. One month before the New Hampshire primary, the supermarket tabloid *Star* printed a story alleging that Clinton, while married, had had an affair for twelve years with aide Gennifer Flowers. Clinton's handlers were warned about the bombshell and tried a preemptive strike by having Bill and Hillary appear together on the popular CBS program *60 Minutes*, which followed the Super Bowl football game. The maneuver worked; Clinton's favorable ratings increased to 67 percent after the broadcast.[24]

Good fortune also helped Clinton's campaign. He would have been an underdog in his bid for the Democratic nomination had the leading contenders—including Governor Mario Cuomo of New York—not all withdrawn from consideration. One year earlier when serious candidates had to plan their prenomination strategies, President Bush had frightened off the establishment Democrats. He appeared to be unbeatable given his enormous popularity after the Persian Gulf War.

In 1996 President Clinton had more going for him than simply incumbency. Robert Dole did not have the luxury of a unified GOP because he did not clinch the nomination with the requisite number of delegates until the March 26 California primary. It was a more difficult than anticipated battle to win the nomination (Dole also had to spend disproportionate funds during the early stages and thus lacked sufficient money to sustain his campaign over the summer months). As Senate Majority Leader Dole was the leading Republican, but he faced a large contingent of rivals who argued he was old, too much a Washington insider, or too fuzzy on the issues that mattered to conservatives.

February 20, 1996, was the date for the New Hampshire primary, but four months earlier—October 1995—a political forum in that state attracted *ten* declared candidates for the GOP nomination.[25] Another aspirant had been Governor Pete Wilson (R–Calif.), but anemic poll standings and no campaign funds had forced him to withdraw quietly from the race the month before.

Had Dole decisively won the New Hampshire primary, he could have quickly put an end to confusion within Republican ranks. Dole was presumed to be the leader, but New Hampshire—not at all typical of the nation—is a conservative state. When Patrick Buchanan upset Senator Dole in New Hampshire with 29 percent of the vote (against Dole's 25 percent and third-placed Lamar Alexander's 23 percent), the Associated Press declared Buchanan the "winner" and he proclaimed, "This is a crucial moment in the political history of the country. We can recapture the party. We can reshape the party. Nothing like this has happened in the Republican Party in my lifetime."[26] Buchanan did not reshape the party, although his victory allowed other candidates and media commentators to raise questions about Dole's leadership prowess. Meanwhile Dole had to respond, defending himself against fellow Republicans, instead of going on the attack against Bill Clinton.

MONEY MATTERS

Although it has mainly been the presidential primaries that have encouraged larger numbers of self-proclaimed candidates who seek the presidency, another reason for the crowded preconvention field of contenders is the advent of public financing of presidential campaigns during both the primary and general election stages. In the decades before public funding, wealthy contributors—called "fat cats"—decided whose candidacy to back based largely on the prospects that a particular contender had good prospects for winning the White House. Although frivolous candidates and extremists might have wanted to contest the presidential nomination, without large contributors and the infusion of public funds, most of those marginal candidates would have been forced to withdraw from the race at an early stage.

Because public funds are now dispersed to any declared candidate according to how much money each candidate raises in small contributions across various states, the system works to the advantage of any candidate—whether extremist, celebrity, or "favorite son" (politicians who want to raise their own national exposure or draw attention to their home state)—who desires to enter the early stage of the preconvention campaign.

Money was not an all-consuming activity for the leading presidential contenders when two major parties dominated the nomination system. But now the free-for-all primaries mean a candidate has to raise a lot of money to be considered viable and, just as importantly, to discourage potential adversaries from contesting the nomination. The system of public funding was established by the Federal Election Campaign Act of 1971 (FECA) and the Revenue Act of 1971 (which created a presidential election fund and allowed taxpayers to check off $1—now $3—of federal income taxes for publicly funded presidential elections). Amendments were added to that legislation in 1974, to create a Federal Election Commission (FEC), and in 1979, this time prompted by the Supreme Court ruling in *Buckley v. Valeo* 424 U.S. 1 (1976), as well as in 1984 and 1993. *Buckley* nullified a ceiling on spending by individuals or groups as a violation of First Amendment speech guarantees, although limits on contributions to candidates and limits on candidates accepting public funds were upheld. Also the Court disallowed a provision whereby Congress appointed four of the six-person FEC (the 1974 amendments overcame this objection by allowing the president to nominate and the Senate to confirm all six).

Public funding extends from prenomination through the general election. During any election cycle, no individual can contribute more than $1,000 to a candidate, $20,000 to a national party committee, or $5,000 to a political action committee, and his or her total contribution cannot exceed $25,000. If a candidate agrees to accept federal funds, personal contributions from those candidates and their immediate families cannot exceed $50,000 at the prenomination stage and another $50,000 during the general election, but candidates who do not accept federal campaign funds can spend unlimited amounts of their own money.

In 1992 billionaire Ross Perot declined to accept any federal funds and personally spent millions of dollars on his campaign, resulting in one of the highest vote percentages (19 percent) of any third-party candidate. His vote share dropped to 8 percent in 1996 after Perot agreed to accept a smaller allocation of federal campaign funds. Unlike his previous presidential campaign, Perot did not have unlimited personal funds to spend on political advertisements and media coverage (and he was excluded from the 1996 presidential debates, which further undermined his ability to reach voters with his limited campaign budget).

For those candidates who accept federal funding, each is limited to spending no more than $10 million during the prenomination stage and $20 million during the general election plus a cost-of-living adjustment from the base year of 1974. However, to qualify for federal funds, candidates have to raise $5,000 in twenty states in contributions not exceeding $250 for a total of $100,000. Only those who meet these fundraising goals are eligible for federal matching grants during the prenomination stage, beginning January 1 of the election year. But not every dollar raised by the candidates is matched, only the first $250, meaning that the maximum federal matching grant would be another $100,000.

In European democracies, campaign funds are usually dispersed by central party organizations to their candidates, which encourages the candidates to follow the party platform and show loyalty to the party program once they are elected to office. But the American system of publicly funded campaigns largely bypasses the party organization and encouraged aspirants for the presidency to go into business for themselves. In an effort to reenergize their party organizations, both Republicans and Democrats made a concerted effort in 1996 to solicit so-called soft campaign contributions, but this time they were aided by a favorable Supreme Court ruling.

Soft money donations from rich individuals and corporations go to the political parties—not the candidates—and have proven to be a huge loophole in the campaign finance laws. Such funds, for example, may be targeted to TV advertisements that praise all the party's candidates or attack the opposition party's candidates. In the case of *Colorado Republican Committee v. Federal Election Commission* (1996), the Supreme Court ruled that the FEC may not limit how much political parties spend to help their candidates unless the FEC proves collusion between the party and its candidate. By extending the free speech guarantees under the First Amendment to party expenditures, the Court rejected the FEC position that spending by political parties was never done independently of their candidates.[27]

Because of the feverish pace of fund-raising by both parties during the 1996 election, soft money expenditures became the largest source of campaign funds, and overall spending on the presidential campaign was projected to hit $600 million, a record. Here is a list of expenditure categories allocated to each party:

1. Federal funds of $12.4 million for the 1996 convention.
2. Federal funds of $74 million for the election campaign.
3. Nonfederal "soft" money of $120 to $150 million for party-promoting activities.
4. Nonfederal convention "host" committee funds of $25 million raised by local businesses to promote the party conventions.
5. Nonfederal "compliance" committee funds of $6 million to defray the cost of legal and accounting fees related to complying with the federal campaign laws.
6. Nonfederal "in-kind" donations of office and business equipment (amount unknown).
7. Nonfederal "independent" expenditures by labor unions and advocacy groups without any coordination with the political party (labor unions expended $35 million to help Democrats, but no estimate was available on which groups or how much money was spent to help Republicans).[28]

DELEGATES AND ACTIVISTS

Critics of the delegate selection process argue that the people who vote in primary elections are not often representative of the party's membership, and certainly are not representative of the entire electorate. A candidate nominated by delegates who were chosen in primaries and a platform written by those kind of delegates may handicap the party's ability to compete in the general election. Those who defend the primary system of delegate selection argue that when the conventions were dominated by state party organizations, the parties too often abandoned their commitment to principle and favored nominees who said all things to all people in order to maximize voter appeal. That happened in the past when large numbers of delegates were mayors, governors, and members of Congress whose main interest was finding a strong candidate to head the ticket and thus wage an effective campaign.

The primary reforms were achieved at a political price, however. The 1972 nominee for the Democratic Party ultimately carried only Massachusetts and the District of Columbia against President Nixon. The delegates to that convention were far more liberal than most Democratic voters on such issues as school busing, welfare, and crime. As Ladd concluded, "The convention that formally nominated McGovern was strikingly unrepresentative of the policy preferences of the mass of Democrats."[29] His observation is confirmed by a Kirkpatrick study which found that Democratic voters in 1972 were closer ideologically to the Republican convention delegates than to those who attended the Democratic convention.[30] Thus the situation that year was the reverse of what was discovered in 1956, a time when Democratic delegates were ideologically more representative of both Republican and Democratic voters than were the delegates to the Republican convention that year.[31]

A study of the 1976 and 1980 convention delegates by Miller and Jennings found, on a wide range of issues, "large absolute differences in terms of what are widely recognized as conservative and liberal positions." Moreover, their findings showed the following:

> [D]ifferential rejection and antipathy, when coupled with the element of differential approval, not only produces the extreme differences between the parties in terms of group evaluations, but it also implies a marked polarization of attitudes towards groups [blacks, gays, unions, for example] going well beyond varying degrees of favorableness. In this sense the opinion cultures of the two elites are truly antagonistic.[32]

Ideological polarization among Republican and Democratic delegates extended also to the conventions of 1984, 1988, and 1992 (Table 3-2). Since 1976, no more than 3 percent of GOP delegates were liberals, whereas conservatives represented 48 percent (1976) to 70 percent (1992) of the total. For Democratic delegates, liberals dominated but to a lesser degree, ranging from 40 percent to 48 percent of the total, although conservatives never rose above 8 percent. Says Miller, the first term of Reagan's presidency "pro-

Table 3-2. Ideological Polarization of Convention Delegates by Party

	1976		1980		1984		1988		1992		1996	
	Dem	*Rep*	*Dem*	*Rep*	*Dem*	*Rep*	*Dem*	*Rep*	*Dem*	*Rep*	*Dem*	*Rep*
Liberal	40%	3%	46%	2%	48%	1%	43%	0%	47%	1%	43%	0%
Conservative	8%	48%	6%	58%	4%	60%	5%	58%	5%	70%	5%	66%

Source: CBS News/*New York Times* polls. Data for 1976–1992 was adapted from Stephen J. Wayne, *The Road to the White House 1996* (New York: St. Martin's Press, 1996), pp. 110–111; data for 1996 from James Bennet, "In Poll, Ardor for President, Faults and All," *New York Times* (Aug. 26, 1996), p. A12.

duced a visible extension of the ideological polarization of the parties that had taken place during the later 1970s . . . [and] there was an increase in the magnitude of difference separating Democratic from Republican elites and Democratic from Republican rank and file."[33]

The data in Table 3-3 shows what happened to elite and mass opinions within both parties between 1980 and 1984. In both years, GOP delegates and identifiers were more conservative than Democratic delegates and identifiers. As shown by the differences in the means, rank-and-file Republicans and Democrats were much closer in their attitudes compared to the delegates. Note that on most issues the gap widened in 1984 as compared to 1980, especially among the delegates. We can infer from these distributions, therefore, that both party elites are unrepresentative of mass opinion.

Looking back, the Miller-Jennings study found that the 1972 imbalance, when Democratic delegates were ideological outliers compared to the party rank and file, had been corrected by the rightward shift of GOP delegates by 1980. Says Miller,

> [In 1980] symmetry had been restored to the two-party system as Republican estrangement came to equal that of the Democrats. Although our data did not

Table 3-3. Mean Scores of Democratic and Republican Delegates and Partisan Identifiers on Five Policy Areas, 1980 and 1984

Policy Domain	Delegates		Identifiers	
	Democrat	*Republican*	*Democrat*	*Republican*
Liberal-Conservative				
1984	32	72	46	61
1980	34	64	48	62
Social Issues				
1984	27	70	54	64
1980	35	69	49	54
Foreign Policy				
1984	15	67	40	57
1980	38	77	59	68
Domestic Spending				
1984	29	56	25	34
New Politics Groups*				
1984	39	64	46	52
1980	18	59	32	43
Traditional Groups*				
1984	21	89	37	66
1980	23	89	42	67

*New Politics Groups were blacks, women's liberation movement, evangelicals (1980 and 1984), gay men/lesbians and antiabortionists (1984 only). Traditional Groups were conservatives, union leaders, liberals, business interests, Democrats, and Republicans. The delegates and identifiers were asked to scale their attitudes toward each of these groups.

Source: Adapted from Warren E. Miller, *Without Consent: Mass-Elite Linkages in Presidential Politics* (Lexington: University Press of Kentucky, 1988), Tables 11 and 14, pp. 35 and 42. The means were based on a scale from 0 (liberal) to 100 (conservative).

support the thesis of a return to the circumstances of 1956, we did argue that the extremism of a very homogeneous ideological Republican elite had produced a situation in which Democratic leaders were virtually as close to the Republican rank and file as were the Republican leaders.[34]

People who are activists in party organizations obviously are more involved in politics, have stronger opinions on policy issues, and are more apt to develop a political ideology. What applies to the delegates who nominate the national ticket also extends to lower echelon functionaries. An ambitious study by Rapoport, Abramowitz, and McGlennon of 17,628 Democratic and Republican delegates to presidential nominating conventions in 11 nonprimary states found wide differences in opinion on 13 policies (Table 3-4).[35] On all policies Republicans were to the right of Democrats and were especially opposed to affirmative action, the Equal Rights Amendment (for women), national health insurance, and ratifying the SALT II treaty with the Soviet Union. Democrats were more hostile to increased defense spending and nuclear power plants. Their research generally agreed with the findings by Barton and Parsons[36] that the GOP is more unified in its ideology, whereas Democrats, although liberal, historically have exhibited more diversity of opinion within their ranks.

PARTY PLATFORMS

The national conventions draft the party platforms, which are statements of past accomplishments and future goals. Voters usually use the

Table 3-4. Issue Positions of Delegates to State Party Conventions in 1980

Issue	Democrats (Mean Value)*	Republicans (Mean Value)
Equal Rights Amendment	2.06	3.96
Amendment banning abortion	3.56	2.85
Increase defense spending	3.09	1.56
National health insurance	2.54	4.50
Nuclear power (energy)	3.27	2.02
Spending cuts/balance budget	3.22	2.00
Affirmative action programs	2.45	3.71
Deregulation of oil and gas	3.10	1.99
Wage and price controls	2.90	3.96
Reduce inflation	3.13	2.35
Draft (military) registration	2.73	2.16
Ratification of SALT II with Soviets	2.57	4.26
U.S. military in Middle East	2.88	2.25

*For each item the delegates were asked to place themselves on a five-point scale, ranging from "strongly favor" (1) to "strongly oppose" (5), so the higher the mean value equals more opposition.

Source: Ronald B. Rapoport, Alan I. Abramowitz, and John McGlennon, eds., *The Life of the Parties: Activists in Presidential Politics* (Lexington: University Press of Kentucky, 1986), p. 168, Table 9.1.

candidates' statements during the campaign to indicate the probable direction of public policy, but often enough the party platforms make very explicit commitments to interests and voter blocs. It was the strategy of the Clinton campaign staff to make sure the 1992 Democratic platform avoided making excessive promises to groups in order to affirm his image as a centrist candidate and avoid giving the Republicans campaign ammunition that Democrats pander to special interests. Voters may not take platforms seriously, but delegates and party leaders do because they reflect the ideological and policy cleavages between the two parties.

Pomper studied party platforms from 1944 to 1968 and found that one-third of the pledges were similar for both parties, about one-half were made by only one of the parties, and the rest showed that Republicans and Democrats held opposing views.[37] In his update for the period 1960 to 1976, conflicting pledges were only 7 percent of the total, whereas nearly three-fourths of them were in the platform of one party but not the other. Paul David's finding that a high percentage of the very specific pledges eventually were enacted into law[38] is confirmed by Pomper and Monroe.[39] Writing a platform is serious business and, for the in-party, says David, "platform drafting has come increasingly under the influence of the President, usually with active participation by White House staff at all stages."[40]

But sometimes the incumbent loses control of that process, as happened to Jimmy Carter in 1980. The Democratic platform was hotly contested because the renomination of President Carter had been challenged by the liberal wing led by Senator Ted Kennedy (D–Mass.). Although Carter was renominated, the convention adopted three minority planks in its platform that he opposed: a prochoice stand on abortion, a $12 billion jobs program, and sanctions against any Democratic candidates who opposed the (unsuccessful) Equal Rights Amendment (for women). Carter had to wage an uphill battle for reelection, forced to explain his position on the platform he personally opposed, whereas the 1980 GOP platform was written to conform with the conservative views of Ronald Reagan.

Perhaps the most contentious debate over a platform in the modern period occurred in 1948 when the Democratic convention that renominated President Truman resisted including a states' rights plank offered by delegates from the South. Instead, the majority adopted a very strong civil rights plank, which caused the southerners to bolt. They walked out of the convention, formed a third party (Dixiecrat), and nominated Strom Thurmond for president (Thurmond is now the Republican senator from South Carolina but was then one of its Democratic senators). Similarly, the 1968 Democratic convention had to cope with strong anti-Vietnam sentiments, and there ensued a four-hour debate over the war. But President Johnson was able to gain convention approval for a plank that supported his war policies even though it hurt the presidential campaign of Vice President Hubert Humphrey.

Organized interests want specific pledges in the platform because so often they result in public policy, and platforms are viewed as serious commitments by the party activists and their presidential contenders. But do they represent the thinking of ordinary citizens? The guarded answer is yes, based on a study by Alan Monroe. He matched promises in the Republican and Democratic platforms from 1960 through 1980 with data from national surveys to determine how often party pledges are supported and opposed by the majority. The findings indicate "a tendency, albeit imperfect, for each party to adopt positions held by a majority of the public" although "[i]t also appears that the Democratic platforms tend to 'err' more frequently than the Republicans in favoring policy changes that the public opposes."[41] With respect to the social agenda, particularly, he notes, "the Democratic alliance, which has developed in the last 20 years, with ethnic minorities and liberals generally on social issues appears to have resulted in adoption of less popular positions on some occasions. Republicans, on the other hand, can limit their civil rights stands to those positions favored by the public as a whole."[42]

RATIFYING CONVENTIONS

In 1992 Bill Clinton was nominated at a convention in New York City where the Democrats took great pains not to get involved in any bloodletting over policy disputes during prime-time television. It contrasted sharply with the Republican convention where President Bush allowed free rein to conservative spokesmen like Patrick Buchanan in an effort to placate the right wing. The media loves controversy and Buchanan provided great copy, but his speech and others left the impression that the GOP was controlled by extremists. To avoid that kind of embarrassment again, in 1996 the GOP under Bob Dole orchestrated a fine-tuned public relations event that was geared to the prime-time needs of the networks, much to the chagrin of the reporters and anchorpersons. This time Patrick Buchanan was offered a non-prime-time spot for his commentary, whereas such celebrity-status Republicans as General Colin Powell, Governors George Bush of Texas and Christine Todd Whitman of New Jersey, and Elizabeth Hanford Dole (whom pollsters found respondents preferred by a 49 percent to 32 percent margin over Hillary Rodham Clinton as First Lady[43]) were highlighted as were the kick-off speeches by Dole and vice presidential candidate Jack Kemp. The Democrats tried to copy the GOP success, by giving time to Sarah Brady (wife of Jim Brady, press secretary who was shot during an assassination attempt on President Reagan) and actor Christopher Reeve, who had been paralyzed in a horse-riding accident.

But despite the showbiz quality of the conventions, the number of viewers on all the networks dropped from four years earlier. The networks were outsmarted by the Republicans in 1996, and there was an outcry from the critics. "Somehow we have very little trouble the rest of the year seeing through this kind of thing, when Hollywood tries to do it with a movie, or a factory does it with some new product," declared Ted Koppel of ABC's *Nightline*. He ended his live coverage abruptly during the second night of the GOP convention to protest the lack of any "real" news.[44]

During the formative years of television, the networks gave the American people gavel-to-gavel coverage of the conventions, because the conventions actually made important decisions; nobody knew—with certainty—who would win the nomination until ballots were taken of the state delegations. CBS began its live convention coverage in 1952, but the convention has become increasingly scripted as presidential primaries have taken hold. And 1952 was the last year either party had a contested battle for its presidential nominee—it took three ballots for the Democrats to nominate Adlai E. Stevenson—but since then both parties have needed only one vote to nominate their standard-bearer. At base, what was then a true nominating convention is now basically a ratifying convention with few surprises to justify any live coverage, let alone day-long coverage. Conventions are now packaged for a sales pitch, which is good for the parties but not for journalists who thrive on back-room deals, cloakroom caucuses, personal rivalries, and the raw politics of a bygone era.

NOMINATION CONTESTS AND ELECTION OUTCOMES

What then is the effect of intraparty competition during the nomination process on that party's ability to win the general election? One interpretation, a favorite among political pundits, is that a difficult primary battle is good preparation for an underdog candidate, one opposing an incumbent president, because he is forced to fine-tune his organization, develop an effective campaign strategy, and highlight salient issues to be exploited in the coming campaign. Yet the downside to that scenario is that a too bloody primary battle may factionalize the party, revealing its ideological splits to public scrutiny, and require the underdog to focus on tangential issues which appeal to primary voters but may alienate the general electorate. It takes a different political strategy for a candidate (who is not the incumbent president) to win primaries but another strategy to broaden his appeal to independents and voters aligned with the opposition party in order to wage an effective general election campaign. With the exception of 1992 for the Democrats, the pattern since 1972 strongly indicates that the second hypothesis is more valid: serious primary competition can place the party nominee at a disadvantage in being able to win the general election (Table 3-5).

Although 5 percent is not a very rigorous criteria by which to define a viable candidacy, in fact there have been a multitude of others who could not garner even that much support. In 1992, for example, although votes for George Bush and Patrick Buchanan totaled 95.3 percent, there were thirty-six others who contested at least one GOP primary. Among Democrats, the total vote for Bill Clinton, Jerry Brown and Paul Tsongas totaled 90 percent, the remaining votes were distributed among fifty-six others. The truly viable presidential candidates are many fewer in number, therefore, and since 1972 generally the field of viable Democratic rivals has been larger than for Republicans. This difference is explained partly by the fact that Republicans were the incumbents in 1972, 1976, 1984, and 1992

Table 3-5. Primary Competition and Election Outcomes, 1972–1996

Year	Party	No. of Viable Contenders (5%+ vote)	Primary Front-runner	Vote Total (%)	Primary Runner-up	Vote Total (%)	Election Outcome
1972	R	3	Nixon	86.9	Ashbrook	5.1	Nixon Wins
	D	4	Humphrey	25.8	McGovern	25.3	McGovern Loses
1976	R	2	Ford	53.3	Reagan	45.9	Ford Loses
	D	6	Carter	38.8	Brown	15.3	Carter Wins
1980	R	3	Reagan	60.8	Bush	23.3	Reagan Wins
	D	2	Carter	51.2	Kennedy	37.1	Carter Loses
1984	R	1	Reagan	98.6		—	Reagan Wins
	D	3	Mondale	37.8	Hart	36.1	Mondale Loses
1988	R	3	Bush	67.9	Dole	19.2	Bush Wins
	D	4	Dukakis	42.8	Jackson	29.1	Dukakis Loses
1992	R	2	Bush	72.5	Buchanan	22.8	Bush Loses
	D	3	Clinton	51.8	Brown	20.1	Clinton Wins
1996	R	3	Dole	58.4	Buchanan	21.6	Dole Loses
	D	1	Clinton	89.7		—	Clinton Wins

Source: Data for 1972–1992 derived by authors from *Congressional Quarterly's Guide to U.S. Elections*, 3rd ed. (Washington, DC: Congressional Quarterly, 1994), pp. 185, 190, 197, 203, 211, 220; data for 1996 from William G. Mayer, "The Presidential Nominations," in Gerald M. Pomper et al., eds., *The Election of 1996: Reports and Interpretations* (Chatham, NJ: Chatham House, 1997), p. 47.

(arguably 1988 also, since Bush was vice president), and incumbents easily beat their strongest challengers.

In 1972 Nixon bested Congressman Ashbrook (R–Ohio) by 87 to 5 percent; nobody of stature challenged Ronald Reagan in 1984, with his 99 percent of the primary vote; and even President Bush defeated Patrick Buchanan handily in 1992, 73 percent to 23 percent. President Clinton faced only token opposition during the 1996 primary season, and ultimately won 90 percent of all the votes cast by rank and file Democrats. The most serious threat to an incumbent faced Gerald Ford in 1976 when a combative conservative named Ronald Reagan collected 46 percent of the primary votes against Ford's 53 percent.

More importantly, party nominees who face serious primary competition are handicapped when they begin campaigning after Labor Day, the traditional beginning of the presidential election campaign. In 1972 George McGovern actually won fewer primary votes than his archrival Hubert Humphrey, was still nominated, and proceeded to be crushed by President Nixon in one of the five biggest landslides in U.S. history. In 1980 President Carter faced a stiff primary challenge from Senator Ted Kennedy (D–Mass.), one that continued on the convention floor, and he subsequently lost to Reagan, who wisely chose GOP runner-up George Bush to be his vice presidential nominee. Civil rights leader Jesse Jackson got 29.1 percent of the votes in the 1988 Democratic primaries, which was impressive enough given that front-runner Michael Dukakis, then Massachusetts governor, won barely 43 percent of the primary vote, but then he lost to George Bush by a sizable margin. Doubtless the upset victory by Patrick Buchanan in the New Hampshire primary stalled the political momentum of Bob Dole's candidacy in 1996 by forcing the Senate Majority Leader to divert his scarce resources to defeating Buchanan rather than attacking Bill Clinton. In the end, Dole won nearly three-fifths of the GOP primary votes, against one-fifth for Buchanan, but then proceeded to lose handily to the incumbent Democrat.

Bill Clinton deserved his reputation as the comeback kid in 1992. In the 1992 primaries Democrats favored Clinton over Jerry Brown, former governor of California, by 52 percent to 20 percent, which was the best margin of victory of any previous Democratic nominee, so the party was relatively unified behind Clinton's candidacy. Although President Bush in 1992 had an easier time defeating Patrick Buchanan in the GOP primaries, nevertheless he was defeated by Clinton, so intraparty factionalism is one but not the only factor in the political equation to explain who wins and who loses. The tone and tactics of the general election campaign also matter, the topic of our next chapter.

SUMMARY

While the Constitution gives few criteria for those running for the presidency, there are a number of traditional *availability standards* that have in the past delimited the number of candidates running for office. Prior to 1960, for example, candidates tended to come from those demographic groups possessing social values that predominated in the political culture. Since the election of John Kennedy, the first Catholic candidate, presidents have tended to come from the South, to be both young and old, wealthy and poor, living in small states and large. Yet all have been white, male, and with the exception of Kennedy, all have been Protestant; all have also been persons of Northern European backgrounds, have been educated, and, most, with the exception of Eisenhower, have been politicians and members of the majority parties. While the public seems willing to accept a qualified candidate who is also a woman, an African American or a Jew, some barriers still remain including resistance to voting for an atheist or homosexual.

The nomination process continues to be as important, or more so, than the general election. Since voter turnout is always lower in the primaries and caucuses, these voters tend to have a disproportionate say in the selection process. Here ideology, issues, and candidate image became very important for voter decisions in the party primaries. When real competition exists in the primaries, it can both help winning candidates in helping to fine-tune their election organization, or hurt the candidates in factionalizing the party, threatening victory in the general election.

Money remains important as a measure of whether or not a candidate is viable. While public funding has helped to expand the field of candidates and wrested some control from the hands of the moneyed interests, allowing so-called "soft-money" to pay for TV advertisements and other party activities, it has circumvented the effectiveness of campaign restrictions.

Delegates who select candidates tend to be ideologues and activists in their parties and do not always reflect the needs of the rank and file. Party platforms are seen as serious statements of purpose by delegates reflecting the ideological and policy cleavages in the party, but, again, do not always reach the rank and file party member. Party conventions that used to be arenas of decision making now often become dominated by the leading candidates to become instruments to sell their campaign message.

NOTES

1. Clinton Rossiter, *The American Presidency* (New York: Harcourt, Brace and World, 1960), p. 201.

2. "Survey Reveals Growing Willingness of Electorate to Disregard a Presidential Candidate's Sex, Race and Religion When Voting," *The Gallup Report* #216 (Sept. 1983), p. 9.

3. Donald R. Matthews, "Presidential Nominations: Process and Outcomes," in James David Barber, ed., *Choosing the President* (Englewood Cliffs, NJ: Prentice-Hall, 1974), pp. 43–44.

4. Robert L. Dudley and Ronald B. Rapoport, "Vice Presidential Candidates and the Home State Advantage: Playing Second Banana at Home and on the Road," *American Journal of Political Science* (May 1989), pp. 537–540.

5. Michael S. Lewis-Beck and Tom W. Rice, "Localism in Presidential Elections: The Home State Advantage," *American Journal of Political Science* 27 (Aug. 1983), pp. 548–556.

6. V.O. Key, Jr., *Politics, Parties, & Pressure Groups* (New York: Crowell, 1964), p. 397.

7. George C. Edwards and Stephen J. Wayne, *Presidential Leadership: Politics and Policy Making*, 3rd ed. (New York: St. Martin's Press, 1994), p. 23.

8. Frank Munger and James Blackhurst, "Factionalism in the National Conventions, 1940–1964: An Analysis of Ideological Consistency in State Delegation Voting," *Journal of Politics* (May 1965), pp. 375–394.

9. Ibid.

10. A classic essay on the transformation in the nomination process was W.G. Carleton, "The Revolution in the Presidential Nominating Convention," *Political Science Quarterly* (June 1957), pp. 224–240.

11. William H. Lucy, "Polls, Primaries, and Presidential Nominations," *Journal of Politics* (Nov. 1973), pp. 830–848.

12. *Congressional Quarterly Weekly Report* (July 10, 1976), p. 1803.

13. Austin Ranney, *Participation in American Presidential Nominations* (Washington, DC: American Enterprise Institute, 1977), p. 7.

14. James I. Lengle, *Representation and Presidential Primaries: The Democratic Party in the Post-Reform Era* (Westport, CT: Greenwood Press, 1981); H.M. Kritzer, "The Representativeness of the 1972 Presidential Primaries," in W. Crotty, ed., *The Party Symbol* (San Francisco: W.H. Freeman, 1980); Austin Ranney, "Turnout and Representation in Presidential Primary Elections," *American Political Science Review* 66 (1972), pp. 21–37; Austin Ranney, "The Representativeness of Primary Electorates," *Midwest Journal of Political Science* 12 (1968), pp. 224–238; Austin Ranney and L.D. Epstein, "The Two Electorates: Voters and Non-Voters in a Wisconsin Primary," *Journal of Politics* 28 (1966), pp. 598–616.

15. Mark J. Wattier, "Ideological Voting in 1980 Republican Primaries," *Journal of Politics* 45 (1983), p. 1020.

16. Mark J. Wattier, "The Simple Act of Voting in 1980 Democratic Presidential Primaries," *American Politics Quarterly* 11 (July 1983), p. 274.

17. John H. Kessel, *Presidential Campaign Politics*, 2nd ed. (Homewood, IL: Dorsey Press, 1984), p. 17.

18. Ibid., pp. 17–18.

19. Ross K. Baker, "Sorting Out and Suiting Up: The Presidential Nominations," in Gerald M. Pomper et al., eds., *The Election of 1992* (Chatham, NJ: Chatham House, 1992), p. 46.

20. Ibid., p. 70.

21. Nelson W. Polsby and Aaron Wildavsky, *Presidential Elections* (Chatham, NJ: Chatham House, 1996), p. 129.

22. Kessel, *Presidential Campaign Politics*, pp. 13–14.

23. Gerald M. Pomper, "The Presidential Nominations," in Gerald M. Pomper et al., eds., *The Election of 1988* (Chatham, NJ: Chatham House, 1989), p. 37.

24. See Eleanor Clift, "Testing Ground," *Newsweek* (March 30, 1992).

25. The ten Republicans included: ex-governor (Tenn.) Lamar Alexander, millionaire Malcolm Forbes, Jr., Congressman (R–Calif.) Robert K. Dornan, columnist Patrick J. Buchanan, African American conservative Alan Keyes, Senators Arlen Specter (R–Pa.), Richard G. Lugar (R–Ind.), and Phil Gramm (R–Tex.), Michigan businessman Morry Taylor, and Dole.

26. Richard L. Berke, "Buchanan Claims Victory over Dole in New Hampshire," *New York Times* (Feb. 21, 1996), pp. 1, C19.

27. Adam Clymer, "Court Rejects Bid to Limit Campaign Spending by Parties," *New York Times* (June 27, 1996), p. C19.

28. Leslie Wayne, "Loopholes Allow Presidential Race to Set a Record," *New York Times* (Sept. 8, 1996), pp. 1, 19.

29. Everett Carll Ladd, Jr., "Reform Is Wrecking the U.S. Party System," *Fortune* (Nov. 1977), pp. 177–181, 184, 188.

30. Jeane Kirkpatrick, "Representative in the American National Conventions: The Case of 1972," *British Journal of Political Science* (July 1975), pp. 313–322.

31. Herbert McClosky, Paul J. Hoffman, and Rosemary O'Hara, "Issue Conflict and Consensus among Party Leaders and Followers," *American Political Science Review* (June 1960), pp. 406–427.

32. Warren E. Miller and M. Kent Jennings, *Parties in Transition: A Longitudinal Study of Party Elites and Party Supporters* (New York: Russell Sage Foundation, 1986), pp. 166–167.

33. Warren E. Miller, *Without Consent: Mass-Elite Linkages in Presidential Politics* (Lexington: University Press of Kentucky, 1988), p. 16.

34. Ibid., p. 37.

35. Ronald B. Rapoport, Alan I. Abramowitz, and John McGlennon, *The Life of the Parties: Activists in Presidential Politics* (Lexington: University Press of Kentucky, 1986).

36. A. Barton and R.W. Parson, "Measuring Belief System Structure," *Public Opinion Quarterly* 41 (1977), 159–180.

37. Gerald Pomper, *Elections in America: Control and Influence in Democratic Politics* (New York: Dodd, Mead, 1970), chaps. 7 and 8.

38. Paul T. David, "Party Platforms as National Plans," *Public Administration Review* (May/June 1971), pp. 303–315.

39. See Gerald M. Pomper, *Elections in America: Control and Influence in Democratic Politics,* rev. ed. (New York: Longman, 1980); Alan D. Monroe, "American Party Platforms and Public Opinion," *American Journal of Political Science* 27 (Feb. 1983), pp. 27–42.

40. David, "Party Platforms as National Plans," p. 305.

41. Alan D. Monroe, "American Party Platforms and Public Opinion," *American Journal of Political Science* 27 (Feb. 1983), p. 32.

42. Ibid, p. 36.

43. R.W. Apple, Jr., "For Star Power, Democrats May Have Trouble Matching the G.O.P. Show," *New York Times* (Aug. 25, 1996), p. 12.

44. James Bennet, "Few Tears for the Death of the Network Convention," *New York Times* (Sept. 1, 1996), p. 4E.

4

The Democratic Connection: Electing a President

We have elected presidents routinely for over two hundred years. Elections have continued without interruption during peacetime and wartime and, except for the first two elections, all involved a choice between at least two candidates. But the exact meaning of elections for presidential leadership has prompted an ongoing debate among political scientists. Some presidency scholars assert the "elitist" viewpoint that presidential elections are simply a means by which people choose between candidates for the highest office.[1] They do not ensure popular control over the policies that are implemented by the White House and, moreover, once elected presidents have to reorder their campaign priorities in the face of unexpected world crises and changing economic conditions at home. Nor does the campaign address all the issues that may confront the president during his term and, besides, voters may choose a particular candidate for very different reasons. Polsby and Wildavsky observed that "voters in presidential elections do not transmit their policy preferences to elected officials with a high degree of reliability. There are few clear mandates in our political system because elections are fought on so many issues and in so many incompletely overlapping constituencies."[2] This elitist view, therefore, doubts that elections can produce mandates on any precise terms.

More than one example can be found to validate this view of electoral politics. In 1980 Ronald Reagan promised to increase defense spending, to enact a massive tax cut, and also to balance the budget by the end of his first term. To reconcile those divergent goals proved impossible, and one enduring legacy of the Reagan years has been the mounting triple-digit deficits that have continued into the 1990s. Today some observers judge Reagan harshly because he failed to fulfill a major campaign pledge, although it was unlikely any president could simultaneously increase military spending, cut taxes, and yet bring federal expenditures and revenues into balance.

Yet the notion that presidential elections have *no* meaning for future policy does not seem justified, and other scholars point out that optimal electoral conditions may yield mandates to guide decision-makers. Presidency scholar Bruce Buchanan made this observation:

> Presidential campaigns such as 1964, 1980, and 1992 suggest that mandate critics may overlook an important possibility. It is that presidential candidates willing to seek the explicit prior approval of voters for one or at most a very few specific policy actions, and willing to do so in a way that leaves little doubt that a large majority is aware of the request before any votes are cast, can transform electoral success into policymaking momentum.[3]

We agree, and argue that presidential elections can shape public expectations about the *direction* and *policy agenda* for the new administration (although not necessarily the specific content of policy). Was there much doubt that the election of Michael Dukakis in 1988 or Bill Clinton in 1992 instead of George Bush would advance the prochoice rather than the prolife agenda on abortion policy? A policy mandate is focused rather than expansive, as President Clinton in 1993 learned with regard to the economy versus gay rights.

In 1992 Bill Clinton won 43.3 percent of the vote, meaning the majority of voters cast ballots against the Democrat. Still he was the victor, although his narrow margin of victory suggested that President Clinton did not have a mandate for radical changes in a wide variety of policy areas. A sign above the desk of candidate Clinton's campaign strategist read, "It's the economy, stupid," meaning that the most important issue in the 1992 campaign was recession and the sorry state of the nation's economy. That alone probably defeated President Bush. If there was a mandate in 1992, it was the economy.

But President Clinton made a political miscalculation at the beginning of his term by proposing to lift the ban on homosexuals in the military. The Joint Chiefs of Staff and key members of Congress balked, public opinion was not supportive, the controversy dominated the headlines, and ultimately the president had to back down. It was probably the major issue, among varying missteps during the early months, responsible for Clinton's historic low approval ratings during his first year in office. The odds are that most Americans who voted for Clinton over Bush did not do so to bring about a new policy on homosexuals in the armed forces.

THE ELECTORAL COLLEGE SYSTEM

The Framers of the Constitution were not concerned about making the president directly accountable to the people. Choosing a president through the electoral college is fairly complicated and puts his election on a federal rather than a national basis. The number of electoral votes is equal to the total number of senators (100) and representatives (435), with 3 more allocated to the District of Columbia by the Twenty-third Amendment. Each state's number of electoral votes equals its number of representatives (which varies according to population size) plus two senators. No state has fewer than three electoral votes (one representative plus two senators). A majority of the total (or 270) is needed to win the highest office, but electors in each state cast their electoral votes as a group. Should no candidate get the 270, then the House of Representatives, with each state casting only one vote, chooses the president from among the three candidates receiving the largest number of electoral votes.

The Constitution authorized each state to appoint electors "in such manner as the legislature thereof may direct." When George Washington was elected in 1789 and 1792 and John Adams succeeded to the presidency in 1796, the electors were chosen by the state legislatures. After 1796, however, various states began to allow the electors to be chosen by popular vote, and by 1832 all the states except South Carolina (which did not abandon the legislative method until 1864) authorized popular election of electors. This development coincided with the rise of national political parties. To assure its electoral victory, the dominant political party in each state changed the law to allow the "general ticket" system, whereby the presidential candidate who wins a plurality (not necessarily a majority) of the state's popular vote would capture all of the state's electoral votes. So today, when you vote for Bill Clinton, you are actually casting one vote for each Democratic elector pledged to support Clinton for president.

The Framers intended that the electors use their independent judgment to choose the best man for president, which occurred when Washington was elected twice. By 1796, however, the political rivalries that had developed between the Federalists and the Anti-Federalists prompted the electors to cast their ballots according to their own partisan preferences. Thus Federalist John Adams was selected over his opponent, Thomas Jefferson, who became the leader of the Anti-Federalists (known later as the Jeffersonian-Republicans or Democratic-Republicans). From this point on, electors acted in the name of their political party.

The possibility does exist that electors may desert their party's presidential candidate and support another person, although he was never nominated by the party. This "faithless elector" problem has occurred but is a minor nuisance, because as yet it has never altered the outcome of a presidential election. Custom reinforced by state law, not to mention their own political careers, assures that most electors remain loyal to the declared presidential candidate of their party.

Another threat to the electoral college is posed when the states modify their laws to permit the voters to choose, in addition to electors pledged to the Republican and Democratic candidates, "unpledged" electors. In 1960, for example, fourteen unpledged electors were chosen in Alabama and Mississippi. It is highly unlikely that slates of unpledged electors could decide a presidential election, but usually that is not the intent. Similar to the scenario when third parties nominate candidates for president, the real purpose of selecting unpledged electors is to "send a message" and attempt to deny the leading contender a majority of electoral votes so the House of Representatives has to choose the president.

The possibility that a third party or independent presidential candidate such as Ross Perot in 1992 and 1996 may distort the workings of the electoral college is one of the criticisms made against the existing system. The arguments against the electoral college may be summarized as follows:

1. The electoral college exaggerates the margin of victory for the winning candidate because electoral votes are allocated on a winner-take-all basis in each state.
2. The electoral college can permit the candidate who received the most popular votes to lose the election by not obtaining the majority of electoral votes, as occurred in 1824, 1876, and 1888.
3. On three occasions (1800, 1824, 1876) the electoral college failed to elect the president.
4. The electoral college benefits the smallest states and the largest states in the country.
5. The electoral college violates the democratic ideal of "one person, one vote" because it effectively disenfranchises the losing candidate's popular votes and because the value of each individual's vote cast for president depends on the state in which the voter resides.
6. The winner-take-all system of allocating electoral votes gives political leverage to pivotal voter groups located in the most populous states.
7. The electoral college discourages minor political parties and independent presidential candidates because it is so difficult for them to win the majority of electoral votes allocated on a state-by-state basis.

Critics of the existing system are more concerned about the niceties of democratic theory than any political consequences that may result from reforming the electoral college. They point out that seventeen times in U.S. history the winning presidential candidate obtained less than a majority of the popular vote cast.[4] Implicit in this criticism is the idea that a president elected with less than a majority of the popular votes cast is somehow illegitimate or is politically weakened even before he takes office. Of more practical concern is the prospect that the electoral college may fail to work as intended or will distort the popular will.

The experience of 1800, when two candidates tied in electoral votes, led to the enactment of the Twelfth Amendment, which now requires the electors to cast two separate ballots, one for president and then one for vice president. Under the Constitution, each elector originally had two votes, and one had to be cast for a candidate who did not reside in the elector's home state. By this method the candidate with the highest number of votes, so long as it was a majority, was president, and the runner-up with the second highest vote total was vice president. Obviously a problem would occur should two candidates tie in the electoral college voting. This happened in 1800, between Thomas Jefferson and Aaron Burr, and as a result the outcome was decided by the House of Representatives. The rival Federalist Party held the majority of seats in Congress and, although Jefferson was the intended presidential candidate of the Democratic-Republican Party, it required thirty-six ballots in the House before Jefferson won, after Federalist leader Alexander Hamilton gave Jefferson his backing.

In 1824 four candidates received electoral votes: Andrew Jackson (99), John Quincy Adams (84), William Crawford (41), and Henry Clay (37). In the 18 states (of 24 in the Union) choosing electors by popular vote, Jackson captured the plurality of popular votes. Nevertheless Clay, who was Speaker of the House of Representatives, threw his support to Adams and the House of Representatives selected John Quincy Adams as president. In 1876 Democrat Samuel J. Tilden received 250,000 more popular votes than Republican Rutherford B. Hayes, but Hayes became president. That year fraud and violence affected voting throughout the nation, especially in the South. An electoral commission was established by Congress to determine which candidate won the disputed electoral votes in Florida, Louisiana, and South Carolina. By a partisan vote the commission awarded all three states' contested electoral votes to Hayes.

Perhaps the most blatant distortion of the popular will occurred in 1888. Incumbent Democrat Grover Cleveland won a plurality of the popular vote (48.6 percent) against Republican Benjamin Harrison (47.8 percent) but lost in the electoral college by a vote of 168 to 233. What happened in 1888 concerns political scientists anew every time a close election occurs. It is possible for a candidate to lose the popular vote in the large states (with many electoral votes) by small margins but win the popular vote in small states by tremendous margins. As a result, a candidate could be the popular-vote winner but lack a majority of electoral votes. Had 25,000 votes in New York State shifted from Lincoln to Stephen A. Douglas in 1860, for example, the election would have been decided by the House of Representatives. Jimmy Carter would have lost to Gerald Ford in 1976 had about 9,000 votes shifted in Hawaii and Ohio.

The existing system favors the smallest states as well as the largest ones, but for very different reasons. Because no state has fewer than three electoral votes, the least populated states hold a larger proportion of electoral votes than they do popular votes. This bias violates the democratic ideal of "one person, one vote" because small states are overrepresented in the electoral college.

More important politically, a few large states represent the majority of 270 electoral votes needed for victory, so candidates focus on winning those key states. After the 1960 census and 1990 census, these states (Table 4-1) had the majority of 270 electoral votes.

Of the 12 states after 1960 that held the majority of electoral votes, 10 remained on the list after 1990. These statistics reflect the shift in population from the North to the South and West. The 32 electoral votes that California, Texas, and Florida gained over the period was exactly the number

Table 4-1. Listing of States with 270 Electoral Votes

After 1960	After 1990
New York—43	California—54
California—40	New York—33
Pennsylvania—29	Texas—32
Illinois—26	Florida—25
Ohio—26	Pennsylvania—23
Texas—25	Illinois—22
Michigan—21	Ohio—21
New Jersey—17	Michigan—18
Massachusetts—14	New Jersey—15
Florida—14	North Carolina—14
Indiana—13	Virginia or Georgia—13
North Carolina—13	
Total = 281	Total = 270

lost, as a group, by New York, Pennsylvania, Illinois, Ohio, Michigan, New Jersey, and Massachusetts.

Racial, ethnic, and religious minorities, and unionized labor historically were concentrated in the highly populated states. These groups tended to be liberal on economic issues, and presidential candidates were encouraged to address their concerns in an effort to win states rich in electoral votes. Although Jews account for about 3 percent of the total vote, for example, disproportionate numbers live in New York, Illinois, and Florida, which gives them political leverage in those key states. This bias violates the democratic ideal that each vote should have "one weight" (or the same value) in shaping the outcome. That is not the case, in reality, because voters in the larger states—including pivotal minority groups—are more important politically than voters in the smaller states. This explains why liberal organizations such as the NAACP and the Americans for Democratic Action (ADA) defended the existing electoral college. In 1977 the ADA gave this justification:

> Perhaps the only way that significant American minorities can have an impact on the political process is as the deciding factor as to which major candidate can win a given state and a given set of electoral votes. In this way, urban interests and rural, blacks, Latinos, and other minorities, the handicapped and the elderly, the young, the poor, the rich, and the middle-aged can all compete for some attention and some share of public policy. If direct election were instituted, the need for taking into account the needs and desires of minorities would no longer exist. Candidates would campaign for the American middle as their particular pollster describes that middle and would be beholden to no group, no cause, and no interest. Those who constitute America's minorities, whether they are farmers or urban dwellers, would all suffer.[5]

Since the 1930s, Jews, blacks, union labor, and Catholics were reliably Democratic in their party affiliation, and these groups were concentrated in the large urbanized states of the Northeast and Midwest. The presence of those voter blocs in the pivotal states constrained Democratic presidential candidates to articulate a liberal policy agenda. But the political dynamics within northern states have changed. In the 1940s, 1950s, and 1960s those minority groups resided in large cities such as Chicago and New York which included so many voters that often the cities could dominate the election outcomes in those states.

In a celebrated case, Mayor Richard J. Daley of Chicago won Illinois for John F. Kennedy (his critics say Daley stole the election) by delivering enough Democratic votes to offset Nixon's support in suburban and downstate Illinois. Were that election to be repeated today, however, and a Democrat receive the same vote margin that Kennedy did in Chicago, the Republican could still win the state. Illinois lost three electoral votes between 1980 and 1990 because it did not grow as fast as the nation, but within Illinois a redistribution of population occurred because large numbers of people moved out of Chicago. There are now more votes in suburban Cook (Chicago) County and the "collar" counties around Cook. A Republican presidential candidate now can lose the majority of votes in Chicago but stitch together suburban and downstate votes to win Illinois. Because suburban and downstate voters are more conservative than residents of Chicago, today GOP presidential candidates may develop a political strategy to win big states like Illinois without having to cater to liberal interests in big cities.

So when a candidate declares his intention to visit every state in the Union, as Richard Nixon did in 1960, it is viewed as a serious political blunder because that strategy undermines the candidate's ability to concentrate on the key states. No presidential candidate since Nixon has repeated his mistake. One study traced both parties' candidates on the campaign trail during the period 1932 to 1976 and determined that in all but one election both candidates devoted substantially more than 50 percent of their campaign appearances to states with large blocs of electoral votes.[6]

A fundamental reform of the electoral college would be *direct popular election* of the president. The proposal, advocated by the late senator Birch Bayh (D–Ind.), provided for the president's election by a nationwide popular vote. A plurality would be enough for election so long as the winner achieved at least 40 percent of the vote cast. If nobody gets the 40 percent, a runoff election would be held between the top two candidates. Jimmy Carter was the first Democratic president to favor this change but, with the 1980 reelection defeat of Senator Bayh, nobody else has emerged as the acknowledged leader promoting direct popular election.

Another option, the *proportional plan*, would allocate each state's electoral votes to the presidential candidates according to their share of the popular vote. A third alternative is the *single-member district system* (in force currently in Maine). Each state is divided into districts equal to its number of representatives; voters in each district choose an elector; and two more electoral votes (for each state's senators) go to the presidential candidate who wins a plurality of the popular votes statewide. Still a fourth possibility is the *national bonus plan*. It would retain the electoral college but weigh it more heavily toward the candidate who wins the popular vote. Under this scheme, a bonus of 102 electoral votes would be given to that candidate who receives the most popular votes, with the existing number of electoral votes (538) allocated on a state-by-state basis as is traditional. In the late 1970s this plan was advocated by a task force of social scientists, including political scientist Thomas Cronin.[7]

Presidential campaigns are waged in the context of long-term electoral constraints and short-term political strategies. Demographic, economic, and social conditions define American culture in ways that bring meaning to U.S. political ideology. Changing the socioeconomic and political makeup of America is a long-term process. Crises such as secession or economic depression can alter fundamentally the political landscape. We next discuss two long-term electoral constraints, namely, realignment and regional shifts, as well as several short-term political strategies, including the choice of a running mate, that may be employed by both parties and their presidential candidates to win the White House.

LONG-TERM ELECTORAL CONSTRAINTS

Realignment

Republicans have won more presidential elections since 1952 than the Democrats, but why? The answer has to do with coalition building and the policy alternatives offered by the two major parties. It also hinges on electoral preferences and the factors that motivate voters.

In the 1950s leading scholars of voting behavior at the University of Michigan Survey Research Center classified presidential elections as (1) maintaining, (2) deviating, or (3) realigning based on their outcomes.[8] In maintaining elections, the party with the largest number of identifiers wins, presumably because most people are supporting their party preference. Because most voters have been Democrats, seven contests are maintaining elections: 1936, 1940, 1944, 1948, 1960, 1964, 1976, and 1992.

A deviating election occurs every time the minority party is able to exploit issues, events, incumbency, or the superior appeal of its candidate to win the presidency: 1952 and 1956 with Eisenhower, 1968 and 1972 with Nixon, 1980 and 1984 with Reagan, and 1988 with Bush. But those elections do not cause many voters to change their political party affiliation.

More enduring are realigning elections, which are extraordinary events: 1800 (Jefferson), 1828 (Jackson), 1860 (Lincoln), 1896 (McKinley), and 1932 (Roosevelt). Here the outcome is shaped by massive shifts in the party identification of voters. V. O. Key referred to such contests as "critical" elections because they are important watersheds in American politics.[9] In realigning elections the relationship between voter choice and public policy is strengthened; historically, they have occurred during crises when issues of huge magnitude shook the nation. The shifting of partisan loyalties by voters increases party conflict in the short term and the parties' ideological makeup over the long run. It was found that "party voting" in Congress—in which a majority of Republicans oppose a majority of Democrats—increased sharply following the 1932 realignment.[10] Because the constituency of each party has been redefined and sharpened, partisan conflict over issues affects the lawmaking process.

The Republican Party's domination of national politics from 1860 to 1932 followed the debate over slavery and the issue of secession. More important to today's politics is the realignment associated with the Great Depression of the 1930s. It forged a New Deal coalition that has sustained the Democratic Party hegemony ever since. Unlike the regional shifting that followed the Civil War, the Depression and FDR's New Deal precipitated a reshuffling along class lines; many working-class people and minority groups became Democrats, whereas the middle-class moved toward the Republican Party. So realigning elections are related more to ideology and issues and less to candidate personality.

Franklin D. Roosevelt won the 1932 election by holding on to the then "solid" South (Democratic since the era of Andrew Jackson) and adding voters who traditionally had supported Republicans or had not voted at all. The regional shift in the electoral college "lock" (see later) reflects changing voting patterns by groups in the population since the 1930s. So much has the New Deal coalition been undermined by political developments in these sixty years that political scientists have been pondering the prospects of a new "realignment" toward the Republican Party or, at least, a "dealignment" away from the Democratic Party. Scholars are certain that voters are moving away from traditional straight-ticket Democratic voting but, if anything, the next realignment may be generational and gradual as a new age cohort of (young) voters enters the electorate.[11]

After Richard Nixon's 1968 victory, GOP strategist and columnist Kevin Phillips wrote *The Emerging Republican Majority,* arguing that electoral realignment was underway.[12] Phillips saw contemporary demographic shifts reestablishing a conservative coalition in American politics. The realignment thesis seemed especially credible after 1980, when Reagan carried a Republican majority into the Senate for the first time since 1952–1953.

Whereas voting analysts who argue realignment theory have a bottom-up perspective, by looking at how the political coalitions of parties are fundamentally changed, a top-down perspective is argued by Steven Skowronek[13] (also see chapter 2), who has a cyclical interpretation of American history. The prevailing political ideology of the country may be dominant or in decline, and the ability of presidents to exert leadership depends on when during a political cycle they assume office. For Skowronek, Lyndon Johnson represented the height of New Deal liberalism, whereas its demise was reflected in the failed leadership of Jimmy Carter. Ronald Reagan, in contrast, represented the ascendancy of conservatism, which continues today even though a Democrat may have won the presidency in 1992 and 1996. Essentially Clinton had to define himself as a "new Democrat" in order to avoid being tainted as an "old" tax-and-spend liberal Democrat.

Barely was the election of 1996 over when *New York Times* reporter R.W. Apple, Jr., offered this postmortem. Regardless of outcome, he wrote, "[i]t is not so much that the nation is witnessing a partisan realignment (except in the South, where the parties have almost completely switched roles). In most elections, in most places, Republicans and Democrats compete on more-or-less equal terms, as long as neither of the candidates is boldly liberal." And Clinton is "the great exemplar of this continuing trend," as Apple explained:

> Having stubbed his toe, politically speaking, on liberal causes in the first two years of his term, he has espoused selected conservative causes. He gave up on homosexuals in the military and an overhaul of the health-insurance system and took on welfare reform, more cops on the beat and fiscal restraint. On the way to re-election, he made himself, or rather his political image, so thoroughly middle-of-the-road that he went into Election Day with a chance to carry conservative states like Indiana, Florida and Arizona [Clinton did carry Florida and Arizona], which have not voted for a Democrat for President since 1964, 1976 and 1948, respectively.[14]

Historically, partisan realignments were caused by singularly important presidential elections, but it seems doubtful that this pattern will be repeated. The American electorate as well as the character of presidential politics has been transformed during the past three decades. Both parties have been weakened by the use of presidential primaries, candidate reliance on the mass media, public funding of presidential elections, and most importantly by a lessened partisan identification among large numbers of voters. The number of "strong" Republican and "strong" Democratic voters has declined, indicating that even party identifiers are less committed to their political party than before.[15] The ability of the "minority" party to capture the presidency is a manifestation of greater split-ticket voting, although GOP success is also related to such considerations as turnout. The turnout in presidential elections has shown a general decline from 1960 (63 percent) to 1988 (51 percent) although in 1992 it bumped upward (55 percent) in large measure because of the interest generated by the independent candidacy of Ross Perot. In 1996, however, turnout dropped to 48.5 percent of eligible voters. Because a higher proportion of nonvoters are Democrats, any shrinkage in the electorate tends to favor the Republican candidates. Democrats retained control of the White House in 1996, but the decline in voting turnout probably helped Republicans hold their majorities in both houses of Congress.

Regional Shifts

Despite the fact that more Americans identify themselves as Democrats than Republicans (although GOP identifiers nearly equaled Democrats in the 1980s), the minority party has won seven of the twelve presidential elections since 1952, whereas from 1932 to 1952 the Democrats won the White

Table 4-2. The Changing Partisan Lock on the Electoral College

Two-Party Distribution of Electoral Votes

Region	1932 Dem	1932 Rep	1936 Dem	1936 Rep	1940 Dem	1940 Rep	1944 Dem	1944 Rep	1948 Dem	1948 Rep	1952 Dem	1952 Rep
North	237 80%	59 20%	288 97%	8 3%	244 82%	52 18%	222 77%	68 23%	129 44%	161 56%	8 3%	276 97%
South	146 100%	0 —	144 100%	0 —	146 100%	0 —	148 100%	0 —	109* 74%	0 —	81 55%	65 45%
West	89 100%	0 —	89 100%	0 —	59 66%	30 34%	62 67%	31 33%	65 70%	28 30%	0 —	101 100%

Region	1956 Dem	1956 Rep	1960 Dem	1960 Rep	1964 Dem	1964 Rep	1968 Dem	1968 Rep	1972 Dem	1972 Rep
North	13 5%	271 95%	205 72%	79 28%	278 100%	0 —	141 53%	125 47%	17 6%	253 94%
South	60* 41%	85 58%	88* 60%	43 29%	98 68%	47 32%	37 26%	74* 51%	0 —	136* 99%
West	0 —	101 100%	10 9%	97 91%	110 96%	5 4%	13 11%	102 89%	0 —	121* 100%

Region	1976 Dem	1976 Rep	1980 Dem	1980 Rep	1984 Dem	1984 Rep	1988 Dem	1988 Rep	1992 Dem	1992 Rep	1996 Dem	1996 Rep
North	166 61%	104 39%	33 12%	237 88%	13 5%	241 95%	90 36%	163 64%	227 95%	12 5%	227 95%	12 5%
South	127 86%	20 14%	12 8%	135 92%	0 —	155 100%	0 —	155 100%	47 29%	116 71%	59 36%	104 64%
West	4 3%	116* 96%	4 3%	117 97%	0 —	129 100%	21 16%	108 84%	96 71%	40 29%	93 68%	43 32%

*States Rights Party won 38 electoral votes in 1948 and 1 Truman elector in Tennessee voted for the States Rights Party in 1948; 1 Stevenson elector in Alabama voted for Walter Jones in 1956; 14 "unpledged" electors voted for Senator Harry F. Byrd in Alabama and 1 Nixon elector in Oklahoma voted for Senator Harry F. Byrd in 1960; American Independent Party won 33 electoral votes and 1 Nixon elector in North Carolina voted for American Independent Party in 1968; 1 Nixon elector in Virginia voted for Libertarian Party in 1972; 1 Ford elector in Washington voted for Ronald Reagan in 1976.

House in every election. Republican success is related to the changing partisan lock on the electoral college (Table 4-2).

In the 1932 to 1952 period the Democratic solid South gave its entire bloc of electoral votes to the party's presidential candidate in every election except 1948, when its segregationist wing bolted the Democratic convention in opposition to a civil rights plank and organized a States Rights (or Dixiecrat) Party, winning one-fourth of the region's electoral votes. The West was almost as loyal; Roosevelt won all its electoral votes in 1932 and 1936, and Republicans captured one-third of its electoral votes in 1940 and 1944 and 30 percent in 1948. Excluding 1948, the average number of electoral votes won by the Democrats was 147 in the South and 75 in the West, which totals 222, or 83 percent of the electoral vote majority (which was then 266).

What happened beginning in 1952 is the shift of the West and especially the South, which have been growing in population at the expense of the North, into the GOP column. The electoral college lock now favors Republicans. The first GOP contender to cut into the solid South was Dwight D. Eisenhower, who won 45 percent of its electoral votes in 1952 and 58 percent in his 1956 landslide reelection. In 1960 and 1968 the region returned to the Democratic column but, despite the tremendous loss by GOP candidate Barry Goldwater in 1964, his winning one-third of the electoral votes in the South marked a turning point in southern politics. The reason, at first, was racial, but eventually the region's general conservatism found a new home in the national Republican Party.

The year 1968 was unusual because segregationist governor George C. Wallace of Alabama contested the White House as the candidate of the American Independent Party. All of his 46 electoral votes came from the southern states, yet Richard Nixon still managed to win the plurality of electoral votes in the South. The McGovern candidacy in 1972 was a debacle for the Democrats in all regions, but four years later another son of the South, former Georgia governor Jimmy Carter, won 86 percent of the electoral votes there. In 1980 and 1984 with Reagan and in 1988 with Bush, the Republicans captured all the electoral votes in the South. And what is noteworthy about 1992 is that, although both Clinton and Gore (Tennessee) are from the South, President Bush won 71 percent of the electoral votes in the region. In 1996 Clinton-Gore did slightly better on their home turf, but Kansan Bob Dole still carried 64 percent of southern electoral votes, although this time Florida voted Democratic. In the West, with 1964 also the exception, during 1952 to 1988 the Republican electoral vote share ranged between 84 and 100 percent, but Bill Clinton cut deeply into Republican territory by winning 71 percent of its electoral votes in 1992 and 68 percent in 1996.

In sum, during the period 1952 to 1988, with the exception of 1964, the electoral vote won by the Republicans averaged 98 in the South and 103 in the West, which totaled 201, or 74 percent of the 270 electoral vote majority now required for victory. With this base of states that vote fairly reliably Republican in presidential elections, the Democrats today face a more challenging task to stitch together the necessary 270 electoral votes, and to do so with minimal or no electoral support among southern states makes the odds of that happening even more problematic. Thus it is no accident that GOP losses in recent decades—1976, 1992, and 1996—occurred when the Democrats nominated centrist candidates from the South.

SHORT-TERM POLITICAL STRATEGIES

The ultimate objective is to win 270 electoral votes, but the immediate problem is to wage an effective presidential campaign in light of the weakened force of partisanship and the population shifts from the Frost Belt to the Sun Belt states. Both parties must devise political strategies reflecting the realities of the electoral map of America, but where the Republicans had to overcome their partisan disadvantage among voters to exploit candidate image, events, or issues to win opposition voters and independents, today the Democrats face a similar challenge in trying to cement a winning coalition without straying too far to the political left. Political strategies involve issue selection, rhetorical appeals and sloganeering, manipulation of the mass media and political advertisements, and a bit of luck. We begin this discussion with one age-old strategy to balance the national ticket with a running mate offering different political assets than the standard-bearer.

Choosing a Vice President

Looking ahead to the general election campaign, perhaps the first strategic decision a presidential candidate makes is the choice of a running mate. The standard-bearer used to wait until the convention to announce that selection as another technique to arouse party loyalists and voter interest, but now that decision is made in advance of the formal proceedings (for example, Dole's choice of Kemp). In recent memory only Adlai Stevenson, the 1956 Democratic nominee, allowed the national convention to make that selection.

The choice of vice presidential candidate is one way to balance the ticket both geographically and ideologically. In 1960 Kennedy chose Senator Lyndon Johnson (D–Tex.) as his running mate to shore the former's position in the South given uncertainties about how that region would react to him as a liberal and a Catholic. It worked: LBJ carried Texas and the Democrats won most southern states (despite the presence of "unpledged" electors committed to states' rights on race), but the attempt to forge a "Boston-Austin axis" in 1988 failed, despite Governor Michael Dukakis (D–Mass.) picking Senator Lloyd Bentsen (D–Tex.) as his teammate. The GOP carried the South including Texas.

Of course George Bush was thankful that Reagan, who was regarded as very conservative in 1980, chose Bush to moderate the image of the ticket. Because Bush had challenged Reagan in the 1980 GOP primaries, his selection prevented any possibility of a disunited Republican Party. Also, Bush was from Texas and Reagan had been governor of California: both states are crucial to winning the White House.

The choice of Senator Albert Gore (D–Tenn.) to run with Clinton operates contrary to conventional wisdom, but made some political sense. Clinton, inexperienced in foreign affairs and the governor of a small state, turned to Gore as a so-called insider with Washington connections. Beyond that, Gore had championed environmental issues, whereas the environmental record of Arkansas is one of the worst among the states. But the most important consideration was strategic. By labeling himself as a new Democrat, Clinton hoped to compete more effectively in the South and break the GOP lock that Nixon, Reagan, and Bush had enjoyed in the region.

In recent years two choices did little to strengthen the national ticket. One was Mondale's selection of Congresswoman Geraldine Ferraro (D–N.Y.) in 1984; she and he were equally liberal and both lived in the northeastern quarter of the nation. Because he was so behind Reagan in the polls, perhaps Mondale needed to take some risk to have any chance at all. Says Richard Brookhiser, "The best justification for Mondale's audacity, though, was that it was audacious. . . . Prudent losers remain losers. The first woman on a major party ticket might shake things up."[16] But that strategy was counterproductive. Throughout the campaign Ferraro was a drag on the ticket and became embroiled in a highly publicized dispute with the Roman Catholic archbishop of New York City because she was a prochoice Catholic.

The other instance in which the running mate became a political liability rather than an asset was Senator Dan Quayle (R–Ind.), Bush's choice in 1988. Not well known outside his home state, opinion polls throughout the campaign indicated that Democrat Lloyd Bentsen was more than a match for Dan Quayle (indeed Bentsen outshone Dukakis in some polls on leadership). Perhaps Bush was trying to appeal to the so-called yuppie vote, but, although Quayle did not cost Bush the election, he never recovered from his image of intellectual lightweight. Polls during his tenure as vice president repeatedly found that most respondents believed he was unfit to be president.[17] Some even speculated that Bush might dump Quayle from the 1992 ticket.

In 1996 GOP candidate Bob Dole chose Jack Kemp as his running mate probably out of a desire to unify the party after the early brutal primary battles. After Dole's overtures to General Colin Powell were rebuffed, Kemp's name recognition and hyperactive style would deflect any concerns about Dole's age (if elected, he, at 73, would have been older than even Ronald Reagan). Beyond that, Dole had been challenged during the GOP primaries by multimillionaire Steve Forbes who championed a flat (one rate) income tax to bolster economic growth. Kemp was a keen advocate of supply-side economics (which favors cutting income taxes), and had endorsed Forbes during the primary season, so Dole's choice won him the backing of Steve Forbes and, as important, meant the Dole-Kemp ticket could make broad appeals based on cutting taxes and avoid divisive social issues such as abortion that might undermine their appeal to Republican women. In the end, Kemp's campaigning in Democratic territory like big cities and among minorities won few adherents, and there was virtually no chance he would carry his home state of New York against Clinton.

Media Bias and Polling Error

Presidential candidates want to win, leading reporters to assume that every move reflects some kind of political calculation, so the mass media has taken on the responsibility of keeping politicians honest. As Paul Taylor put it, "Our [journalistic] habits of mind are shaped by what Lionel Trilling once described as the 'adversary culture.' . . . We are progressive reformers, deeply skeptical of all the major institutions of society except our own."[18] As a result, media critic Thomas E. Patterson has documented (Figure 4-1) a steady increase in "negative" reporting of presidential campaigns over the past four decades.

In 1960 three-fourths of the references to Nixon or Kennedy were positive, whereas, by 1992, only 40 percent of the comments about Clinton and Bush were favorable. Says Patterson, "The dominant schema for the reporter is structured around the notion that politics is a strategic game. When journalists encounter new information during an election, they tend to interpret it within a schematic framework according to which candi-

Figure 4-1. "Bad News" and "Good News" Coverage of the Presidential Candidates, 1960–1992
Note: Figure is based on favorable and unfavorable references to the major-party nominees in 4,263 *Time* and *Newsweek* paragraphs during the 1960–1992 period. "Horse-race" references are excluded; all other evaluative references are included.

Source: Thomas E. Patterson, *Out of Order* (New York: Knopf, 1993), Figure 1.1, p. 20.

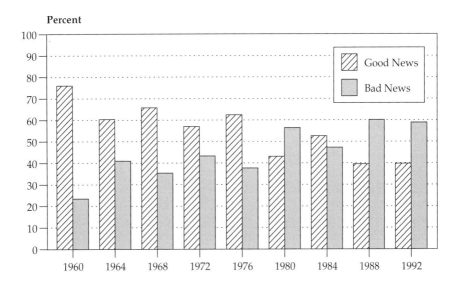

dates compete for advantage. The candidates play the game well or poorly."[19]

One of Patterson's major complaints about the media is its disproportionate attention to character flaws or what are nothing more than misstatements by the candidates. One famous gaffe that did some harm was President Ford's comment during the second presidential debate of 1976 in which he said Soviet control over its satellite nations had lessened and there was "no Soviet dominance of Eastern Europe." Afterwards polls by a 44 to 33 percent margin[20] indicated that Ford had won the debate and few people placed any significance on his Eastern Europe comment, but, according to the press, Ford made a blunder. At a press conference the next day, the first eleven questions focused on that remark and tried to get Ford to admit his mistake, and within twenty-four hours a follow-up survey found that President Ford had lost his debate with Jimmy Carter, now by the lopsided margin of 17 to 63 percent.[21] Most people did not think Ford made a gaffe until they were told by the press.

Although presidential elections are supposed to offer the electorate a policy choice and educate voters on the issues and their implications for the nation, that kind of coverage is not given high priority by the leading newspapers or television networks. What is news is defined by media elites under the guise of First Amendment guarantees of free speech and free press. Sadly, however, although the Constitution protects the mass media from government intervention, the Constitution cannot guarantee that the mass media will serve the public interest or nurture democratic processes.

The mass media thrives on personalities, personal rivalries, scandalous behavior, or missteps (figuratively and literally: when Bob Dole fell off a stage during a campaign rally, it was filmed for the evening news) and the horse race that ends at the finish line (Election Day). An extensive analysis by presidency watcher Bruce Buchanan of media coverage during the 1992 election campaign shows that the candidates were two to three times more likely to discuss domestic, economic, and foreign policy as compared to the coverage given to those topics in the printed and electronic media (Table 4-3). Also, Clinton, Bush, and Perot were three times more likely than the media to discuss their qualifications for office or their stands on issues of the campaign. Rather the media gave much more attention to "nonissues" and various aspects of the horse race. Besides focusing on the conduct of the campaign, the candidates' ability to campaign, or their election prospects, the media gave significant attention to poll standings and offered commentary on the "viability" of each campaign, topics that were practically ignored by the three contenders.

Coupled with the media bias in the coverage of presidential elections is the related problem of misleading opinion polls that may cause a bandwagon stampede among voters to the projected winner or, equally plausible, may discourage many Americans from voting if the outcome is widely viewed as a foregone conclusion. Could the turnout in the presidential election of 1996—technically the lowest turnout since 1924 and ar-

Table 4-3. 1992 Media Coverage of Candidates; Candidate versus Media
Emphasis

	Candidates* %	Media[†] %
Issues		
Domestic policy	31	7
Economic policy	28	11
Foreign policy	9	3
Nonissue	32	79
Other topics		
Candidate qualifications		
Records	31	11
Character	5	5
Issue stances	44	13
Campaign horse race		
Campaign conduct	8	12
Campaign ability	1	5
Strength in polls	0	14
Prospects for election	3	5
General viability	2	22
General assessments	6	13
Number of assessments	4,256	22,889

*Assessments of Bill Clinton, George Bush, and Ross Perot, coded from their speeches, spot ads, and position books during post–Labor Day general election period. Includes both assessments of rivals and self–assessments by the candidates, 9/2–11/3/1992.

[†]Assessments of the three candidates coded from ABC, CBS, NBC, CNN, or PBS newscasts, the *New York Times*, the *Washington Post*, or the *Wall Street Journal*, 9/2–11/3/1992.

Source: Bruce Buchanan, *Renewing Presidential Politics: Campaigns, Media, and the Public Interest* (New York: Rowman & Littlefield, 1996), p. 148, Table 8.4. Reprinted with Permission.

guably the lowest since the popular vote for president was introduced in the 1830s[22]—be related to the avalanche of news reports about the horse race and particularly the double-digit lead that Clinton established over Dole in the early months of 1996?

Since 1952 the opinion polls have correctly predicted the winner in most instances[23]—even in 1996 no established poll had forecast a Dole victory. But the polls have been wrong on occasion, as Stephen J. Wayne observes: "Very close elections in 1960, 1968, and 1976, however, resulted in several pollsters making wrong predictions. In 1980, the size of Reagan's victory was substantially underestimated in some nationwide polls, whereas in 1992, Clinton's margin was overestimated by some pollsters who failed to allocate properly the undecided vote among the three candidates."[24]

Some pollsters unfortunately did not show greater restraint in 1996 despite their mistakes in 1992 because, once again, the voters had to evaluate three candidates. The actual results of the 1996 election were 49.2% for Clinton, 40.8% for Dole, 8.5% for Perot, and 2 percent for other candidates, but as a group seven major polls (ABC, CNN/*USA Today*/Gallup, Harris, *New York Times*/CBS, Pew Research Center, Reuters/Zogby) *underestimated* support for the Republican. Their combined average forecast was 49 percent for Clinton, 37 percent for Dole, and 8 percent for Perot, with 6 percent undecided or going to other candidates. The worst offender was the *New York Times*/CBS News final preelection poll that predicted 50 to 53 percent for Clinton and 34 to 35 percent for Dole. As for what caused this systematic polling error: "A last-minute break of previously undecided voters toward Mr. Dole, a drop in voter turnout that left the electorate disproportionately Republican, and the perennial challenge of distinguishing likely voters from unlikely voters all created potential trouble for pollsters."[25]

More important than predicting the election outcome with exact precision is the larger question of how the constant drumbeat of the horse race based on polls, which may or may not be valid, affects the presidential campaign. Indeed, CNN and *USA Today* resorted to *daily* tracking polls to measure presumably every nuance of the horse race, a practice that caused some concern when CNN/*USA Today* reported a 16-point shift between Clinton and Dole within days. On Saturday (September 29, 1996) Clinton led Dole by only 9 percentage points, but three days later (Tuesday, October 1) Clinton expanded his lead to 25 points, and such dramatic changes are quickly publicized by the media, as Clinton-Gore spokesman Joe Lockhart recalls: "I spent most of Saturday answering questions about, 'Why is it closing?'" He added: "It's gone beyond ridiculous."[26]

Surely this trend in polling would disturb any serious student of democratic politics. Do such wide swings in the horse race (even if accurate) suggest that voters have formulated compelling reasons why they prefer one candidate over the other? Or does this volatility imply that the electorate either is not really paying attention to the campaign or needs additional information in order to arrive at a firm judgment? Polls offer a snapshot of public opinion at one given time, but a presidential campaign stretches for months, and the entire process can be short-circuited by popular misperceptions based on preliminary polls.

Early polls less carefully differentiate between likely voters and nonvoters, so results can distort political reality. What matters is the horse race as judged by voters, not by the public at large. Although these distortions may be recognized by the pollsters, and by experts with both campaigns, they are largely ignored by the news media, even though they have the potential of affecting the conduct of the presidential campaign and, in some cases, the outcome. For 1996, as political scientist Everett C. Ladd, who heads the Roper Center for Public Opinion Research at the University of Connecticut, observed, "A large body of polling data collectively showed a landslide contest, about a 15-point Clinton lead, on average, across the autumn. The electorate was told throughout the campaign that it was over. Clinton voters may have been made complacent, or the Dole campaign demoralized."[27]

Campaign Tactics and Attack Ads

In developing a winning campaign strategy, presidential candidates need to energize their political base without offending independent voters; trying to win over votes from the opposition party is more problematic. In general, Democrats emphasize bread-and-butter appeals such as jobs, wages, and benefits for the working class, whereas the Republicans have tried to shift the debate to social issues that exploit divisions within the Democratic Party: crime; family values, school prayer, and abortion.

Tax cutting also is a perennial GOP pledge (e.g., George Bush declared, "Read my lips, no new taxes" in 1988, and Bob Dole advocated a 15 percent tax cut in 1996). Foreign policy and national security are also areas in which the Republicans historically (until the end of the Cold War with the Soviet Union) held the advantage over Democrats. In 1980 Reagan used the Soviet invasion of Afghanistan and the Iran hostage crisis to question President Carter's leadership ability and advocate more defense spending. Compared to the inexperience of his rival, Governor Michael Dukakis (D–Mass.), Bush in 1988 could point to his own extraordinary high-level involvement in foreign affairs.

A new issue that should benefit the Democrats is environmentalism, but the Bush campaign in 1988 effectively discredited Dukakis's environmental record. The GOP aired TV advertisements alleging pollution in Boston Harbor that involved "deceptive use of visuals" which, nonetheless, were effective: "The ad succeeded on two levels. It inoculated Bush in an issue area that, because of the Reagan administration's record, had been a political soft spot for Republicans. By pinning the blame for the lack of pollution enforcement on Dukakis, the ad also questioned Dukakis' record on the environment and his managerial capacities as governor."[28]

In 1992 the Bush campaign tried to make an issue of the pathetic condition of Arkansas's environmental protection laws during Clinton's tenure as governor, but this attempt fell short. One reason was Clinton's choice of Al Gore to be his running mate; Gore's well-known advocacy of environmental causes, notably global warming, was enthusiastically received by the environmentalists and assured that the issue would get favorable attention by the press. In a postmortem of the failed 1992 campaign, GOP strategist Fred Steeper made this observation:

> Maybe the biggest effect [of Gore's selection] was on our strategy, by your putting an environmentalist on the ticket. In fact, we had been going after Clinton on his environmental record in Arkansas, which some felt was inconsistent, but the selection of Gore provided you with protection on the environmental issue. At one time I thought for dead certain that we'd be running a chicken waste commercial sometime in September or October. In fact, some people were looking forward to it. Part of the reason we didn't was because of Gore being on the ticket. Plus, we were also accusing the Clinton/Gore ticket of being environmental extremists, and some thought it might be contradictory.[29]

So-called negative political advertisements are commonly used today to attack one's opponent rather than to outline the candidate's own priorities or policies. Many commentators believe their extensive use in 1988 against the hapless Michael Dukakis started this ominous trend, as presidency scholar Myron Levine explains:

Negative advertising was the dominant hallmark of the 1988 race. The Bush campaign charged Dukakis with having run a "revolving door" prison program as governor. An advertisement sponsored by an independent PAC went even further by showing the picture of one criminal, Willie Horton, a black man, and detailing the heinous crimes Horton committed when he had escaped while on furlough. The Bush campaign further denied Dukakis's claim to having led an economic revival in the "Massachusetts miracle"; instead, they portrayed the state under Dukakis's leadership as "Taxachusetts." They also charged Dukakis with being soft on national defense and being an incompetent manager who presided over the pollution of Boston Harbor.[30]

An extensive analysis of political advertisements by Darrell West verifies their increased use since 1952. The percentages of "prominent" ads that were judged to be "negative" since then are 1952—25 percent, 1956—38 percent, 1960—12 percent, 1964—50 percent, 1968—69 percent, 1972—33 percent, 1976—33 percent, 1980—60 percent, 1984—74 percent, 1988—83 percent, and 1992—66 percent.[31] In other words, the level of negativism jumped from the 1950s to the 1960s, moderated somewhat during the 1970s, but then escalated to new highs in the 1980s, culminating with the Bush-Dukakis campaign of 1988.

One infamous attack ad dates back to the Johnson campaign of 1964 against Barry Goldwater. To scare voters into thinking Goldwater was an extremist who would allow military commanders to use tactical nuclear weapons against Communists in Vietnam, the "Daisy Girl" ad showed a little girl in a meadow plucking petals from a daisy and counting softly to herself. When she got to zero, there was an explosion, the girl disappeared, and then a mushroom-shaped cloud representing a nuclear blast covered the screen. After Goldwater's camp protested, the commercial was withdrawn (it was aired only once), but the political damage to the Republican was done.

Yet four years later political advertisements also were utilized for an entirely different purpose—to recreate the public persona of Richard Nixon. As chronicled by Joe McGinnis in his book *The Selling of the President,* that advertising strategy was designed to create a "new" Nixon (not the "old" Nixon who had lost his 1960 presidential race and his 1962 bid to become governor of California):

> America still saw him as the 1960 Nixon. If he were to come at the people again, as candidate, it would have to be as something new; not this scarred, discarded figure from their past. . . . This would be Richard Nixon, the leader, returning from exile. Perhaps not beloved, but respected. Firm but not harsh; just but compassionate. With flashes of warmth spaced evenly throughout.[32]

Richard Nixon was never a lovable American politician, given his background as a vicious campaigner during the anticommunist era of the 1940s, but his image problem dated back to his lackluster appearance in the first series of presidential debates in 1960. According to two media experts, "The recollection of the shadowy, shifty-eyed Nixon projected in the first debate of 1960 has forced the attention of consultants on appearance

in debates." As a result of Nixon's poor appearance (attributed to his recent release from the hospital), a survey indicated that people who heard
the debate on the radio believed Nixon had won, whereas those who
watched the televised debate thought that Kennedy beat Nixon.[33]

Ever since then, candidates are prepared to make their best showing
before the TV audience. They now are served by media consultants,
speech coaches, specialists in makeup and body language (even the height
of the podiums are adjusted to diminish the appearance that one of the
candidates is taller), and mock debates are convened between the presidential contender and a friendly adversary. Perhaps the sterile quality of
the modern presidential and vice presidential debates have undermined
their effect as an educational forum.

Presidential debates do not change many minds; instead, they generally reinforce the public's prior disposition toward the candidates. No debates took place in 1964, 1968, or 1972 (Nixon learned his lesson!), but they
have continued ever since. In 1980 the debates helped Ronald Reagan portray a warm image that reassured many voters, and the former actor
clearly outperformed the incumbent, as Jimmy Carter later recollected:
"In the debate itself it was hard to judge the general demeanor that was
projected to the viewers. Reagan was, 'Aw, shucks, this and that. I'm a
grandfather, and . . . I love peace,' etc. He had his memorized lines, and
he pushes a button and they come out. Apparently he made a better impression on the TV audience than I did."[34]

With the emphasis on playing it safe rather than scoring debate
points, the candidates normally are so well scripted that, regardless of
who is declared the winner, the encounter has little effect on the overall
campaign. But they are political risks because, as the Ford gaffe showed,
every once in a while a misstatement by a candidate or a well-placed one-
liner by the opponent can hurt. At one moment in their televised vice presidential debate in 1988, Democrat Lloyd Bentsen devastated Republican
Dan Quayle when, after Quayle compared his own personal experience in
military service with that of JFK, (Quayle served in the National Guard to
avoid going to Vietnam) Bentsen shot back, "You're no John Kennedy."
The media effect was immediate and dramatic.

Coalition Building

In the wake of the 1932 realignment, the Democratic Party forged a
New Deal coalition comprised of unions, Catholics and Jews, immigrants
and African Americans (who abandoned their loyalty to the Republican
Party that resulted after Lincoln's 1860 realignment), the big city working
classes, and the intellectual community. The New Deal had more of an impact on younger voters who grew up during the Roosevelt-Truman era
than on older citizens whose formative years, earlier in the century, were
under Republican presidents. And importantly white southerners (African
Americans were disenfranchised throughout the South at that time) retained their Democratic loyalties that dated back to Andrew Jackson.

Some of those social groups remain loyal to the Democratic Party, but six decades have passed since the Great Depression and the advent of the Franklin Roosevelt welfare state, with the result that the New Deal coalition has begun to crumble. Exit polls (taken as voters leave the polls on Election Day) indicate how those various social groups have voted in more recent presidential elections (Table 4-4).

The exit polls since 1976 show that the Democratic Party has retained the loyalty of African Americans, union households, self-identified liberals, people who call themselves Democrats, income-earners in the lowest income range, and probably easterners. Following the 1996 elections, the Northeast became almost solidly Democratic because so few congressional Republicans withstood the Clinton landslide. All these social groups comprised the New Deal coalition of the 1930s and 1940s, but there have been some additions. Hispanics, the newest wave of immigrants, vote Democratic, but peoples from Spanish-speaking countries are not entirely homogeneous. Mexicans and Puerto Ricans are generally Democratic, but Cubans are solidly Republican[35] because they fled the communist takeover by Fidel Castro and, moreover, many Cuban immigrants are middle-class professionals.

The GOP draws votes from self-identified Republicans and independents (until Clinton narrowly won the independent vote), conservatives, Asian Americans (whose educational level and income profile is high relative to any social group), and higher income earners generally. The changing voting behavior from the lowest to the highest income earners shows, for all six elections, nearly a perfect relationship: the percentage of Democratic votes decreases and the percentage of Republican votes increases as incomes go up. Until Clinton, westerners also tended to vote Republican, but the major regional shift since the New Deal has been the movement of southerners into the GOP column. Most southerners voted against the Clinton-Gore ticket in 1992 and were loyal to the Republicans in 1988, 1984, and 1980. Only in 1976, when the Democrats nominated a favorite son of the South (Jimmy Carter of Georgia), did most southerners vote Democratic. The loss of the South means the national Democratic Party will have to rely more heavily on the West Coast, Midwest, and East Coast states to achieve a winning coalition in presidential elections.

Voters from nonunion households (a larger number than from union households) voted Republican in 1976 and 1980 and split their vote in 1992 and 1996. Although Democrats have retained the loyalty of unionists, still a sizable bloc of union households has voted Republican in recent elections. Those pro-Republican union voters—popularly called "Reagan Democrats" by the media—cast 45 percent and 46 percent of their ballots for Reagan, respectively, in 1980 and 1984. Not only has the percentage of unionized jobs in the United States been on the decline, but the rank and file union member can no longer be characterized as a monolithic force in American politics.

One brighter prospect for the Democrats is the possibility that the gender gap may be widening in their favor. Men were strongly inclined

Table 4-4. How Social Groups Voted in Presidential Elections, 1976–1996

	1996 %		1992 %		1988 %		1984 %		1980 %		1976 %	
Group	Dem	Rep	Dem	Rep	Dem	Rep	Dem	Rep	Dem	Rep	Dem	Rep
Democrats	84	10	77	10	83	17	74	26	67	27	80	20
Republicans	13	80	10	73	8	92	7	93	11	85	11	89
Independents	43	35	38	32	43	57	36	64	31	56	48	52
Liberal	78	11	68	14	82	18	71	29	60	28	74	26
Moderate	57	33	47	31	51	49	46	54	43	49	53	47
Conservatives	20	71	18	64	19	81	18	82	23	73	30	70
Male	43	44	41	38	42	58	38	62	38	55	52	48
Female	54	38	45	37	49	51	42	58	46	47	52	48
White	43	46	39	40	40	60	34	66	36	56	48	52
Black	84	12	83	10	89	11	91	9	83	14	83	17
Hispanic	72	21	61	25	70	30	66	34	56	37	82	18
Asian	43	48	31	54								
Union	59	30	55	24	57	43	54	46	48	45	62	38
Nonunion	46	45	41	40					36	56	48	52
East			47	35	49	51	47	53	44	48	54	46
Midwest			42	37	47	53	38	62	42	52	49	51
South			41	43	41	59	36	64	45	52	54	46
West			43	34	47	53	38	62	36	54	50	50
1st $*	59	28	58	23	63	37	54	46	52	42	62	38
2nd $	53	36	45	35	51	49	42	58	48	43	57	43
3rd $	48	40	41	38	43	57	40	60	39	54	50	50
4th $	47	45	40	41	43	57	32	68	33	59	38	62
5th $	44	48	36	48	39	61	31	69	26	66		
6th $	38	54			33	67						
1st age†	53	34	46	33	47	53	39	61	45	44	49	51
2nd age	48	41	41	36	46	54	43	57	44	44	56	44
3rd age	48	41	41	38	42	58	42	58	38	55	52	48
4th age	48	44	43	39	49	51	39	61	39	55	48	52
5th age			50	39			36	64	41	55	48	52

Source: Exit polls are reported in "Presidential Election: How Social Groups Voted 1976–1996," *The Public Perspective,* A Roper Center Review of Public Opinion and Polling 8 (Dec./Jan. 1997), pp. 8–10.

*The number and ranges for income categories were changed over time, so 1st refers to the lowest category and 6th to the highest.

†The number and ranges for age categories were changed over time, so 1st refers to the youngest category and 5th to the oldest category.

to vote Democratic during the 1930s and 1940s because most were employed in blue-collar or unionized jobs, and women did not vote all that differently than men during those early elections. No gender gap existed when Carter opposed Ford, but men were decidedly more pro-Reagan in 1980. Four years later the Reagan landslide buried any gender gap, and in 1988 again men were more enthusiastic about George Bush, although most women voted Republican as well. Both men and women favored

Clinton in 1992, but a gender gap was beginning to develop to the point that men narrowly preferred Dole over Clinton in 1992, whereas the pro-Clinton margin among women was sixteen percentage points.

In summary, the shift by southerners toward the Republican Party is the most dramatic reversal of the New Deal coalition, although the GOP, particularly under Reagan, was successful in chipping away Democratic votes from union labor and Catholics.[36] One explanation why these voters, particularly (white) southerners, have left the national Democratic Party (southerners still vote Democratic in many state and local level elections) is that economic security issues—the mainstay of the New Deal coalition—are no longer as important. New social issues—race relations, crime, taxes, patriotism, lifestyle—have become more important and, on these questions, the liberalism of the national Democratic Party is not in favor with those voter blocs. Clinton was able to overcome this ideological baggage during the 1992 campaign, and again in 1996, by asserting that he was a new Democrat as opposed to crime and welfare dependency as any Republican. If issues are the reason why voters are not as loyal to Democratic presidential candidates, then presumably they are aware that Republicans are conservative and Democrats are liberal and they are choosing accordingly.

ELECTION OUTCOMES AND POLICY MANDATES

Voters evaluate the presidential contenders based on their party affiliation, candidate image, the past performance of incumbents (called "retrospective" voting), and the issues. After a realigning election, party is very important because most voters have endorsed the policy direction of the majority party and not the minority party. Voting Democratic during the 1930s and 1940s was an endorsement of the New Deal-Fair Deal programs of Roosevelt and Truman because the 1932 realignment signaled that most Americans wanted a fundamentally new direction in public policy, with an activist federal government promoting economic security for the average citizen. However, although the 1932 election was profoundly important to the future of American politics and policy, most voters at that time would probably not pass the test we now apply to assess the "rationality" of voters. Yes, they rejected Hoover; yes, they endorsed a new liberal ideology; no, they did not give FDR a "mandate" to carry out a specific programmatic agenda.[37]

Some kind of policy mandate exists in every presidential campaign, although no contest since 1932 qualifies as a realigning election. In some elections—1964, 1980, 1992—the exact policy that voters endorse is easily recognized, whereas in other elections the message is garbled because voters judged the contenders according to personality traits rather than issues or past performance and not promises for the future. Of the twelve presidential elections between 1952 and 1996, candidate image was the key influence in two races, issue saliency was primary in three instances, five were based largely on positive or negative evaluations of the incumbent, and the two closest elections involved unique variables including the candidates' personal background characteristics.

Candidate Image: 1952 and 1956

When voters choose between presidential contenders based on the images of those candidates, the rational voter ideal is strained. Is there any relationship between how people perceive a candidate's leadership ability, charm, or charisma and the public policy debate? The Eisenhower victories in 1952 and 1956 were a testimony to his celebrity status, although voters were not totally unaware of Ike's position on key issues. The seminal work on electoral behavior at that time pointed to three reasons why Eisenhower won in 1952.[38] First was a strongly anti-Democratic attitude because the "second Truman term was characterized by a growing criticism of the President and his Administration on the question of honesty in government." Secondly was Eisenhower's stature as a military hero in World War II, which yielded "a strongly positive feeling toward him in all elements of the population" even before Ike declared his candidacy. The phrase "I Like Ike" typified the public feeling during the 1950s. And third was foreign policy, the Korean War in particular:

> Frustration and resentment over the stalemated Korean War, which had never been well understood by the American people, were widespread and intense. As the action in Korea dragged into its third year, it became an increasingly partisan issue, with the Republican leadership arguing either that this country should never have been involved in Korea in the first place or that the Democratic Administration should have brought our involvement there to a successful conclusion.[39]

The GOP used the rallying cry "Corruption, Korea, and Communism" to dramatize charges against the Truman administration, and thus encouraged retrospective voting, so the votes cast for the GOP did not represent a future policy agenda, other than the fact that Eisenhower did promise to "go to Korea" and ultimately did sign an armistice ending the conflict. Issues were less important to Ike's 1956 reelection victory, whereas "the popular appeal of Eisenhower was unquestionably of paramount importance" because his landslide win did not translate into Republican gains in the Congress.[40]

Issue Saliency: 1964, 1968, 1972

Traditional political wisdom held that candidates would occupy the center ideologically to attract votes from all segments of the electorate,[41] although this strategy would blur the differences between Democrats and Republicans and prevent the voters from making a policy choice when casting their ballots. Conventional wisdom, however, did not explain the outcomes of 1964, 1968, and 1972 in which issues were dominant and, regarding the Johnson-Goldwater contest in 1964 and the Nixon-McGovern battle in 1972, that heightened policy choice led to landslide victories of historic magnitude by the incumbents.

Citizens were more alert to issues in these three campaigns. For the period 1956 to 1972[42] Pomper found a stronger linkage between voters' attitudes and party preference beginning with the 1964 Goldwater-Johnson campaign, and he concluded that the electorate became more aware that Democrats are generally "liberal" and Republicans are generally "conservative" on public policies. This finding contrasts with the 1950s research by Converse that the majority of voters were not ideological.[43] The trend of greater issue voting at the expense of party loyalty also was documented in the important study *The Changing American Voter*.[44] Issue voting began with the 1964 presidential election and continued through 1972, but in 1976 party voting returned as the more important predictor of how people evaluated Gerald Ford and Jimmy Carter. Similarly, an examination of 1964 and 1968 led Richard Boyd to conclude that the choice of Goldwater by the Republicans and the entrance of George Wallace as the American-Independent Party candidate in 1968 heightened voters' awareness of issues when they cast their ballots in those elections.[45]

David RePass pointed out that federal aid to education, federal job guarantees, and housing policy shaped the outcome of the 1964 election.[46] The key issues of 1968 were racial desegregation, the Vietnam War, and law and order. Although many people could not differentiate between Humphrey and Nixon on the issues, Vietnam in particular, those who backed Wallace did so expressly because of his rightist stands on all three policies.[47] The election of 1972 factionalized the Democratic Party just as it polarized the general electorate. McGovern's opposition to the Vietnam War and advocacy of abortion and marijuana legalization caused "policy disagreements strong enough to cause massive defections among rank and file [Democratic] Party supporters" whose views were closer to Richard Nixon's.[48] Apart from the issues, other observers believe that McGovern "may have been hurt by voters' perceptions of the people standing by him: too many young people, too many blacks, too many welfare mothers."[49]

Retrospective Voting: 1980, 1984, 1988, 1992, 1996

A healthy economy and the absence of war loom large when the public votes retrospectively. Those considerations handicapped Jimmy Carter in 1980 and George Bush in 1992 and virtually guaranteed the reelection of Ronald Reagan in 1984 and victory by George Bush in 1988. When the incumbent is unpopular, it is more difficult for the challenger to claim a policy mandate, as 1980 and 1992 show.

In 1980 Ronald Reagan carried 44 states with 489 electoral votes and received 51 percent of the popular vote compared to 41 percent for Carter and 7 percent for independent candidate John Anderson. The last time an incumbent Democrat lost reelection was 1888: Grover Cleveland was defeated by Benjamin Harrison. According to George Gallup, "the Reagan landslide was the result not so much of an ideological shift to the right among the electorate as of dissatisfaction with the leadership of the nation and a desire for change."[50] A study by Frankovic concluded that "disapproval and dislike of the incumbent outweighed any other single explanation for supporting Ronald Reagan on Election Day."[51]

As for a mandate for conservatism, Frankovic agreed that "Reagan was not elected because of increasing conservatism of the country."[52] Still the media pundits proclaimed a Reagan mandate and the congressional Democrats became cowed by the GOP winning back control of the Senate, so commentators missed the point that the mandate supposedly given to Reagan was selective. During the 1980 campaign, voters were more aware of Reagan's views on policy than Carter's, and the majority agreed with Reagan that the United States should be more forceful when dealing with the Soviet Union and that inflation was the major economic problem facing the country. Thus Frankovic concluded, "The new President does not have a mandate for conservative policies; instead, he has a mandate to be different from Jimmy Carter."[53]

In the 1984 presidential election, according to Abramson, Aldrich, and Rohde, the most important issues were economic (inflation and unemployment), foreign affairs and defense were a close second, and social welfare issues also got the attention of the voters.[54] The Reagan-Bush team were the benefactors as the recession of 1981–1982 was over, the economy was rebounding, there was peace and the perception that America had regained its stature as a world power.

The 1988 presidential campaign was dominated by negative advertisements against Massachusetts governor Michael Dukakis, the Democrat, whose old-fashioned liberalism made him an easy target for the GOP. George Bush made *liberal* a dirty word and blasted Dukakis for his membership in the ACLU, his support of legalized abortion, his advocacy of gun controls, and his opposition to reciting the Pledge of Allegiance in schools. As we noted earlier, most effective and controversial were TV ads charging that Dukakis was soft on crime and particularly one about Willie Horton, a black prisoner released on furlough who kidnapped a white couple, stabbing the man and raping the woman. Dukakis was painted into a political corner, but the voters nonetheless were given a real choice, as Abramson, Aldrich, and Rohde explain:

> Clearly, the election offered policy alternatives, and as we shall see, voters saw clear policy differences between Bush and Dukakis. Although voters could not reelect Reagan, they could vote to continue his policies. Electing Dukakis would not overturn Reagan's reforms, but it would clearly lead to major revisions. Americans could also vote to support the traditional values espoused by Bush or the more liberal views advanced by Dukakis.[55]

No doubt the negative ads used by the Republicans helped sharpen the contrast between Bush and Dukakis. With the economy seeming to be rebounding, the GOP could shift its focus to social issues almost exclusively, although the critics felt that the Horton-type ads brought the level of campaign rhetoric to a new low. Yet Myron Levine argues, to the contrary, that "it is elitist for self-proclaimed experts to assume that they know just what issues voters should have focused on in an election. For many voters, crime was a more pressing matter than was the subject of the mounting budget deficit."[56]

The economy can be a double-edged sword. Carter blamed Ford for recession, won in 1976, and then lost in 1980 to Reagan, who asked the voters if they were more prosperous compared to four years earlier. George Bush rode the coattails of a popular incumbent and an upbeat economy to the White House in 1988, only to face reelection as the country struggled to rebound from the latest economic downturn. The economy was virtually the whole story that year. When 1992 began, 82 percent of respondents told pollsters that the economy was in bad shape, and at the end of the presidential campaign 75 percent still held that view. Although Bush was a more popular president than Jimmy Carter was by the time the GOP convened its party convention in August 1992, "the public's evaluation of how Bush was managing the economy had actually fallen below Carter's all-time low."[57] When all was said and done, says Frankovic, "1992 turned out to be a very simple election. It was a referendum on the incumbent president—and George Bush lost."[58]

It is also paradoxical that in 1988 Bush opposed Michael Dukakis, who conducted one of the most disorganized campaigns of any modern Democrat, but four years later President Bush then proceeded to wage a lackluster campaign. In the three-way race of 1992, with the uncertainties caused by Ross Perot's candidacy, it was not impossible for Bush to close the gap, or win. "George Bush lost an election that he should have won," Maggiotto and Wekken argue, but failed because he had no strategy and attacked Clinton on the wrong issues:

> By the time of the campaign, however, Republican strategists concluded that it was too late to provide a positive rationale for the election of George Bush. Aside from a widely-praised "agenda for American renewal" unveiled at a September 10 speech to the Detroit Economic Club, there was little emphasis on an economic plan. Instead, the strategists insisted, they needed to go negative. In other words, the reason to reelect George Bush was to avoid being governed by Bill Clinton. Thus, the campaign emphasized trust and taxes. Although there was some responsiveness in the electorate to these themes, they could not make up for the lack of a compelling positive message, a reason to support Bush and not just oppose Clinton. And the attempts to stain Clinton confirmed the impression among many in the public that Bush was not serious about economic policy.[59]

Two Close Elections: 1960 and 1976

The outcomes of the 1960 and 1976 presidential elections were close, which suggests the presidential candidates were not far apart on the major issues. In both cases, but especially in 1976, the incumbent Republican

Party waged its campaign in the midst of recession, one during 1960–1961 (following an earlier recession in 1957–1958) and a worse economic downturn during 1975–1976.

In 1960 any number of influences (for example, Kennedy's superior performance on the first televised debates of the modern era) could have resulted in his 100,000-vote margin of victory but, on net, major voter blocs did not stray much from their vote in 1956—except one group. The key factor in 1960 was Kennedy's religion, and his candidacy got disproportionately more support from Catholics in the large states of the North, even though his Catholicism lost Kennedy even more votes among Protestant southerners.[60] But the southern electorate still followed its traditional loyalty to the Democratic Party, thus giving most of its votes to Kennedy.

The 1976 election came less than two years after President Nixon resigned and Vice President Gerald Ford succeeded to the highest office. The Watergate scandals tarred the GOP (which suffered big losses in the 1974 congressional elections), and politically the decision by President Ford to pardon Richard Nixon was disastrous. Ford had to fight an uphill battle, but he nearly won because a good deal of retrospective voting was going on. On many issues, however, Carter and Ford were close to each other and occupied the middle of the road, but not all issues were equally salient for voters in 1976. The social issues were less important (than in 1972) and voters focused more on economic problems such as unemployment, which gave Carter the advantage. The Democratic Party was perceived by voters as more able and willing to deal with the growing joblessness than the Republicans.[61]

Jimmy Carter took advantage of the post-Watergate backlash and was portrayed as a political outsider beholden to no one in Washington, D.C. With origins in the Deep South, regional pride also worked in his favor. Carter won the entire South (except Virginia), a feat no other Democrat including Clinton achieved, and Scammon and Wattenberg concluded that his southern origins were the primary reason why white southern Protestants deviated from their recent loyalty to Republican presidential candidates and gave Carter their votes. But Scammon and Wattenberg doubted that the South would support Carter indefinitely for that reason because "looking to the future, we can say that if a relatively few Southern conservatives perceive Carter as a liberal in 1980 and vote conservative instead of Southern, Carter could be in serious trouble."[62] Which is likely what happened in 1980 as Carter faced the very conservative Ronald Reagan, although other factors such as double-digit inflation rates, his failed rescue attempt of Americans who were held hostage (a total of 444 days) by Iranian militants, and the invasion of Afghanistan by the Soviets fueled the long-standing perception that Carter was not up to the job of president.

To conclude, the debate over so-called rational voting has been overly critical of ordinary citizens for their failure to differentiate between the two parties when the presidential candidates deserve some of the blame. Citizens lack the time and inclination to become fully informed about all the nuances of public policy and where candidates stand, and the task is no easier when the contenders deliberately confuse the issues and equivocate. But as the elections of 1964, 1968, and 1972 show, voters respond to issue cues when candidates offer real policy differences, and differences can be communicated effectively through televised advertisements. Ads may be simplistic; they may reduce complex problems to slogans; they may be deemed negative in content. But they help to define the policy alternatives represented by each party and their presidential candidates.

Elections are a blunt instrument for democratic governance, but they are not irrelevant. They set the agenda and direction for policy, if not the specifics of programs. The 1980 defeat of Carter signaled to President Reagan that the inflation fight had to be his first priority, and it was. Reagan also promised to cut taxes, increase military expenditures, and reorder domestic spending, and he redeemed those pledges as president. The 1984 landslide that engulfed Mondale was attributed to the "peace and prosperity" of the Reagan years, but his declaration to the Democratic national convention that a Mondale administration would raise income taxes (even for the worthy cause of reducing the deficit) doomed his candidacy. Bush's loss was largely attributed to a recession and a start-and-stop economic recovery, which Bill Clinton fully understood, but once elected the Democrat also carried through on his promise to "reinvent" government and, although too late and unsuccessful, submitted to Congress a plan for universal health care coverage.

Instead of going back to the heady days of the 1950s when political scientists favored "responsible parties" that offered the electorate alternatives on a wide range of policies, as political "mandates" were traditionally viewed, Bruce Buchanan's concept of a focused "policy mandate" that links campaign promises on specific issues to follow-up action by the winning candidate is a more realistic way to judge the impact of elections on democratic governance.[63] Even this limited concept of policy mandate requires presidential campaigns to be driven by issues that resonate with the voters and are communicated by positive political commercials that inform the electorate.

PRESIDENTIAL SUCCESSION WITHOUT ELECTION

The number of vice presidents who succeed to the presidency is mainly explained by the fact that eight presidents have died in office—William Henry Harrison, Taylor, Lincoln, Garfield, McKinley, Harding, FDR, and Kennedy—and the resignation of Nixon. None have been removed from office under Article II of the Constitution, designating "treason, bribery, or other high crimes and misdemeanors" as grounds for impeachment, although President Andrew Johnson came close. He was impeached by a majority vote in the House of Representatives, but the Senate fell one vote short of the needed two-thirds for conviction. President Nixon, who faced impeachment proceedings in the House of Representatives, chose to resign, and his departure afforded the first opportunity to use the provisions of the Twenty-fifth Amendment, which dictates vice presidential succession after resignation or death. Ratified in 1967, the Twenty-fifth Amendment was the fourth attempt to resolve the question of presidential succession (others were the Succession Acts of 1792, 1886, and 1947).

Under the Twenty-fifth Amendment, should the vice presidency be vacant, the president can nominate a vice president who assumes office after a majority vote in the House and Senate. When Vice President Spiro Agnew resigned in 1973 following charges that, as a Baltimore County official and governor of Maryland, he evaded income taxes and accepted bribes, President Nixon consulted with congressional leaders and selected the House Minority Leader, Gerald Ford (R–Mich.), as his new vice president.

When Nixon resigned in 1974, Ford assumed the presidency and proceeded to nominate Governor Nelson Rockefeller of New York, who was confirmed as vice president. By virtue of the Twenty-fifth Amendment, it is highly unlikely that the nation would suffer a double vacancy in both offices of president and vice president. It also assures that the president and vice president will represent the same political party and most likely be compatible personalities.

A more thorny issue pertains to presidential disability, and again the Twenty-fifth Amendment provides a satisfactory resolution to this matter, although questions persist about its implementation. William McKinley lingered for about eight days after being shot by an assassin, and President Garfield was disabled for eighty days before he died, after an assassin's bullet lodged in his spinal column. President Woodrow Wilson was stricken by a paralyzing stroke from about September 25, 1919, until the end of his term in March 1921. During the disabilities of Garfield and Wilson their vice presidents hesitated to assume presidential powers, and the cabinet in both instances did not force the issue. It was also unclear whether legally Garfield and Wilson could have resumed their duties had they recovered, which was not addressed by the Constitution.

Pursuant to the Twenty-fifth Amendment, a president now communicates in writing with the Speaker of the House and the president pro tempore of the Senate that he is unable to discharge his duties. His disability also can be determined by the vice president acting with a majority of the cabinet or "of such other body as Congress may by law provide"; again, written communications are made to the Speaker and president pro tempore. In either case the powers and duties of the presidency are exercised by the vice president as "acting president." If his disability ends, the president makes this known in writing to the speaker and president pro tempore, whereupon he resumes the powers and duties of office, unless, that is, the following takes place:

> [T]he Vice President and a majority of either the principal officers of the executive department, or of such other body as Congress may by law pro-

vide, transmit within four days to the President pro tempore . . . and the Speaker . . . their written declaration that the President is unable to discharge the powers and duties of his office. Thereupon Congress shall decide the issue, assembling within 48 hours for that purpose if not in session. If the Congress, within 21 days after receipt of the latter written declaration, or, if . . . not in session, within 21 days after Congress is required to assemble, determines by two-thirds vote of both Houses that the President is unable to discharge the powers and duties of his office, the Vice President shall continue to discharge the same as Acting President; otherwise, the President shall resume the powers and duties of his office.

Before this amendment was enacted, Congress did not seem the least concerned about electoral accountability in matters of presidential succession. When a double vacancy in the presidency and vice presidency occurred under the Succession Act of 1792, the president pro tempore became "acting president." Provided in the Succession Act of 1886, the presidency was to be assumed by members of the cabinet, beginning first with the secretary of state. The Succession Act of 1947 was the least desirable resolution of the problem. In the case of a double vacancy, succession would pass to the Speaker, then to the president pro tempore, and then to the various cabinet members.

The 1947 act, like the 1886 law, allowed cabinet members who were appointed to office to become president. But this latest statute also violated separation of powers, by making members of Congress the chief executive, and also allowed for the possibility (if, for example, Democrats controlled the House and Republicans the Senate) that different parties would control the presidency and vice presidency.

Most observers were thankful when the Twenty-fifth Amendment was added in 1967, although its procedures are not perfect either. When Gerald Ford and Nelson Rockefeller were president and vice president, Senator Pastore (D–R.I.) made this observation: "For the first time in the history of this great nation the President and Vice President will both be appointed—not elected by the people and not responsive to any mandate from the citizens."[64] Had the Succession Act of 1947 been in force, however, in this situation the president would have been the Democratic Speaker of the House despite the fact that Nixon, a Republican, had been elected president, which would be a more serious blow to the notion of electoral accountability.

SUMMARY

The election of presidents becomes routine in the American system and has occurred in times of war and peace. The real question for political scientists, however, is what the election actually means. Elections become blunt instruments for democratic governance, but are not irrelevant. They set the agenda and direction for policy, if not the specifics for a president's programs. While few clear mandates come out of most elections, candidate victories in 1964, 1980, and 1992 did translate into policymaking. In other words, presidential elections can shape public expectations about the direction and policy agenda for the new administration.

Presidential campaigns are waged in the context of long-term electoral constraints and short-term political strategies. Realignment is one of the long-term electoral constraints that may change the complexion of the political system as we experienced in 1800, 1828, 1860, and 1932, but they occur only in infrequently and, because parties have been weakened by the use of presidential primaries, candidate reliance on mass media, public funding, and lesser party identification among voters, it is unlikely these realigning elections will happen in the near future.

Regional shifts also seldom occur, but they can be as important as realigning elections, as we have seen since the New Deal period. The West and South, for example, have changed hands from Democratic Party dominance to regions dominated by the Republican Party, which means that 74 percent of the electoral vote has also changed hands.

Other constraints on elections in the shorter term occur because of mass media coverage, coalition building, issue saliency, and emphasis on candidate image. The elections of 1964, 1968, and 1972 indicate that when candidates offer clear policy stands that differentiate one from another, voters will respond to the election cues.

NOTES

1. Richard Pious, *The American Presidency* (New York: Basic Books, 1979), p. 86.
2. Nelson Polsby and Aaron Wildavsky, *Presidential Elections*, 9th ed. (Chatham, NJ: Chatham House, 1996), p. 315.
3. Bruce Buchanan, *Renewing Presidential Politics* (Lanham, MD: Rowman & Littlefield, 1996), p. 71.
4. Those presidents involved included: John Quincy Adams (1824), Polk (1844), Taylor (1848), Buchanan (1856), Lincoln (1860), Hayes (1876), Garfield (1880), Cleveland (1884 and 1892), Benjamin Harrison (1888), Wilson (1912 and 1916), Truman (1948), Kennedy (1960), Nixon (1968), and Bill Clinton in 1992 and 1996.
5. Cited in Thomas E. Cronin, "Choosing a President," *The Center Magazine* (Sept./Oct. 1978), p. 9.
6. Raymond Tatalovich, "Electoral Votes and Presidential Campaign Trails, 1932–1976," *American Politics Quarterly* (Oct. 1979), pp. 489–498.
7. Its advantages are discussed in Thomas E. Cronin, "Choosing a President," *The Center Magazine* (Sept./Oct. 1978), pp. 5–15.
8. Angus Campbell, Philip E. Converse, Warren E. Miller, and Donald E. Stokes, *The American Voter: An Abridgement* (New York: Wiley, 1964), pp. 274–279.
9. V.O. Key, "A Theory of Critical Elections," *Journal of Politics* 17, 1 (Feb. 1955), pp. 3–18.
10. Wayne Shannon, *Party, Constituency, and Congressional Voting* (Baton Rouge: Louisiana State University Press, 1968), pp. 42–43.
11. "Partisan Identification as Electoral Backdrop," *The Public Perspective,* A Roper Center Review of Public Opinion and Polling 7 (Oct./Nov. 1996), pp. 26–26.
12. Kevin Phillips, *The Emerging Republican Majority* (New Rochelle, NY: Arlington House, 1969).
13. Stephen Skowronek, *The Politics Presidents Make: Leadership from John Adams to George Bush* (Cambridge, MA: Harvard University Press, 1993).
14. R.W. Apple, Jr., "Nation Is Still Locked onto Rightward Path, Leaving Liberals Beside Road," *New York Times* (Nov. 5, 1996), p. A14.

15. Philip Converse, *The Dynamics of Party Support: Cohort-Analyzing Party Identification* (Beverly Hills, CA: Sage, 1976).

16. Richard Brookhiser, *The Outside Story* (Garden City, NY: Doubleday, 1986), p. 155.

17. *The Gallup Poll Monthly* 328 (Jan. 1993), p. 12. From August 1988 through January 1993 no more than 46 percent ever believed Quayle "is qualified to serve as president," whereas the majority in 9 of the 13 surveys taken said he was not qualified.

18. Paul Taylor, *See How They Run* (New York: Knopf, 1990), p. 23.

19. Ibid., p. 57.

20. Reported in Thomas E. Patterson, *Out of Order* (New York: Knopf, 1993), p. 57.

21. Ibid. Also see Frederick T. Steeper, "Public Response to Gerald Ford's Statements on Eastern Europe in the Second Debate," in George F. Bishop, Robert G. Meadow, and Marilyn Jackson-Beeck, eds., *The Presidential Debates: Media, Electoral, and Policy Perspectives* (New York: Praeger, 1978), pp. 84–87.

22. Everett C. Ladd, "The Status-Quo Election: Introduction," *The Public Perspective*, A Roper Center Review of Public Opinion and Polling 8 (Dec./Jan. 1997), pp. 4–5.

23. Stephen J. Wayne, *The Road to the White House 1996* (New York: St. Martin's Press, 1996), p. 265.

24. Ibid., p. 264.

25. Michael R. Kagay, "Experts See a Need for Refining Election Polls," *New York Times* (Dec. 15, 1996), p. 22.

26. James Bennet, "Polling Provoking Debate in News Media on Its Use," *New York Times* (Oct. 4, 1996), p. A10.

27. Ibid.

28. Myron A. Levine, *Presidential Campaigns and Elections* (Itasca, IL: F.E. Peacock, 1995), p. 247.

29. Charles T. Royer, ed., *Campaign for President: The Managers Look at '92* (Hollis, NH: Hollis, 1994), p. 264.

30. Levine, *Presidential Campaigns and Elections*, pp. 25–26.

31. Darrell M. West, *Air Wars: Television Advertising in Election Campaigns, 1952–1992* (Washington, DC: Congressional Quarterly, 1993), pp. 46–51.

32. Joe McGinnis, *The Selling of the President* (New York: Simon & Schuster, 1969), p. 34.

33. Kathleen Hall Jamieson and David S. Birdsell, *Presidential Debates* (New York: Oxford University Press, 1988), pp. 183–184.

34. Jimmy Carter, *Keeping Faith* (New York: Bantam, 1982), p. 565.

35. Dario Moreno and Christopher L. Warren, "The Conservative Enclave: Cubans in Florida," in Rodolfo O. de la Garza and Louis DeSipio, eds., *From Rhetoric to Reality: Latino Politics in the 1988 Elections* (Boulder, CO: Westview Press, 1992), pp. 127–145.

36. For polling data on Catholics, see *The Gallup Report* 278 (Nov. 1988), pp. 6–7.

37. Sidney M. Milkis and Michael Nelson, *The American Presidency: Origins and Development, 1776–1990* (Washington, DC: CQ Press, 1990), p. 267.

38. Angus Campbell, Philip E. Converse, Warren E. Miller, and Donald E. Stokes, *The American Voter* (New York: Wiley, 1960), pp. 537–538.

39. Angus Campbell, Philip E. Converse, Warren E. Miller, and Donald E. Stokes, *The American Voter, an Abridgement* (New York: Wiley, 1964), p. 272.

40. Ibid.

41. Anthony Downs, *An Economic Theory of Democracy* (New York: Harper & Row, 1957).

42. Gerald Pomper, *Voters' Choice: Varieties of American Electoral Behavior* (New York: Dodd Mead, 1975).

43. Philip E. Converse, "The Nature of Belief Systems in Mass Publics," in David E. Apter, ed., *Ideology and Discontent* (New York: Free Press, 1964), chap. 6. Also see Angus Campbell, Philip E. Converse, Warren E. Miller, and Donald E. Stokes, *The American Voter, an Abridgement*, p. 144.

44. Norman Nie, Sidney Verba, and John R. Petrocik, *The Changing American Voter* (Cambridge, MA: Harvard University Press, 1979).

45. Richard W. Boyd, "Popular Control of Public Policy: A Normal Vote Analysis of the 1968 Election," *American Political Science Review* 66 (1972), pp. 429–449.

46. David E. RePass, "Issue Salience and Party Choice," *American Political Science Review* 65 (1971), pp. 389–400.

47. Philip E. Converse, Warren E. Miller, Jerrold R. Rusk, and Arthur C. Wolfe, "Continuity and Change in American Politics: Parties and Issues in the 1968 Election," *American Political Science Review* 63 (1969), pp. 1083–1105.

48. Arthur Miller, Warren E. Miller, Alden S. Raine, and Thad H. Brown, "A Majority Party in Disarray: Policy Polarization in the 1972 Election," *American Political Science Review* 70 (1976), pp. 753–778.

49. Samuel Popkin, John W. Gorman, Charles Phillips, and Jeffrey A. Smith, "Comment: What Have You Done for Me Lately? Toward an Investment Theory of Voting," *American Political Science Review* 70 (1976), pp. 779–813.

50. Gallup Opinion Index, Report 183 (Dec. 1980), p. 2.

51. Kathleen A. Frankovic, "Public Opinion Trends," in Gerald M. Pomper, ed., *The Election of 1980* (Chatham, NJ: Chatham House, 1981), p. 97.

52. Ibid., p. 113.

53. Ibid., p. 117.

54. Paul R. Abramson, John H. Aldrich, and David W. Rohde, *Change and Continuity in the 1984 Elections* (Washington, DC: Congressional Quarterly Press, 1987), pp. 165–168.

55. Paul R. Abramson, John H. Aldrich, and David W. Rohde, *Change and Continuity in the 1988 Elections* (Washington, DC: CQ Press, 1990), p. 3.

56. Myron A. Levine, *Presidential Campaigns and Elections* (Itasca, IL: F.E. Peacock, 1992), p. 207.

57. Kathleen A. Frankovic, "Public Opinion in the 1992 Campaign," in Gerald M. Pomper, ed., *The Election of 1992* (Chatham, NJ: Chatham House, 1993), pp. 112–113.

58. Ibid., p. 130.

59. Michael A. Maggiotto and Gary D. Wekkin, "'His to Lose': The Failure of George Herbert Walker Bush, 1992," *The American Review of Politics* 14 (1993), pp. 179, 194.

60. Angus Campbell, Philip E. Converse, Warren E. Miller, and Donald E. Stokes, *Elections and the Political Order* (New York: Wiley, 1966), pp. 86–93.

61. Benjamin I. Page, *Choices and Echoes in Presidential Elections* (Chicago: University of Chicago Press, 1978), pp. 91–97. Also see Arthur Miller and Warren Miller, "Partisanship and Performance: Rational Choice in the 1976 Presidential Election," paper delivered at the annual meeting, American Political Science Association, Washington, DC, Sept. 1977.

62. Richard M. Scammon and Ben J. Wattenberg, "Jimmy Carter's Problem," *Public Opinion* (March/April 1978), pp. 3–8.

63. See Bruce Buchanan, *Renewing Presidential Politics: Campaigns, Media, and the Public Interest* (Lanham, MD: Rowman & Littlefield, 1996).

64. Quoted in Arthur Schlesinger, Jr., "On the Presidential Succession," *Political Science Quarterly* (Sept. 1974), p. 476.

5

Opinion/Party Leader: The Limits of Presidential Persuasion

What we define as the presidential role of opinion/party leader is often-times subdivided into the roles of "chief of state," "chief of party," and "voice of the people."[1] More is gained analytically by aggregating those related activities into one role than trying to study each of them separately. Fundamental to all three orientations—chief of state, chief of party, and voice of the people—is their direct relationship to the people. Thus opinion/party leadership has the objective of generating public support for the office of the presidency, the incumbent president, the public policies he advocates, and his party's candidates for Congress. This omnibus role operates at those four levels.

Opinion/party leader is the weakest role of the five we discuss in this volume. Effective use of presidential power in this role had to await the historical development of political parties and the mass media (see Table 5-1), but it also depends on the personal skills of the incumbent. Few presidents have been the master of public opinion throughout their terms of office, and where presidents have been successful as opinion/party leaders it has depended on their own influence. No president can *command* respect, let alone affection, and little authority exists in this role for his use.

AUTHORITY

Common sense dictates that presidential leadership can be enhanced when public opinion is effectively mobilized behind his programs. We can point to Theodore Roosevelt's campaign against the business monopolies, Wilson's championing Progressive causes, and Franklin Roosevelt's promise of a New Deal for all Americans as examples. But this kind of linkage between presidential leadership and public opinion cannot be traced to the Constitution or the intentions of the Framers. The delegates who gathered in Philadelphia in 1787 to write the Constitution were wary

Table 5-1. Significant Historical Developments in Opinion-Party Leader Role

President	Historical Event or Decision
Washington	—Head of state
	—Grand tour around the country
	—Federalist Party dominant
	—Caucus nomination of president
Jefferson	—1800 Jeffersonian-Republican Party realignment
	—First grassroots party organization
Jackson	—1828 Democratic Party realignment
	—Democratic Party established
	—Universal white manhood suffrage
	—Democratic Party nominating convention
	—President as "tribune" of the people
	—Popular selection of electoral college
Lincoln	—1860 Republican Party realignment
	—Republican Party (Grand Old Party) established
McKinley	—1896 Republican Party realignment
T. Roosevelt	—White House press room created
	—"Bully pulpit" leadership style
Wilson	—Responsible party doctrine
	—"Rhetorical" presidency begins
	—First press conference
	—First midterm (1918) campaigning by president in congressional general elections
Hoover	—First aide as press secretary
F.D. Roosevelt	—1932 Democratic Party realignment
	—Fireside radio chats
	—Press conference institutionalized
	—First (1938) party "purge" in primary elections
Eisenhower	—Office of press secretary created
	—First televised (taped) press conferences
Kennedy	—First televised (live) press conferences

of direct democracy, which explains why the role of opinion/party leader is not alluded to in the Constitution.

The president's election by the electoral college resulted after the Framers debated and discarded other options. They disapproved his selection by the Congress on the grounds that the executive's independence would be jeopardized. They also feared his election by the populace. At the Constitutional Convention the main advocate of popular election of the president was James Wilson of Pennsylvania, but his views did not prevail because, as Charles Thach argues, "the force of anti-democratic sentiment was too strong."[2] There was also a widespread concern that a direct dialogue between the president and the people would give rise to demagogues and demagoguery, and not the kind of reasoned argument necessary for the survival of good government.[3]

Beyond that, the Framers believed Congress—not the executive—

should be the primary instrument of representative government. Yet today's pundits often infer that the problems of "gridlock," "stalemate,"and "deadlock" should be blamed on divided government (when Republican presidents are opposed by Democratic majorities in Congress), ignoring the fact that Congress has a rightful place under the U.S. system of government to assert its own priorities with respect to public policy. Those advocating this position argue that only the president, and the vice president, are elected by the entire nation; consequently, only they and not a Congress elected from 435 House districts and 50 states, can claim a popular mandate to govern. This notion is contrary to the original intent of the Framers that the majority would be represented through the collective deliberations of Congress.

The debate over which branch of government better represents public opinion is a modern development because the presidential "majority" has, says Willmoore Kendall, "been *engrafted* on our political system: it was not intended by the Framers, not even present to their minds as something to be 'frustrated' and have 'barriers' put in its way. It is, in other words, insofar as we can satisfy ourselves that it exists *qua* majority and eventuates in 'mandates,' something new in our politics."[4] Despite the periods of soul searching following the abuse of presidential power during the Vietnam War and Watergate, there has been such glorification of the modern president. Thus we now talk commonly about a plebiscitary presidency, meaning that presidents routinely can claim they speak for the popular majority because the public pulse is recorded daily by opinion polls.[5]

The evolution of opinion/party leadership requires us to abandon another intellectual underpinning of the Constitution as well, namely fear of party. The word *party* in the eighteenth century derived its meaning from partisanship, and the Framers saw factionalism as disruptive to the stability of a new nation. The primary cause of faction, argued James Madison in *The Federalist No. 10,* was human nature:

> A zeal for different opinion concerning religion, concerning government, and many other points, as well of speculation as of practice . . . have . . . divided mankind into parties, inflamed them with mutual animosity, and rendered them much more disposed to vex and oppress each other than to cooperate for their common good.

For Madison, the political cause of divisiveness was "liberty" but because he did not want to destroy personal liberties, his solution was to design governmental arrangements that suppressed the ill effects of factions. When political parties evolved in America, therefore, they did so outside the formal structure of government.

The strongest party presidents have been Jefferson, Jackson, Wilson, and Franklin D. Roosevelt. The election of 1800 effectively ended Federalist rule, and it ushered in America's first real experience with party government. Thomas Jefferson was able to achieve major legislative successes because he could marshal the necessary votes in Congress from the

Jeffersonian-Republicans. With Jefferson, people began to view the president as the titular head of his party.

The 1800 realignment brought into power the Jeffersonian-Republicans, considered to be the first modern political party because, unlike the Federalists, they developed a grassroots organization that mobilized voters and recruited candidates for local, state, and federal offices.

Jacksonian Democracy

Eventually the Jeffersonians became known as the Democrats, following the 1828 realignment, which elected Andrew Jackson. President Jackson strengthened the role of opinion/party leader in important ways. The era of Andrew Jackson was a time when presidential politics reached the average (white) citizen and saw political parties strengthened. He was the first Democrat by name (whose party was known as The Democracy), and in 1831 Jackson was the first president to be nominated by the prototype of the modern party convention.

Jackson's victory in 1828 and his reelection in 1832 had a major impact on the course of party politics in the United States and "made possible a new drawing of party lines," allowing a "reconstitution of parties on broad national lines, and a reformulation of political opinions such as had not been since the close of the War of 1812."[6] This realignment also marked the beginning of a loyal opposition in national politics. It meant that even though Whigs and Democrats disagreed over such policies as the Bank of the United States and federal funding of internal improvements (roads), they largely agreed on the essentials of the U.S. constitutional system.

Following Jefferson's style, Andrew Jackson was a president who acted as tribune for public opinion, as both the people's educator and defender. Jackson even favored abolishing the electoral college in favor of direct popular election, and for obvious reasons. As he reasoned,

> To the people belongs the right of electing their Chief Magistrate; it was never designed that their choice should in any case be defeated, either by the intervention of electoral colleges or by the agency confided, under certain contingencies, to the House of Representatives. . . . So far, therefore, as the people can with convenience speak, it is safer for them to express their own will.[7]

Jackson also favored limiting a president's tenure to one term of four to six years, which reflected his commitment to rotation of public offices as a major cornerstone of his republican creed. The federal government ought to be returned to the people through mass participation in politics and, toward that end, President Jackson defended the spoils system because the duties of officials could be made "so plain and simple that men of intelligence may readily qualify themselves for their performance."[8] Although he did not invent the concept, Jackson did nationalize the patronage system by bringing numerous new-style democratic politicians with him to Washington, D.C. Using patronage built Jackson's political base and helped "restore faith in the government."[9] He was also an enthusiastic supporter of universal manhood suffrage and, as a presidential candidate, he encouraged the enfranchisement of adult males throughout the country.

In summary, Andrew Jackson's egalitarianism and belief in the common sense of ordinary citizens led him as president to articulate the grievances of workingmen, small farmers and merchants, and debtors, and to encourage them to participate in party politics through such devices as the nominating convention, officeholder rotation, the patronage or spoils system, and universal manhood suffrage.

Modern Party Leaders

Another Democratic president who relied heavily on his party to rally public opinion was Woodrow Wilson. A highly regarded academic before entering politics, Wilson understood the importance of parties for democracy. Wilson wanted to strengthen both political parties, believing that presidential power is greatest when the chief executive asserts leadership derived from his party and the public. This exalted statement by Wilson shows him to be the first president to conceptualize opinion/party leadership as a role:

> [The President] cannot escape being the leader of his party except by incapacity and lack of personal force, because he is at once the choice of the party and the nation. He is the party nominee, and the only party nominee for whom the whole nation votes. . . . He can dominate his party by being spokesman for the real sentiment and purpose of the country, by giving direction to opinion, by giving the country at once the information and the statements of policy which will enable it to form judgments alike of parties and of men.[10]

Here is likely the first declaration by a president that his electoral majority should guide public policy and Congress should follow his leadership rather than assert a different policy agenda. The key to Wilson's opinion/party leadership was "unified government" in which the same party controls the executive and legislature and both branches cooperate to fulfill the mandate resulting from the presidential election.

Wilson tried to apply this concept to government. He urged the Democratic Party caucus in the House of Representatives to formulate legislative strategy and he encouraged progressives in his party to seek leadership positions in Congress. The Democratic majorities that gained control of both houses of Congress in 1913 were essential to that legislative approach. He also began the practice, now commonly accepted, of a president campaigning for his party's candidates for Congress during the midterm elections, but was ineffective in his efforts: Republicans regained control of both houses of Congress in the elections of 1918.

Franklin D. Roosevelt tried to expand on Wilson's midterm campaign efforts, persuading Democratic voters in the Democratic party primary to replace those conservative Democrats who had blocked his legislative program. He took this initiative, which became identified by his opponents as Roosevelt's *purge* (a term associated then with bloody purges in Russia as the Communists solidified their power), during the 1938 midterm congressional elections. This failed effort had been precipitated by another Roosevelt defeat in Congress when many southern Democrats refused to support FDR's Supreme Court packing plan of 1937. In one of his famous fireside chats, the president declared his intention to get involved in the upcoming Democratic primary contests:

> As the head of the Democratic party . . . charged with the responsibility of the definitely liberal declaration of principles set forth in the 1936 Democratic platform, I feel that I have every right to speak in those few instances where there may be a clear issue between candidates for a Democratic nomination involving these principles, or involving a clear misuse of my own name.[11]

But Roosevelt's attempt failed; all but one of the senators and congressmen he marked for defeat won their reelection. As a result of what Professor Koenig called "Franklin Roosevelt's grisly and unforgettable failure, no President has ventured onto the purge trail since his day."[12]

There was one exception, however. In 1970 Nixon tried to defeat anti-Vietnam senator Robert Goodell (R–N.Y.) in the Republican primary. Nixon's "action, limited as it was, alienated several important Republican senators from the Nixon administration. Many conservative and liberal Republicans in the Senate criticized the President's purge campaign and actively supported Goodell's candidacy."[13] (Goodell was defeated by Conservative Party candidate James Buckley, who pledged to support Nixon's policies.)

The role of opinion/party leader is affected by a degree of ambiguity because people expect the president to represent the nation, but they understand he also will act in ways to gain the partisan advantage. The practice of presidents campaigning for members of Congress indicates that the role of opinion/party leader has become routinized.

Although the public may accept a president campaigning for his party's candidates to Congress in a general election, to go beyond those parameters and get involved in state and local elections can be politically risky. Mayoral or gubernatorial elections deal almost entirely with local issues, and for presidents to take sides in those contests may seem illegitimate—like a carpetbagger who tries to influence local affairs although he or she does not live there.

This kind of situation embarrassed President Clinton after he, and wife Hillary, made campaign appearances in New York City to help the reelection bid of incumbent mayor David Dinkins who faced a serious challenge from Republican Rudolph Giuliani. The Dinkins loss coupled with Democratic defeats in elections for governor in New Jersey and Virginia led news commentators to raise questions about Clinton's nonexistent "coattails."

The fusion of civic and political responsibilities in the presidential role of opinion/party leader bolsters the standing of a president and, knowing this, incumbents seeking reelection may limit their campaigning and adopt a "Rose Garden" (stay close to home) strategy. This approach was relied on extensively by President Nixon during the 1972 campaign and by President Clinton through the spring and summer of 1996. By staying close to the White House, the president tries to convey the impression that he is burdened with the pressing matters of state while the opponent, with no responsibilities, has the luxury of being a full-time campaigner. The record indicates that from 1932 to 1976 incumbents were on the campaign trail less than their challengers.[14]

DECISION MAKING

Public opinion is shaped in large measure by the daily newspapers, magazines, radio stations, and especially television networks that comprise the mass media. There are media outlets for specialized publics, and most daily newspapers target a local market. Some magazines are aimed at ethnic or racial groups (*Ebony*), at women (*Cosmopolitan*), at economic interests (*Fortune, Nation's Business*), and youth (*Rolling Stone*). Much of the literature is disseminated by interest groups for their own members. As an example, *The American Rifleman, The American Hunter,* and *The American Marksman* are all magazines distributed by the National Rifle Association. Thus size, diversity, and range of the mass media in the United States make it impossible for any president to dominate news sources let alone control the messages Americans receive about him, his policies, and the government.

Journalists and commentators span the ideological spectrum, to include such liberals as Anthony Lewis and Tom Wicker and such conservatives as George Will, William Safire, and radio commentator Rush Limbaugh. Limbaugh became a constant thorn in the side of President Clinton, and on one occasion Clinton dialed Limbaugh's radio call-in program from Air Force One and "unleashed an unusually bitter, 23-minute attack on the press, the Reverend Jerry Falwell [an evangelical minister who once headed Moral Majority] and Rush Limbaugh in particular." Said Clinton: "I don't suppose there's any public figure that's ever been subject to any more violent personal attacks than I have, at least in modern times, anybody who's been President."[15]

The concepts of gatekeeping and agenda setting are used to describe how the media can influence the content of so-called news either by avoiding some issues or by focusing undue attention on others. Public perceptions of all politicians are colored by the views of journalists, the slant given to interpreting their activities, and the use of code words to infer their motives. What events mean also depends on press interpretation.

Media Bias and Attack Journalism

Is the mass media biased? There is, first, a "structural" bias, which, given the highly competitive nature of news reporting, breeds a style of political coverage that, at best, tends to be superficial but can become highly negative and overly critical of the White House. Some presidential scholars think "structural" media bias is far more pervasive than the second type, a "political" and ideological bias.[16] Certainly President Roosevelt believed the newspapers of his day were politically biased. He exploited the radio through his fireside chats to reach the American people directly because he feared the majority of newspaper editors, who were largely Republican in their sympathies, would not report his New Deal programs accurately. This partisan preference by newspaper owners has persisted, and usually newspaper dailies endorse Republican presidential candidates.[17]

Reporters, however, may not agree with their editors, as Polsby and Wildavsky note: "Although the papers are generally conservative and Republican, political correspondents are comparatively more liberal and Democratic."[18] Today the Washington press corps is more liberal and Democratic than the public and, according to Lichter and Rothman, these "media elite" hold views opposite those of newspaper editors. The journalists, surveyed by Lichter and Rothman, for example, had overwhelmingly favored Democrats for president every year from 1964 through 1976; they even preferred George McGovern in 1972 by a margin of 81 to 19 percent, although three-fifths of American voters cast ballots for Richard Nixon that year.[19]

The ideological bent of the Washington press corps has not been diminished in the 1990s: 89 percent voted for Bill Clinton in 1992 and only 7 percent backed George Bush. Moreover, only 2 percent called themselves conservative and 4 percent were identified as Republicans, compared to 50 percent who were registered Democrats, 37 percent who were Independents, and the 91 percent who were self-proclaimed liberals or moderates.[20]

The structural bias in news reporting means the news, particularly on television, must have entertainment value because TV advertising revenues are related to the Nielsen ratings of the national audience just as newspapers depend on their circulation and advertisements. Because so many Americans read and comprehend political concepts at a grade school level, the problem for the mass media is to sell a product that the majority of people can consume easily. Thus the mass media—and television more so than newspapers or magazines—is encouraged to focus on personalities and interpersonal rivalries, on dramatic visuals like action-filled film footage rather than thousands of words of analysis, and on simplifying complex problems into understandable slogans or themes.

The common complaint is that this coverage gives too little attention to issues and rarely any detailed examination of public policy. It is simply easier to frame issues as partisan conflicts between House Speaker Newt

Gingrich (R–Ga.) and President Clinton than to detail the specifics on which they disagree. After the partial shutdowns of the federal government during the budget stalemate of 1995, for example, media commentators repeatedly alleged that the public welfare was put at risk by partisan infighting among politicians and extremism exhibited by GOP first-term members of Congress. The mass media generally did not portray that conflict as reflecting a legitimate difference of opinion between Democrats and Republicans over taxes, spending, and achieving a balanced budget.

Grossman and Kumar did a content analysis of news stories in the *New York Times*, in *Time Magazine*, and on CBS News and concluded that "[t]he number of negative articles has grown, but the favorable still outnumber the unfavorable. Johnson's successors have not received the same level of favorable coverage that he did early in his term, but in the post-Vietnam and Watergate period, the balance of press coverage of the White House has been favorable. Yet Presidents Ford and Carter, like their predecessors, complained about media treatment of their administrations."[21] Maybe Ford and Carter had reason to complain about their rough treatment from the press, according to Mark Rozell. President Ford never recovered after his pardon of Richard Nixon, although his failed efforts at public relations were the result of many factors beyond his control. According to Rozell,

> Ford came to the presidency with too many disadvantages to be able to "manage" press relations: lack of a campaign to unify the staff and build a rapport with journalists, lack of an ordinary transition period to plan press strategy. . . . press expectations that could not be met such as the need to eliminate all Nixon "holdovers" and public policies, a divisive staff and press secretaries who did not have previous experience as government information officers, and the "bumbler" image that, once formed, became unchangeable.[22]

By focusing on his every misstep, the press portrayed Ford as a not very coordinated or bright human being.

The press also was very quick to judge Jimmy Carter as less than qualified to be president and "the White House could not fundamentally change the journalistic portrait of the president. . . . In the journalistic reviews of Carter we found that a negative press image began to develop in the first year of the term. Once this image became established it appeared that journalists assessed almost all of Carter's actions in light of this perspective."[23]

The media has been more critical of presidents in recent years. A steady barrage of negative stories about the president, scandals and conflict inside the White House, and policy failures is bound to take its toll on the incumbent. Objectivity and professionalism has been replaced with "attack journalism" and cynicism as to what politics is all about. It is not just the major errors of judgment but also the smallest, most innocent gaffes by a candidate that provoke a feeding frenzy among the press corps; according to Larry Sabato,

It has become a spectacle without equal in modern American politics: the news media, print and broadcast, go after a wounded politician like sharks in a feeding frenzy. The wounds may have been self-inflicted, and the politician may richly deserve his or her fate, but the journalists now take center stage in the process, creating the news as much as reporting it.[24]

Why the press chooses to exaggerate what may be simply a misstatement has to do with the skeptical—indeed cynical—view that causes it to scrutinize closely every president. This ethos among journalists is a by-product of the Vietnam War and Watergate when the media blindly accepted the statements from President Johnson that U.S. troops were winning the war and when the media failed to investigate aggressively George McGovern's charges that Watergate was serious. As a consequence, today's reporters take nothing for granted, and any action by presidential candidates is assumed to have some ulterior motive.

In his first two years President Clinton more than once attacked the press. One outburst came during an interview with *Rolling Stone* magazine in December 1993. As the interview was about to end, William Greider made this comment: "Believe it or not, I got a call this morning from a guy whose son was one of your Faces of Hope [one of the citizens Clinton met during the campaign and invited to the inaugural]. He was very dejected, disappointed. I told him I was coming over here to see you, and he said, 'Ask him what he's willing to stand up for and die on.' I think there's a feeling that—." Whereupon "The president, standing a foot away from Greider, turned and glared at him. Clinton's face reddened, and his voice rose to a furious pitch as he delivered a scalding rebuke—an angry, emotional presidential encounter, the kind of which few have ever witnessed." As the president charged,

> But that is the press's fault, too, damn it. I have fought more damn battles here for more things than any president has in 20 years, with the possible exception of Reagan's first budget, and not gotten one damn bit of credit from the knee-jerk liberal press, and I am sick and tired of it, and you can put that in the damn article.[25]

PUBLIC INPUTS

The president is the best known political leader in the country, and most people support him more often than not. Research indicates that various social, economic, and political influences affect how public opinion evaluates presidential performance and that public attitudes toward the presidency as an institution of government are grounded in deep-seated emotional underpinnings.

The leading advocate of this view is Fred Greenstein, who claims the president serves six psychological functions for the people.[26] First, by combining the roles of political leader and head of state in one highly visible national figure, the president simplifies our understanding of government and politics. The president also acts as an emotional outlet for us to identify with his life in personal ways. Through vicarious participation a president shows us that somebody is in charge and we are not left in the hands of fate. The president further symbolizes our national unity, and represents to the ordinary citizen social stability. Finally, Greenstein maintains, in light of the Watergate scandal, that the president is a convenient lightning rod for public discontents, so any policy failure can be easily personalized.

How Children View Presidents

The attachments Americans have for the president begin early in life when children are socialized politically in the norms they will use as adults. In the 1960s, research detailed how children evaluate presidents,[27] but only sampled suburban, middle-class, and white children, failing to assess the feelings of minorities and the poor. Suburban, white, and middle-class children hold idealized and positive views of the president, and their primary orientation toward government is captured through authority figures—mainly the president—who are trustworthy and benevolent.

For white children in less affluent circumstances, later research found them to be more negative in their feelings about the president. These children may even have a negative reaction to the president.[28]

As children mature, they acquire a more realistic picture of politics and government and their political knowledge increases, but apparently the favorable disposition most children have toward the president carries over into adulthood. Research in the 1970s found that support among children for President Nixon had fallen, showing the pervasive impact of Watergate and the widespread negative commentary about the White House.[29] Vietnam and Watergate had similar effects on adult opinions toward government. In 1973 Watergate likely caused more people to express greater confidence in Congress than in the White House (Figures 5-1a and 5-1b). But this question is not a perfect barometer of public attitudes toward the *president* because respondents are being asked to evaluate *institutions* of government. It is also noteworthy that when the word "White House" is substituted for "executive branch," the level of public confidence increases because a reference to the White House is likely to be associated with the president, whereas the executive branch might mean the federal bureaucracy to some respondents.

How Adults View Presidents

Virtually all adults can name the president (98 percent) and vice president (87 percent), although a majority of people cannot identify their U.S. senators or the representative from their district.[30] The president is also regularly mentioned as one of America's "most admired" persons in popular surveys; further, the public also admires the activist presidents. Not many people could explain why Washington or Lincoln are among the

Figure 5-1a. Percentage of Public Expressing "A Great Deal of Confidence" in Leaders of White House (Harris) and Executive Branch (NORC)

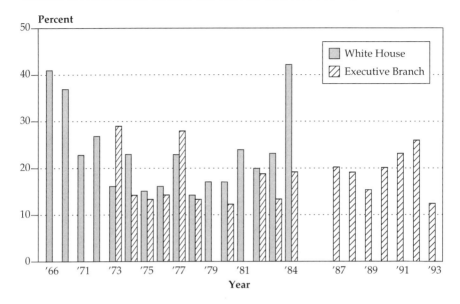

Figure 5-1b. Percentage of Public Expressing "A Great Deal of Confidence" in Leaders of Congress

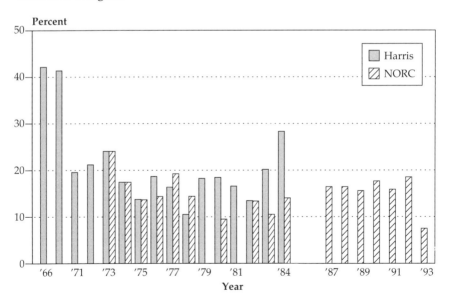

great presidents, but they believe it, which indicates that the mythology surrounding those men makes them larger than life heroes.

Gallup polls taken during the 1940s and 1950s showed that Americans identified Franklin Roosevelt, Abraham Lincoln, and George Washington as America's "greatest" presidents, but Dwight Eisenhower scored even higher than Woodrow Wilson did.[31] Similarly, in a 1975 Gallup poll, respondents ranked Kennedy higher than Lincoln, FDR, or Washington, and Eisenhower scored more points than Jefferson and Wilson.[32] On the one hand, these polls suggest that citizens are overly impressed with recent incumbents and cannot make genuine comparisons with their historical counterparts. Not only are contemporary presidents ranked higher than they probably deserve, but as time passes, contemporary presidents tend to gain in public favor when compared to their own popularity during their term(s) of office (see Table 5-2). On the other hand, seven presidents who have been ranked by professional historians as "great" or "near great" in the 1962 Schlesinger poll (see Table 2-1) were also named by the 1975 Gallup poll.

Approval Ratings

Popular support for the president is tracked by a Gallup Poll question that has been asked since the late 1930s: "Do you approve or disapprove of the way [name] is handling his job as president?" There is a tendency for public approval to decline over the four-year term (Figure 5-2) for all presidents. John Mueller attributed this common pattern of steadily declining approval to a "coalition of minorities" effect.[33] A president is not elected by a majority but rather by a coalition of minorities— a collection of voter blocs and interests. Because presidents are forced to address a wide variety of controversies during their tenure, Mueller believed, inevitably they alienate various groups who voted for their election. A differing interpretation is offered by James Stimson.[34] While he

Table 5-2. Changing Approval Ratings for Presidents over Time

President	Approval Rating over Term(s)[a]				
	100 Days[b]	High	Low	Final	Average
Roosevelt	—	84%	54%	66%	68%
Truman	—	87	23	31	46
Eisenhower	73%	79	49	59	66
Kennedy	83	83	57	58	70
Johnson	79	80	35	49	54
Nixon	62	68	24	24	48
Ford	47	71	37	53	46
Carter	63	75	21	34	47
Reagan	68	68	35	63	52
Bush	56	89	29	56	61
Clinton[c]	55	60	37	58	49

[a]Source: The Gallup Report 280 (Jan. 1989), p. 13.

[b]Source: The Gallup Poll Monthly 331 (April 1993), p. 4. This is the approval rating after 100 days in office.

[c]Data on Clinton was provided to the authors by The Gallup Organization, Princeton, NJ.

Figure 5.2. Yearly Average for Presidential Approval Ratings, 1945–1996.

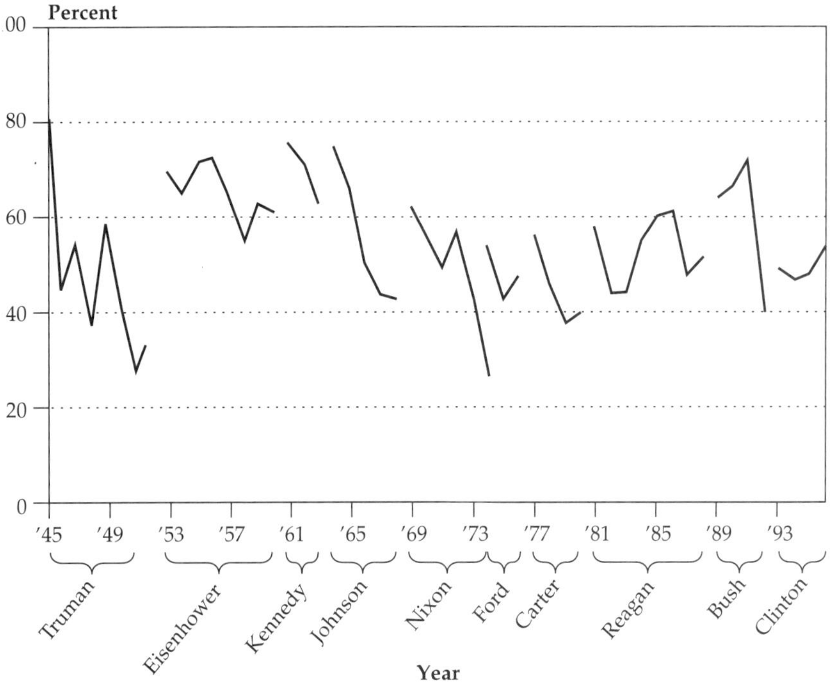

also argues that popularity declines over the four years for all presidents, he maintains that there is in almost every case some recovery at the end of a president's term. This pattern is so much a part of the popular approval of the presidency that the cycle occurs regardless of a what a president does. Stimson adds that the initial high presidential popularity is a result of the expectations of the less informed, and that a president's actual popularity is found after it "bottoms out" near the end of the term, reducing popular support to approximately the plurality that elected the president.

The downward trend begins after a honeymoon period that starts the term of a newly elected president. When the first polls are taken after Inauguration Day, invariably more people approve of his performance than the percentage that actually voted for him two months earlier, a pattern that continues through the early months of his term. Polls taken after the 100-days benchmark (Table 5-2) show that all presidents since Eisenhower had higher levels of approval compared to the voting percentage they won by on Election Day five months earlier. Because a president enjoys very high approval ratings from people who identify with his political party—Republicans give high support to Republican presidents and Democrats do the same for Democratic presidents—the bonus of approval a president enjoys during the honeymoon is likely due to those who identify with the candidate of the *losing* party. They give the winner the benefit of the doubt, but ultimately those out-party identifiers are the people who later turn against the incumbent. Tatalovich and Gitelson found the rate of disaffection in the first terms of Eisenhower, Nixon, and Reagan was greatest among Democrats, suggesting that Republicans have a unique problem of mobilizing public opinion by having to rely more heavily on Independent voters.[35]

The inevitable downward trend in public approval can be reversed temporarily by the so-called rally-round-the-flag effect. International crises, particularly where military force is involved, prompts a short-term sharp rise in presidential popularity as the nation unifies around executive leadership (see Table 13-4). An emotional response must be triggered in people who rally to support the president during wartime or foreign crises—some kind of instinctive patriotism—because the public does not react in the same way when the president confronts a domestic crisis. Theodore J. Lowi observed that incidents like urban riots or racial disturbances, although they may involve violence, usually hurt the incumbent's approval ratings,[36] which implies that people may apply different criteria to the handling of lawlessness or social unrest. Empirical research also finds that scandals in the administration harm the president's standing in opinion polls.[37]

The key to sustained presidential popularity is "peace and prosperity," argues Sam Kernell.[38] Economic growth helps and recession hurts, but presidents gain from the absence of wartime conditions. When a war begins, Americans rally behind their commander in chief, but a prolonged war with mounting U.S. casualties is a sure recipe for falling approval ratings. Both the Korean and Vietnam Wars hurt the incumbent—Harry Truman and Lyndon Johnson, respectively—because no decisive victories occurred in the short term. As a result both Truman and Johnson chose not to seek reelection.

Of the twin economic plagues—unemployment and inflation—rising prices cause greater loss of support for a president than increasing joblessness, but everything is relative and depends on public perceptions. If people are used to an inflation rate of 2 percent, then a 6 percent rate would be viewed as disastrous, but if people don't expect unemployment to fall much below 6 percent, they might tolerate its rise by one percentage point. If we plot the unemployment rate against the approval rate for President Bush, the relationship is negative; Bush's popularity dropped as the jobless rate began rising.[39] Clinton faced an anomaly because the jobless rate steadily declined during his first term, but Clinton's popularity did not rebound until early in 1996 (see chapter 6).

Current events also can affect a president's standing in the opinion polls. Brody and Page have explained the approval ratings according to their "news discrepancy" theory: public support rises or falls depending on the balance between good and bad news in the mass media. During the Johnson and Nixon years, poll-to-poll changes in presidential popularity were predicted based on the discrepancy between the approval rating in the previous month and the "goodness or badness" of news content in the current period, but the results were more conclusive for Johnson than for

Nixon.[40] This theory may explain why Bill Clinton's popularity stagnated over the first three years of his presidency (see Chapter 6).

Midterm Elections

A president's popularity affects his party's fortunes in the midterm congressional elections. Indeed, the historic record (Table 5-3) suggests a president is more often a political liability than an asset to his party's candidates for Congress. Since the Civil War—with the exception of 1934—the party of the president always loses seats during the midterm elections to the House of Representatives. Originally the theory was advanced that midterm House losses were a function of voter turnout.[41] In the midterm election, voting turnout invariably declines, and more people choose between their congressional candidates on the basis of party preference. The decline in turnout results from marginal voters, which allows those people who are loyal to a party to have disproportionate impact on the outcome.

This surge-and-decline theory made sense during the 1950s and early 1960s when more voters were identified strongly with a political party, but today Independents are a sizable minority of the electorate. As a re-

Table 5-3. Gains and Loses in Congress by President's Party in Presidential and Midterm Congressional Elections, 1932–1994

Presidential Elections[a]			Midterm Congressional Elections[b]		
Year	House	Senate	Year	House	Senate
1932(D)	+90	+13	1934(D)	+9	+10
1936(D)	+12	+7	1938(D)	−71	−6
1940(D)	+7	−3	1942(D)	−55	−9
1944(D)	+24	−2	1946(D)	−55	−12
1948(D)	+75	+9	1950(D)	−29	−6
1952(R)	+22	+1	1954(R)	−18	−1
1956(R)	−3	0	1958(R)	−48	−13
1960(D)	−20	+1	1962(D)	−4	+3
1964(D)	+37	+1	1966(D)	−47	−4
1968(R)	+2	+7	1970(R)	−12	+2
1972(R)	+12	−2	1974(R)	−48	−5
1976(D)	+1	+1	1978(D)	−15	−3
1980(R)	+35	+12	1982(R)	−26	+1
1984(R)	+17	−1	1986(R)	−5	−8
1988(R)	−3	−1	1990(R)	−8	−1
1992(D)	−8	0	1994(D)	−53	−8
Rep. Avg.	+12	+2		−24	−4
Dem. Avg.	+24	+3		−36	−4

[a]Source: Derived through 1984 from Gary King and Lyn Ragsdale, *The Elusive Executive* (Washington, DC: CQ Press, 1988), Table 7.20. Data for 1988 and 1992 from other sources.

[b]Source: Harold W. Stanley and Richard G. Niemi, *Vital Statistics on American Politics*, 4th ed. (Washington, DC: CQ Press, 1994), Table 7.4, p. 205. Data for 1994 from other sources.

sult, the winning presidential candidate tends to have shorter "coattails" than was once the case[42] (see Table 5-3) because more voters split their ticket when choosing between the executive and legislative branches. Although fewer partisans ride into office on a winning president's coattails, inevitably a certain number of his party members in Congress lose their seats in the midterm election.

The latest round of research suggests an explanation, namely that the midterm election is basically a referendum on the president's performance in office and, as a consequence, his party's losses are linked to his declining popularity. For every 10 percent loss in the president's approval rating between his election and the following midterm election, Tufte determined, his party will lose 1.3 percent of its share of the House vote, which translates into a 2.6 percent loss in its share of House seats.[43]

EXPERTISE

The opinion/party leader was the last role to evolve, in the mid to late nineteenth century when the development of the telegraph, telephone, typewriter, and the electronic printing press led to mass-circulation newspapers. Thus it was not too long ago when the dominant mode of presidential leadership was elite-to-elite interaction—not public appeals.

Theodore Roosevelt's Legacy

Theodore Roosevelt pioneered many of the White House public relations techniques, believing that presidents ought to advocate popular reforms. One commentator summarized the impact of TR (as he was known) this way: "To a superactive, but squeaky-voiced Roosevelt, the presidential podium was a 'bully pulpit,' and his pontifical moral judgments echoed throughout the land. From his office, the President preached righteousness, national honor, prestige, patriotism, 'square deal,' world peace, and progressivism. So articulate and vehement was the Rough Rider, that he virtually drenched Congress with words."[44]

Teddy Roosevelt was the first president to use the junket as a calculated publicity stunt (in 1907 he traveled down the Mississippi River with his Inland Waterways Commission), and twice during his tenure Roosevelt made extended nationwide speaking tours to educate the citizenry about his programs and to publicize ideas he felt would not get attention in the newspapers. Another first was his creation of a press office in the White House. Roosevelt met with reporters to provide background information or float trial balloons to test their political acceptance, and he never allowed White House news to be distributed without his express approval. To assure good coverage, he also made a point of becoming acquainted with the leading journalists. These various techniques—now called the art of news management—have been used more aggressively by his successors, although not always as successfully.

Press Conference

A press conference offers a forum for the president to respond to questions asked by reporters. During Woodrow Wilson's term in office, reporters gathered by general invitation in the Oval Office for the first time for a question-and-answer session.

Modern press conferences were begun by Franklin Roosevelt (see Table 5-4) whose heavy reliance on them partly reflected the urgency of the times. He scheduled press meetings almost twice weekly and abandoned Hoover's practice of requiring written questions. However, Roosevelt did establish his own ground rules. Any "background" information was not to be attributed to the White House and "off the record" materials were for the reporters' use only. At his first press conference Roosevelt mandated that nothing he said could be "quoted" without his express permission.[45] An unwritten rule among reporters stipulated that the president not be photographed below the waist. The White House and the journalists came to an understanding that focusing on FDR's physical disability might undermine his rapport with the people at a time when Americans needed to believe in him.

Table 5-4. Press Conferences by Modern Presidents

President and Years	Total and Monthly Average
Hoover	268
1929–1933	5.6
Roosevelt	998
1933–1945	6.9
Truman	334
1945–1953	3.6
Eisenhower	193
1953–1961	2.0
Kennedy	65
1961–1963	1.9
Johnson	135
1963–1969	2.2
Nixon	39
1969–1974	0.6
Ford	39
1974–1977	1.3
Carter	59
1977–1981	1.2
Reagan	53
1981–1989	0.6
Bush	64
1989–1993	1.3
Clinton	29
1993–1995(April)	1.1

Source: Harold W. Stanley and Richard G. Niemi, *Vital Statistics on American Politics,* 5th ed. (Washington, DC: CQ Press, 1995), Table 2-4, p. 53.

Roosevelt was a hard act to follow. Truman tried, but was less effective, because he was not so manipulative and would reveal his quarrelsome nature. Under Eisenhower the press conference was taped for television and presented to the people—with minor editing. Roosevelt averaged seven press conferences per month, but the frequency was cut to under four by Truman and to twice monthly under Eisenhower. Eisenhower timed press conferences strategically, and all presidents since have scheduled their press conferences for maximum political effect rather than as a routine forum for keeping reporters informed.

Even John F. Kennedy—a master at public relations—held fewer press conferences than Eisenhower, but his were televised live with no editing. JFK's skills brought to mind a Hollywood epic, as Elmer Cornwell remarks:

> The reporters grew to feel that they were extras in the recurring drama. . . .
> So efficient had the transcript system become that the first five or six pages
> were ready for use by the time "Thank you, Mr. President" was uttered, and
> stories could be written from the conference by newsmen who had not even
> bothered to attend. The point had almost been reached, in short, at which the
> only real excuse for holding the conference was the vast unseen audience.[46]

Like FDR, Kennedy viewed the press conference as a means of reaching the public directly because he too was concerned with the Republican press treating him fairly.[47]

President Johnson's preference for holding impromptu news conferences with small groups of reporters at almost any time and any place came to annoy the press because not all reporters could be on hand and TV coverage was precluded. This approach allowed LBJ to badger reporters in his familiar one-one-one manner in order to blunt criticism as he escalated the Vietnam War.

The real PR master, though, was Ronald Reagan, a former Hollywood actor who was labeled "The Great Communicator" because he was able to simplify complex problems, relating them as stories understandable to the ordinary voter. Not good at answering impromptu questions before an audience of reporters, Reagan preferred making speeches to the people on prime-time television, avoiding any direct confrontations with the press.

The press conference survives, but barely, because having a critical press corps question the president is a risky business. Now the tendency is to avoid press conferences whenever political scandals or contentious issues arise, although the White House cannot always anticipate the flow of news. When President Clinton scheduled a meeting with reporters during Christmas week in 1993, he planned to give a year-end review of his achievements. His approval rating was beginning to rise, but just before the holidays the newspapers gave substantial coverage to a story from two Arkansas state police officers, members of the governor's security detail, who said they had arranged sexual rendezvous for Clinton. When the press conference began, Clinton was unable to pursue his agenda but had to respond to several questions about renewed allegations of his infidelity.

Press Secretary

The task of protecting the president from the media and promoting his achievements falls to the press secretary, a position dating back to Herbert Hoover, who delegated those duties to one of his White House secretaries. The press secretary now must have some experience in the mass media and, better yet, contacts among the Washington press corps.

By many accounts the most effective modern press secretary was James C. Haggerty, who served Eisenhower during his two terms: "He gave the media as much news as he could . . . but he also was loyal and painstaking in his work performed for Eisenhower. He was also consulted by Eisenhower as a trusted aide during his eight-year term."[48] Only one press secretary (Pierre Salinger) served Kennedy during his thousand days in office and one served Carter (Jody Powell), but it has been rare for a president to have only one person in this position during the entire term. Turnover among press secretaries may be symptomatic of the controversies that envelop the modern presidency.

So many deceptions came from the Johnson White House about the Vietnam War that a credibility gap developed between the president and the press despite the efforts of three press secretaries. Ron Ziegler, who served President Nixon, had his credibility destroyed by Watergate because of his lack of knowledge of the incident, indicating he was not privy to high-level decision making. Jerald TerHorst, Ford's first press secretary, resigned one month after his appointment because he could not defend Ford's pardon of former President Nixon. President Reagan, who first chose James Brady as his press secretary, was served by the highly regarded Marlin Fitzwater, who took over for Brady when he was disabled in the 1981 assassination attempt on Reagan's life. Bill Clinton has had two press secretaries: Dee Dee Myers, who found media decisions taken out of her hands by then director of communications, George Stephanopoulos, and Michael McCurry.

The press secretary plays four roles for the president: (1) conduit, (2) staff, (3) policymaker, and (4) agent.[49] Being a conduit who transmits information routinely to the media is the press secretary's most important duty. Daily press briefings are held, and a press secretary who has the confidence of the president, as Michael McCurry does in the Clinton administration, can speak for him on a wide variety of topics. Daily press briefings also allow the administration to set the agenda for news coverage. With fast-breaking stories and the tight news deadlines for the evening TV broadcast or newspaper publication, the media has little choice but to report verbatim the White House position. As a staffer, the press secretary is supposed to coordinate all contacts by the White House with the press. Most press secretaries have not been policymakers, although those who served Eisenhower, Kennedy, and Carter were more involved. The press secretary also serves an agent for the president, the White House staff, and the media and, as such, must assure that the legitimate needs of the working press are met while defending the administration's viewpoint.

The press secretary stands at the apex of a gigantic public relations apparatus in the executive branch. The tasks of the Press Office, which handles regular contacts with the press, the appointments secretary to the president, and the White House photo office are obvious. Other units sustain contacts with non-Washington-based media outlets and act as liaison with ethnic, racial, or women's groups (Office of Public Liaison), monitor day-to-day political activities (Office of Political Affairs), and service the PR needs of the vice president and the First Lady.

Art of News Management

The relationship between the president and the news media is symbiotic. The media wants news and the president needs to sell his image. But one commentator has observed correctly that this relationship is doomed because "to each, the other is a convenient means; but their ends are usually quite different."[50] Lyndon Johnson once told Richard Nixon that he never understood why, after wining and dining reporters at the White House, the press remained his enemy. But Nixon understood; he believed reporters were after a story and a negative story made better copy than a positive one.[51]

The adverse experiences of Clinton during his first year illustrate how quickly press relations can deteriorate. On the one hand, his observance of the public pulse was obsessive as each policy move was calibrated by White House pollster Stanley Greenberg. Yet President Clinton never had a honeymoon with the press. After such snafus as the allegation that Clinton delayed air traffic at the Los Angeles airport so he could get a $200 haircut and the attempt to fire White House travel aides, *Time* ran a cover story headlined "The Incredible Shrinking President,"[52] and Eleanor Clift of *Newsweek* observed, "Clinton's press staff made the mistake of not only ignoring White House reporters but actively disdaining them. . . . No surprise, then, that when Clinton began to stumble this spring, the White House press corps was positively gleeful."[53] Mark Rozell explains why he thinks the media treated Clinton and Carter—both Democrats—so badly:

> President Clinton is receiving much press criticism for not living up to impossible measures of achievement. The expectation that a president achieve the bulk of his policy agenda in the first 100 days in office is one such possible measure that persists in press accounts of each chief executive. The frequent criticism of Clinton for not putting an immediate end to governmental gridlock . . . is also reminiscent of the press coverage that Jimmy Carter received when the Democratic-controlled Congress did not automatically march in step to the president's proposals. In both cases there is little press acknowledgment of the complexity of the policy process and issues that mitigate against executive-legislative cooperation even during a period in which one party dominates the government.[54]

The art of news management is defined by Grossman and Kumar as the "manipulation by the President and his advisers of the kinds of information that will be made available to reporters and of the forums in which information is given to them."[55] Thus it involves controlling access to the president, manipulating the timing, content, and setting of information provided, courting the favor of reporters, journalists, and news broadcasters, and ultimately—if all fails—attacking the credibility of the media.

News management became a fine art under Ronald Reagan, partly because he was so willing to be programmed by his White House handlers whereas others such as Carter and Clinton have been too quick with offhand comments to be controlled. Observers agree that Reagan joins the ranks of FDR and JFK as America's most successful opinion/party leaders. Opinion/party leadership, then, depends on an effective media strategy, an able PR staff, and a president with an engaging public persona.

Six ingredients made up Reagan's media strategy. First, his staffers each morning would decide on the story line of the day, and the daily briefings by the White House press secretary would focus on that story. Second, Reagan's aides framed the story by preparing a script to guide the president's remarks and providing visuals for TV use. Third, the White House paid close attention to non-Washington media outlets, which are more sympathetic in their coverage. Fourth, staffers kept the press at a distance and controlled access to Reagan, even to the point of banning questions from reporters at photo opportunities. Fifth, the president used press appearances to report good news, leaving it to members of the Cabinet to respond to reporters whenever any scandal or problem arose. Sixth, unlike the hostility toward the press that permeated the Nixon White House, Reagan and his staffers were committed to maintaining good rapport with the mass media. As NBC correspondent Andrea Mitchell put it, "There is a remarkable lack of animus in this White House."[56]

Yet the most important advantage for Reagan was "Ronald Reagan" himself. As presidency scholar Robert DiClerico observes, Reagan "was no ordinary president. On the contrary, he possessed two qualities—a captivating personality and extraordinary rhetorical skills—the combination of which we have not seen since Roosevelt and *are not likely to see very often*. These qualities made him exceedingly popular as a person."[57]

CRISIS

The public's extraordinary commitment to the presidency is revealed whenever a president is stricken by illness or by an assassin's bullet. Assassination attempts have been made against nine presidents—including two attempts against Ford and one against Reagan—and four presidents (Lincoln, Garfield, McKinley, and Kennedy) were killed. Following the attempt on Reagan's life in 1981, his popularity jumped from 60 percent in early March to 68 percent in May. By June, with Reagan recovering from his wounds, his approval rating fell back to 59 percent.[58]

Kennedy's Assassination

People reacted emotionally and physically when they heard about JFK's assassination in 1963. People recorded having a variety of personal reactions:[59]

- "Felt sorry that a strong young man had been killed at the height of his powers"   88%

- "Felt ashamed that this could happen in our country"   83%

- "Felt the loss of someone very close and dear"   79%

- "Felt angry that anyone should do such a terrible deed"   73%

- "Worried about how his death would affect the political situation in this country"   47%

- "Worried about how his death would affect our relations with other countries"   44%

- "Felt worried about how the United States would carry on without its leader"   31%

This survey found that people experienced loss of appetite, insomnia, headaches, rapid heart rate, and described themselves as nervous and tense. In other words, the Kennedy assassination affected people more in a personal way than in terms of policy or politics. Such mass outpourings of emotion do not accompany the deaths of other public figures.

Watergate

Watergate was another kind of political crisis that affected the nation deeply and, although Nixon's behavior was scandalous, opinion polls indicate the degree to which Americans wanted to believe in their president despite mounting evidence to the contrary. The impact of Watergate on public opinion was shown in Gallup polls taken during 1973 and 1974.[60] From a high of 67 percent in January 1973 following his landslide reelection, Nixon's popularity fell steadily to a record low of 24 percent in July 1974, the month before he resigned. Despite Democratic presidential candidate George McGovern's insistence that Watergate was a serious offense, a September 1972 Gallup Poll found that only 52 percent had heard or read about it and, further, eight in ten Americans did not think it was an important enough reason for them to vote for McGovern. After White House aide John Dean implicated the president in his testimony before Congress, Nixon's approval ratings fell below 40 percent; when Nixon fired the first Watergate special prosecutor (Archibald Cox) in October 1973, his popularity dropped to under 30 percent.

By June 1973 polls indicated that 98 percent of the public had heard or read about Watergate, and a plurality believed it revealed corruption in the Nixon administration. Based on the polls that tracked public attitudes from June 1973 until his resignation in August 1974, 15 to 23 percent of the respondents still thought Nixon had "no knowledge" of the affair, and only 8 to 11 percent believed he had "planned" Watergate. A majority (ranging from 54 to 73 percent) felt Nixon either had known about Watergate in advance or had tried to cover it up. As a result, just two months after his landslide victory over George McGovern, a plurality said they wanted Vice President Gerald Ford to assume the highest office.

Despite Nixon's culpability, the American people seemed to resist his forced removal by impeachment. Not until August 1974, just days before Nixon announced his resignation, did a bare majority (57 percent) favor his removal. As late as June 1973 fully 69 percent said "no" when asked by Gallup: "Do you think President Nixon should be impeached and compelled to leave the presidency, or not?" By this time the House of Representatives was preparing articles of impeachment. Robert Sherrill observed that Congress "moved with extreme reluctance and only after many felonies and subversions of statutory law had been traced to the White House. If a Democratic Congress was that hesitant to move against a Republican President so plainly guilty of having violated the law ... then it is clear that the impeachment process has little appeal to Congress."[61]

Nor was impeachment an appealing option to the public. Although a majority of Americans believed the seriousness of Nixon's crimes warranted a trial for impeachment, less than a majority actually was willing to see him removed from office. Once Nixon became a private citizen, however, public opinion turned against him and favored Nixon's prosecution to the extent allowed by the law. No doubt this sentiment was fueled by the very act of resignation (which implied guilt) coupled with Nixon's pardon by President Ford "for all offenses against the United States which he ... has committed or may have committed." Ford's popularity plunged twenty-two percentage points after he decided to issue the pardon.

SUMMARY

That opinion/party leadership is the weakest presidential role is readily apparent. Presidents who are or have been able to sustain high popularity and good press relations are few in number—Kennedy and Reagan—and at times even these masters of public relations stumbled. A president's approval rating invariably declines because too many forces beyond White House control affect public perceptions: economic prosperity or recession, peace or war, scandals or policy failures. The media is not manipulated so easily by the White House, and reporters are more determined to show the underside of presidential power. The age of innocence is over, as is the age of heroes. Eisenhower and Kennedy had celebrity status, and society at that time also accorded them more deferential treatment so, although there were stories about JFK's personal indiscretions,[62] the media did not investigate and broadcast those rumors across country.

Scholars once believed that heightened visibility is related to presidential leadership, but that linkage is not so obvious. The president clearly is America's best known political figure—the "personal" president—but his ability to persuade the public has not grown commensurate with expectations that he be an effective leader. With each passing day Americans are reminded, by the press and by events, that the president is a mortal being.

NOTES

1. A classic study of presidential roles is Clinton Rossiter, *The American Presidency,* 2nd ed. (New York: Harcourt, Brace and World, 1960), chap. 1.

2. Charles C. Thach, *The Creation of the Presidency* (Baltimore: John Hopkins Press, 1922), p. 86.

3. See Jeffrey Tulis, *The Rhetorical Presidency* (Princeton, NJ: Princeton University Press, 1987).

4. Willmoore Kendall, "The Two Majorities," *Midwest Journal of Political Science* 4 (Nov. 1960), p. 336.

5. Paul Brace and Barbara Hinckley, *Follow the Leader* (New York: Basic Books, 1992).

6. William MacDonald, *Jacksonian Democracy: 1829–1837* (New York: Harper and Brothers, 1906), pp. 185–186.

7. Quoted in Francis N. Thorpe, ed., *The Statesmanship of Andrew Jackson* (New York: Tandy-Thomas, 1909), p. 42.

8. Quoted in Arthur M. Schlesinger, Jr., *The Age of Jackson* (Boston: Little, Brown, 1945), p. 46.

9. Ibid.

10. Quoted in Rowland Egger, *The President of the United States* (New York: McGraw-Hill, 1972), p. 172.

11. Cited in Louis W. Koenig, *The Chief Executive,* 3rd ed. (New York: Harcourt Brace Jovanovich, 1975), p. 132.

12. Ibid., p. 133.

13. Sidney M. Milkis, *The President and the Parties* (New York: Oxford University Press, 1993), p. 229.

14. Raymond Tatalovich, "Electoral Votes and Presidential Campaign Trails, 1932–1976," *American Politics Quarterly* 7 (Oct. 1979), pp. 489–498.

15. Douglas Jehl, "Clinton Calls Show to Assail Press, Falwell and Limbaugh," *New York Times* (June 25, 1994), p. 10.

16. George C. Edwards, III,and Stephen J. Wayne, *Presidential Leadership* (New York: St. Martin's Press, 1994), pp. 157–161.

17. Milton C. Cummings, Jr., and David Wise, *Democracy Under Pressure* (New York: Harcourt Brace Jovanovich, 1981), p. 282; John P. Robinson, "The Press as King-Maker: What Surveys from Last Five Campaigns Show," *Journalism Quarterly* 51 (Winter 1974), pp. 587–594, 606. Also see "11 Dailies Support Ford; 80 for Carter," *Editor and Publisher* (Oct. 30, 1976), pp. 5, 12–13; John Consoli, "Reagan Backed by 443 Dailies; Carter Trails with 126; Anderson with 30 and 439 Undecided," *Editor and Publisher* (Nov. 1, 1980), pp. 9–13; "A Newspaper Majority for Reagan," *Editor and Publisher* (Nov. 3, 1984), pp. 9–12; Andrew Randolf, "Majority of Newspapers Don't Endorse," *Editor and Publisher* (Oct. 29, 1988), pp. 9–10.

18. Nelson W. Polsby and Aaron Wildavsky, *Presidential Elections,* 8th ed. (New York: Free Press, 1991), p. 74.

19. S. Robert Lichter and Stanley Rothman, "Media and Business Elites," *Public Opinion* (Oct./Nov. 1981), pp. 42–46, 59–60. Also see William Schneider and I.A. Lewis, "Views on the News," *Public Opinion* (Aug./Sept. 1985), pp. 6–11, 58; Stephen Hess, *The Washington Reporters* (Washington, DC: The Brookings Institution, 1981), p. 87.

20. Rowan Scarborough, "Leftist press? Suspicions Right," *Washington Times* (April 16, 1996), p. A1.

21. Michael Baruch Grossman and Martha Joynt Kumar, *Portraying the President: The White House and the News Media* (Baltimore: Johns Hopkins University Press, 1981), p. 253.

22. Mark J. Rozell, *The Press and the Ford Presidency* (Ann Arbor: University of Michigan Press, 1992), p. 208.

23. Mark J. Rozell, *The Press and The Carter Presidency* (Boulder, CO: Westview Press, 1989), p. 231.

24. Larry Sabato, *Feeding Frenzy: How Attack Journalism Has Transformed American Politics* (New York: Free Press, 1991), p. 1.

25. Jann S. Wenner and William Greider, "The Rolling Stone Interview: President Clinton," *Rolling Stone* (Dec. 9, 1993), p. 47.

26. Originally five functions were outlined in Fred I. Greenstein, "The Psychological Functions of the Presidency for Citizens," in Elmer E. Cornwell, *The American Presidency: Vital Center* (Glenview, IL: Scott, Foresman, 1966). The sixth function of "lightning rod" was added in his "What the President Means to Americans," in James David Barber, ed., *Choosing the President* (Englewood Cliffs, NJ: Prentice-Hall, 1974), pp. 146–147.

27. See Fred I. Greenstein, *Children and Politics* (New Haven: Yale University Press, 1965); Robert D. Hess and Judith V. Torney, *The Development of Political Attitudes in Children* (New York: Anchor Books, 1968); David Easton and Jack Dennis, *Children in the Political System* (New York: McGraw-Hill, 1969).

28. Dean Jaros, Herbert Hirsch, and Frederic J. Fleron, Jr., "The Malevolent Leader: Political Socialization in an American Sub-Culture," *American Political Science Review* (June 1968), p. 569.

29. See Jack Dennis and Carol Webster, "Children's Images of the President and of Government in 1962 and 1974," *American Politics Quarterly* (Oct. 1975); Dean Jaros and John Shoemaker, "The Malevolent Unindicted Co-Conspirator: Watergate and Appalachian Youth," *American Politics Quarterly* (Oct. 1975), pp. 483–506; F. Christopher Arterton, "The Impact of Watergate on Children's Attitudes toward Political Authority," *Political Science Quarterly* (June 1974), pp. 269–288; F. Christopher Arterton, "Watergate and Children's Attitudes toward Authority Revisited," *Political Science Quarterly* (Fall 1975), pp. 477-496.

30. Fred I. Greenstein, "What the President Means to Americans," in James D. Barber, ed., *Choosing the President* (Englewood Cliffs, NJ: Prentice-Hall, 1974), p. 125.

31. See Hadley Cantril, ed., *Public Opinion 1935–1946* (Princeton, NJ: Princeton University Press, 1951, p. 590; American Institute of Public Opinion, Survey No. 558 (Jan. 4, 1956). Cited in James MacGregor Burns, *Presidential Government* (Boston: Houghton Mifflin, 1973), p. 100.

32. American Institute of Public Opinion, *Public Opinion 1972–1977*, Vol. I (Wilmington, DE: Scholarly Resources, 1978), pp. 641–643.

33. John E. Mueller, "Presidential Popularity from Truman to Johnson," *American Political Science Review* (March 1970), pp. 136-148.

34. James A. Stimson, "Public Support for American Presidents: A Cyclical Model," *Public Opinion Quarterly* (Spring 1976), pp. 1–21.

35. Raymond Tatalovich and Alan R. Gitelson, "Political Party Linkages to Presidential Popularity: Assessing the 'Coalition of Minorities' Thesis," *Journal of Politics* 52 (Feb. 1990), pp. 233–242.

36. Theodore J. Lowi, *American Government: Incomplete Conquest* (Hinsdale, IL: Dryden Press, 1976), pp. 440–442.

37. Paul Brace and Barbara Hinckley, *Follow the Leader* (New York: Basic Books, 1992), p. 28.

38. Samuel Kernell, "Explaining Presidential Popularity: How Ad Hoc Theorizing, Misplaced Emphasis, and Insufficient Care in Measuring One's Variables Refuted Common Sense and Led Conventional Wisdom down the Path of Anomalies," *American Political Science Review* (June 1978), pp. 506–522.

39. John P. Frendreis and Raymond Tatalovich, *The Modern Presidency and Economic Policy* (Itasca, IL: F.E. Peacock, 1994), p. 239.

40. Richard A. Brody and Benjamin I. Page, "The Impact of Events on Presidential Popularity: The Johnson and Nixon Administration," in Aaron Wildavsky, ed., *Perspectives on the Presidency* (Boston: Little, Brown, 1975), pp. 136–148.

41. Angus Campbell, "Surge and Decline: A Study of Electoral Change," *Public Opinion Quarterly* (Fall 1960), pp. 397–418.

42. See George C. Edwards, III, "Impact of Presidential Coattails on Outcomes in Congressional Elections," *American Politics Quarterly* 7 (Jan. 1979); John A. Ferejohn and Morris P. Fiorina, "Incumbency and Realignment in Congressional Elections," in John E. Chubb and Paul E. Peterson, eds., *The New Direction in American Politics* (Washington, DC: The Brookings Institution, 1985), p. 99.

43. Edward R. Tufte, "Determinants of the Outcomes of Midterm Congressional Elections," *American Political Science Review* (Sept. 1975), pp. 812–826.

44. Thomas Bailey, *Presidential Greatness* (New York: Appleton Century, 1967), p. 201.

45. See Samuel Kernell, *Going Public: New Strategies of Presidential Leadership*, 2nd ed. (Washington, DC: CQ Press, 1993), pp. 53–70.

46. Elmer E. Cornwell, Jr., *Presidential Leadership of Public Opinion* (Bloomington: Indiana University Press, 1966), p. 192.

47. Richard Rovere, "Letter from Washington," *New Yorker* (Feb. 4, 1961), p. 112.

48. William C. Spragens, *The Presidency and the Mass Media in the Age of Television* (Washington, DC: University Press of America, 1979), p. 253.

49. See Michael Baruch Grossman and Martha Joynt Kumar, *Portraying the President: The White House and the News Media* (Baltimore: Johns Hopkins University Press, 1981), pp. 136–147.

50. James C. Thomson, Jr., "Government and Press: Good News about a Bad Marriage," *New York Times Magazine* (Nov. 25, 1973), p. 44.

51. From an interview between Richard Nixon and Howard K. Smith, "Every Four Years: A Study of the Presidency," part 2, PBS Television Documentary on the Presidency, 1980.

52. "The Incredible Shrinking President," *Time* (June 7, 1993), p. 22.

53. Eleanor Clift, "Don't Mess with the 'Media,'" *Newsweek* (June 7, 1993), p. 23.

54. Mark J. Rozell, "The Limits of White House Image Control," *Political Science Quarterly* 108 (Fall 1993), p. 480.

55. Grossman and Kumar, *Portraying the President*, p. 280.

56. Quoted in Mark Hertsgaard, *On Bended Knee* (New York: Farrar Straus Giroux, 1988), p. 42.

57. Robert E. DiClerico, "The Role of Media in Heightened Expectations and Diminished Leadership Capacity," in Richard W. Waterman, ed., *The Presidency Reconsidered* (Itasca, IL: F.E. Peacock, 1993), p. 133. Also see pp. 127–133.

58. *The Gallup Report* 187 (April 1981), pp. 2–3, and 189 (June 1981), pp. 11–13.

59. Paul B. Sheatsley and Jacob J. Feldman, "The Assassination of President Kennedy: A Preliminary Report on Public Reactions and Behavior," *Public Opinion Quarterly* (Summer 1964), pp. 189–215.

60. This discussion is drawn from Raymond Tatalovich and Byron W. Daynes, *Presidential Power in the United States* (Monterey, CA: Brooks/Cole, 1984), pp. 120–122.

61. Robert Sherrill, *Governing America* (New York: Harcourt Brace Jovanovich, 1978), p. 318.

62. See Nigel Hamilton, *JFK: Reckless Youth* (New York: Random House, 1993).

6

Insight on Opinion/Party Leader: Clinton's Popularity and the Economy

This Insight shows how and why presidential popularity depends on factors beyond the control of the White House. It is ironic—and inconsistent with recent political history—that the prosperity during his first term did *not* translate into higher approval ratings for President Clinton until he began his reelection campaign in 1996. An article of faith among presidency scholars, as Kernell verified,[1] is that "peace and prosperity" are the twin pillars of presidential popularity. During Clinton's first term, peace and prosperity were present. Even though U.S. troops were stationed in Bosnia, they were not involved in ground combat and the nation was never at war, unlike the Persian Gulf War that erupted under President Bush.

Using five standard measures of economic performance, Frendreis and Tatalovich ranked all administrations from Truman through Bush on each criteria and then derived an overall ranking (see Table 6-1).[2] Compared to the "best" performance (Johnson, 1965–1968) and the "worst" (Bush, 1989–1992), our recalculation shows that Clinton's first term would rank eighth overall, still better than Bush's four years. Since the turn of the century, the Dow Jones Industrial Average showed its third best performance during the period from 1993 to 1996 (rising 85.8 percent). Better records were posted from 1933 to 1936—but then Americans were experiencing the Great Depression and the market was rising after the 1929 stock market crash—and during Coolidge's 1924 to 1928 tenure.[3]

The negative relationship between rising unemployment and declining presidential popularity caused political troubles for President Bush. As we noted earlier, campaign aide George Stephanopoulos in 1992 had a sign posed in the Clinton campaign headquarters as a constant reminder that "It's the economy, stupid!". When Bush was inaugurated in January 1989, the unemployment rate was 5.4 percent and remained at or below that level until July 1990, when it began a gradual but steady rise. By year-end the jobless rate stood at 6.3 percent, but public attention was

Table 6-1. Comparing the Clinton Economic Performance against the Best and Worst Administration Records since World War II[a]

	Unemployment % (rank)	Inflation % (rank)	Economic Growth % (rank)	Productivity $ (rank)	Current Account Balance (rank)	Overall Ranking[b]
Johnson 1965–1968	3.9 (1)	2.9 (5)	4.6 (2)	2.8 (3)	+11.6 (3)	1
Clinton 1993–1996	6.0 (7)	2.9 (5)	2.6 (6)	0.5 (11)	−561.6 (12)	8
Bush 1989–1992	6.2 (8)	4.4 (8)	1.0 (12)	0.6 (10)	−257.6 (10)	12

[a]Macroeconomic Indicators are (1) four-year average unemployment rate, (2) four-year percentage change in Consumer Price Index over each year, (3) four-year average percentage change in real gross national product over each year, (4) four-year average percentage change in productivity (real output per hour per employee) over each year, and (5) the net surplus or deficit over four years in billions of dollars.

[b]Frendreis and Tatalovich originally had ranked the Johnson term as the best (1 of 11) and the Bush term as the worst (11 of 11) overall based on eleven presidents. For Clinton, we recalculated the rankings for each president based now on twelve administrations, and the ranking alongside each economic indicator shows where Johnson, Clinton, and Bush placed in this new distribution. Each macroeconomic indicator was ranked from best (1) to worst (12) and the overall rank was derived from an "average" ranking for each president. In this new order Johnson still ranked 1 of 12 but now Bush dropped to 12 of 12.

Source: Data on Johnson and Bush in John P. Frendreis and Raymond Tatalovich, *The Modern Presidency and Economic Policy* (Itasca, IL: F.E. Peacock, 1994), pp. 308–309. Data on Clinton were calculated by the authors from the *Economic Report of the President* (February 1997) and the *Survey of Current Business*. As explained below, whereas the growth rate for Johnson and Bush was real Gross National Product, the growth rate for Clinton was reported as real Gross Domestic Product.

diverted temporarily by the Persian Gulf crisis and the outbreak of war. The economy had no effect on the commander in chief because Bush garnered an 89 percent approval rating in March 1991 despite a 6.8 percent unemployment rate. Once the war ended, however, the public became aware that the nation was gripped by recession. Unemployment reached 7.3 percent at the end of 1991 and hit 7.8 percent—the high—in June 1992. Because the economy eased away from recession very slowly, joblessness inched downward to only 7.4 percent by Election Day, and a plot of the unemployment rate against Bush's approval rating shows that his popularity plunged sharply from its March 1991 high.[4]

The economy defeated President Bush in 1992, and its impact on presidential popularity was a textbook example of why incumbents rarely survive an economic downturn or raging inflation. For Bill Clinton, however, a good economy did not work as one would have expected. It assured Clinton's reelection in 1996, but the improving economy did not elevate his popularity during most of his first term. Indeed, some scholars have observed that citizens are apt to punish incumbents more for bad economic times and to reward them less for prosperity.[5] This is shown visually by plotting the unemployment rate against the overall popularity of President Clinton in addition to the specific level of public "approval" for his "handling" of the economy (Figure 6-1).

At first glance there may appear to be some relationship between the economy and Clinton's popularity, although nothing as pronounced as what Bush experienced. But compare the first two years against the second two years. During 1993–1994 the unemployment rate dropped from 7.3 percent in January 1993 to 5.6 percent in November 1994—when Republicans captured both houses of Congress. Can the economy be the reason why the Democrats were punished on Election Day?

Apparently it was one factor because 54 percent of Americans told the *New York Times*/CBS News poll that the "economy, jobs or inflation" was the most important problem facing the country.[6] The last time in recent memory the index was that high was in 1980, when 59 percent of the public expressed those feelings (and Reagan defeated Carter), whereas it fell to 41 percent in 1984 when Reagan was reelected and to 17 percent in 1988 when Bush was elected. In contrast, the figure stood at 23 percent in 1996 when Clinton faced reelection.

Can we blame President Clinton? Likely so, because his approval ratings *decreased* during his first two years despite the marked improvement in the unemployment rate. Clinton was inaugurated with 58 percent ap-

Figure 6-1. Monthly Unemployment Rates, Average Overall Approval Ratings, and Average Approval Ratings, and Average Approval Ratings for Handling Economy during Clinton's First Term
Sources: Unemployment rate: Bureau of Labor Statistics
Approval ratings: The Gallup Organization

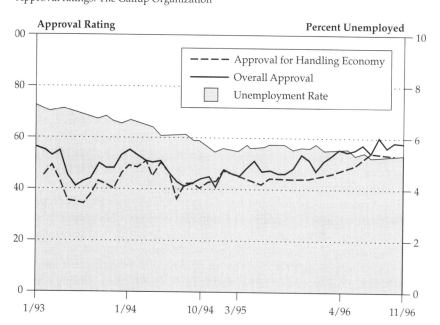

proval—a major improvement on his 43 percent of the popular vote—but then dropped to 51 percent in early February, rose again to 59 percent later in February, but then fell below 50 percent until September 1993. From September 1993 through May 1994 Clinton's approval ratings fluctuated between 47 and 54 percent, but then declined to 39 percent in August/September, rebounding to 46 percent as voters headed to the polls in November.

The decline in joblessness over the last two years of Clinton's term was much less impressive; it was 5.6 percent in January 1995 and 5.3 percent in December 1996. Thus the unemployment rate seemingly stabilized even though Clinton's popularity finally started rising. January 1996 marked the beginning of a sustained majority approval, which continued into the early months of 1997. During the second half of his term the jobless rate initially fell to 5.4 percent by March, but then hovered around 5.6 or 5.7 percent until year-end. From February 1996 through May the jobless rate stayed at 5.5 percent but then dropped slightly, hitting 5.2 percent during the crucial preelection months of August, September, and October. So the economy gave Clinton a belated boost to his popularity just in time for Election Day, but can we attribute that relationship to Clinton's stewardship of economic policy? Probably not, given how people responded when pollsters asked them that question.

The trend line on Clinton's handling of the economy shows his stewardship was assessed below his overall popularity during his entire first term. It was not until August 1996 when a majority of Americans approved his handling of the economy, and three months later only 53 percent did so. If the economy were the key to explaining Clinton's popularity, one would think people would have given him higher ratings on handling the economy, as compared to his overall approval rating. In other words, the relationship between the unemployment rate and Clinton's handling of the economy is more tenuous than even the relationship between joblessness and his general popularity.

No president has the requisite *authority* to actually manage the national economy (see chapter 15), although he may have a so-called election mandate to try. Clinton did, largely because President Bush had abdicated that responsibility. According to one commentator, "the story of the 1992 campaign is fundamentally shaped by the failure of Bush's campaign to address voter concerns about the economy."[7] When asked, "Which candidate do you think would do the best job solving the country's economic problems?" more than one-third chose Clinton with Ross Perot closely behind, whereas no more than 25 percent of the respondents picked President Bush.[8]

Two polls showing 79 percent and 86 percent of respondents naming the economy as the most important problem led another analyst to conclude that "[t]o an extraordinary degree, voters were focused on economic issues in 1992."[9] One poll taken in the early months of 1992, for example, found 57 percent believing the economy was getting worse, 34 percent saying it was about the same, and only 9 percent viewing the economy as better.[10] What prompted those widespread perceptions was anxiety about the macroeconomy rather than one's own economic predicament. As Gerald Pomper maintains, "Instead of self-interest, the key element of the economic issue was a concern for the national welfare."[11] Simply put, pollster Kathleen Frankovic summarizes the dynamics of the 1992 election this way: "George Bush's problem stemmed from the voters' belief that the economy was the country's most important problem and that the president was managing it badly."[12]

An aspect of authority is the use of presidential rhetoric to set the policy agenda for the administration and for pending legislation. When Ronald Reagan campaigned against President Carter in 1980, he rhetorically asked the voters—"Are you better off today than you were four years ago?" That question effectively framed Carter's failed economic game plan for the American people, but as Reagan approached his own reelection he used the same analogy to remind voters how much better the economy had become under his leadership.

Championing his economic success appeared difficult for Clinton, and as late as 1996 news commentators wondered if the economy would benefit his reelection. "Reagan would talk about how he disciplined Government, how he cut taxes, so there was a story in people's head about why he deserved the credit," argued Democratic pollster Geoffrey Garin. "This Administration says they reduced the deficit, which led to lower interest rates, and they opened up foreign markets, but they never establish a cause and effect between this and the state of the economy."[13]

It seems obvious that *expertise* has limited effect in shaping public attitudes toward the economy. The "leading economic indicators" are published regularly by the Bureau of Labor Statistics, the Commerce Department, and the Federal Reserve Board and highly publicized by the news media. Neither good nor bad news could be suppressed by the Clinton administration, and there was some bad economic news. Although unemployment declined and the stock market set new highs, wages continued to stagnate, the gap between the top and bottom income earners widened (as more people fell below the poverty line), the rate of economic growth slowed, and the balance of trade worsened considerably.[14]

In 1995 the average increase in worker compensation was 2.9 percent, the smallest since 1980, and barely enough to keep ahead of rising prices (the Consumer Price Index rose by 2.5 percent in 1995). "White-collar workers beat inflation," observed Labor Secretary Robert B. Reich. "Blue-collar workers didn't."[15] To have income inequality widen under a Democratic president is telling and could have posed problems had GOP presidential nominee Bob Dole been able to use economic populism to rally working-class voters. Clinton's advisors were concerned and in mid-1995 Treasury Secretary Robert E. Rubin addressed the issue: "It's the problem the President works on the most," he said. "Because median real wages have not behaved well, too many Americans don't feel in their own lives what has happened in the economy."[16] Even though Americans pulled out of the recession of 1990–1991, not since the Civil War had economic growth been so weak for so long, and economists generally agreed that the upper limit for growth in the gross domestic product (without high inflation) ranged from 2.2 to 2.5 percent, nearly half of the 4 percent plus annual growth rate experienced during the 1950s and 1960s.[17]

The nation's trade imbalance (imports exceeding exports) continued to worsen, making the $111 billion deficit for 1995 the biggest in seven years. Although small progress was made in narrowing the trade gap with Japan—a pledge Clinton made in his 1992 campaign—a new trade deficit was emerging with mainland China. It was left to Clinton's economic aides to interpret those statistics in the best possible light. "We've got a significant education job to do with the American people," said Commerce Secretary Ron Brown. "There's a lack of understanding of how dependent our economy is on exports and healthy trade. That's why we've taken such aggressive action to open markets around the world."[18]

Expertise might involve efforts to manage the economic news, but as we already noted (chapter 5) Clinton blamed the mass media for not appreciating all his efforts and also lashed out against his radio talk-show critics. Clinton's problems with the press may have been his own doing because he repeated the mistake made by Jimmy Carter when Carter flip-flopped in 1977 over the need for a tax cut to stimulate the economy. On economic policy the Clinton administration did not speak with one voice.

President Clinton did not give his undivided attention to the economic agenda. In his presidential race Clinton had detailed an ambitious economic game plan, including promises to reduce the budget deficit, legislate middle-class tax cuts, and urge more federal spending on job training, education, and research. One month before his inaugural, Clinton at a televised conference in Little Rock called for a "national economic strategy" to create jobs, raise incomes, and reduce inequality. Once he took office, however, "[t]ime and again, he was forced into hard choices about economic policy. In almost every instance, he took the route favored by Wall Street, business executives and conventional economists, not the ones that ordinary people might have favored and that almost certainly would have been easier to defend politically."[19] He abandoned his campaign pledge to cut taxes on the middle class and reneged on another promise to organized labor (which wanted trade restrictions) by aligning with congressional Republicans to implement the North American Free Trade Agreement (NAFTA) with Canada and Mexico.

To jump-start the economy early in his first year, President Clinton proposed a fiscal stimulus package of expenditures, but congressional Republicans successfully labeled his program as wasteful pork barrel spending and, in the Senate, used a filibuster to kill the proposal. Nor did the White House strengthen its own case with so many contradictory statements on deficit reduction, economic growth, taxes, and spending cutbacks (Clinton challenged anyone to find more areas to cut in his own budget). "The Clinton administration has lost control of its agenda," remarked Stan Greenberg, Clinton's pollster.[20] All these mixed signals during the critical first year led presidency scholar George Edwards to con-

clude that "[o]ne of the most serious limitations of the Clinton administration has been its lack of rhetoric definition. The administration's failure
to structure choice effectively for the public and for Congress is a consequence of its ill-defined projections of itself."[21]

With the Clinton administation unable or unwilling to focus exclusively on its economic agenda, other *decision-makers*, notably the mass media, were able to define the Clinton presidency based on other policy missteps. To begin with, Clinton squandered his honeymoon by making very
controversial policy decisions—notably the attempt to allow homosexuals to serve openly in the armed forces—which dominated the headlines
for months. Almost every day there were signs that Bill Clinton was not
the polished and smooth political operator his reputation had implied.
His White House team did sloppy work on appointments, like two attorney general nominees who withdrew after it was learned they did not pay
Social Security taxes for domestic help and the president's about-face
when critics labeled one of Clinton's choices for an assistant attorney general a "quota queen" on racial preferences. The media focused on Clinton's Arkansas "cronies" and their inadequacies as managers, which led
during the first eighteen months to two major shake-ups in his White
House operations.

The so-called character issue surrounding "Slick Willie" came racing
back onto the front pages and the evening news as revelations were un-
earthed that both Clinton and his wife Hillary (whose approval ratings,
typically lower than her husband's,[22] may well make her the least popular of any modern First Lady) were deeply involved in unethical, if not illegal, behavior in the Whitewater land development scheme when he was
governor of Arkansas. The White House was forced by events to appoint
an independent counsel to investigate the charges, and Republicans in
Congress demanded—and Democrats finally relented—that hearings on
Whitewater be held.

The allegations which surfaced in the primary campaign that Clinton was a Vietnam draft dodger came back to haunt him at the D-Day
commemoration of the Allied offensive during World War II. An untold
number of rumors that he was unfaithful to his wife (as first publicized
with the accusation by Gennifer Flowers during the New Hampshire
primary that she had had an affair with Clinton) regained credibility
during the spring of 1994 when Paula Jones, a former state employee,
brought charges of sexual harassment against Clinton. That forced him
to solicit private funds to pay for his legal defense, the first time a sitting
president faced the prospects of a trial on charges based on his prior behavior.

Toward the end of Clinton's term he could point to some diplomatic
successes, but foreign policy also had troubled beginnings after his inauguration. Clinton reversed himself on such issues as human rights in
China, inspections of North Korean nuclear capability, military rule in
Haiti, the problem of Haitian immigration, and the civil war in Bosnia,
leaving the distinct impression that Clinton and his foreign policy team

were inexperienced or, worse, lacked any sense of direction in foreign policy.

For its part, *public inputs* were a negative force because apparently people harbored reasons other than the economy for their assessment of the president. People may not have trusted Bill Clinton. Indeed, the public gave him the lowest levels of trust of any presidential candidate dating back to 1976.[23] Presidency scholar George Edwards concluded,

> There seems to be an almost visceral level of mistrust and dislike for Clinton, a rejection of him not as a leader or politician but as a person. Much of the aversion to Bill Clinton appears to be based on cultural issues such as gays in the military, abortion, and doubts about the president's character. These controversies broke early and set the tone of the administration for many, and the issue of character is never far from the headlines."[24]

The ongoing Whitewater investigation by Independent Counsel Ken Starr, the resignation (and later conviction) of Webster Hubbell (who had been a law partner with Hillary Rodham Clinton) as associate attorney general in March 1994, and the Senate Whitewater hearings during the summer months had the expected effect on the Clinton White House. By August 1994 a majority of Americans believed the Clintons were hiding something about their Whitewater involvement.[25]

Looking ahead to the election campaign, a correspondent for the *New York Times* speculated in early 1996 that "there is another, perhaps more important reason that the economy may not be the central force this year that it has been in past Presidential elections, and it is an anomaly that political analysts are just beginning to discuss. The public seems to be giving President Clinton little credit for his economic accomplishments and little blame for the economy's shortcomings."[26] According to a *USA Today*/CNN/Gallup Poll in May 1994, 56 percent said his policies had "no effect" on the economy as compared to 24 percent who said they helped the economy; 16 percent indicated they hurt the recovery.[27] The newspaper offered many reasons why economic growth had not translated into higher popularity for Clinton, but the reaction from a teacher in Loveland, Ohio, may have hit on the essential truth: "I don't think there ever was a majority of people behind him and what he wanted to do. Then you add on the extra personal baggage he's brought with him and you can see how he's just never going to be a popular president."[28]

In assessing Clinton's popularity amid prosperity, *crisis* was an irrelevant consideration. There was no sense of economic urgency that would have helped President Clinton, nor enough economic anxiety to undermine the general perception that the economy was moving in the right direction. In 1988 Democrat Michael Dukakis alleged that the Reagan-Bush prosperity yielded a "swiss cheese" economy that left too many Americans behind, but that strategy never worked. Similarly, a late 1995 *New York Times* poll found that 49 percent of Americans believed it unlikely that today's youth would have a better life than their parents,[29] and for a time Patrick J. Buchanan seized on that economic anxiety—dramatized by

a wave of corporate layoffs and downsizings—to defeat Bob Dole in the
New Hampshire primary. But Dole still won the GOP nomination, although his advocacy of a 15 percent tax cut to spur economic growth never
captured the imagination of the American people.

It was only a matter of time before economic reality and public perceptions would mesh and, for President Clinton, it was better late than
never. The results of the *New York Times*/CBS News polls parallel the
Gallup polls (see Figure 6-1) by indicating that in September 1996 the majority of Americans now approved of the way Clinton was handling the
economy. The 55 percent (up from 46 percent two weeks earlier) was the
president's highest rating on his economic stewardship.

Of the 72 percent who believed the economy was good or fairly good
(the highest proportion since 1988), 57 percent preferred Clinton over
Dole. Clinton also did better than Dole among people who were concerned that a family member would be unemployed in the next year. Of
the 19 percent who were so concerned, 58 percent favored Clinton,
whereas the margin was closer (49 percent for Clinton and 38 percent for
Dole) among the 80 percent of the sample that was not overly concerned
about family unemployment. Only with respect to long-term economic
anxiety did Dole do marginally better. The 57 percent who were optimistic
about the standard of living for the next generation planned to vote for
Clinton by the same (57 percent) margin, whereas Dole beat Clinton (43 to
41 percent) among the 40 percent of the sample that was pessimistic about
future generations.[30] A comparison of poll results from December 1995
showed that "feelings of economic insecurity among the American public
have ebbed somewhat," although the September 1996 polls "documented
the considerable economic anxiety that continues among the American
public."[31]

So unclear were economic forces in shaping the 1996 presidential
election that some well-known scholars who developed economic models
to forecast election outcomes were uncertain or wrong about political developments in 1996. The "misery index"—inflation rate, unemployment
rate, and prime lending rate combined—stood at 16.5 percent in mid-1996,
down slightly from the 17.5 percent figure that helped defeat President
Bush. Lewis Beck of the University of Iowa was unable to make a firm prediction between Clinton or Dole; Ray Fair, an econometrician at Yale University, tentatively predicted a narrow Dole victory despite polls showing
a substantial Clinton lead.[32]

Those readings were taken in May, but six months later Clinton's reelection was heralded as a triumph of the economy over character.[33]
Robert Dole's pledge to cut taxes by 15 percent was always viewed with
skepticism, and the September 1996 *New York Times*/CBS News poll
found that 64 percent believed that, even if elected, Dole could not cut
taxes that much.[34] On Election Day, exit polls showed that the majority of
voters believed Clinton was not honest and trustworthy and 6 in 10 said
he had not told the truth about Whitewater. But the majority of voters also
declared that issues mattered more than character, and the issues they

cited as most important were the economy and jobs followed by Medicare and Social Security. In the final analysis, Dole's greatest obstacle was the economy. The exit poll found that 6 in 10 respondents said the economy was good (only 19 percent of voters who said so in the 1992 presidential election) and 7 in 10 of that group of optimists cast ballots for President Clinton.[35]

NOTES

1. Samuel Kernell, "Explaining Presidential Popularity: How Ad Hoc Theorizing, Misplaced Emphasis, and Insufficient Care in Measuring One's Variables Refuted Common Sense and Led Conventional Wisdom down the Path of Anomalies," *American Political Science Review* 72 (1978), pp. 506–522.

2. See average four-year rankings of each administration from Truman through Bush on inflation, economic growth, unemployment, (international) balance of payments, and productivity in John P. Frendreis and Raymond Tatalovich, *The Modern Presidency and Economic Policy* (Itasca, IL: F.E. Peacock, 1994), pp. 308–309.

3. Floyd Norris, "History Lesson: Dow Up, Incumbent Wins," *New York Times* (Nov. 5, 1996), p. C8.

4. Frendreis and Tatalovich, *The Modern Presidency and Economic Policy*, Figure 9.1, p. 239.

5 Howard S. Bloom and H. Douglas Price, "Voter Response to Short-Run Economic Conditions: The Asymmetric Effect of Prosperity and Recession," *American Political Science Review* 69 (Dec. 1975), pp. 1240–1254.

6. David E. Rosenbaum and Steve Lohr, "With a Stable Economy, Clinton Hopes for Credit," *New York Times* (Aug. 3, 1996), p. 38.

7. F. Christopher Arterton, "Campaign '92: Strategies and Tactics of the Candidates," in Gerald M. Pomper, ed., *The Election of 1992* (Chatham, NJ: Chatham House, 1993), p. 77.

8. Kathleen A. Frankovic, "Public Opinion in the 1992 Campaign," in Gerald M. Pomper, ed., *The Election of 1992* (Chatham, NJ: Chatham House, 1993), p. 125.

9. Bruce Buchanan, *Renewing Presidential Politics* (New York: Rowman & Littlefield, 1996), p. 6.

10. Reported in "1992: Again, Widespread Dissatisfaction," *The Public Perspective*, A Roper Center Review of Public Opinion and Polling 7 (Oct./Nov., 1996), p. 18.

11. Pomper, "The Presidential Election," in *The Election of 1992*, pp. 145–146.

12. Frankovic, "Public Opinion in the 1992 Campaign," p. 124.

13. Quoted in David E. Rosenbaum, "Can the President Capitalize on the Economy's Strength," *New York Times* (April 1, 1996), p. A9.

14. Rosenbaum and Lohr, "With a Stable Economy, Clinton Hopes for Credit," pp. 1, 38.

15. Robert D. Hershey, Jr., "Index of Pay and Benefits Increased 2.9% Last Year," *New York Times* (Feb. 14, 1996), p. C6.

16. Quoted in David E. Sanger, "Clinton and the Economy," *New York Times* (July 28, 1995), p. C5.

17. Louis Uchitelle, "It's a Slow-Growth Economy, Stupid," *New York Times* (March 17, 1996), p. E5.

18. Richard W. Stevenson, "Nation's Trade Deficit Widens, but Gap with Japan Improves," *New York Times* (Feb. 29, 1996), p. C4.

19. Rosenbaum and Lohr, "With a Stable Economy, Clinton Hopes for Credit," p. 1.

20. Quoted in George C. Edwards, III, "Frustration and Folly: Bill Clinton and the Public Presidency," in Colin Campbell and Bert A. Rockman, eds., *The Clinton Presidency: First Appraisals* (Chatham, NJ: Chatham House, 1996), p. 249.

21. Ibid.

22. *The Gallup Poll Monthly* (Jan. 1996), p. 3.

23. Bert A. Rockman, "Leadership Style and the Clinton Presidency," in Colin Campbell and Bert A. Rockman, eds., *The Clinton Presidency: First Appraisals* (Chatham, NJ: Chatham House, 1996), p. 334.

24. Edwards, "Frustration and Folly: Bill Clinton and the Public Presidency," p. 240.

25. Reported in *Time* (Aug. 15, 1994), p. 18.

26. David E. Rosenbaum, "Can the President Capitalize on the Economy's Strength?" *New York Times* (April 1, 1996), p. A9.

27. Richard Benedetto, "Few Credit Clinton for Economy," *USA Today* (May 25, 1994), pp. 1A, 6A.

28. Ibid., p. 6A.

29. Rosenbaum and Lohr, "With a Stable Economy, Clinton Hopes for Credit," p. 38.

30. Richard L. Berke, "Majority Give Clinton Credit on the Economy, Poll Finds," *New York Times* (Sept. 6, 1996), pp. A1, A11.

31. "Public Still Worries, but Less, about Economy," *New York Times* (Sept. 6, 1996), p. A11.

32. Bill Montague, "Economy Spins Control in elections," *USA Today* (May 30, 1996), p. 6B; also see Peter Passell, "Sideshows Aside, Economy Is Still Key to Election," *New York Times* (Jan. 2, 1997), p. C3.

33. R.W. Apple, Jr., "The Economy, Again, Helps Clinton," *New York Times* (Nov. 6, 1996), pp. A1, A13.

34. Berke, "Majority Give Clinton Credit on the Economy, Poll Finds," p. A11.

35. James Bennet, "Voter Interviews Suggest Clinton Was Persuasive on Path of U.S.," *New York Times* (Nov. 6, 1996), pp. A11, A17.

7

Legislative Leader:
An Uncertain Mandate
for Presidential Power

Over the years the president has become known variously as "legislative leader," "chief legislator," and even "initiator-in-chief."[1] These titles imply an active relationship between the president and Congress, with policymaking at its core. Historical developments of legislative leadership indicate that the more assertive presidents have shaped the customary practices and public expectations that have come to define this role (Table 7–1). Presidency scholars Edward Corwin and Louis Koenig once suggested that "virtually all presidents who have made a major impact on American history have done so in great degree as legislative leaders,"[2] and they pointed specifically to Andrew Jackson, Theodore Roosevelt, Woodrow Wilson, and Franklin D. Roosevelt.

Political conflict has been a notable attribute of the legislative relationship between the two branches of government. Historian Arthur Schlesinger, Jr., makes the analogy to guerrilla warfare, with Congress attacking in ambush against the commanding forces and firepower of the executive.[3] The causes of this contentious behavior are many: the president may veto important acts of Congress, or refuse to appoint persons having legislative support to administrative positions, or neglect to consult with representatives or senators on policy issues. Conflict also results because the president and members of Congress are elected from constituencies of various sizes and have differing terms of office. Because all representatives must face the electorate every two years, they may be especially anxious about constituency interests when voting on legislation; senators, however, can afford to be more aloof, since they enjoy six-year terms, with only one-third of the Senate reelected every two years.

The separation of powers system has been characterized as "separate institutions sharing power," but those institutional rivalries can be aggravated by ideological and partisan tensions between the president and Congress. Even though Democratic President Kennedy had Democratic majorities in both houses of Congress, his domestic New Frontier programs of 1961 were largely obstructed by the southern Democrats who

Table 7-1. Significant Historical Developments in Legislative Leader Role

President	Historical Event or Decision
Washington	• Legislative agenda setting with Secretary of Treasury Alexander Hamilton's economic program • Used veto power against bills he deemed unconstitutional • Delivered State of the Union Address to Congress in person
Jefferson	• Used Jeffersonian-Republican "caucus" in Congress to gain support for his legislative program • Ended practice of delivering State of the Union Address to Congress in person
Jackson	• Used veto power against bills for policy or political reasons • Added "signing statement" as caveat to enactment
Theodore Roosevelt	• Square Deal domestic program
Wilson	• Used Democratic Party "caucus" in Congress to enact progressive legislative program • Began modern practice of delivering State of the Union Address to Congress in person
Franklin Roosevelt	• New Deal domestic program • First "100 days" as benchmark for legislative success • Conservative coalition between southern Democrats and Republicans was born
Truman	• Fair Deal domestic program
Eisenhower	• Failed to give Congress his legislative program in the first year • Established the Office of Congressional Relations (OCR)
Kennedy	• New Frontier domestic program
Lyndon Johnson	• The Great Society domestic program and War on Poverty
Nixon	• Advent of the era of divided government: different parties control the executive and legislative branch
Clinton	• Granted a statutory line-item veto by the 104th Congress

held key power positions within the committee system. Many of his legislative proposals were defeated by the "conservative coalition" of Republicans and southern Democrats who generally were hostile to his liberal social-welfare agenda.

At that time presidency scholars in the "idealist" or heroic camp (see Table 2-1) blasted Congress as a bastion of conservatism, localism, and special interests, and one well-known liberal senator even penned a book calling Congress the "sapless" branch of government.[4] Thirty years later, however, the political scenario changed radically when President George Bush confronted a very liberal Congress, this time dominated by a more ideologically unified Democratic Party.

But conflict is not the entire story of executive-legislative relations because much legislation is enacted even when divided government—different parties having control of the Congress and the presidency—exists, and presidency scholars have begun to rethink their assumptions about what variables undergird presidential success as legislative leader. It was once assumed that one political party controlling a unified government was the essential element for legislative success but, although party remains a prominent factor in explaining the degree of conflict or cooperation between the branches, partisanship alone does not account for all the variations in the executive-legislative dynamics of enacting law. Moreover, regardless of party or ideology, cooperation does occur when bills affecting national security and foreign affairs are debated and when the nation is faced with a diplomatic or military crisis. After the preliminary round of partisan debate was over, for example, Congress formally supported President Bush during the 1990 Persian Gulf War.

Success as legislative leader requires an appreciation of the subtle uses of political persuasion, for no president has enough authority in this role to meet his needs. Although most presidents have enjoyed modest records of legislative achievement, certain presidents have achieved tremendous successes in shaping the lawmaking process for their own ends. By comparing the leadership styles of two presidents (Jefferson and Johnson) who wielded legislative power effectively with the styles of two other presidents (Carter and Bush), who were decidedly less effective, we can begin to understand the complexities of legislative leadership in a separation of powers system.

FOUR CASES OF LEGISLATIVE LEADERSHIP

Jefferson

Thomas Jefferson was the first president to exert recognized leadership in Congress. To do so he had to create a legislative "party" by assisting in the election of Jeffersonian-Republicans to Congress and, once elected, maintain constant contacts with his congressional supporters to assure acceptance of his proposals. The Jeffersonian-Republicans were a rather loosely knit group sharing a common dislike for the Federalist "aristocrats" and what they represented.[5] However the Jeffersonians were a heterogeneous and often disunited group in Congress who did not support Jefferson's program in every instance. Jefferson's success with Congress was based partly on his personal involvement in the legislative process, his understanding of congressional politics, and his ability to bargain and persuade.

Congress itself was very different during that period. Committee chairs were not very strong, nor were leadership positions routinized. There were no formalized party leaders, party whips, or party committees. High membership turnover, conflicting constituency interests, and internal procedures encouraged party factionalism.[6] The Jeffersonians had also designated informal floor leaders in Congress such as John Randolph, although as many as twenty men functioned as "leaders" for the administration during the Jefferson years.[7] The party leaders worked closely with Jefferson and, because he was swept into office with party majorities in both the House and Senate, he had a base of support from which to operate.

The president's major legislative accomplishments involved passage of the 1803 Louisiana Purchase and establishing a government for that new territory. Jefferson called Congress into session three weeks early to capitalize on the groundswell of public support for the treaty. It took the Senate only four days to approve the document, with voting strictly along party lines. The bill establishing governing procedures for the Louisiana Territory also was enacted despite Federalist opposition.

Key to Jefferson's success as legislative leader was his attitude toward Congress as well as his personal involvement in the lawmaking process. To many his attitude appeared "deferential"[8] because Jefferson vetoed no bills and, in an early presidential message, indicated that "nothing shall be wanting on my part to inform . . . the legislative judgment, nor to carry the judgment into faithful execution."[9] His overtures to the legislature were indirect; his suggestions to the Congress were frequent, but Jefferson did not let it be known they were his ideas. He also kept his legislative role from public view[10] (because he had been so critical of Alexander Hamilton, Washington's secretary of the treasury, for directly intervening in the workings of Congress).

Other critics of Jefferson perceived his assertiveness and manipulations of the legislative process behind the scenes. Jefferson was actively engaged in legislative affairs, and he enjoyed it. He visited Congress and personally met with legislators, helped recruit party leaders, wrote many of his own bills, and supplied information to committees when needed. He would ask cabinet members to lobby Congress and testify before committees. Jefferson made use of social contacts to win congressional support, and dinner parties at his residence became well-known settings for encouraging unity among the Jeffersonians.

As effective as Jefferson was as a legislative leader, however, even his influence had its limits. Opposition to his policies grew among Federalists, and occasionally Jeffersonian-Republicans grew tired of presidential lobbying. The greatest threat to party unity faced by Jefferson concerned floor leader John Randolph, who publicly opposed the president on two issues: Jefferson's compromise settlement of the Yazoo land claim controversy in 1804–1805 and the unsuccessful impeachment of Federalist Supreme Court Justice Samuel Chase. Jefferson offered a compromise to the Georgia state legislature over its questionable cession of the disputed Yazoo lands, but Randolph fought the compromise from the very beginning. The president also was upset with Randolph's mishandling of the Chase impeachment, which resulted in the Justice's acquittal in the Senate.

Jefferson had his greatest success as legislative leader during his first five years, a time when the United States came as close to having party government as it ever has. In the House of Representatives the Jeffersonians were able to select the Speaker, who then appointed all the standing committees and their chairs,[11] allowing power to become centralized within the party organization. This arrangement benefited Jefferson and, after his first year in office, he wrote that Congress had "carried into execution steadily almost all the propositions submitted to them in my message at the opening of the session."[12] By 1805, however, his control over Congress waned after he announced his retirement would take effect after his second term.

Johnson

The "modern" Congresses of the 1960s were highly institutionalized[13] and very different than the "premodern" Congresses of the nineteenth century or the "postreformed" Congresses that followed in the 1970s. When Lyndon Johnson was president, formal party leadership positions and a decentralized committee system characterized the legislative system. Republicans and southern Democrats frequently voted together as the conservative coalition against social-welfare programs such as JFK's New Frontier. That President Johnson could overcome these obstacles and fashion an impressive number of legislative victories for his Great Society domestic program was due chiefly to the size of his Democratic majorities in Congress, a large freshman class that was elected on LBJ's 1964 coattails, and Johnson's political instincts and sophisticated knowledge of how Congress works.

In the election of 1964 Lyndon Johnson's margin of victory over Barry Goldwater was one of the five biggest landslides in U.S. history, so his coattails carried many new liberal Democrats into the Congress.[14] Democrats in the 89th Congress had the largest majorities in the House (295 to 140) and the Senate (68 to 32) since 1937. Moreover President Johnson was popular with the American people, enjoying an approval rating of 66 percent in 1965.[15]

Lyndon Johnson assumed office in 1963 following President Kennedy's assassination, thus beginning his tenure with an extraordinary degree of national unity. The early 1960s were also a time of economic prosperity (the most prosperous decade since World War II), which provided rising federal revenues and a positive mood for Johnson's Great Society proposals. Congress was responsive to Johnson because he had spent 23 years there including his 8 years as Senate Majority Leader. Unlike Kennedy, Johnson, as a Texan, had good rapport with the senior southern Democrats in both chambers. Thus Johnson, as president, could work with relatively few congressional leaders, including the inner club of southern Democrats who effectively controlled the Senate, and be assured of the votes needed from the rank and file for his programs. Whenever southern Democrats refused support for a Johnson program, specifically on civil rights legislation, Johnson would cultivate bipartisan support by working closely with Minority Leader Senator Everett McKinley Dirksen (R–Ill.).

Lyndon Johnson knew the congressional machinery and the key law-makers to approach to get things done. The president made demands on Congress but he also serviced its members.[16] A liaison officer was assigned to members of Congress to determine what the administration could do for them. Johnson's personal touches with leaders and members of both parties gave him added leverage. He posed for color photographs at the White House to give to legislators and their wives who were invited to the White House for dinner. He signed bills in public before cameras to publicize those legislators who supported him and made telephone calls to thank those who had delivered crucial votes. In 1965, as one example, Johnson invited every senator and representative to the White House for buffets and briefings. Over five hundred accepted these invitations to come with their spouses during five weeks in February and March.

Johnson was an activist legislative leader who courted the Congress personally. He delighted in shepherding a bill through the legislative process, confronting committee chairs when necessary and appealing to the rank and file. Most political scientists, however, tend to view Johnson's personal skills as a secondary factor given the size of his party's majorities. Indeed, some critics suggest that, with the votes he had to spare, Johnson should have won more victories in 1965 and 1967.[17] The historical record (Table 7–2) does show that Johnson was more effective than his Democratic predecessor and his immediate GOP successors in terms of the number of bills signed into law. As far as victories on key roll call (recorded) votes in Congress, LBJ's success in the 89th Congress (1965–1966) was better than any president during the entire 1953 to 1995 period.

SUMMARY.   The legislative achievements of Jefferson and Johnson were related to conditions of unified government and party government. Both houses of Congress and the White House were controlled by the same political party, and the Jeffersonian-Republicans in 1801 and the Democrats in 1965 had large vote margins over the minority Federalists or Republicans, respectively. It was the realigning election of 1800 ending Federalist domination of politics that was most responsible for Jefferson's secure position with Congress; LBJ's landslide victory over a GOP opponent who was branded as an extremist secured Johnson's position vis-à-vis Congress. Also crucial to Jefferson's success was his leadership of a new political party dedicated to following another set of governing principles. For Johnson, his landslide election was also responsible for bringing into office a large freshman class of Democrats who owed their political survival to the man in the White House. As a group, moreover, the new members of Congress were liberals eager to approve Johnson's ambitious Great Society legislative program.

Both Jefferson and Johnson were hands-on legislative leaders who enjoyed following the congressional process, personally lobbying the leadership, and setting the policy agenda for Congress. Johnson was aware that a newly elected president needs to hit the ground running and not

Table 7-2. Presidential Success Rates on Key Roll Call Votes and on
　　　　　Legislation, 1953–1996

| President/Year | Success on Votes | Success on Legislation | |
		N Submitted	Approved
Eisenhower			
1953	89.0%	44	72.7%
1954	82.8	232	64.7
1955	75.0	207	46.3
1956	70.0	225	45.7
1957	68.0	206	36.9
1958	76.0	234	47.0
1959	52.0	228	40.8
1960	65.0	183	30.6
Kennedy			
1961	81.0	355	48.4
1962	85.4	298	44.6
1963	87.1	404	27.2
Johnson			
1964	88.0	217	57.6
1965	93.0	469	68.9
1966	79.0	371	55.8
1967	79.0	431	47.6
1968	75.0	414	55.8
Nixon			
1969	74.0	171	32.2
1970	77.0	210	46.1
1971	75.0	202	19.8
1972	66.0	116	44.0
1973	50.6	183	31.1
1974	59.6	97	34.0
Ford			
1974	58.2	64	35.9
1975	61.0	—	—
1976	53.8	—	—
Carter			
1977	75.4	—	—
1978	78.3	—	—
1979	76.8	—	—
1980	75.1	—	—
Reagan			
1981	82.4	—	—
1982	72.4	—	—
1983	67.1	—	—
1984	65.8	—	—
1985	59.9	—	—
1986	56.1	—	—
1987	43.5	—	—
1988	47.4	—	—

Table 7-2. Presidential Success Rates on Key Roll Call Votes and on
          Legislation, 1953–1996 *(continued)*

| President/Year | Success on Votes | Success on Legislation | |
		N Submitted	Approved
Bush			
1989	62.6	—	—
1990	46.8	—	—
1991	54.2	—	—
1992	43.0	—	—
Clinton			
1993	86.4	—	—
1994	86.4	—	—
1995	36.2	—	—
1996	55.1	—	—

Source: *Congressional Quarterly Almanac, 1991* (Washington DC: Congressional Quarterly Press, 1991), p. 9-B. and "Success Rate History," *Congressional Quarterly Weekly Report* (Dec. 21, 1996), p, 3455.

waste his electoral mandate or the honeymoon period during the beginning of his term. But Johnson also had the advantage of succeeding to office at a time of genuine political crisis, Kennedy's murder, so the country rallied behind its new leader. Jefferson had his occasional problems with congressional leaders who rebelled against his leadership, and Jefferson as well as Johnson saw their legislative influence wane over the course of their tenure in office. But Johnson unlike such presidents as Kennedy and Jimmy Carter, was able to neutralize the conservative coalition by appealing to southern Democrats for support. Furthermore, Johnson had a relatively good working relationship with the Republicans in Congress.

The size of the party majorities that supported Jefferson and Johnson allowed them to govern as legislative leaders without being unduly obstructed by the minority party. The task of legislative leadership is more complicated and requires more subtlety when a president has a smaller legislative majority of his own party or he confronts the opposition party in control of the legislative branch. These were the fundamental causes for legislative gridlock under Presidents Carter and Bush.

Carter

Presidency scholar George Edwards draws a sharp contrast between Lyndon Johnson, the "ultimate professional, the 'insider'" and Jimmy Carter as the "amateur outsider with no Washington experience at all."[18] In terms of victories on key roll call votes (Table 7-2), Carter's best year was only 3.3 percent better than Johnson's worst year.

Unlike LBJ, Jimmy Carter's only previous experience with legislative assemblies was his four years in the Georgia state senate and his one term as Georgia's governor. As governor his difficulties in dealing with the state legislature were similar to the kinds of problems he faced with Congress. One incisive study of Carter points out that he was reluctant to "wheel and deal" with politicians in the legislature and also had difficulties fashioning winning legislative coalitions.[19] Carter, unlike Johnson, was unable to establish legislative priorities for his agenda or to forcefully communicate his intentions. As one representative indicated, "with almost no exception every issue that has come down from the White House or agency has been viewed as *the* big issue."[20]

Carter was depicted by the press as indecisive and irresolute in his dealings with others. He did not always consult with members of Congress or vigorously lobby them, which is why the president suffered some very close victories, too many narrow defeats, and much unnecessary criticism. As then Majority Leader Jim Wright (D-Tex.) said of Carter in 1978: "In dealing with Congress, he doesn't twist arms nor promise favors. Some in his Cabinet can be disdainful of congressional advice. And that has cost him some support."[21]

Not all of Carter's problems had to do with his personal style. The Congress in 1977 was a different institution than it had been during Johnson's term. Congressional scholars have characterized the post-1973 Congress as a "postreformed" Congress[22] because it democratized its internal procedures. In the aftermath of Vietnam and Watergate the Congress also reasserted its authority over war-making and budgeting. Moreover, congressional Democrats owed Carter very little because Jimmy Carter in 1976 ran well behind most Democrats who sought reelection.

The Democratic leadership in Congress no longer could dictate terms to its rank and file but had to contend with the newly reformed but fragmented decision-making process. Standing committees lost power to their subcommittees, and long-standing legislative caucuses such as the liberal Democratic Study Group and the House Wednesday Group of moderate Republicans were joined by many special interest groups such as the Black Caucus and Hispanic Caucus. Also, the conservative coalition gained enough strength to block some of Carter's liberal proposals, with the assistance of new ideological factions such as the Conservative Democratic Forum ("Boll Weevils") and the moderate Committee of Northeast-Midwest Republicans ("Gypsy Moths").

The 1970s reforms limited the power of the standing committee chairs at just the time when liberal Democrats were gaining enough seniority to fill those positions. No president could influence the legislative process simply by dealing with a few chairs and party leaders. Now each legislative leader had to contend with a large number of rank and file members who shared power in the Congress.

The hit-and-miss legislative strategy during Carter's first year sent negative signals to the Washington establishment, the press corps, and the electorate. President Carter tried to veto water projects for the West but backed down, wanted a 50 percent tax rebate but changed his mind, and failed to check with Speaker "Tip" O'Neill before firing an O'Neill protégé from an administrative position. Such blunders made the president the brunt of Washington jokes, and one Democratic member of Congress was heard to remark, "[e]very night is Amateur Night at the White House."[23]

Eventually Carter learned from his mistakes. White House liaison decidedly improved by 1978, and the president began to lobby Congress in order to win some narrow victories. For example, he was able to get defeated a plan to build the B-1 bomber by calling committee chairmen and contacting all the Democrats on the House Appropriations Committee. To win Senate approval for his Panama Canal Treaties, Carter unleashed his entire administration including the vice president, several cabinet secretaries, and White House staffers to rally public opinion.

Carter also corrected one of his worst legislative mistakes by cutting the number of priority bills, thereby allowing his liaison staff to concentrate their limited resources on fewer bills. His legislative liaison staff became more effective in using bargaining and patronage and in developing a working relationship with Democratic leaders in Congress. Commenting on the improved Carter liaison efforts, one observer noted, "[W]hat began as a comedy of errors has definitely matured. . . . Now people on the Hill are more willing to work with Frank Moore [assistant to the president for congressional liaison]."[24]

Bush

A completely different set of problems afflicted the legislative leadership of George Bush who faced a divided government and intense partisanship on Capitol Hill. At first Bush's open and bipartisan approach was welcomed by Congress, as President Bush declared in his inaugural address: "To my friends—and yes, I do mean friends—in the loyal opposition—and yes, I mean loyal: I put out my hand."[25] But Bush's bipartisan overtures did not last long. The fundamental problem was the political antagonisms generated by the Democratic-controlled 102nd Congress. A *New York Times* columnist summarized it this way:

> A furious exchange over the presidential campaign was a typical punctuation mark for the end of a Congress that began with stately speeches about the Gulf war but dissolved quickly into partisan wrangling over the economy. Then it descended into dismal reflection over the House bank scandal and the Senate Judiciary Committee's handling of the Clarence Thomas-Anita Hill confrontation over allegations of sexual harassment.[26]

George Bush did his utmost to protect a presidency under siege by the Congress. As Secretary of Defense Dick Cheney stated,"[t]he president . . . genuinely respects the role of Congress, but he also has decided to stand up forthrightly to preserve the powers of his own office."[27] This attitude was bound to lead to frequent clashes between the branches, and the veto became a primary weapon of the Bush presidency. He was particularly successful with it, casting thirty-five vetoes before any were overridden.[28] Bush's reliance on veto power, however, bears out the ominous prediction from Robert Spitzer that "[a]s a substantive power, it is potent, but politically dangerous for presidents who use it too much."[29]

The consequence of George Bush's rancor against the Congress was legislative disaster. Bush's presidential support score in Congress for 1992 (see Table 7–1), indicating how often legislators voted on bills in conformity with the president's wishes, was the second lowest since the 1950s, and his 1990 score was the fourth worst in terms of getting legislators to support his policy positions. None of his major 1992 legislative requests from the State of the Union Message—health care reform, education proposals, or economic recovery package—were acted on.[30]

The basic reason for Bush's gridlock with the 102nd Congress was the gulf between the policy agenda of a Republican administration and a Democratic Congress. As journalist Helen Dewar described the tumultuous relationship between Bush and the Democrats,

> More often than not, Congress' Democratic majority rejects Bush's proposals, Bush vetoes proposals from the Democrats, and Congress cannot override the vetoes. . . . Bills are delayed or killed, and vital matters ignored, trivialized or manipulated for partisan advantage.[31]

SUMMARY.   Having the same political party control the presidency and Congress is helpful but, as the Carter experience shows, it is no guarantee that policy gridlock will not develop between the two governing branches. For Bush, who faced divided government and for Carter, who enjoyed unified government, the overriding problem was ideological and not partisan. In the wake of Ronald Reagan's presidency, both legislative parties became ideologically monolithic to the point that the old conservative coalition vanished. With African Americans now vital to Democratic election victories in the South, southern Democrats became increasingly liberal voting alongside their northern brethren to oppose GOP policies. Congressional Republicans also became much more conservative. Thus Bush faced the nearly impossible task of trying to bridge that ideological chasm. It is doubtful that any amount of political acumen or personal lobbying on his part would have made much difference to his final legislative record.

The Carter problem was different in kind, not in content. According to one interpretation, Jimmy Carter was a "trusteeship" president who naively wanted to do what was right, not what was politically right. He was forced to tackle "new" issues that were not amenable to solutions based on Democratic liberalism.[32] Environmentalism, the energy crisis, and stagflation (slow growth with high inflation), for example, were problems that could not be resolved by debating left/right principles. This explanation does not absolve Carter's lack of legislative skills or his inexperience but accounts partly for his unwillingness to be joined ideologically with many of the Democratic leaders of Congress.

AUTHORITY

The president has little real authority to exert over Congress. Article II, Section 3, of the Constitution allows the president to "give to the Congress information of the State of the Union, and recommend to their consideration such measures as he shall judge necessary and expedient." He is also given authority to call the Congress into special session and to adjourn Congress in instances when the House and Senate disagree over adjournment. The clearest source of legal authority is his veto power, but the veto does not allow a president to initiate policy.

Congress was granted an array of enumerated legislative powers in Article I, Section 8, of the Constitution, including the power to lay and collect taxes, borrow money, regulate interstate and foreign commerce, coin money, and declare war, and to do whatever is "necessary and proper" for carrying out every power specified in Article I. Because Congress lays legal claim to both enumerated and implied powers, the president must use political resources in order to shape the legislative process.

We talk routinely about the legislative leader role, but not every president has been so involved in lawmaking. George Washington, for one, remained aloof in his dealings with Congress. Although Washington did give an annual State of the Union Address to a joint session of Congress, he made only three recommendations to Congress during his eight years in office. Moreover, he relied extensively on Secretary of the Treasury Alexander Hamilton to mobilize the votes behind Federalist policies. Some 150 years later, Dwight D. Eisenhower believed so strongly in the separation of powers, he neglected to present a legislative program to the Congress for its consideration in 1953, his first year in office.

Veto

Veto power was not an original invention of the Framers of the Constitution because the governors of the royal colonies and the English monarch held an "absolute" veto over legislation passed by the colonial assemblies (absolute vetoes could not be overridden by the legislatures). The Constitutional Convention generally supported a qualified presidential veto, but few delegates were willing to accept an absolute veto, believing veto power would serve to preserve the executive branch from legislative meddling.

Early presidents rarely exercised the veto, however, and, when they did, they used it to reject legislation they thought unconstitutional. Washington vetoed two bills, but John Adams and Jefferson never cast a veto (Table 7-3). That tradition was ended with President Andrew Jackson. His twelve vetoes set a record unbroken until the Andrew Johnson presidency. More important than Jackson's number of vetoes, however, was his justification for them. He established a new precedent by using veto power to shape public policy or to reject legislation he did not like.

A minor innovation added by President Jackson was his use of a "signing statement" in 1830 to a bill he signed into law, which was designed to limit the bill's impact. Congress was unable to react to it because the House had already recessed. A signing statement is akin to an item veto, which forty-three governors now have. Similar attempts were made by such presidents as Tyler, Wilson, Nixon, Carter, Reagan, and Bush to circumvent legislative intent despite the fact that legal scholars generally believe the practice is not constitutional.[33]

Table 7-3. The Use of Presidential Vetoes, 1789–1996

President	All Bills Vetoed	Regular Vetoes	Pocket Vetoes	Regular Vetoes Overridden
Washington	2	2	0	0
J. Adams	0	0	0	0
Jefferson	0	0	0	0
Madison	7	5	2	0
Monroe	1	1	0	0
J.Q. Adams	0	0	0	0
Jackson	12	5	7	0
Van Buren	1	0	1	0
W.H. Harrison	0	0	0	0
Tyler	10	6	4	1
Polk	3	2	1	0
Taylor	0	0	0	0
Fillmore	0	0	0	0
Pierce	9	9	0	5
Buchanan	7	4	3	0
Lincoln	7	2	5	0
A. Johnson	29	21	8	15
Grant	93	45	48	4
Hayes	13	12	1	1
Garfield	0	0	0	0
Arthur	12	4	8	1
Cleveland (1st term)	414	304	110	2
B. Harrison	44	19	25	1
Cleveland (2nd term)	170	42	128	5
McKinley	42	6	36	0
T. Roosevelt	82	42	40	1
Taft	39	30	9	1
Wilson	44	33	11	6
Harding	6	5	1	0
Coolidge	50	20	30	4
Hoover	37	21	16	3
F.D. Roosevelt	635	372	263	9
Truman	258	191	67	12
Eisenhower	188	79	109	2
Kennedy	21	12	9	0
Johnson	29	18	11	0
Nixon	43	24	19	5
Ford	68	49	19	12
Carter	31	13	18	2
Reagan	68	41	27	8
Bush	46	27	19	1
Clinton	17	17	0	1
TOTALS	2,538	1,483	1,055	102

Source: *Congressional Quarterly's Guide to the Presidency* (Washington, DC: Congressional Quarterly,1989), p. 451. Data on Bush is from *Congressional Quarterly Weekly Report,* (Dec. 19, 1992) pp. 3925–3926; Data on Clinton from *Weekly Compilation of Presidential Documents 1995–1996.*

The veto is extremely effective: only about 7 percent of all 1,483 vetoes (Table 7-3) have been overridden by two-thirds vote in the House and Senate. Because a veto that is sustained by either house of Congress means that nobody won the legislative struggle, a more effective presidential tactic is to threaten its use as a way of influencing the legislative process. In his battle with the Republican 104th Congress over welfare reform, President Clinton actually vetoed the first bill to reach his desk and threatened additional vetoes unless the more punitive aspects of the bill were removed.

It is unclear whether the use of the veto is an index of presidential strength or weakness for the legislative leader. Although presidents who are considered great, near great, or even above average accounted for most of the vetoes cast (Table 7–4), only two presidents—Franklin Roosevelt and Grover Cleveland—were responsible for nearly one-half of all the regular vetoes cast. After Roosevelt and Cleveland, both active presidents and more passive presidents are represented among the presidents who have vetoed the largest numbers of bills, including Presidents Truman, Eisenhower, Ford, Grant, Theodore Roosevelt, Benjamin Harrison, Wilson, and Coolidge. A partisan pattern clearly exists, with Democrats more than twice as likely to use the veto as Republicans. President Clinton thus seems to be the exception, having vetoed only fifteen bills, which is fewer than any president going back to Warren G. Harding. This did not stop congressional Republicans, however, from referring to Clinton as "Veto Bill."[34]

Table 7-4. Classification of 2,521 Presidential Vetoes from 1789 to 1992 according to Party Affiliation and Ranking by Historians*

Variable	Number	Percentage	Number per President	Number per year
Party				
Republican	867	34.4	48.2	10.3
Democratic	1634	64.8	128.5	22.7
Other	20	0.8	2.0	0.4
Ranking[†]				
Great	644	25.4	161.0	20.1
Near great	396	15.7	99.0	12.4
Above average	833	32.8	92.6	16.0
Average	287	11.3	31.9	8.3
Below average	69	2.7	13.8	4.1
Failure	178	7.0	35.6	7.7
Not ranked (after 1981)[‡]	131	5.2	43.7	8.2

* Robert Murray and Tim Blessing," The Presidential Performance Study: A Progress Report," *Journal of American History* (Dec. 1983), pp. 540–541. This categorization of presidential vetoes is based on the data in Table 7-3.

[†]See Table 2-2.

[‡]Reagan, Bush, and Clinton veto numbers are from Table 7-3.

Presidents since U.S. Grant have advocated the item veto to eliminate unnecessary pork barrel spending programs from omnibus appropriations bills. It would take a constitutional amendment to establish permanently an item veto, but the Republican-controlled 104th Congress approved and President Clinton signed the first statutory line-item veto for a president. Some critics in Congress, including Senator Robert Byrd (D–W.Va.), filed suit on constitutional grounds, but that legislation ingeniously disaggregated billions of dollars into multiple accounts, protecting from the item veto such major spending programs as Medicare and Social Security, which account for about two-thirds of federal expenditures in a year.[35]

Excessive use of the regular veto can damage the prospects for a productive executive-legislative relationship, and periods of divided government seemingly heighten political animosities between the branches of government. Of recent presidents, Ford had the highest number of regular vetoes, followed by Eisenhower and Bush; each of these presidents experienced divided government. Eisenhower faced a Democratic Congress for six years; Ford and Bush did so during their entire time in office.

DECISION MAKING

Despite veto power, Congress remains the dominant power in its relationship with the president. One study, now a classic, which documented that Congress—not the president—was the primary initiator of legislation, examined some ninety statutes from the 1880s until the 1940s.[36] Despite such strong legislative leaders as Wilson and the two Roosevelts holding office during that era, it concluded that only about 20 percent of the laws were considered "presidential influence preponderant." Nearly 40 percent of the enactments were deemed "congressional influence preponderant," and another 30 percent reflected "joint presidential-congressional influence." Moreover, 77 of the 90 bills originated in Congress and not in the executive branch.[37]

A follow-up study by Moe and Teel for the period 1940 to 1967[38] evaluated legislation in twelve policy areas and similarly concluded that Congress had substantial impact in virtually every policy area. A somewhat different conclusion was drawn in another study covering the twenty years from 1945 to 1964.[39] It focused on sixty-three major statutes but concluded that only 11 percent could be attributed to Congress alone, whereas 41 percent originated within the executive branch and the remaining 44 percent had input from both branches of government.[40] Despite the differing approaches employed, all three analyses indicate that Congress had a substantial if not dominant impact on the legislative process affecting a range of significant public policies.

If that kind of analysis of domestic policy was applied to foreign and military policy, however, the results might suggest the creative role of Congress is reduced when national security is involved. In a seminal article from the 1960s, "The Two Presidencies," political scientist Aaron Wildavsky made the argument that the executive dominates over foreign affairs[41] but Congress predominates over domestic policy. This thesis was validated in an updated analysis by LeLoup and Shull, focusing on the years 1965 to 1975. Even though there were four times as many domestic bills as foreign policy or defense bills, they found the president had greater dominance over foreign and defense legislation.[42]

Unified or Divided Government

The party leadership in the House and Senate serves as a vital communications link between the congressional parties and the president. Both Ronald Reagan and Bill Clinton, for example, recognized the importance of working through their own party leadership to facilitate passage of legislation. Richard Berke observed of Bill Clinton's efforts to stay in close contact with congressional leaders that "at times it can be hard to figure out who is working for whom."[43]

Conventional wisdom has it that a president under unified government has a better chance of getting his program enacted. On average, presidential support scores are much higher among his congressional partisans than among legislators who belong to the opposition party (Table 7-5). But party is a double-edged sword because Republicans and Democrats in the Congress are not nearly as unified behind their party lead-

Table 7-5. Average Presidential Support Scores by Party in the First Year

Year/President	Senate		House of Representatives	
	Republicans	*Democrats*	*Republicans*	*Democrats*
1953/Eisenhower	78%	55%	80%	55%
1957/Eisenhower	80	60	60	54
1961/Kennedy	42	73	41	81
1965/Johnson	55	75	46	83
1969/Nixon	74	55	65	56
1973/Nixon	70	42	67	39
1974/Ford	67	45	59	48
1977/Carter	58	77	46	69
1981/Reagan	84	52	72	46
1985/Reagan	80	36	69	31
Bush/1991	84	56	72	38
Clinton/1993	29	87	39	77

Source: Harold W. Stanley and Richard G. Niemi, eds., *Vital Statistics on American Politics,* 4th ed. (Washington, DC: CQ Press, 1994), pp. 276–277, Table 8-12. These percentages are the number of congressional votes supporting the president divided by the total number of votes on which the president took a position. The percentages are calculated to eliminate the effects of absences as follows: support = (support)/(support + opposition).

For the Clinton score, see "Presidential Support: When Congress Had to Choose, It Voted to Back Clinton,"*1993 Congressional Quarterly Almanac* (Washington, DC: CQ Press, 1994), pp. 3C–7C.

ership as legislators are in such parliamentary systems as Great Britain or Canada. There cohesion within the legislative parties is so reliable that in Britain, for example, a party vote occurs whenever *at least* 90 percent of Conservatives oppose 90 percent of Labourites in the House of Commons. In the U.S. Congress a party vote occurs any time a bare majority of Republicans oppose a bare majority of Democrats when voting on legislation. In other words, even though the frequency of party votes in Congress has been increasing during the 1980s and into the 1990s (Figure 7–1), by definition 49 percent of Democrats or Republicans could desert their own leadership and their president and vote with the members of the opposition party.

Since World War II any presumed benefits from unified government have accrued to Democratic presidents because, until Clinton, it was more likely that Republican presidents would have to deal with divided government at some time during their tenure. Since 1933 Democratic presidents had Democratic Congresses for all but six of these years—1946–1948 under Truman, and 1995–1996 and 1997–1998 under Clinton—whereas Republican presidents were able to work with Republican Congresses for only two years—1953–1955 under Eisenhower—and a Republican Senate for another six years—1981–1986 under Reagan. Nixon, Ford, and Bush confronted Democratic majorities in both House and Senate during their entire tenures in office. As a consequence, the aggregate support scores for representatives and senators during each year show that the typical member regardless of his or her party backed Ford and Bush on less than 60 percent of the roll calls on which they took a position (Figure 7-2). For Kennedy, Johnson, Carter, and Clinton—during his first two years—as legislative leaders under conditions of unified government, the average

Figure 7-1. Percentage of Partisan Senate and House Roll Calls 1954–1995*
Source: *CQ Weekly Report* (Jan. 27, 1996).
*Partisan votes are those in which a majority of each party oppose each other.

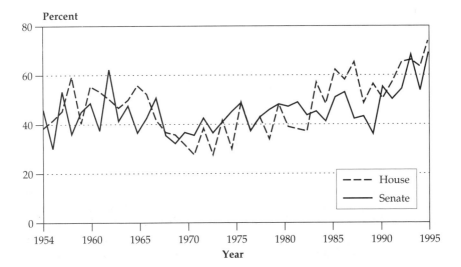

Figure 7-2. Average Presidential Support Score by Year 1956–1996*
*A presidential support score measures the times a president won a victory on a roll call
vote on those votes on which he took a clear position.
Source: *Congressional Quarterly Weekly Report* 54 (50), (1996), p. 3428.

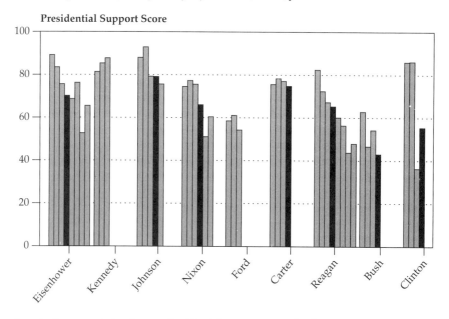

level of support for the typical legislator approached or exceeded 80 percent. Clinton's steep decline to a 36 percent average support score occurred after the Republicans took control of both chambers.

The avalanche of legislation enacted during the New Deal under FDR
and the Great Society under Johnson was a product of unified government, and those experiences further convinced that generation of presidency scholars who were enamored with the idealist or heroic school of
thought (see Table 2-1) that party control of government is essential to effective lawmaking and "deadlock," "gridlock," or "stalemate" will result
whenever different parties control the executive and legislative branches.

Recent studies by David Mayhew and Charles Jones, however, cast
doubt on those assumptions. When Nixon was first elected in 1968, for instance, the era of divided government arrived, becoming in the last thirty
years more typical than unified government. Both Mayhew and Jones
wanted to determine why legislative deadlock has *not* characterized the
political system. Mayhew studied the volume of legislation as well as congressional investigations of executive branch wrongdoing over five
decades, concluding that Congress was equally productive during eras of
divided or unified rule.[44] His wake-up call to presidential scholars
prompted Jones to use Mayhew's case studies and detail what legislative
role was played by both houses of Congress (and their various committees) and by the president in enacting landmark statutes. Jones concluded
that it was rare for any president, Republican or Democrat, to have his
way with Congress on the shaping of legislation. Jones applauded this

finding rather than joining the naysayers who wanted to transform the U.S. separation of powers system into a parliamentary regime. Said Jones,

> I conclude that it is more important to make the separated system work well than to change systems. The preferred institutional interaction is that of balanced participation, with both branches actively involved in the policy process. The United States has the most intricate lawmaking system in the world. It will not be made better through simplification. Preponderance of one branch over the other should be a cause for concern, not celebration.[45]

PUBLIC INPUTS

The lawmaking process allows innumerable opportunities for public opinion, social movements, and interest groups to shape the outcome of pending legislation. A president must always be on guard to counteract such influences.

Accessing Congress

The very organization of Congress facilitates inputs from constituency groups. Although not representative of the plurality of society, frequent elections open access points to the Congress allowing ethnic, religious, racial, and other minorities to bring their grievances before the legislative assembly. Individual spokespersons have articulated many of society's pressing interests including African American Congressman Ronald V. Dellums (D–Calif.) who gave voice to civil rights and Representative Patricia Schroeder (D–Colo.) who did the same for women's rights. How members of Congress vote on abortion legislation is affected by their religious background, with Catholics generally opposed to it.[46]

Senators and representatives are recruited, nominated, and elected by local and state parties or their own personal organizations, which are more attuned to constituency opinions than to the needs of the president. An influential study argues that reelection is the primary motivation of members of Congress,[47] and that all-consuming focus—reelection—encourages them to strive for an electorally safe district by directly servicing their constituents.[48]

An insightful essay by legislative scholar Michael Mezey argues that students of the presidency have a fundamentally different view of the lawmaking process than congressional scholars.[49] Analysts of the presidency expect him to dominate Congress, whereas experts on the legislative process know the White House is only one, and hardly the most important, influence on legislative voting behavior.

To assess presidential leadership over Congress, presidency scholars examine a president's popular vote as an expression of an electoral mandate to pursue a certain agenda, his approval ratings at the time when roll calls are taken, and the party identification of each member of Congress.

This scholarship also takes account of presidential skill at legislative relations, but George Edwards argues persuasively that any alleged skills operate "at the margins" of legislative leadership.[50]

In their research, congressional scholars have been guided by their understanding that all senators or representatives are constrained by a "field of forces," or political pressures, from their attitudes about the issue in question, their constituencies, other legislative colleagues, party leaders, their staff, interest groups, and the White House.[51] Bond and Fleisher undertook to evaluate these divergent "presidency-centered" and "Congress-centered" models, and their results validated the latter by a wide margin. As Bond and Fleisher conclude,

> [O]ur explanation of presidential success on floor votes centers on the shared preferences between a president and the Congress defined by the partisan-ideological predisposition of the members. The election of a president advocating policies that run against congressional predispositions generates substantial conflict. While unified party control is no guarantee of success on any given vote, the probability of defeat increases significantly when the branches are controlled by different parties. From this perspective, the selection of one bundle of policy preferences over a competing set of policies has a major impact on presidential-congressional relations.[52]

In other words, the party and ideological makeup of Congress is the most important predictor of long-term success, but elections determine the composition of the legislative branch, and a presidential candidate, even when the incumbent, does not have much impact on whether certain types of Democrats or Republicans win office. If anything, evidence shows that presidents have far shorter electoral coattails than was the case in the 1930s and 1940s. Bill Clinton won reelection by eight percentage points, but the Republicans retained their control of both houses of Congress.

Interests

To establish a working majority behind his legislative program, a president tries to cooperate with the party leadership in Congress. In the 1950s, for example, Senate Majority Leader Lyndon Johnson did not exploit his position for partisan advantage because he believed he had a responsibility to help Dwight Eisenhower govern the country. When Johnson became president, he expected Everett McKinley Dirksen (R–Ill.), the Senate Minority Leader, to rally Republican senators behind his civil rights program. Many political scientists believe parties ameliorate the worst effects of factionalism through their efforts to create a majority coalition. To the degree that party in Congress is weakened, the influence of special interests will be strengthened.

A *Time* essay in 1978 focused on "the startling increase in the influence of special interest lobbies" in Congress and suggested this development was the primary reason why so many of President Carter's proposals had been defeated or stalled.[53] Interest groups of all kinds have increased steadily. Among the 22,289 nonprofit associations in 1990, the largest organizations have professional staffs in Washington, D.C., who monitor legislative developments.[54] Likely the number of lobbyists on Capitol Hill is higher because the definition of a lobbyist changes. According to the head of the American League of Lobbyists, in 1989 some 47,000 lawyers and 11,500 PR specialists as well as paid Washington consultants engaged in what one would call lobbying, yet only 6,000 register annually as lobbyists.[55] By another recent estimate, approximately 70 percent of the 14,500 persons mentioned in *Washington Representatives*[56] are not formally listed as lobbyists.[57]

Legislators are influenced by special interests because they provide the financial and personnel resources needed to wage a campaign for reelection. Organized interests like labor unions, which were especially mobilized in 1996 to defeat the first-term Republicans elected to office, trade associations, and professional groups have always been capable of devoting resources to protect their legislative interests. The dimensions of this problem have taken a quantum jump with the rise of political action committees (PACs) coupled with the escalation in campaign costs. In the 1960s and 1970s there were relatively few PACs—608 in 1974 but PACs increased to 4,430 in 1995–1996,[58] and they increased their contributions to members of Congress from $8.5 million in 1972 to more than $124.2 million in 1995–1996.[59] Unlike presidential campaigns, no public funding is available for congressional elections, making PAC funds virtually essential to every member of Congress.

Thus the two factors strongly affecting the likelihood that a president can exert any power—decision making and now public inputs—work to his distinct disadvantage as legislative leader. Nor is the situation much improved when we consider his ability to exploit legislative expertise.

EXPERTISE

No president can monopolize information and expert opinion in the role of legislative leader. Nonetheless, a president can gain some leverage over Congress by using staffers who specialize in legislative liaison and by manipulating the information sent to Congress by the executive branch. In the case of highly technical and complex legislation, expertise is relevant. When Congress appropriates funds for the space shuttle, for example, it can only assume the National Aeronautics and Space Administration (NASA) has the capability to actually launch it. In a famous episode that led to structural reform, David Stockman, Reagan's director of the Office of Management and Budget, thoroughly dominated the 1981 budgetary debate, promising the Reagan tax cut, increasing military spending while at the same time decreasing domestic expenditures. The result, Stockman maintained, would be a balanced budget by the end of his first term. Members of Congress did not know that Stockman had altered the statistics by revising the economic assumptions in his computer forecasts until he finally produced, on paper, the balanced budget. That manipulation of economic forecasts and budgetary estimates led Congress to consult its own experts in the Congressional Budget Office (CBO), which generally had more accurate economic forecasts than the OMB during the 1980s.

Political scientist David Price, now a Congressman (D–N.C.), in the 1970s studied fourteen major bills to assess the policy role of the Congress, executive branch, and special interests in the various stages of program development.[60] He found that the executive had a decisive advantage for "information gathering." Congress does have alternative sources of technical advice, however, in such congressional agencies as the CBO, Congressional Research Service (CRS), General Accounting Office (GAO), and, prior to the 104th Congress, the Office of Technology Assessment (OTA).

Office of Congressional Relations (OCR)

To strengthen their legislative liaison with members of Congress, presidents have come to rely on the Office of Congressional Relations. Its establishment by President Eisenhower in 1953 signaled the further routinization of legislative leadership. For a president to promote his legislative agenda effectively requires continued liaison with OCR staffers who have the requisite knowledge about the legislative process and the substance of legislation. Eisenhower made use of professionals in the OCR who were very familiar with the lawmaking process, yet OCR focused its energies mainly on preventing the enactment of legislation that Eisenhower opposed and on protecting him from demanding members of Congress.[61]

John F. Kennedy, who wanted to make the OCR more proactive to further his legislative agenda, chose the politically astute Lawrence O'Brien to head the agency. O'Brien's model was continued by his successors. As Eric Davis observed,

> The decisions O'Brien made regarding the organization and functioning of the White House Congressional Relations Office established the framework within which the liaison effort was conducted not only in the Kennedy White House, but also under Presidents Johnson, Nixon, and Ford. Indeed, the continuity in the organization and functioning of the liaison staffs across the transition from a Democratic to a Republican administration in 1969 is noteworthy.[62]

Lyndon Johnson, however, could not resist acting as his own legislative liaison because, given his previous experience as Senate Majority Leader, he believed no one else in his administration knew more about Congress. LBJ had the philosophy that the only way to deal with Congress was "continuously, incessantly, and without interruption."[63]

Under Ronald Reagan, the (renamed) Office of Legislative Affairs (OLA) also was effectively orchestrated, first by Max Friedersdorf, formerly Gerald Ford's liaison head, who contributed immeasurably to Reagan's 1981 legislative successes. The president augmented the OLA's efforts by personally contacting congressional Republicans and, just as important, the Reagan administration had a highly focused economic agenda in 1981. The effectiveness of Reagan's liaison team declined after 1986: Democrats won back control of the Senate and Reagan's legislative priorities were more diffuse.

Frederick McClure took charge of the OLA for President Bush, but staffers had their hands full given the often contentious relationship between the president and Congress. Part of the problem was that Bush distanced himself from legislative developments.

In Clinton's first term, the legislative liaison staff played a more limited role. President Clinton in 1995–1996 had to cope with the Republican 104th Congress, making effective legislative contacts more infrequent. Turnover among Clinton's aides included the resignation of two congressional liaisons. Moreover, when Clinton selected former Congressman Leon Panetta (D–Calif.) as his chief of staff and George Stephanopoulos (formerly an aide to House Minority Leader Richard Gephardt, D–Mo.) as a presidential aide, they became the primary contacts with Democratic members of Congress needing liaison with the administration.[64]

Since legislative liaison was institutionalized in 1953, OCR and its successor OLA have performed the same functions under Republican and Democratic presidents. Regular contact with members of Congress at all levels is central to its approach because most presidents want input into the subcommittees, committees, and floor deliberations. OCR tries to assure legislative support for the executive's program and provides information about the president's program to members of Congress. Over the years OCR staffers have coordinated the liaison activities of departmental and agency personnel, including their regular contacts with state and local party leaders and interest groups. When the OCR enjoys close rapport with the president, it is able to speak with greater authority regarding his wishes to members of Congress.

CRISIS

Crisis is an unreliable factor in legislative leadership. The strongest presidents have profited from domestic turmoil, and presidency scholar Louis Koenig reminds us that "in the gravity of the peril, national opinion demands action and the population looks to the President for initiative and brooks no denial."[65] In 1958 a concerned Congress speedily passed the National Defense Education Act to increase educational opportunities for graduate students, a direct response to the Soviet launch of the first Sputnik satellite in 1957. The political crisis after Kennedy's assassination helped President Johnson persuade Congress to pass social-welfare programs that had been stalled during the Kennedy administration. The murder of civil rights leader Martin Luther King, Jr., in 1968 also prompted Congress to finally consider, and approve, an Open Housing Act. Congress also acted quickly when President Reagan requested emergency legislation to stop a nationwide railroad strike in September 1982 that threatened the jobs of over one million people, promised to cost nearly $1 billion a day, and would inconvenience nearly 250,000 commuters across the nation. President Reagan asked Congress to pass a law ordering the 26,000 striking engineers back to work, and Congress did it.

Cooperation between president and Congress during crisis does not always take place because the two may disagree about whether there *is* a crisis and, moreover, weak presidents may be unable to take advantage fully of crisis conditions. The threat of imminent Civil War did little to strengthen James Buchanan's leadership, and the debate over Reconstruction after the Civil War only undermined Andrew Johnson's already faltering leadership in Congress. Nor was Herbert Hoover able to exploit the disastrous beginning of the Great Depression to strengthen his legislative leadership. Even in the midst of the Great Depression and following Franklin Roosevelt's landslide reelection victory in 1936, the constitutional dilemma triggered by the Supreme Court's invalidation of many key New Deal laws was not enough to persuade Congress to approve Roosevelt's controversial court packing plan. Although Democrats held large majorities in both chambers of Congress, enough southern Democrats and Republicans were concerned that Roosevelt's action threatened the separation of powers to defeat his proposal to increase the size of the Supreme Court by adding new pro–New Deal justices.

Thus the impact of crisis on legislative leadership depends on a collective feeling of urgency, a common definition of the situation as a crisis, and a Congress ready to answer the president's initiatives.

The Myth of "100 Days"

The economic collapse of the 1930s Great Depression gave President Roosevelt political leverage to rally his newly elected Democratic Congress into enacting an unprecedented number of laws during the first 100 days, of 1933. In FDR's first 100 days, 15 presidential messages were sent to Congress, 15 major laws were enacted, 10 speeches were delivered, and biweekly press conferences and cabinet meetings were held.[66] The Roosevelt legislative record, however, gave rise to one of the most enduring myths of American politics, one largely perpetuated by the media commentators and political pundits every time a new president is elected. The popular press now expects all presidents to achieve what FDR achieved immediately upon taking office.

But Roosevelt confronted a genuine crisis of historic proportions, whereas his successors have been legislative leaders during essentially normal periods of tranquility and relative prosperity. To impose the FDR 100-days standard on modern presidents is to doom them to legislative failure. Such was the case when the press described President Carter an ineffective legislative leader, a label that stayed with him through his years in office. Even President Clinton had to publicize a laundry list of accomplishments following his first three months in office because of this myth.

Its persistence is yet another manifestation of the inflated presidency today (see Table 2-1), one based on unrealistically high expectations.

This myth can be put to rest by documenting how many bills were signed into law during the first 100 days of each administration from 1933 to 1993 (Table 7-6). Legislative output during Franklin Roosevelt's first three months and under Harry Truman during and after World War II was unprecedented. It has never been repeated by any Republican or Democrat since.

Nobody would doubt that the 89th Congress passed Johnson's Great Society legislation, but most of his landmark legislation was not passed during the first 100 days of his term. There is, in fact, a tendency for more legislation to be enacted during the 100 days of Democrats Kennedy, Carter, and Clinton than the corresponding period for Republicans Nixon, Reagan, and Bush.

Although President Reagan's ability to gain congressional enactment of his plan to reduce income taxes and raise military spending led some observers to make favorable comparisons between him and Franklin Roosevelt, the fact remains that the legislative output under Reagan during his first three months was lower than any modern president including Dwight D. Eisenhower, who as we noted earlier, failed to give Congress a comprehensive legislative program during his first year.

Table 7-6. Myth of the First 100 Days

Year	Public Laws	Joint Resolutions	Total
1933	38	10	48
1937	58	24	82
1941	36	8	44
1945	42	5	47
1949	38	15	53
1953	16	5	21
1957	17	9	26
1961	22	4	26
1965	11	3	14
1969	7	3	10
1973	10	16	26
1977	14	7	21
1981	6	3	9
1985	11	17	28
1989	7	11	18
1993	12	10	22
Average	22	9	31

Source: *United States Statutes at Large* (Washington, DC: U.S. Government Printing Office, various years). Public laws are the acts passed by each Congress, whereas joint resolutions are almost entirely devoted to honorific designations (albeit a few proposed constitutional amendments) such as "National Recognition Day for Veterans of the Vietnam Era" in 1981, "Education Day, U.S.A." in 1985, and "Women's History Month" in 1993. The relevant measure of serious legislation is the number of public laws enacted.

SUMMARY

A president lacks the authority to force Congress to enact his programs and, instead, must rely on political resources to shape the legislative arena to his advantage. The president shapes the congressional agenda through his State of the Union Address, "special" messages to Congress, the executive budget, and the policy agenda he campaigned for. He can expect more votes from members of his legislative party than from the opposition, but no president can rely on unified support from his own partisans. Today, unlike the 1930s and 1940s, divided government is more the norm than the exception. Future presidents may have to develop bipartisan or nonpartisan legislative strategies when dealing with Congress. President Bush failed to do so and, as he began his second term, President Clinton made bipartisan overtures to the GOP-controlled 105th Congress.

Congressional parties are not disciplined organizations like parliamentary parties. Legislators are constantly pulled away from close alignment with their party leaders, but presidents are confronted in the legislative process by voter groups, constituency pressures, and special interests that have become even more powerful since the 1970s. A modern president can rely on his liaison staff to lobby Congress, but he cannot monopolize all the information used by its members to assess the technical and political desirability of his legislative proposals. Crises may strengthen presidential leadership of Congress, but this contingency is not reliable in terms of day-to-day lawmaking. To understand the role of legislative leader, therefore, we must appreciate how the myriad of political conditions increase or decrease the president's influence on the legislative branch to support his programs. Thus the dynamics of legislative leadership go well beyond the formal legal relationship between the president and Congress.

NOTES

1. It was Howard Lee McBain who allegedly used the term "chief legislator" for the first time in his 1927 book, *The Living Constitution* (New York: Macmillan, 1948), pp. 115–118.

2. Edward C. Corwin and Louis W. Koenig, *The Presidency Today* (New York: New York University Press, 1956), p. 83.

3. Arthur Schlesinger, Jr. and Alfred deGrazia, *Congress and the Presidency: Their Role in Modern Times* (Washington, DC: American Enterprise Institute for Public Policy Research, 1967), pp. 4–5.

4. Joseph S. Clark, *Congress: The Sapless Branch* (New York: Harper & Row, 1965).

5. William M. Goldsmith, *The Growth of Presidential Power: A Documented History* (New York: Chelsea House, 1974), vol. 1, p. 347.

6. See James Sterling Young, *The Washington Community, 1800–1828* (New York: Columbia University Press, 1966), p. 147.

7. Robert M. Johnstone, Jr., *Jefferson and the Presidency: Leadership in the Young Republic* (Ithaca, NY: Cornell University Press, 1978), p. 133.

8. James W. Davis and Delbert Ringquist, *The President and Congress: Toward New Power Balance* (Woodbury, NY: Barron's Educational Series, 1975), p. 21.

9. James D. Richardson, *Messages and Papers of the Presidents* (Washington, DC: U.S. Government Printing Office, 1897), vol. 1, pp. 331–332.

10. Noble E. Cunningham, Jr., *The Process of Government under Jefferson* (Princeton, NJ: Princeton University Press, 1978), p. 192.

11. "Rules and Orders for Conducting Business in the House of Representatives," U.S. Congress, *House Journal* (Dec. 17, 1805), vol. 5, p. 200.

12. Noble E. Cunningham, *The Jeffersonian Republicans in Power, 1801–1809* (Chapel Hill: University of North Carolina Press, 1963), p. 74.

13. See the seminal work by Nelson W. Polsby on this topic, "The Institutionalization of the U.S. House of Representatives," *The American Political Science Review* (March 1968), pp. 144–168.

14. Milton Cummings, ed., *The National Election of 1964* (Washington, DC: The Brookings Institution, 1966), pp. 247–248.

15. Johnson's five-year average approval rating, however, was only 56 percent.

16. See Ralph K. Huitt, "White House Channels to the Hill," in Harvey G. Mansfield, Sr., ed., *Congress against the President* (New York: Praeger, 1975), p. 263.

17. George Edwards, one of those critics, argued that Kennedy actually had more support from northern Democrats than Johnson did, in spite of the increased number of liberals elected in 1964. Obviously Edwards's analysis deemphasizes the importance of a president's personal skills as a factor underlying effectiveness in this role George C. Edwards III, "Presidential Legislative Skills as a Source of Influence in Congress," *Presidential Studies Quarterly* (Spring 1980), pp. 220–222.

18. Ibid., p. 214.

19. Gary M. Fink, *Prelude to the Presidency: The Political Character and Legislative Leadership Style of Governor Jimmy Carter* (Westport, CT: Greenwood Press, 1980), p. 108.

20. *Washington Post*, (Nov. 13, 1977), p. B12 in Robert E. DiClerico, *The American President*, 3rd ed. (Englewood Cliffs, NJ: Prentice Hall, 1990), p. 72.

21. Quoted in Richard E. Cohen, "The Carter-Congress Rift—Who's Really to Blame," *National Journal* (April 22, 1978), p. 630.

22. Roger H. Davidson, *The Postreform Congress* (New York: St. Martin's Press, 1992).

23. Charles Mohr, "Carter's First Nine Months: Charges of Ineptitude Rise," *New York Times* (Oct. 23, 1977), p. 36.

24. Larry Light, "White House Lobby Gets Its Act Together," *Congressional Quarterly Weekly Report* (Feb. 3, 1979), p. 200.

25. See *Congressional Quarterly Almanac, 1989*, pp. 7-C, 8-C, 9-C in Ryan J. Barilleaux and Mary E. Stuckey,eds., *Leadership and the Bush Presidency* (Westport, CT: Praeger,1992), p. 64.

26. Adam Clymer, "Bills Sent to Bush as 102d Congress Wraps Up Its Work," *New York Times* (Oct. 9, 1992), p. A1.

27. See Chuck Alston, "Bush Crusades on Many Fronts to Retake President's Turf," *Congressional Quarterly Weekly Report* (Feb. 3, 1990), p. 291.

28. See "Veto Cloud Loomed Large over 1992 Floor Fights," *Congressional Quarterly Weekly Review* (Dec. 19, 1992), p. 3854.

29. Robert J. Spitzer, *The Presidential Veto* (Albany, NY: SUNY Press, 1988), p. 145.

30. Phillip A. Davis, "Politics, Drop in Senate Support Put Bush's Ratings in Cellar," *Congressional Quarterly Weekly Report* (Dec. 19, 1992), p. 3841.

31. Helen Dewar, "The Politics of Gridlock," *Washington Post National Weekly Edition* (Aug. 10–16, 1992), p. 6.

32. Charles O. Jones, *The Trusteeship Presidency: Jimmy Carter and the United States Congress* (Baton Rouge: Louisiana State University Press, 1988).

33. Richard A. Watson, *Presidential Vetoes and Public Policy* (Lawrence: University Press of Kansas, 1993), pp. 166–167.

34. "Election Watch," *Salt Lake Tribune* (March 31, 1996), p. A21.

35. See Jerry Gray, "How It Works: Using the Line-Item Veto," *New York Times* (March 29, 1996), p. A11.

36. Lawrence H. Chamberlain, *The President, Congress and Legislation* (New York: Columbia University Press, 1946).

37. Ibid., p. 454. Another 10 percent of the bills were classified by Chamberlain as "Pressure Group Influence Preponderant."

38. Ronald C. Moe and Steven C. Teal, "Congress as Policy-Maker: A Necessary Reappraisal," *Political Science Quarterly* (Sept. 1970), pp. 443–470.

39. William M. Goldsmith, *The Growth of Presidential Power: A Documented History* (New York: Chelsea House, 1974), vol. 3, p. 1400.

40. The remaining 3 percent was attributed to interest group influence. Ibid.

41. Aaron Wildavsky, "The Two Presidencies," *Trans-Action* (Dec. 1966), pp. 7–14.

42. Lance T. LeLoup and Steven A. Shull, "Congress versus the Executive: The Two Presidencies' Reconsidered," *Social Science Quarterly* (March 1979), pp. 704–719.

43. Richard L. Berke, "Courting Congress Nonstop, Clinton Looks for an Alliance," *New York Times* (March 8, 1993), p. A1.

44. David R. Mayhew, *Divided We Govern* (New Haven, CT: Yale University Press, 1991).

45. Charles O. Jones, *The Presidency in a Separated System* (Washington, DC: The Brookings Institution, 1994), p. 297.

46. Raymond Tatalovich and David Schier, "The Persistence of Ideological Cleavage in Voting on Abortion Legislation in the House of Representatives, 1973–1988," *American Politics Quarterly* 21 (1993), pp. 125–139.

47. Richard E. Fenno, Jr., *Home Style* (Boston: Little, Brown, 1978).

48. Morris P. Fiorina, *Congress: Keystone of the Washington Establishment* (New Haven, CT: Yale University Press, 1977).

49. Michael L. Mezey, "The President and the Congress: A Review Article," *Legislative Studies Quarterly* 10 (1985), pp. 519–536.

50. George C. Edwards, III, *At the Margins: Presidential Leadership of Congress* (New Haven, CT: Yale University Press, 1989).

51. John W. Kingdon, *Congressmen's Voting Decisions*, 3rd ed. (Ann Arbor: University of Michigan Press, 1989).

52. Jon R. Bond and Richard Fleisher, *The President in the Legislative Arena* (Chicago: University of Chicago Press, 1990), p. 230.

53. See "The Swarming Lobbyists," *Time* (Aug. 7, 1978), pp. 14–22.

54. U.S. Bureau of Census, *Statistical Abstract of the United States, 1991*, 11th ed. (Washington, DC: U.S. Government Printing Office, 1991), p. 786.

55. See Marcus D. Rosenbaum, *Editorial Research Reports* 2 (23) (Dec. 15, 1989) (Washington, DC: Congressional Quarterly, 1989), p. 699.

56. Arthur C. Close,ed., *Washington Representatives* (Washington, DC: Columbia Books, 1991), p. 3.

57. See "*Lobbying:* Committee Moves to Tighten Registration Loopholes," *Congressional Quarterly Weekly Report* (June 27, 1992), p. 1858.

58. For the 1974 figure, see Federal Election commission press release, January 17, 1990, from M. Margaret Conway, "PACs in the Political Process," in Allan J. Cigler and Burdett A. Loomis, *Interest Group Politics*, 3rd ed. (Washington, DC: Congressional Quarterly, 1991), p. 200; for the 1995–1996 figure, see Federal Election Commission News Release, September 27, 1996, "1995–96 PAC Contributions Increase $17 Million over 1993–94," at http://www.fec.gov/press/pac1.8tx.htm, p. 1.

59. For the 1974 figure, see Conway, "PACs in the Political Process," p. 205; for the 1995–1996 figure see Federal Election Commission News Release, September 27, 1996, "PAC Financial election Commission News Release, September 27, 1996, "PAC Financial Activity," p. 1 at http://www.fec.gov/press/pace 1.htm.

60. David Price, *Who Makes the Laws?* (Cambridge, MA: Schenkman, 1972), table 7, pp. 290–291.

61. Eric L. Davis, *Building Presidential Coalitions in Congress: Legislative Liaison in the Johnson White House*,Ph.D. diss., Stanford University, 1977, p. 33.

62. Eric L. Davis, "Congressional Liaison: The People and the Institutions," in Anthony King, ed., *Both Ends of the Avenue* (Washington, DC: American Enterprise Institute, 1983),p. 62.

63. Doris Kearns, *Lyndon Johnson and the American Dream* (New York: Harper & Row, 1976), pp. 236–237.

64. Jennifer Senior, "White House Liaison Fights Irrelevance," *The Hill*. Capitol Hill Publishing, January 10, 1996, p. 1. Lexis source.

65. Robert Sherrill, *Why They Call It Politics* (New York: Harcourt Brace Jovanovich, 1972), p. 67.

66. Arthur Schlesinger, Jr., *The Coming of the New Deal* (Boston: Houghton Mifflin, 1959), pp. 20–21.

8

Insight on Legislative Leader: Clinton and Health Care Reform

Health care first became an issue in 1992 in a special election for U.S. Senate in Pennsylvania when an unknown Democrat, Harris Wofford, defeated former governor and sitting U.S. attorney general Richard Thornburg, who was the overwhelming favorite. After trailing in the polls by forty points, Wofford focused his campaign efforts on the sole issue of health care, which turned the race around. Intentionally vague on the details, he called for universal health care coverage, rallying from seemingly inevitable defeat to finish with 55 percent of the vote. Health care was also the most important domestic issue coming out of the 1992 presidential election. As reflected in national polls in the early 1990s, almost 90 percent of Americans wanted the health care system fundamentally changed or completely rebuilt,[1] a finding that remained constant through the 1992 campaign period and influenced presidential choice among the electorate.[2] It became in essence Bill Clinton's issue. With the White House and both houses of Congress under Democratic control, how could Bill Clinton fail to obtain health care reform?

By 1994 health care became the "first or second most important non-economic problem" facing the nation.[3] It was a "countable problem" with "systemic indicators " of a failing health care system.[4] The number of uninsured Americans had reached 35 million by 1991, the proportion of gross national product (GNP) devoted to health care was greater than 14 percent, and health care costs were forecast to exceed $1.6 trillion by the year 2000.[5]

The 103rd Congress began with high expectations for its work with the Clinton administration on health care reform. One enthusiastic congressman even suggested this anticipated working relationship posed "a real opportunity to have an impact on the future of the country."[6] The president moved cautiously, not wanting to repeat the problems Jimmy Carter had had with Congress and hoping to avoid self-inflicted damage in his working relationship with the Hill.[7]

Surprisingly, the president had numerous early allies in developing the health care issue. The American Medical Association (AMA) viewed reform as a way to free physicians from the constraints of insurance companies. No mention was made about the dangers of so-called socialized medicine that had dominated the Medicaid debates of the 1960s. Labor unions had supported the idea of national health insurance for a number of years. Smaller insurance companies, facing possible extinction as health maintenance organizations (HMOs) continued to control more and more of the market, also supported the proposed reform. Big business, which provided the majority of health care benefits to the nation's work force, realized the disproportionate burden they were carrying under the present system. Even the conservative forces of the U.S. Chamber of Commerce, opposed to all forms and functions of welfare, supported health care reform for a time.[8] Such political opponents as Newt Gingrich (R–Ga.) lent his support as well, noting that "it reminds me of *The Music Man*—I have the same sense of excitement."[9] How then did health care reform fail to materialize? It was supposed to be a hallmark of Clinton's presidency; instead, it remains the unfinished and unsolved problem of his administration to date.

Clinton decided to use his *authority* to take an aggressive tack by making health care, per his campaign promise, an early agenda item of his administration. But it was eight months into his first term before he delivered his health care speech before the Congress, which was not followed promptly by proposed legislation. That would have to wait. In the interim, White House staffers seemed unprepared to answer the question "Where is the legislation?"[10] The call for a new national mandate on health that set a bipartisan tone after a summer of heated budget battles was severely hampered by the decision to delay legislation.

His health care speech of September 22 (1993) given to Congress and the nation, proposed legislation that would focus on six principles: security, simplicity, savings, choice, quality, and responsibility. Clinton's speech, considered at the time the most important of his presidency, served as a test of his power vis-à-vis Congress and called for universal health care coverage. Clinton outlined the parameters for health care reform, developing a sense of optimism and common purpose in Congress. As reported, Clinton succeeded in convincing members of Congress that the issue was not whether to overhaul the health care system, but how to do it. In doing so, "he created a sense that change is inevitable" and there were reports that Democrats and Republicans alike agreed on his outline.[11] Once the speech was delivered, Clinton ran into a number of difficulties. He was unable to help people understand the proposal, nor could he generate the bipartisan support he needed for major policy initiatives as his predecessors had. Even with a majority of Congress of his party, Clinton could not manifest his legislative prerogative into support that could pass health care reform.[12] He did appoint a task force to develop the legislation. The White House Task Force on National Health Care Reform, chaired by First Lady Hillary Rodham Clinton and Clinton supporter Ira Magaziner, was asked to develop a plan in the president's first 100 days. One of the primary problems with this selection was that none of the principals had experience with the presidential advisory process, a lack of experience that would prove to be the task force's downfall in many ways.[13]

The presidential advisory system permits the president to appoint the people best able to articulate and champion his ideas and does not require the approval of the Senate. Advisory systems also help communicate these ideas to important constituencies that can assist in ensuring the success of the president's proposals and prepare for a defense against a proposals' critics.[14] On the downside, advisors can isolate the president from reality and from the critics. Moreover, an advisory group may also become a policy advocate in its own right as the process moves along, losing sight of some of the original goals and intent. The system set up under the Task Force on National Health Care Reform resulted in an uncontrollable force of five hundred members that came from inside and outside of government. The sizable membership was divided into a number of working groups to carry out their mandate. Attempts to keep membership and activities of the working groups secret was challenged as a violation of federal law, and the assumption that the president could develop input insulated from Congress and the public quickly eroded Clinton's leadership position.[15] The proposed legislation emerged after a laborious and contentious five months during which time the task force's credibility was called into question. No support for the forthcoming proposals was developed outside the task force and the president's position drifted from his campaign image as a centrist new Democrat, providing Congress a target on which to focus in the months following the delivery of the 1,350-page plan—the proposed Health Care Security Act of October 1993.[16]

The plan itself focused on universal coverage, cost containment, benefit packages, a revamping of the insurance system, mandatory health alliances, and a broad array of taxes to fund the proposal (see Table 8-1); it was, indeed, a "gold-plated" package that was unconvincing to a set of interests that had shifted their previous support into ardent opposition.[17]

The White House focused on the 15 percent of the American public without access to health care, families with incomes in the $15,000 to $30,000 range. The fears of the middle class about this plan related to rising health care costs and government control of health care. Two of their other concerns—loss of coverage and rationing of services—were not emphasized in the task force's campaign.[18] This decision-making mode tried to impose a broad activist approach to the health care problem on an increasingly conservative Congress that had favored incremental changes over sweeping reform in the previous decades.

Using Mrs. Clinton to represent the president before Congress was deemed a good decision at first. However, the failure to produce legislation and the questions about her Arkansas law practice encouraged a backlash against the First Lady precipitated by those who reported they had not voted for her and felt she should not play such a role.

Mrs. Clinton's nature and demeanor was also a concern to some people. Clearly, Mrs. Clinton is unlike previous presidents' wives—with the possible exception of Eleanor Roosevelt—and the segment of the popula-

Table 8-1. Basic Provisions of the Clinton Health Care Plan

Provision	Description
Universal Coverage	Guaranteed coverage for all Americans by 1998.
Cost Containment	Limit the growth in insurance premiums using a national rate set by a health board.
Benefits	Package of benefits including doctor visits, hospital care, prescription drug and necessary mental care.
	Limited home health care, preventive care, health care, reproductive care and abortion.
Insurance Changes	Prohibit insurance companies from refusing coverage.
	Equality in rating to ensure equal fees regardless of age, gender, and so on.
Mandatory Alliances	Except for workers in firms with more than five thousand employees, all insurance would be purchased through regional health alliances. The alliances would be established by states and contract services through existing health plans.
Taxes	Several new taxes, including 75 cents increase on a pack of cigarettes, 1 percent payroll tax on large companies not participating in health alliances, taxes on alliances to increase academic health centers.

tion discomforted by a well-educated, assertive, and intelligent First Lady, who could hold her own and claim praise among members of Congress,[19] expressed their concerns by opposing the task force's health care proposals. In the aftermath of the health care battles, Hillary Rodham Clinton became a more subdued First Lady in the public realm, although in the private realm she remained a strong advisor to the president.

Another miscalculation on the part of the president was the creation of the task force under the direction of Mrs. Clinton and Ira Magaziner instead of using the existing structures of the Department of Health and Human Services, the National Institute of Health, or other health-related agencies.[20] Instead, a 500-member task force was put in place and the value of a small decision group, capable of reaching consensus in a timely fashion, was overshadowed by a new behemoth of an organization at a time when concern for downsizing government was reaching a feverish pitch. The task force membership, the 535 members of Congress, the many decision-makers in the Executive branch, and the committee staff in Congress added up to far too many people involved in the decision making about health care. The support available in existing agency structures could not be leveraged at a critical time because of their early exclusion from the process.

An air of aloofness and secrecy also surrounded the task force: key health care leaders were not involved or kept abreast of the workings of the group. An image problem consequently developed about the task force as early supporters such as labor unions became disenfranchised and shifted their interests to other issues.

The decision to characterize the pharmaceutical industry and health insurance providers as greedy and to justify a tax increase on the wealthy in 1993 also backfired when it was recast into big government demanding more from business. Early supporters in these industries and among special interests, such as the National Federation of Independent Businesses (NFIB), quickly took offense and retreated from the health care proposals.[21] The decision to operate the task force in its own sphere and not take special interest concerns into account presented a coordination and acceptability problem from which the program never recovered. Moreover, not consulting with moderates in Congress pushed some would-be supporters away from overall support of a more conservative set of plans that were developed and put forward during 1994. Political winds suggested a distancing from the president because of the glacial pace of health care reform, and the conservative mood of the nation seemed to predominate as the midterm elections of 1994 loomed on the horizon.[22]

Clinton's choice of Ira Magaziner to cochair the task force seemed to imply that the president understood the level of *expertise* that would be needed in the months ahead. Magaziner was considered one of the quintessential "policy wonks" of the Clinton era, a new breed of technocrat focused on process and scientific analyses to support value preferences.[23] But the art of the policy process was lost on Magaziner, who, despite his expertise, could not build a coalition among early supporters, such as the AMA, or share control of the process.

In the House, alternative plans challenged the president's expertise, especially among single-payer advocates who favored universal coverage, freedom to choose physicians, and contained costs—ideas supported by 70 percent of the American public.[24] The White House's reluctance to support a more bipartisan option resulted in pitting White House experts against the industry and the Hill.[25] Clinton's team failed to realize that their opposition was equal in its set of expert resources. The task force relied on public deference to the White House's experts, and by doing so did not engage in a public debate that would draw on the rationale for his proposal. Treating the proposal as a campaign based on promises of security and a better tomorrow, expertise became lost as the process rapidly became politicized.[26]

The inability to use the early momentum generated from more than two days of personal lobbying of Congress by Clinton, who had brought 250 talk-show hosts from around the country to the White House in order to brief them on the program, led to an erosion of the veil of expertise surrounding the task force. With 59 percent of the polity in support of the plan in late September 1993, it seemed as if the decision was not to overhaul health care, but how to complete the plan.[27]

The 500-member task force was still laboring through its process during this period. Although the president was stumping for the program, a completed program never appeared. The task force turned inward. It did not rely on experts from the Department of Health and Human Services nor from Congress. As we noted earlier the task force was thus seen as uncooperative and not part of a consensus-building process that would use all forms of *expertise* in building toward major policy change.

The role of the First Lady also complicated the matter. Was she an expert on health care, a policy wonk, or a power symbol from 1600 Pennsylvania Avenue? As one report notes, she was another "source of discomfort." Some "found her intimidating—hard to argue with and uninterested in the points they made."[28] She was viewed as apart from the rest of the task force members and unwilling to compromise on her expectations. Mrs. Clinton's identity with the program also made it difficult for Congress to be critical. Challenges came, instead, to the Secretary of Health and Human Services, Donna Shalala, creating bad feelings between the secretary and the task force.[29] Hillary Rodham Clinton's supposed expertise never seemed to materialize, and close viewers began to doubt her role.

In addition, a clash between experts developed as Magaziner and Mrs. Clinton also excluded the insurance industry, physicians' groups and health care administrators. The task force leadership seemed in disarray, out of control. The Clintons were viewed as inflexible, and Mrs. Clinton was seen as inexperienced in the process itself as her affect swung between conciliatory and confrontational. As more moderate political advisors began to see the policy process was in trouble, it also became apparent that the president was paying less heed to advice from his political insiders than advice from Magaziner and his wife. He thus adopted a plan that was considered implausible to pass in Congress.[30] In retrospect, one White House staffer noted, "We would have been in the reality zone a long time ago" if not for Mrs. Clinton and her "health care cult."[31]

In hindsight, it appears that simple matters were unattended to and became major chinks in the thin armor of the White House. By not sending the president to the AMA's annual meeting in New Orleans, the major support needed from the nation's physicians became mired in misinformation and a groundswell of opposition from what had early on been a major supporting group.[32] By ignoring their many requests for updates on the task force's progress, an adversarial relationship was created with key media correspondents. A daily update would have allowed for trial balloons, control of the information flow, and a working relationship.

The complexity of the issue also made it a matter of one expert contending with another. The complexity of the proposal meant no one was sure they understood what was going on, even the most ardent supporters. Key legislators reported they too were in a conundrum, unable to finesse the issue and faced with the political reality of having to explain it to every one of their constituents.[33] This was the sort of issue that involved the entire nation and many *decision-makers,* and no one knew where the proposal would really lead. In Congress, the battle spawned a set of turf wars as committees began to examine the plans' impact based on their jurisdictions. Six different House committees examined each issue of the health care bill including Ways and Means that looked at the taxing and Medicare sections; Energy and Commerce that examined the Medicaid,

general revenue, insurance, and malpractice sections; Education and Labor that worked on the employer benefits section; Judiciary that handled
the malpractice section; Post Office and Civil Service that examined the
federal employees segment; and Government Operations that attended to
the new agencies section. In the Senate, five standing committees considered different parts of the health care bill including the Finance Committee that made recommendations on the taxes, Medicare, and Medicaid
segments; Labor and Human Resources that looked at the general revenues section; Commerce, Science, and Transportation that scrutinized
the insurance and malpractice sections of the bill; Labor and Human Resources that considered employer benefits; Judiciary that handled the
malpractice section; and Government Affairs that probed the federal employees issue and the new agencies section.

The level of distrust, stemming from the general level of cynicism
about government, grew as the 1994 elections got closer, compounding
the problem. Seizing his opportunity, Newt Gingrich, then minority
House whip, realized he now had a window of opportunity and an issue
to hang around the Democrats and the president during the 1994 election.
Tirelessly he led the opposition in the House, focusing considerable attention on special interest groups that were unsure of the outcomes and
complexity of the legislation. Key among these groups was the AMA,
whose 450 delegates were all contacted by Gingrich and, in time, became
supportive of the Gingrich position.[34] The president, without question,
had the resources to offset Gingrich, but he never used them, waiting instead for public support for his position, which never materialized.[35] Opponents continued to chip away at specifics, shifting the debate away from
the original concern of a health care system overhaul.

In the end, it could be argued that none of the government experts got
the problem properly focused. The experts began to operate in the interest of those they represented, not in the interest of the public. The National
Health Care Task Force was not simply another group of experts, but
many of the same people who had a role in creating the nation's health
care crisis. The subgovernment, or "iron triangle" of special interests and
government sympathizers dominated the process.[36] No real Democratic
approach to the problem resulted. The power structure stayed intact; the
experts went on to another series of problems and the chairs around the
table simply were reordered. Given the magnitude of the health care problem facing the nation, the final result could be likened to rearranging the
deck chairs on the *Titanic*.

If everyone wanted health care reform, why did it not occur? Was the
public ready for health care reform and was the president ready to use the
public's interest to generate the support he needed to forward his proposal? In midsummer 1994 when the legislation was before Congress,
eight out of ten Americans polled remained strongly in favor of a health
care plan and continued to endorse universal coverage.[37] Why then was
the power of *public input* not a force to bear on Congress that would lead
to the passage of legislation?

A major concern centered on the expense of the proposal, with the general public preferring taxes that would not cover the proposed plan's costs, yet still favoring the concept.[38] Polls indicated overwhelming public support throughout the debate, but many believed their taxes would increase and their own health care costs would rise.[39] Thus public input in support of the president was soft and provided fodder for an opposition case based on the anxieties elaborated by the public.

The apex of public support was the period immediately following the president's September 22, 1993, speech to the joint session of Congress and during the time Mrs. Clinton was testifying before congressional committees.[40] But before the plan was submitted to Congress, support began to wane and the previously discussed perceptions that the task force itself was in disarray did not help build further support. The previous year 54 percent of voters had reported they preferred lower taxes and fewer services from government. The health care proposal seemed counter to this preference. Clinton did not have an election mandate, or even the impression of a mandate that other presidents had enjoyed, and he was in no position to use public support to coerce Congress into responding boldly with quick action on health care reform. The public's position on government expenditures and fewer governmental services was, as George C. Edwards notes, hardly the thrust preferred by an activist Democratic president.[41]

Clinton's use of a campaign approach to sell his health care plan to the polity, in which the president took legislative leadership directly to the people, was a first in many ways. Yet despite his success in this format, he could not take the momentum and rally it into a solidified public input back to the Congress.[42] The going public strategy ideally would have offset actions by special interests, but the Clinton team was unable to coordinate the timing between Clinton's road trips and the policy process.[43] The timing was so far off that by the time the plan arrived in Congress, the public had tired of the issue. Public support, which had been in the 80 percent range earlier in the health care process, was now 45 percent in support when the final 1,342 page bill—the Health Care Security Act—arrived on the Hill on October 27, 1993, nine months after Hillary Rodham Clinton had been appointed with the task of developing legislation in 100 days.

The public's lack of focus was made worse by the confusing details of the plan. The public's interest in policy issues is often a function of its ability to understand the outcomes. Public input in technical issue areas is hampered as complexity increases,[44] and the administration's proposal was so massive and so complicated that the people felt excluded from the process. The debate over health care costs alone was overwhelming. Hit by attacks and counterattacks in the media, the public was not informed that the real rising costs of health care were not in provider services, but in the increasing technology.[45] Thus by August 1994 only 39 percent of Americans favored the Clinton proposal; 48 percent opposed it.[46] In September 1994 Clinton's public approval rating for managing the health care issue—his highest priority—was 36 percent in support and 60 percent opposed.[47] In addition, the Clintons were being maligned for their investments, their personal lives, and, by some, for their self-righteousness, arrogance, and hypocritical stances.[48] Coupled with the public's skepticism and distrust of politicians, which was reaching a feverish pitch as the midterm election grew closer, public input had shifted almost 50 percent in less than two years, from 80 percent support in 1992 to 30 percent support by August 1994.[49]

The health care *crisis* that faced the nation and drew attention during the 1992 election was, and remains, a national dilemma. Opposition to the Clinton plan resulted in the largest nonelection expenditures by special interest groups. Advertising by opponents exceeded $60 million, more than the combined candidate costs of the 1992 presidential campaign.[50] Opponents outspent supporters by two to one, leaving the White House unprepared for an organized response. The White House was unable to exploit the crisis variable to overcome the narrow appeals of special interests that were more effectively conveying their messages to the public. It was an opportunity lost, and the opportunity may not come again any time soon.

Special interests were organized and beating on the doors of Congress before the White House recognized the magnitude of its campaign. The National Federation of Independent Businesses (NFIB), among others, organized its members to contact their elected officials in Washington and in their district offices. Major health care actors, such as the AMA and many insurance companies, were unsure where they stood on the plan, but rather than court their favor, the White House seemed to draw into a shell, letting special interests control the agenda.

The White House, in retrospect, was in disarray. The tools of the political campaign resulted in the health care industry spending over $300 million during the time frame encompassed by the debate in Congress.[51] The protection of the status quo became sacrosanct for the opposition, and the move to stop health care reform resulted in a series of miscues from the White House including the First Lady's verbal assault on the negative television ads. The advertisements became so critical to the opposition's growing support and the loss of support for the plan that Mrs. Clinton lashed out, stating, "They have the gall to run TV ads that there is a better way, the very industry that brought us to the brink of bankruptcy because of the way they financed health care."[52] The president, with no other strategy in mind, joined in these criticisms, an approach that backfired on the White House, heightening the sense of crisis and completely undercutting Mrs. Clinton's leadership potential. Moreover, as Graham Wilson points out, the naïveté of the Clintons included a failure to understand Newman's law, "that every dollar of what some people call waste is someone else's income."[53]

The confusion in the fall of 1993 and into 1994 left Bill Clinton emptyhanded and, in turn, left Congress empty-handed. Congressional attempts to forward alternatives also failed to materialize any meaningful alternative support either in Congress or from the White House. Even task force cochair Magaziner left the scene, claiming that the politics of health care reform was not his task,[54] and Democratic senator Patrick Moynihan threatened to hold health care hostage in the Senate Finance Committee.[55] As PACS contributed $26 million to congressional candidates,[56] Republicans in Congress gained control of the agenda, forcing Democrats to distance themselves from the president in order to save their own careers. By late September, Senator Mitchell, who was to champion the bill for the president before retiring, announced the legislation was dead for the 103rd Congress.[57] Consultants for the opposition—the new force in the policy process—had overturned what had appeared to be an assured legislative success for Bill Clinton. Instead, it became a legislative low point in his first term.

Bill Clinton was not the first president to fail in trying to provide universal health care. Harry Truman repeatedly failed to get a plan approved every time he proposed one in the late 1940s and early 1950s. John F. Kennedy could not get Medicare out of committees in Congress and to the floor for a vote. Lyndon Johnson, a champion legislator, had to make major compromises and lost a considerable amount of his clout on the Hill to get Medicare through Congress in 1965. Likewise, both Richard Nixon and Gerald Ford failed in their efforts to push universal employer-based health plans through Congress.[58]

The health care reform debacle shows that the best laid plans do not always result in legislation. In this instance Clinton found, as legislative leader, his authority was inadequate to overcome the interest group opposition and public opposition from citizens who wanted health care, but never fully supported the Clinton plan, indicating how flawed the decision calculus was at many points in the process. Despite the fact he intended to make health care an early agenda item, delay and ill-timed decisions and a lack of focus allowed other decision-makers to prepare competing proposals that undercut the Administration's plan; moreover, Clinton and staffers found their expertise was undercut by the complexity of their program and public distrust and general cynicism about government and politics. Moreover, the lack of a game plan to offset the opposition—a situation termed by former presidential hopeful Michael Dukakis as "unmatched in American political history"[59]—was yet another reason for the policy failure. For a president to be successful, the president as legislative leader must act in timely fashion, in concert with Congress and special interests, and provide proposals the public can understand; this did not happen. As a result of these miscues, the White House could not sustain the definition of this problem as a crisis and lost political leverage as a result.

Clinton fell victim to his own inflexibility, to the large and complex program, and to what Hillary Rodham Clinton suggested was "paid media and paid direct mail."[60] Any prospect for exploiting a possible health care crisis for legislative leverage, moreover, was lost because the president failed to capitalize on his window of opportunity.

NOTES

1. Robert J. Blendon, Robert Leitman, Ian Morrison, and Karen Donelan, "Satisfaction with Health Systems in Ten Nations," *Health Affairs* 9 (2) (1990), pp. 185–192.

2. Mollyann Brodie and Robert J. Blendon, "The Public's Contribution to Congressional Gridlock on Health Care Reform," *Journal of Health Politics, Policy and Law*, 20 (2) (1995), pp. 403–410.

3. Lawrence R. Jacobs and Robert Y. Shapiro, "Don't Blame the Public for Failed Health Care Reform," *Journal of Health Politics, Policy and Law*, 20 (2) (1995), pp. 411–423.

4. John W. Kingdon, *Agendas, Alternatives, and Public Policies.* (Boston: Little Brown. 1984), pp. 20, 98; Lisa Disch, "Publicity-Stunt Participation and Sound Bite Polemics: The Health Care Debate, 1993–1994, *Journal of Health Politics, Policy and Law* 21 (1) (1996), pp. 3–33.

5. Alissa J. Rubin, "Are U.S. Taxpayers Ready for Health-Care Reform?" *Congressional Quarterly Weekly Report*, (April 17, 1993), p. 959.

6. Barbara Sinclair, "Trying to Govern Positively in a Negative Era: Clinton and the 103rd Congress,"in Colin Campbell and Bert A. Rockman, eds., *The Clinton Presidency: First Appraisals* (Chatham, NJ: Chatham House, 1996), p. 96.

7. Ibid.

8. Cathie Martin, "Mandating Social Change: The Struggle within Corporate America over National Health Care Reform," paper presented at the annual meeting of the American Political Science Association, New York, September 1994; Julie Kosterlitz, "Stress Fractures," *National Journal* (Feb. 19, 1994), p. 413; Graham K. Wilson, "The Clinton Administration and Interest Groups," in Campbell and Rockman, *The Clinton Presidency: First Appraisals.* p. 226.

9. Alisa J. Rubin and Janet Hook, "Clinton Sets Health Agenda: Security for Everyone," *Congressional Quarterly Weekly Report* (Sept. 25, 1993), p. 2552.

10. Gwen Ifill, "Events Steal Health Plan's Thunder," *New York Times* (Oct. 18, 1993), p. C10.

11. Rubin and Hook, "Clinton Sets Health Agenda," p. 2551.

12. George C. Edwards, III, "Frustrations and Folly: The Public Presidency," in Colin Campbell and Bert A. Rockman, eds., *The Clinton Presidency: First Appraisals* (Chatham, NJ: Chatham House, 1996), pp. 256–258.

13. Paul J. Quirk and Joseph Hinchliffe, "Domestic Policy: The Trials of a Centrist Democrat," in Colin Campbell and Bert A. Rockman, eds., *The Clinton Presidency: First Appraisals* (Chatham, NJ: Chatham House, 1996), pp. 274–275.

14. Grant McConnell, *Private Power and American Democracy* (New York: Knopf, 1966); Harold Seidman, *Politics, Position and Power: The Dynamics of Federal Organization* (New York: Oxford University Press, 1980), pp. 280–281.

15. Ibid.

16. Ibid.

17. William Schneider, "A Fatal Flaw in Clinton's Health Plan," *National Journal* (Dec. 12, 1993, p. 2696; Alissa J. Rubin et al., "Clinton's Health Care Bill," *National Journal* (Feb. 26, 1994), pp. 492–504.

18. Edwards, "Frustrations and Folly," p. 252.

19. Allisa J.Rubin, "Mrs. Clinton Conquers Hill, Sets Debate in Motion," *Congressional Quarterly Weekly Report* (Oct. 2, 1993), pp. 2640–2643.

20. Charles O. Jones, "Campaigning to Govern: The Clinton Style," in Colin Campbell and Bert A. Rockman, eds., *The Clinton Presidency* (Chatham, NJ: Chatham House, 1996), p. 38.

21. Edwards, "Frustrations and Folly," pp. 229–242.

22. Alissa J. Rubin and Beth Donovan, "Leaders Tell Clinton Measure Must Have Slower Approach," *Congressional Quarterly Weekly Report* (July 23, 1994), pp. 2041–2042; Alissa J. Rubin, "Uncertainty, Deep Divisions Cloud Opening of Debate," *Congressional Quarterly Weekly Report* (Aug. 13, 1994), pp. 2344–2353.

23. Berton Lee Lamb, Nina Burkhardt, and Jonathan G. Taylor, "Quants and Wonks in Environmental Disputes: Are Scientists Experts or Advocates?" in Dennis L. Soden ed., *At the Nexus: Science Policy* (Commack, NY: Nova Science Publishers, 1996), p. 174.

24. Michael Tomasky,"Why Health Care Reform Failed," *Dissent* (Spring 1996), pp. 49–51.

25. Ibid.

26. Lawrence R. Jacobs, "Taking Heads and Sleeping Citizens: Health Policy Making in a Democracy," *Journal of Health Politics, Policy and Law* 21(1) (1996), p. 131.

27. Edwards, "Frustrations and Folly," p. 251.

28. Elizabeth Drew, *On the Edge: The Clinton Presidency* (New York: Simon & Schuster, 1994), p. 30.

29. Dana Priest, "Shalala's Health Plan Testimony Is Given Bruising Reception on Hill," *Washington Post* (Oct. 7, 1994), p. A4.

30. Robert Pear, "A White House Fight," *New York Times* (May 25, 1993), p. A1; Robert Pear, "Health Planners at White House Consider Lid on Medicare Costs," *New York Times* (Aug. 30, 1993), p. A1.

31. Michael Wines, "First Lady's Health Strategy: Accept Less or Gamble It All?" *New York Times*, (July 5, 1994), p. A4.

32. Robert Pear, "In Noting Absence, A.M.A. Sees Snub," *New York Times*, (Dec. 7, 1993), p. A24.

33. Richard E. Cohen, "Ready, Aim, Reform," *National Journal*, (Oct. 10, 1993), p. 2581.

34. "The Health Care Debate: The Doctors," *New York Times*, (Aug. 5, 1994), p. I8.

35. "Heath Care Reform: The Lost Chance," *Newsweek*, (Sept. 19, 1994), p. 32.

36. Vincente Navarro, "Why Congress Did Not Enact Health Care Reform," *Journal of Health Politics, Policy and Law*, 20(2) (1995), pp. 455–456.

37. Maureen Dowd, "The Health Care Debate: The Public; Strong Support for Health Plans," *New York Times* (July 20, 1994), p. A1.

38. Alissa J. Rubin, "Are U.S. Taxpayers Ready for Health-Care Reform?" *Congressional Quarterly Weekly Report* (April 17, 1993), pp.955–959.

39. Adam Clymer, "Poll Finds Public Is Still Doubtful over Costs of Clinton Health Plan," *New York Times* (March 15, 1994), p. A1.

40. Edwards, "Frustrations and Folly," p. 246.

41. Ibid.

42. Michael Dukakis, "Health Care Reform: Where Do We Go from Here?" *Journal of Health Politics, Policy and Law* 20 (3) (1995), p. 789.

43. Samuel Kernell, *Going Public: New Strategies of Presidential Leadership* (Washington, DC: CQ Press, 1986).

44. Dennis L. Soden, *Managing Florida's Coastal Resources: Technical Complexity and Public Attitudes* (Gainesville: Florida Sea Grant College, 1990).

45. Norman Daniels, "The Articulation of Values and Principles Involved in Health Care Reform,"*Journal of Medicine and Philosophy* 19 (5) (1994), p. 432.

46. Edwards, "Frustrations and Folly," p. 245.

47. Ibid., p. 240.

48. Ibid., p. 241–242.

49. The 1992 and 1994 public opinion figures came from Gallup polls and the *New York Times*\CNN polls for those years.

50. Wilson, "The Clinton Administration and Interest Groups," p. 215.

51. Ibid., p. 54; Wilson, p. 215.

52. Adam Clymer, "Hillary Clinton Accuses Insurers of Lying about Health Proposal," *New York Times* (Nov. 2, 1993), p. A1.

53. Wilson, p. 227.

54. Julie Kosterlitz, "The Big Sell," *National Journal*, (May 14, 1994), pp. 118–123.

55. Jason DeParle, "Moynihan Says Clinton Isn't Serious about Welfare Reform," *New York Times* (Jan. 8, 1993), p. A8.

56. Ibid.

57. Alissa J. Rubin, "Chances for Limited Measure Slight as Congress Returns," *Congressional Quarterly Weekly Report* (Sept. 10, 1994), pp. 2523–2524; Quirk and Hinchcliffe, "Domestic Policy," p. 277.

58. Dukakis, "Health Care Reform," p. 790

59. Dukakis, "Health Care Reform," pp. 790–791.

60. Cited in Wilson, p. 228.

9

Chief Executive: The Struggle against Congressional Government

The chief executive at first glance appears quite powerful because the Framers' intent was that a single executive not share power with any advisory body. Yet the president in this role is often frustrated because the Constitution fragments control over the bureaucracy, making it difficult for any president to dominate the executive branch of government. Not only does the president share jurisdiction over the bureaucracy with the Congress but, as presidency scholar James MacGregor Burns explains; "One finds lines of authority running horizontally from committee or Congressman to department or bureau chief" dispersing authority throughout the bureaucracy.[1] Historical developments in the chief executive role (Table 9-1), however, have added substantially to the meager grant of powers in Article II.

The role of chief executive is complicated by the very size of the national government. In addition to the 3 million civilian federal employees (Table 9-2), a presidential administration interacts with some of the 13 million employees of state and local governments and another 6 to 7 million more in the private sector who are contracted to undertake government projects. This bureaucracy is so huge, complex, chaotic, and dispersed that no one president can manage it alone (see Figure 9–1). Harry Truman was especially sensitive to the problem. He would show visitors a wall chart depicting more than a hundred offices that directly reported to him; his response: "I cannot even see all these men, let alone actually study what they are doing."[2]

AUTHORITY

The president is expected to manage a bureaucracy, supervise subordinates, and implement public policies, yet he has little constitutional au-

Table 9–1. Significant Historical Developments in the Chief Executive Role

Presidents	Historical Event or Development
Washington	• First cabinet
Jefferson	• First impoundment of appropriated funds
Jackson	• Informal "kitchen cabinet" advisors
	• Began spoils system of patronage employment
	• Asserted presidential removal power
Arthur	• Civil Service Act of 1883
Harding	• Budget and Accounting Act of 1921
	• Bureau of the Budget established
F.D.Roosevelt	• Executive Office of the President created
	• Granted reorganization authority
Truman	• Council of Economic Advisers created
	• National Security Council created
Eisenhower	• White House Chief of Staff created
Nixon	• Office of Management and Budget created
	• Transformed OMB from neutral competent to politicized agency of the White House
	• Congressional Budget and Impoundment Control Act of 1974
Carter	• Civil Service Reform Act of 1978
	• Senior Executive Service created
Reagan	• Politicized the bureaucracy by appointing ideological loyalists to key positions
	• Immigration and Naturalization Service v. Chadha (1983) held legislative veto unconstitutional
	• Began regulatory clearance by White House of agency rules
Clinton	• Five-year plan to reinvent government by cutting $108 billion and 252,000 employees

thority to carry out such duties. Authority based on statute and custom can be fragile, especially when executive-legislative tensions heighten. In the Constitution, presidential authority as chief executive is found in two clauses of Article II, namely, one specifying that "the executive power shall be vested in a President of the United States of America" and another stating that the president has the responsibility to "take care that the laws be faithfully executed." Although the Framers chose to give Congress powers in very precise language in Article I, the vague language of Article II makes it unclear exactly what a president was supposed to do.

APPOINTMENT.   A modern president may have to fill as many as 100,000 jobs, but most of these are military commissions and appointments to advisory bodies. Because there is civil service protection for over 90 percent of federal employees, presidential appointments are limited to approximately 5,200 top-level policymaking positions.[3]

One further complication involves the small number of political appointments—less than 2 percent—scattered throughout the federal bu-

Table 9–2. Civilian Employment in the Federal Government, 1816–1990

Year	Total Employees	President
1816	4,837	Madison
1851	26,274	Fillmore
1881	100,020	Arthur
1901	239,476	T. Roosevelt
1921	561,142	Harding
1930	601,319	Hoover
1940	1,042,420	F. Roosevelt
1945	3,816,310	Truman
1950	1,960,708	Truman
1955	2,397,309	Eisenhower
1960	2,398,704	Eisenhower
1965	2,527,915	Johnson
1970	2,981,574	Nixon
1975	2,882,000	Ford
1980	2,987,000	Carter
1985	3,020,531	Reagan
1990	3,128,267	Bush
1995	2,918,675	Clinton

Sources: U.S. Bureau of the Census, *Historical Statistics of the United States: Colonial Times to 1970* (Washington, DC: U.S. Government Printing Office, 1975), p.1102; *Statistical Abstract of the United States, 1981* (Washington DC: U.S. Government Printing Office, 1981), p. 266; *Statisitical Abstract of the United States, 1987* (Washington, D.C.: U.S. Government Printing Office 1987) p. 311; *Statistical Abstract of the United States, 1993* (Washington DC: U.S. Government Printing Office, 1993), p. 343; *Statistical Abstract of the United States, 1996* (Washington, DC: U.S. Government Printing Office, 1996), p. 345.

reaucracy, meaning it is no easy task—although not an impossible one, as President Reagan showed us—for a chief executive to assume direct control over a particular agency. Although he was no novice when it came to organizational experience, President Eisenhower found this dilemma troublesome because two decades had passed since a Republican had occupied the White House. Civil servants and political appointees recruited during the Roosevelt and Truman administrations, Eisenhower believed, did not share his moderate political views, and he had to find ways to release some of these positions from civil service protection. At his request, Congress implemented new "Schedule C" positions that allowed Eisenhower to remove some "supergrade" (GS16-GS18) positions from the civil service and make them available for political appointees, which has allowed approximately 1,100 more positions for presidential appointment.[4]

Once administrative positions are available, it is necessary to find appointees who are loyal, offer managerial experience, and represent important political constituencies. Most presidents limit their search to their own political party. Whenever a president does appoint somebody from the other party to high office, the intent may be to convey the impression that his administration has broad-based, bipartisan support. This was one reason President Bush appointed former Democratic National Chairman

FIGURE 9–1. Executive Branch of Government (1994)

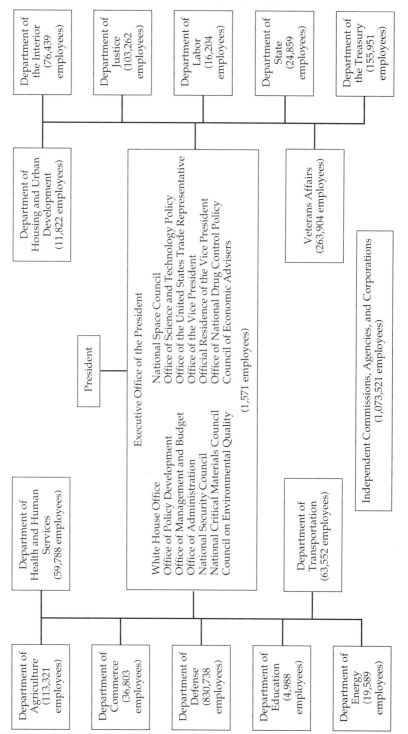

Source: *Statistal Abstract of the United States, 1996* (Washington, D.C.: U.S. Government Printing Office, 1996) p. 345. For the employment data in the Executive Office of the White House, see *World Almanac and Book of Facts, 1997*. (Mahwah, N.J.: World Almanac Books, Inc., 1997).

Robert S. Strauss as ambassador to the Soviet Union. Clinton's choice of ex-Senator William Cohen (R–Me.) as secretary of defense in his second term was consistent with the president's rhetoric that Republicans and Democrats should stop bickering and cooperate to resolve the nation's problems.

Political constraints on his appointment power are imposed on the president by special interests and voter blocs. When nominating a secretary of agriculture, for example, Republican presidents look to the American Farm Bureau Federation for guidance, just as Democratic presidents cannot ignore the advice of the AFL-CIO when naming a secretary of labor. In recent administrations both parties have recruited African Americans to head the Department of Housing and Urban Development (HUD). (e.g., Johnson, Carter, Reagan, and Clinton).

The Constitution requires that certain appointees be confirmed by the Senate, by majority vote, but generally the president is allowed to name his cabinet without much Senate interference.[5] Rejection does happen, however, when a nominee has extremist views or is involved in a conflict of interest. Bill Clinton had problems finding an acceptable woman nominee for attorney general. His first choice, Zoe Baird, withdrew her name from consideration in the face of public criticism for her hiring of two illegal aliens to assist with child care and chauffeuring duties.

Clinton did not do much better with his second nominee, federal district judge Kimba M. Wood of New York. She too had employed an illegal alien as a baby-sitter even though it happened before the law was changed making the practice illegal.[6] Finally Clinton was able to nominate, and see confirmed, Janet Reno—a 54-year-old Harvard-educated attorney with 15 years experience as a Florida state prosecutor from Dade County.[7] Unmarried, she did not have the domestic problems faced by prior nominees and, moreover, Reno had the backing of the National Organization for Women (NOW) and the First Lady. [8]

JUDICIAL APPOINTMENTS.   Court appointments ensure a president's judicial legacy long after he has retired from office. But positions on the court have been filled for many other reasons as well. FDR tried unsuccessfully to pack the Supreme Court in order to put pro–New Deal justices on the bench. Harry Truman and Dwight Eisenhower also made judicial appointments for patronage reasons rather than as an expression of their personal ideologies, whereas Richard Nixon campaigned in 1968 to put "law and order" judges on the bench.

Although Supreme Court appointments are the most visible and important judicial selections a president can make, staffing the federal district and appellate courts can be very important in setting the direction and tone of the court system. In a departure from past practices of appointing white males, for example, Jimmy Carter, although he did not have the opportunity to appooint any Supreme Court justice, opened the way for minorities and women to be represented on the federal judiciary. During his term Carter appointed 202 district and 56 appellate judges, about 40 percent of the total, in which the percentage of women judges rose from 1 to 7 percent and African Americans from 4 to 9 percent.[9] Clinton followed Carter's example in his initial appointment of 187 judges[10]: 60 percent were women or racial minorities. [11]

Presidents can also shape the ideological makeup of the federal judiciary, as shown by the twelve years of GOP rule under Reagan and Bush. By his fourth year President Clinton had appointed 187 federal judges or 22 percent of the total, but 57 percent of the federal judges already seated had been appointed by Republicans Reagan or Bush.[12] Clinton made 101 appointments to the federal bench in one year—the most of any president since 1979[13]—but that number cannot compare with Reagan who, in eight years, appointed four Supreme Court justices, 168 full-time appeals judges, and 575 district court judges.[14]

Franklin D. Roosevelt's famous confrontation with the Supreme Court resulted after the high court had struck down twelve key New Deal laws. FDR asked for legislation allowing him to restructure the judiciary by packing the Supreme Court with up to six additional members for every justice who failed to retire by the age of seventy[15] and also by expanding the lower federal judiciary with fifty additional judges.[16] Congress refused, but after twelve years in office FDR nonetheless succeeded in shaping the Court to his liking by appointing eight Supreme Court justices and selecting a new chief justice.[17]

Although Roosevelt attracted the headlines for doing this, David O'Brien, for one, argues that any judicial appointment can be as political as FDR's insofar as all presidents who appoint judges can be said to "pack the court" with persons who reflect their party and ideology.[18] Lyndon Johnson wanted judges who would enforce his civil rights policies; Ronald Reagan recruited those who shared his brand of conservatism and supported his social policy agenda, particularly judges with prolife views on abortion. Reagan's successor, George Bush, emphasized family values and law and order as judicial criteria [19] but, as it turned out, his Supreme Court appointee Justice David Souter has been much more liberal in his voting record than Bush had hoped.

There are now two women on the Court. Presidents Ford and Nixon were urged by their wives, Betty Ford and Pat Nixon, to appoint the first woman member of the Supreme Court,[20] but both men refused to act, allowing Ronald Reagan to appoint Sandra Day O'Connor as the first woman associate justice to the Supreme Court.[21] The second was Clinton's successful nomination of Ruth Bader Ginsburg as an associate justice. Lyndon Johnson broke the racial barrier by appointing former NAACP counsel Thurgood Marshall, a liberal justice who was succeeded by Bush appointee Republican and African American Clarence Thomas, who votes conservatively on most issues.

An informal barrier to presidential judicial appointments is in the hands of the American Bar Association (ABA), which is asked to rate the judicial nominees as "qualified," if not "highly qualified." The association rarely labels a nominee as "unqualified" because its evaluation takes place after the presidential nomination.[22] The FBI also provides the Senate Judiciary Committee with a background check on the nominee.

The Senate, when controlled by the opposition party, may stall judicial nominations in the last year of a lame duck president's term or when the incumbent faces reelection. Clinton encountered that problem in 1996 when the Republican-controlled Senate stopped him from naming any judges to the appeals courts and allowed only seventeen appointments to district court by midyear, a record low rate of approval for presidential judicial appointments.[23]

Presidents can miscalculate the prospective voting behavior of their nominees[24] as Eisenhower did in two instances. He was both surprised and troubled by the judicial rulings of two of his high court appointments—Associate Justice William Brennan and Chief Justice Earl Warren—because they expressed very liberal political and constitutional views.[25] But Eisenhower was less guided by their ideologies, because Brennan was to be Ike's token Democrat on the Court and Warren, as governor of California, was offered his seat as payment for giving Eisenhower critical California support in the 1952 election.[26] President Nixon also suffered personally from a decision rendered by his own appointees on the Supreme Court. In *U.S. v. Nixon* (1974), three of his four appointees voted against him.[27]

REMOVAL POWER.   No mention is made of a removal power in the Constitution, except impeachment. Thus the presidential power to remove was originally more tenuous than his power to appoint. Alexander Hamilton in *Federalist No. 77* argued that the removal power could be presumed from the power to appoint, and in the first Congress James Madison contended that the removal power is implied in the presidential authority to "take care that the laws be faithfully executed," a viewpoint shared by the majority of his colleagues in the first Congress.

This view was supported, although only temporarily, by the 1926 landmark decision in *Myers, Administratrix v. U.S.*[28] President Wilson in 1917 had appointed Frank S. Myers to the position of first-class postmaster in Portland, Oregon, for a four-year term. Before Myers's term expired, Wilson removed him from office even though an 1876 statute mandated against such removals. The majority opinion delivered by Chief Justice (and former president) William Howard Taft argued that because the Constitution did not limit the removal power and the removal power is as important as the appointment power, a president should have an unchecked power to remove subordinates from office. The 1876 law limiting his removal power, therefore, was unconstitutional.

This 1926 decision was modified nine years later in the equally famous case of *Humphrey's Executor (Rathbun) v. U.S.* (1935). President Roosevelt had asked Hoover appointee William E. Humphrey to resign from the Federal Trade Commission (FTC) in 1933, although Humphrey's term would not end until 1938. Roosevelt believed FTC policies could best be

implemented by appointees loyal to the New Deal, but Humphrey refused to resign. FDR then removed him from office. The constitutional
question was whether a president could remove an FTC member when
the law that created the FTC stipulated a commissioner could only be removed for inefficiency, neglect of duty, and malfeasance of office. Justice
Sutherland, for the majority, concluded that the intent of Congress was to
establish an independent body of experts that possessed quasi-judicial
and quasi-legislative powers beyond the control of the president. The
Court essentially said that presidential removal power varies according to
the nature of the office in question.

Since *Humphrey's Executor,* few other removal cases have come before
the court.[29] *Wiener v. U.S.* (1958), one of the few cases since *Humphrey's,*
prevented President Eisenhower from removing a member of the War
Claims Commission. Wiener, who was appointed by Truman, protested
that the president was not given removal power in either the statute that
created the War Claims Commission or the Constitution. The Court
agreed that officials of the commission could only be removed for cause.
In 1988, however, the Court allowed the secretary of defense to remove an
employee of the National Security Agency for engaging in a homosexual
relationship with a foreign national, even though the 1959 National Security Agency Act had not specifically provided for such removal. Here it
declared that "the power of removal from office is incidental to the power
of appointment."[30]

PRESIDENTIAL REMOVALS.   *Humphrey's Executor* protected members
of the "independent" regulatory commissions from being arbitrarily fired
by a president,[31] but cabinet members are not so immune. Prior to President Jackson's firing of Treasury Secretary Duane, the Senate was more
sympathetic to the need for presidents to remove their own cabinet officers. Although Jackson had removed 252 officers within the executive
branch (more removals than all his predecessors combined), his firing of
Secretary Duane, for refusing to follow his order to remove deposits from
the Second Bank of the United States and distribute them among state
banks, prompted Senate opposition to President Jackson in 1833. The Senate censured Jackson for assuming executive powers not granted to him.[32]
His ultimate victory secured the right of presidents to remove members
from their own cabinet.

Removing a cabinet member today may still incur political costs. Although cabinet members can be legally removed, doing so may damage a
president's rapport with the clientele groups loyal to the department he
or she heads. For example, President George Bush, who proclaimed himself to be the "education president" found he had no choice but to let his
education secretary, Lauro Cavazos, go when it appeared that Cavazos
was not encouraging education reforms assertively.[33]

Resignation accomplishes the same objective but with fewer political
costs to the president. In 1993 Bill Clinton wanted Secretary of Defense Les
Aspin to step down from his post. When Aspin resigned in December

1993 with Clinton standing by his side, Aspin cited "personal reasons" for his departure.[34]

DECISION MAKING

The decision-makers who participate in the formation of policy and the administration of law are the president, his advisors, the federal bureaucracy and subnational political leaders, and may also include the Congress, the Supreme Court, and those clientele who receive benefits from federal programs. What measure of control a president exerts over the permanent government depends on how he structures the relationship between his cabinet and the White House staff as well as the degree of support he receives from the Congress and, where he is legally challenged, from the courts.

The Permanent Government

Virtually the entire federal bureaucracy is established by laws of Congress, which detail the workings of the federal civil service including merit exams, promotions, confirmation of appointments, salaries, hiring and firing procedures, and retirement benefits. The federal civil service system was established when Congress passed the Pendleton Act in 1883, following the assassination of President Garfield by a disgruntled job seeker. This law originally applied to only 10 percent of federal employees but today extends to over 90 percent of the civilian work force. The system was intended to assure that federal employees would be recruited according to merit rather than party patronage and to guarantee job security to federal employees. The system handicapped a president who wanted fundamental policy changes because it was difficult for the chief executive to reassign key personnel, institute cost-effective methods, or reward superior job performance.

In an effort to redress these deficiencies, President Carter proposed new reforms that Congress enacted as the Civil Service Reform Act of 1978. The major change was the creation of a Senior Executive Service (SES) covering approximately 8,500 high-level "careerists" in middle management.[35] The managerial objective was to increase their productivity by offering merit pay raises and bonuses for superior performance. That benign objective was altered by the Reagan administration, which took advantage of the SES flexibility to gain political control of the bureaucracy.[36] Obviously there was increased politicalization of the senior civil service during this time. Between 1981 and 1985 careerists in the civil service declined 18 percent and the number of political appointees increased 169 percent.[37]

Whereas President Nixon tried a reorganization strategy to gain control of the permanent government, President Reagan used the more obvious approach of appointing ideological loyalists to the upper echelons of the bureaucracy. In 1970 Rockman and Aberbach examined "supergrade" and appointive positions and found they were largely liberal and Democratic in composition, which reflected the impact of nearly four decades of Democratic rule.[38] They did a follow-up study in the mid-1980s to assess the impact of Reagan's appointments and concluded that "the Reagan administration was able to sort out SES career personnel in the social service agencies [previously dominated by liberal Democratic civil servants] very well, putting Republicans at the very top and placing the SES Democrats in those agencies in slightly lower . . . positions."[39]

George Bush was described as the most "openly pro–civil service President since Herbert Hoover"[40] and he relied more extensively on the civil service to fill top-level careerist positions than either Reagan or Carter. Yet George Bush was not unlike his Republican predecessors in fearing partisan political activities by rank-and-file civil servants. The Hatch Act of 1939 was a reaction to the New Deal hirings by Roosevelt, which Congress feared was becoming a huge political patronage army amid revelations that some federal workers had to make kickbacks to keep their jobs. Once before President Ford had vetoed legislation to lift the ban and President Bush did the same in 1990. After Clinton was elected, however, congressional Democrats renewed their campaign to revise the Hatch Act, and this time they were successful. President Clinton signed the amended legislation at the end of 1993. The new law tightens on-the-job partisan activities by federal employees but eases the prohibitions on off-duty political activities.[41]

IMPOUNDMENT.   A president impounds funds when he refuses to spend the money appropriated by Congress. President Jefferson is credited with the first impoundment, and various presidents did so during the nineteenth and early twentieth centuries. But the practice and its arguable constitutional basis was not tested in litigation until the modern era. Richard Nixon received the most attention for impounding because he did so extensively, exceeding $30 billion in his first term and $12.2 billion in 1972 alone.[42] The Supreme Court reviewed several cases involving funds earmarked for local water pollution control and ruled against Nixon.[43] The Court said that presidential impoundments infringed on congressional control over appropriations. As a result, Congress proceeded to enact the Congressional Budget and Impoundment Control Act of 1974, which undercut presidential authority to impound funds.

REORGANIZATION PLANS.   Congress through the "necessary and proper" clause of Article I has the authority to oversee presidential plans to reorganize the federal government. In the past, reorganization was used to reduce personnel on commissions, limit the autonomy of certain agencies, reduce funding for some bureaus, and reduce the number of supergrade positions in the civil service. Authority to implement a reorganization plan— unless rejected by a "legislative veto"—was first granted to Franklin Roosevelt, but his successes have not been matched by any other presidents.

Likely the most ambitious reorganization plan was proposed by Richard Nixon. Its fundamental objective was to weaken the clientele Departments of Agriculture, Commerce, Labor, and Transportation and reallocate their functions to four "super" departments: Community Development, Economic Affairs, Human Resources, and Natural Resources. If enacted (it was not), Nixon's proposed new cabinet arrangement would have included eight rather than the eleven existing departments.

President Clinton, bolstered by the Gore Task Force Report of 1993, proposed cutting the federal work force by 12 percent and reducing costs by $108 billion. He recommended various department consolidations and reorganizations, abolishing some agencies, and introducing a more efficient budgeting process.[44] Clinton could not get the Congress to support any overall "reinventing government" measure, but he managed piecemeal to introduce separate measures to realize some of his objectives.[45]

CONGRESSIONAL OVERSIGHT.   The Legislative Reorganization Acts of 1946 and 1970 granted Congress oversight responsibility to closely watch bureau and agency activities. Yet legislative oversight is not given priority despite general agreement in Congress that it ought to be conducted.[46] Following the Watergate scandals of the early 1970s Congress did accelerate its use of the legislative veto to oversee administration and shape policy outcomes. This procedural device, first adopted in 1932, allowed the House and Senate (a "two-house veto"), the House or Senate (a "one-house veto"), or a committee or subcommittee of either or both the House and Senate (a "committee veto") to disapprove a particular action by an agency, a bureau, or the president himself. The Supreme Court declared the legislative veto unconstitutional in *Immigration and Naturalization Service (INS) v. Chadha* (1983).[47] The Burger Court argued that the one-house legislative veto violated Article I of the Constitution, which stipulates that the legislative process require passage by both chambers of the Congress and presentation to the president for his approval or disapproval. Although the Court specifically ruled on the one-house legislative veto, its decision potentially affects all kinds of legislative vetoes in more than two hundred public laws.

Yet Congress was in no rush to respond to the *Chadha* decision. One study found that, 12 months after *Chadha*, 30 legislative vetoes had been incorporated in 11 bills,[48] another study revealed that 16 months after the ruling, some 53 legislative vetoes had been tacked onto statutory laws.[49] By 1992 Congress had successfully resisted altering any of the two hundred major pieces of legislation mentioned in the *Chadha* case. But Congress has considered substitutes for the legislative veto that allow it to control the implementation of public policy[50] including use of joint resolutions, the "report and wait" provision which demands that agencies report certain actions to Congress, and delaying the action for a period of time.

Autonomous Bureaucrats

Bureaucratic decision-makers within federal agencies ought to be subordinate to the chief executive in the formal chain of command, but politically they may be able to develop substantial autonomy from direct presidential control. Most agencies and their careerists survive longer than any president, and over time these agencies tend to enjoy close political relationships with clientele or beneficiary groups they serve as well as supportive alliances with the standing committees of Congress.

Sometimes agency heads are so influential, they are virtually immune from presidential control. Probably nobody in official Washington achieved such political leverage over the White House and Congress like J. Edgar Hoover, who was director of the Federal Bureau of Investigation for the half century from its establishment until his retirement in the 1970s. Hoover turned the FBI into a personal fiefdom and used his secret sources and confidential information to intimidate and frighten his enemies.[51] None of his successors have even come close to reestablishing that kind of personalized power base.

A more common problem involves the independent regulatory commissions, established by Congress to be exempt from the president's direct supervision. Beginning with the 1887 Interstate Commerce Commission (which was abolished by the 104th Congress), Federal Trade Commission, Federal Communications Commission, and others, their members must be bipartisan and are appointed by the president with Senate approval to long and staggered terms so that no chief executive can easily replace a majority during one presidential term.

Subnational Governments and Clientele Groups

The chief executive's responsibility for policy implementation is not limited to the federal bureaucracy. National programs such as the Interstate Highway System, for example, involve federal money, but the actual construction is under the direction of state and local highway departments and private clientele groups—construction contractors and cement companies. In addition, almost all federal grant-in-aid programs to states and localities involve complex relationships among these levels of government and private firms, or nonprofit organizations, and consultants who participate in program design and policy implementation. To interact with the 50 states, 3,042 counties, 19,200 municipalities, 16,691 townships, 29,532 special districts, and 14,721 school districts in the nation,[52] the federal government operates through regional offices, which further subdivides authority.

Advisory System

As we explained earlier, one way scholars differentiate between the historical presidents and the modern presidency (beginning with FDR) is the development of the institutionalized presidency. Specialized staff agencies whose only responsibility is to service the chief executive were launched in 1939 when Roosevelt established the Executive Office of the President. Before that time chief executives were expected to carry out their duties with a few secretaries and clerks and with the advice of the formal cabinet and any informal kitchen cabinet associates they might confide in.

THE CABINET.   The oldest advisory institution to the president is the cabinet, first created in the Washington administration with four officials: secretary of state, secretary of the treasury, secretary of war, and attorney general. The number of departments in the cabinet has increased to four-teen[53] (Table 9–3), but there has been no corresponding increase in its in-fluence. No tradition of collective importance exists similar to what is found in parliamentary governments.

Although the cabinet does not act as a collective advisory body to the president, individual secretaries can be very influential. Quite often these cabinet members come from the so-called inner cabinet—Justice, State, Defense, and Treasury—that was represented in President Washington's original cabinet.

The first secretary of the treasury, Alexander Hamilton, virtually acted as a prime minister in assisting George Washington, and doubtless Clinton's reshuffling of his cabinet at the outset of his second term was de-signed to establish Treasury Secretary Robert Rubin as his most important advisor. Other strong-willed cabinet members who shared influence with the White House inner circle have included at least four secretaries of state:—Dean Acheson under Truman, John Foster Dulles under Eisen-hower, Henry Kissinger in the Nixon cabinet, and James Baker (a close personal friend as well) under Bush.

Turnover among cabinet persons has been a concern of most presi-dents since the era of Franklin Roosevelt (Table 9–4). No department has been immune, but overall the department heads of Commerce, Justice, as well as Health and Human Services have suffered the greatest turnover rate, whereas the secretary of state has experienced the greatest longevity in office.

In looking at those presidents who have been reelected to office—Roo-sevelt, Eisenhower, Nixon, Reagan, and Clinton—it appears that cabinet stability is higher during their first terms than in their second. Truman, the sole exception, had frequent turnovers during his first term because he suc-ceeded to office on the death of Roosevelt and thus wanted to shape the cabinet membership more to his liking. Truman's second term showed in-creased cabinet stability. The best records for retaining the original mem-bers of the cabinet were established by FDR, Eisenhower, and Clinton, fol-lowed closely behind by Kennedy (with Johnson) and Reagan.

Some observers contend that the cabinet no longer is an important source for policy or advice and has little use except "for public relations symbolism."[54] We should not underestimate the importance of its repre-

Table 9–3. The Cabinet, 1995

Department	Year Created	President	1995 Budget Rank	1994 Personnel Rank
State	1789	Washington	13	10
Treasury	1789	Washington	1	3
Interior	1849	Polk	12	7
Agriculture	1862	Lincoln	4	5
Justice	1870	Grant	11	6
Commerce (formerly Department of Commerce and Labor, 1903)	1913	Wilson	14	9
Labor (formerly Department of Commerce and Labor, 1903)	1913	Wilson	8	12
Defense (consolidated Department of War, 1789, and Department of Navy, 1798)	1947	Truman	3	1
Housing and Urban Development	1965	Johnson	9	13
Transportation	1966	Johnson	6	8
Energy	1977	Carter	10	11
Health and Human Services (formerly Department of Health, Education and Welfare, 1953)	1980	Carter	2	4
Education (separated from Department of Health, Education and Welfare, 1953)	1979	Carter	7	14
Veterans Affairs (formerly Veterans Administration, 1930)	1989	Bush	5	2

Source: U.S. Bureau of the Census, *Statistical Abstract of the United States: 1995*, 115th ed. (Washington, D.C.: U.S. Government Printing Office, 1995), pp. 337, 350.

sentative function, however, because cabinet members can represent factions within the president's own party, long established interest groups within the party coalition, or important newly emerging voter blocs such as women, who occupied positions such as attorney general, secretary of energy, and secretary of health and human services in the first Clinton term. After his reelection Clinton appointed Madeleine Albright as the first woman secretary of state.

Since the 1930s, however, presidents have come to rely more and more on their White House staff at the expense of the cabinet. Even those presidents like Richard Nixon who declared in 1968 that the cabinet would play an important role in all significant decisions of his presidency did not find the cabinet was able to overcome the importance of their own staff.[55]

Table 9-4. Cabinet Turnover by Presidential Term, 1933–1995

Years	F.D. Roosevelt 33–36	37–40	41–44	Truman 45–48	49–52	Eisenhower 53–56	57–60	Kennedy/ Johnson 61–64	Johnson 65–68	Nixon 69–72	Nixon/ Ford 73–76	Carter 77–80	Reagan 81–84	85–88	Bush 89–92	Clinton 93–96	Ratio: Total Years / No. of People
State	1	1	1	3	1	1	2	1	1	1	1	2	2	1	2	1	60/22 = 2.8
Treasury	1	3	3	1	1	2	1	3	3	2	2	1	3	1	2		60/28 = 2.2
War	2	1	1	3													16/8 = 2.0
Justice	1	2	2	2	3	1	2	2	2	2	4	2	1	3	2	1	60/33 = 1.8
Postmaster General	1	1	2	3	1	1	1	2	3								40/16 = 2.5
Navy	1	1	3	1													16/6 = 2.7
Interior	1	1	2	2	2	1	1	1	1	2	3	1	2	2	1	1	61/24 = 2.6
Agriculture	1	2	3	3	1	1	1	1	1	2	2	1	1	2	2	2	61/25 = 2.4
Commerce	1	1	1	4	1	1	3	1	4	2	3	2	1	2	2	2	61/33 = 1.8
Labor	1	1		3	1	2	1	2	1	2	3	1	1	3	2	1	61/26 = 2.3
Defense				4	4	3	1	2	1	3	1	1	2	1	2		50/22 = 2.3
HEW/HHS						2	2	2	2	2	2	2	2	1	1		41/21 = 2.0
HUD									1	2	2	1	1	1	1		29/11 = 2.6
Transportation									1	2	2	2	2	1	1		29/12 = 2.4
Education												1	2	2	1		17/7 = 2.4
Energy											2	2	2	1	1		17/8 = 2.3
Total	11	15	16	28	15	13	18	14	24	20	27	21	18	27	19	17	
Turnover Ratio: no. of people/ no. of positions	1.1	1.5	1.6	2.5	1.7	1.3	1.8	1.4	2	1.7	2.5	1.6	1.4	2.1	1.5	1.3	

Sources: *Congress and the Nation*, vol. 5, 1977–1980 (Washington, D.C.: Congressional Quarterly Press, 1981), p.111; *Congress and the Nation*, vol 7, 1985–1988 (Washington, D.C.: Congressional Quarterly Press 1990), p.1045; *Congressional Quarterly Almanac*, vol. 47, 1991 (Washington, D.C.: Congressional Quarterly Press), 1992, p. 9; *Facts on File*, (January 28, 1993, March 7, 1996).

VICE PRESIDENT.   For Bill Clinton, Vice President Al Gore has become one of his closest advisors. Gore has programmatic responsibility including his chairing of the commission on "reinventing government." But this kind of close working relationship between the president and vice president is more the exception than the rule. This office was inserted into the Constitution by the Committee on Postponed Matters of the Constitutional Convention as a means for succession should a president be impeached, resign, become disabled, or die in office.[56] It was an office, as John Adams allegedly commented when he was vice president to George Washington, that is "nothing" but could become "everything." "Cactus Jack" Garner, FDR's first vice president, was less delicate when he said the vice presidency was "not worth a bucket of warm spit."[57]

It was President Carter, the outsider with no Washington connections, who chose the experienced Senator Walter Mondale (D–Minn.) as his vice president and thereby established a new pattern for presidential-vice presidential relations. Mondale was given major policy responsibility and had his quarters close to the Oval Office so he could meet with Carter on a regular basis. In effect, Carter told Mondale that he was welcome in any meeting of importance throughout the administration.[58] As a result Vice President Mondale exerted significant influence on decisions affecting SALT, South Africa, the Middle East, and legislative strategies.[59]

KITCHEN CABINETS.   The kitchen cabinet is any informal group of presidential advisors, a tradition dating back to President Andrew Jackson's time.[60] Those who fill these roles can come from both inside or outside the government. They may be recruited from inside or outside the government and are often close friends or family members.

The First Lady can also fill this role as did Edith Wilson after her husband was incapacitated from a stroke. She selected the important issues to bring to the president's attention and effectively made the important decisions during this difficult period. Rosalyn Carter was the only First Lady to attend cabinet meetings regularly, but it was Hillary Rodham Clinton who cast aside the traditional role of First Lady and became a power in her own right within the Clinton administration. She helped manage the president's daily schedule, assisted in setting his political agenda, advised him on top-level appointments, was involved in writing some of his speeches, and even personally lobbied members of Congress.[61] In an unprecedented action that proved very controversial, Bill Clinton asked his wife to chair a task force to develop ambitious health care reform proposals. As we discussed in Chapter 8, her political activism took its toll with public opinion. One 1996 survey found that her overall job rating was 47 percent positive but 52 percent negative.[62]

For most presidents a groupthink mentality affects his inner circle of advisors because they share similar social and political attributes. One study found that 96 percent of the top White House staffers were white males and young to middle aged, 86 percent were college educated, 60 percent came from the private sector, and 77 percent had resided on the East Coast.[63] Perhaps most important, however, is that each member of the presidential inner circle is chosen because he or she has shown extraordinary loyalty to the president.

Executive Office of the President (EOP)

Unlike the line departments responsible for enforcing laws and implementing public policies, presidential staff agencies with advisory functions are located in the Executive Office of the President. Franklin Roosevelt appointed a three-person President's Committee on Administrative Management, chaired by Louis Brownlow, and in 1937 the Brownlow Committee issued its report proclaiming that the president "needs help" and recommending that he be assigned six assistants to help him administer the executive branch. That was the rationale for the 1939 Executive Order 8248 by which President Roosevelt created an Executive Office of the President with five units: White House Office, Liaison Office for Personnel Management, Office of Government Reports, Bureau of the Budget (transferred from the Treasury Department), and National Resources Planning Board. Today EOP contains fourteen units (Table 9–5) and has become so highly specialized that Professor John Hart characterizes it as the "presidential branch" of government.[64]

Table 9–5. Executive Office of the President, 1995

Office	Year Created	President
White House Office	1939	Roosevelt
Office of Management and Budget (formerly Bureau of the Budget, established in 1921)	1970	Nixon
Council of Economic Advisers	1946	Truman
National Security Council	1947	Truman
Office of Science and Technology Policy (formerly Office of Science and Technology, established 1962–1973)	1975	Ford
Council on Environmental Quality	1969	Nixon
Office of Administration	1977	Carter
Office of United States Trade Representative (formerly Office of Special Representative for Trade Negotiations, 1963–78)	1979	Carter
Office of the Vice President	1939	Roosevelt
Office of National Drug Control Policy	1988	Reagan

Source: *U.S. Government Manual 1995/1996* (Washington, D.C.: U.S. Government Printing Office, 1995), pp. 91–109.

OFFICE OF MANAGEMENT AND BUDGET (OMB).   The most institutionalized component of EOP is the Bureau of the Budget (BOB), renamed the Office of Management and Budget (OMB) by Richard Nixon. Established by the Budget and Accounting Act of 1921, its major responsibility is to formulate the annual "executive budget" that presidents usually submit to Congress in February. BOB reached the high point of its influence under Truman and Eisenhower when the bureau extended its authority over "central clearance" by screening on behalf of the White House agency legislative requests before any were forwarded to Congress.[65]

The Nixon administration also politicized the OMB by appointing directors who were political loyalists rather than careerists within the agency and then by using them to defend Nixon's budgetary priorities. He began a pattern that continues into the Clinton administration. Carter appointed a longtime friend and small town Georgia banker as his OMB director; Reagan appointed David Stockman, a conservative ex-Congressman who championed tax cuts and Reaganomics until he had a change of heart; Clinton took charge of OMB by appointing Leon Panetta, who had been a legislative staffer and then a member of Congress (D–Calif.,) as its head.

But nothing could forestall a fundamental change in the way OMB operated, and its experience, more than any other, gave rise to a serious debate among academics about the desirability of direct White House involvement with federal agencies—line bureaus in the departments or institutionalized units (such as OMB) within EOP. Nixon's takeover of OMB led Hugh Heclo to decry the assault on its "neutral competence" as he raised this issue: "Has OMB balanced the demands placed on it for policy advocacy outside and for quiet diplomacy within government? Has it succeeded in being a close member of the President's political family yet maintaining itself as a detached staff for the ongoing Presidency?"[66] Because every president must rely on agencies like OMB to achieve their policy objectives, they would be better served by careerists who are professional and whose tenure and morale are secure.

The counter-argument by Richard Nathan and Terry Moe[67] is that the chief executive can never take charge of the permanent government unless he "politicizes" its ranks by replacing careerists with political appointees who are loyal to his policy agenda. Of course this debate has been fueled because the Democratic presidents with their ambitious social-welfare agendas were succeeded by Republicans who wanted to shrink government, reduce welfarism, return programs to the states, and rely on the private sector. Nixon and Reagan both entered office, for example, thinking the bureaucracy was filled with liberal-leaning Democratic sympathizers who would resist implementing their policies.

It was Carter who paved the way for Reagan to politicize OMB operations further by creating a Regulatory Analysis Review Group to ensure White House oversight of agency regulations. President Reagan handed down Executive Order 12291 of 1981, allowing the OMB to review all major rules and regulations proposed by agencies to determine whether their benefits outweighed their costs,[68] and Executive Order 12495 of 1985, which required agencies for submit any proposed regulations or new rules to the OMB and to explain how they were consistent with administration policies. As for the impact of the new "regulatory clearance" procedures, the number of approvals declined from 1981 (87.3 percent) to 1985 (70.7 percent), which, given the number of rules evaluated by OMB (12,233), was a substantial decrease.[69]

The Council of Economic Advisers (CEA) was created by the Employment Act of 1946. Intended to advise the president on economic growth, prices, and unemployment, its three members are almost always academic economists who must be confirmed by the Senate. The National Security Council (NSC) was established by the National Security Act of 1947 to coordinate domestic, foreign, and military policies affecting national security.

Ever since Nixon created his Domestic Council in 1970, a unit has been devoted to those concerns. But unlike the OMB, CEA, or NSC, this unit invariably changes its name, and its responsibilities vary according to the domestic priorities of the chief executive. As Shirley Anne Warshaw explains,

> Presidents who are committed to changing the direction of domestic policy, whether decreasing government's role as Reagan sought or reframing that role as Clinton sought, have domestic policy advisors with constant access to the president. Their staffs are generally large and are in constant dialogue with the departments. In contrast, presidents who have little or only minimal interest in domestic policy, such as Ford and Bush, have relegated their domestic policy advisors to second-class status in the White House and generally have little direct contact with them. The domestic policy staffs are relatively small and have few interactions with the departments.[70]

Bill Clinton devised an elaborate domestic apparatus. Within the White House Office of Policy Development he located the Domestic Policy Council along with a newly created National Economic Council and the Office of Environmental Policy.[71]

WHITE HOUSE OFFICE.   The White House Office (WHO) has grown from the six generalists the Brownlow Committee recommended in 1937 to a large and highly specialized organization of public relations experts, speechwriters, political operatives, legislative liaisons, people responsible for community outreach, and specialists in intergovernmental relations, to name only a few examples (Table 9–6). Before EOP was established in 1939, the personal staff assigned to the president had no formal positions and, moreover, to augment its small size President Roosevelt had to borrow other aides from the regular departments. The situation is vastly different today, according to John Hart: "What was essentially intended to be a conduit between the president and the enhanced management capacity in the Executive Office has instead become the management itself. The White House Office is now the directing force of the presidential branch, and the important units within the EOP are very much satellite agencies of the White House Office."[72]

Table 9–6. Unit Offices within the White House Office, 1996

Office of the Chief of Staff
—including divisions for Policy; Strategic Planning and Communications;
Speechwriting and Research
General Counsel
White House Personnel Security Office
Office of Legislative Affairs
—including divisions for House Liaison Office; Senate Liaison Office
Office of National Affairs
Office of the Press Secretary
—including divisions for Media Affairs; News Analysis
Office of the Deputy Chief of Staff for Policy and Political Affairs
Office of Cabinet Affairs
Office of Intergovernmental Affairs
Office of Public Liaison
Office of Political Affairs
Office of Staff Secretary
Office of Correspondence
—including divisions for Agency Liaison; Gifts; Greetings/Inquiries/Comment
Line; Mail Analysis; Presidential Letters; Presidential Messages; Presidential Support; Student Correspondence; and Volunteer Office
Executive Clerk
Records Management
Office of the Deputy Chief of Staff for White House Operations
Office of Management and Administration
—including divisions for White House Administration; White House Intern Program; White House Military Office; Photography Office; White House Telephone
Services; Travel Office; and Visitor's Office
Office of Presidential Personnel
Office of Scheduling and Advance
Office of the First Lady
—including Office of the Press Secretary to the First Lady
Office of National Aids Policy
White House Fellowship Office
White House Post Office
President's Foreign Intelligence Advisory Board
The Board
Ushers Office

Source: *Federal Yellow Book* 40, (1) (New York: Leadership Directories, 1996), pp. I-9–I-14.

THE "COMPETITIVE" MODEL.   Franklin D. Roosevelt adopted a unique
method of presidential administration that has not been duplicated since.
He wanted a highly flexible and informal organization and his two underlying principles were "competition" and "tension." To maximize his access
to information, FDR would pit officials with opposite ideologies against
each other, for example soliciting advice from conservative Secretary of the
Treasury Will Woodin and liberal presidential assistant Harry Hopkins.
    Ideological rivalry was evident when FDR appointed codirectors of
the Office of Production Management. He put in charge of this unit con-

servative William Knudsen of General Motors and liberal Sidney Hillman from the Congress of Industrial Organizations (CIO). This was typical of the Roosevelt style. He also would deliberately overlap bureaucratic jurisdictions by creating a new agency to compete with an existing one. Thus, instead of allowing the Treasury Department to supervise the stock exchanges, he delegated that responsibility to a newly created Securities and Exchange Commission (SEC). Roosevelt did not abide by clear jurisdictional lines and often elicited information by directly contacting individuals throughout his bureaucracy.

Although this management style was used effectively by Roosevelt, it was more appropriate to his era when the vast array of welfare programs and government regulations were being established. Moreover, the federal bureaucracy that FDR managed was small by the standards of today. So his competitive model had to give way to more stable and institutionalized relationships among the president, his cabinet, and White House staff.

CABINET GOVERNMENT.   President Eisenhower had been a career military man who understood organization. Thus he utilized a hierarchical model with lines of authority pyramiding down through his staff to the subordinates. His system was orderly and, unlike FDR, Eisenhower did not relish conflict or dissent among his staff and thus stressed the need for collegiality and teamwork. One of Eisenhower's primary administrative skills was his ability to get the White House staff and cabinet to work together, without the institutional conflicts that emerged in later administrations. Eisenhower believed in cabinet government, and he regularly chaired meetings of the entire cabinet to discuss policy, to elicit their reactions, and to develop a unity of purpose and a team spirit. To assist him in arranging the formal agenda for business, Eisenhower created the position of cabinet secretariat. The secretaries were expected to report on how they planned to implement the president's directives. No other president so effectively used the cabinet as a collective decision-making body.

Eisenhower also appointed the first chief of staff, naming former New Hampshire governor Sherman Adams to that post. Adams screened domestic matters for Eisenhower, and all appointments, policy decisions, and cabinet secretaries' reports passed through his hands first. One exception to this was Secretary of State John Foster Dulles, who reported directly to the president. Although some have criticized the Eisenhower system and particularly the role played by Adams,[73] Stephen Hess argues that this model really gave Eisenhower "considerable freedom of action by giving his subordinates considerable latitude to act."[74]

SPOKES-OF-THE-WHEEL MODEL.   President Kennedy dismantled much of Eisenhower's structure, doing away with the cabinet secretariat and appointing no chief of staff. Kennedy probably best represents the collegial, or spokes-of-the-wheel model, which was more compatible with his personalized and less formal style. JFK wanted to be at the center of all the decisions, with his White House staffers and cabinet members coming to him with information and policy options for a final decision. There was no pretense of cabinet government in his administration. As Kennedy once remarked: "Cabinet meetings . . . are simply useless. Why should the Postmaster General sit there and listen to a discussion of the problems of Laos? . . . I don't know how Presidents functioned with them or relied on them in the past."[75]

Kennedy relied extensively on individual advisors who were assigned to specialized areas such as national security or legislative affairs. This arrangement permitted Kennedy to depend less on any inner circle of advisors than perhaps any other contemporary president. One advantage of his fluid management system was that President Kennedy could direct his staff to focus on whatever problem had top priority. The primary disadvantage of his model, however, is system overload. Being at the hub of the wheel of decision making means every immediate issue can be brought to the president's attention, which exhausts his time and energy and allows little room for reflection. Since JFK, all presidents have agreed with Eisenhower that delegation is essential to White House management.

White House-Cabinet Relations

Trying to structure a working relationship between the White House staff and members of the cabinet lies at the heart of presidential management. The optimal strategy would be "powersharing" whereby presidents take advantage of the organizational strengths of both White House staff and cabinet members, as Warshaw explains:

> Neither the Cabinet nor the White House staff alone appear to be the appropriate mechanism for policy development. The answer would seem to lie in a well-structured system of powersharing in which both the Cabinet and the White House staff share policy development responsibility. The Cabinet provides the president the technical expertise in policy development and implementation, while the White House staff provides the president the assurance that departmental policies meet administration goals and objectives, and are in concert with presidential political ends.[76]

Many presidents tried to find the managerial formula for success, but few have succeeded (Table 9-7).

It is now commonplace to follow Eisenhower's example and appoint a White House chief of staff to manage the Executive Office of the President. Especially strong-willed men were appointed by Nixon (H.R. Haldeman); Bush (John Sununu, before he was forced to resign in late 1991 and was replaced with the more collegial Sam Skinner); and Reagan (Donald Regan, who served two years in his second term before being forced to resign after the Iran-contra affair, when a collegial Howard Baker took that position).

Table 9–7. Presidents' Relationships to Cabinet and Staff

Executive Relationships		Presidents					
		Nixon	Ford	Carter	Reagan	Bush	Clinton
President	• Involved in White House Staffing	X	X	X	X	X	X
	• Uninvolved						
White House Staff	• Strong	X			X	X	
	• Weak		X	X			X
Cabinet	• White House Controlled	X			X	X	
	• Independent Actors		X	X			X
Subcabinet	• Cabinet Controlled	X§	X	X		X	
	• White House Controlled				X		X
Staffing Model	• Spokes of the Wheel		X*	X*			X*
	• Hierarchy	X			X	X	
Chief of Staff	• Dominant	X	X		X	X	
	• Collegial						
	• Weak			X†			X‡

* These presidents later went to the hierarchical model.

† Carter at first had no chief of staff, until 1979, when he appointed Hamilton Jordan, a collegial chief of staff.

‡ Clinton's chief of staff was at first weak, but later was replaced by a dominant chief of staff.

§ Moved to White House control in the first administration.

Source: Shirley Anne Warshaw, *Powersharing: White House-Cabinet Relations in the Modern Presidency* (Albany, NY: SUNY Press, 1996); and *The Domestic Presidency: Policy Making in the White House* (Boston: Allyn & Bacon, 1997).

Jimmy Carter experimented with cabinet government at the beginning of his term but, after disarray engulfed his administration, he turned in mid-1979 to his Georgia friend Hamilton Jordan as his de facto chief of staff. Bill Clinton at first called on his congenial friend from Arkansas, Thomas P. "Mack" McLarty, III, who tried to facilitate Clinton's spokes-of-the-wheel decision-making style, which resulted in a series of administrative missteps during the first year and ultimately forced McLarty to step aside. To bring order to White House operations, Clinton then picked the politically astute Leon Panetta, and the situation decidedly improved during the last two years of Clinton's first term.

Not just Clinton but also Ford and Carter originally attempted a spokes-of-the-wheel decision-making style. For Ford, who became president upon the resignation of Richard Nixon, it was his way of repudiating Nixon's imperial style of governing. But eventually all three presidents shifted to a hierarchical arrangement, allowing the White House more control over the policy agenda. Republican presidents have generally favored more hierarchy in how they structure White House and cabinet relations.

Every president has been personally involved in choosing his White House staffers, but the chief executive has failed to exert hands-on control over appointments that involve recruitment of under-secretaries or deputy secretaries to subcabinet positions. Under Nixon, Ford, Carter, and Bush cabinet members were typically given discretion to recruit their own subcabinet officials. The results of this for Carter were especially disastrous. Because Carter's cabinet secretaries tended to recruit their subcabinets from policy advocates aligned with the relevant clientele groups, they continually pulled the cabinet members away from the presidential orbit into being spokespersons for their own constituencies. In this regard Clinton learned from Reagan, whose White House took charge of recruiting nominees for both cabinet and subcabinet positions.

Reagan wrote a new chapter on White House-cabinet relations by creating a system for presidential control. Concludes Warshaw, "Ford, Bush and Clinton did not succeed at all at powersharing. Nixon and Carter experimented with a White House staff that had minimal policy responsibilities and found the system unsatisfactory. Ronald Reagan was the only one of the six presidents who attempted a powersharing relationship."[77]

PUBLIC INPUTS

A chief executive cannot easily mobilize the public at large to gain control over the bureaucracy even though most Americans have a negative image of the federal government. When Roper in 1986 surveyed people about their impressions of the word bureaucrat, 41 percent indicated it had a "negative" connotation, whereas 11 percent had a "favorable" impression of the term."[78]

Although public administration may lack the political sex appeal to arouse public opinion, nonetheless special interests and voter blocs are alert to policy implementation and law enforcement. When considering membership on such so-called independent regulatory commissions as the Federal Trade Commission (FTC), Federal Communications Commission (FCC), or the Securities and Exchange Commission (SEC), which are supposed to regulate those sectors of the economy in the public interest, "rarely does the President appoint, and the Senate confirm, a commissioner if the regulated industry is politically aligned against him."[79]

Until the late 1970s when President Carter appointed proconsumer advocates to the FTC, the history of FTC enforcement was a classic example of how a regulatory commission supposedly independent of direct presidential control could be "captured" by the industry it was intended to regulate. At the turn of the century, a public uproar about monopolistic practices and unfair competition led to the establishment of the FTC.

Since then its very existence has symbolized to the general public that their public interests were being safeguarded when, in reality, the day-by-day decisions by the FTC are shaped by the concerns of the industries, not the consumers.[80]

In the 1990s, with pressure building on the Clinton administration to accommodate Republican demands that the federal budget be balanced by the year 2002, there was renewed interest in slowing the growth of entitlements such as Medicaid, Social Security, federal pensions, veterans benefits, and the like, by recalculating the Consumer Price Index (CPI) because those entitlements had COLAs (cost-of-living adjustments) guaranteeing that the benefits would increase with rising prices. Most economists believed, however, that the CPI overestimated inflation, and the Bureau of Labor Statistics (BLS) had been studying the problem. But it was Federal Reserve Board chairman Alan Greenspan who publicly advocated recalculating the CPI in order to save billions of dollars in federal expenditures, thus easing the burden of deficit reduction. Whatever the public may have thought about the question, the American Association of Retired Persons (AARP) quickly condemned any change in the CPI that would lower entitlements for beneficiaries and suddenly both the Clinton administration and the Republican 105th Congress refused to endorse the concept openly, each preferring to let the other end of Pennsylvania Avenue take the first step.

At base, public opinion is not easily mobilized behind a chief executive's objectives, whereas organized interests do monitor policy implementation in which they have an economic stake. Particularly where they are the clientele served by a particular program—retirees who get pensions or farmers who get price supports—they rally their membership, friendly legislators, and even agency personnel to block any action that threatens their self-interest.

EXPERTISE

Expertise also is an uneven resource for the chief executive. Congress lacks the capability to detail administrative regulations in highly technical areas, and so the executive branch must rely on data collected by public and private institutions. Sometimes those databases can be unreliable. The first FBI report on hate crimes in 1991, for example, was judged to be inaccurate because the FBI depended on local law enforcement agencies to volunteer that data, and few did.

But unreliable data may give the president greater leverage to control the situation at hand. Adam Bryant challenges the figures released by the Department of Transportation regarding the cost of the impending 1997 airline strike at American Airlines. The president intervened, stopping some 9,000 airline pilots from walking off the job. Clinton took his authority from the 1926 Railway Labor Act that required showing the labor dispute would "threaten substantially" interstate commerce, depriving sections of the United States of essential transportation. The seriousness of the situation was revealed in Department of Transportation figures suggesting that the strike would cost $200 million and inconvenience some 43,000 passengers a day. The $200 million a day figure is, as Bryant revealed, the passenger revenue from the entire U.S. industry, whereas American Airlines only controls 20 percent of the industry. A more realistic figure for the cost of the impending strike would probably have been around $83 million a day, but there would then have been questions about whether Clinton had the authority under this act to intervene.[81] Such manipulation of the data by the president allowed him to act as he wished, but at the cost of distorting the crisis at hand.

Another problem with government regulation is its enforcement. Much regulatory enforcement depends on the expertise and know-how of the very industries that are being regulated because federal agencies lack sufficient staff to monitor the private economy. This problem was widely documented during the 1960s by investigatory studies done by the Ralph Nader Study Group, a consumer advocate organization.[82] Essentially the same story—inadequate federal regulatory personnel, too much reliance on voluntary compliance by an industry, and too cozy a relationship between the regulators and the regulated—surfaces every time a major accident or bureaucratic blunder takes place.

THE VALUJET CRASH.   One disaster that raised questions about how effectively the Federal Aviation Administration (FAA) was enforcing airline safety was the May 12, 1996, crash of ValuJet Flight 592 in the Florida Everglades that killed all 110 people aboard. Immediately there were charges about the FAA's ability to regulate airline safety. Probably few of the millions of Americans who fly the nation's airlines were aware that the FAA is given the dual responsibility of promoting air travel as well as regulating air safety, whereas in countries such as Canada and Britain, these two functions are divided. Nor do many people know the FAA has 2,500 safety inspectors who are responsible for checking the airworthiness of over 7,300 commercial airliners, 11,000 charter planes, and the nearly 200,000 general (civilian) aviation aircraft in the United States.

Although no definitive conclusion has emerged on what caused the crash, most speculation centered on as many as 136 oxygen canisters (used for emergency oxygen masks) that were loaded improperly into the cargo hold of Flight 592, although ValuJet was not authorized to carry hazardous materials. The investigation discovered that nearly half of the FAA's 600 hazardous-materials inspectors performed no on-site inspections but relied instead on paperwork provided by the airlines. Moreover, there were no fire-detection devices in the cargo hold despite recommendations made in 1988 by the National Transportation Safety Board (NTSB), restimulating the long-standing tensions between the NTSB and the FAA because the FAA is not obligated to follow NTSB recommendations. Instead, the FAA is required by Congress to do a cost-benefit analysis by implementing any NTSB recommendation, and apparently an early FAA statistical analysis did not warrant following that advice.

Immediately after the crash both Secretary of Transportation Federico Pena and FAA administrator David Hinson made public statements that ValuJet planes were safe, but then the news media publicized internal FAA reports from February and May that expressed safety concerns about the airline. The February 14 FAA report had recommended "an immediate . . . re-certification of this airline," citing "the absence of adequate policies and procedures for the maintenance personnel to follow" and noting "an absence of engine trend monitoring data" and possibly inadequate airworthiness-maintenance programs that used "reliability based procedures without a reliability program."

Following the crash, a whistle-blower emerged from the Department of Transportation (DOT). DOT's inspector general authored a *Newsweek* article that questioned FAA practices and indicated she had stopped flying ValuJet because of the problems the FAA had uncovered in February. Within a month Transportation Secretary Pena urged Congress to change the FAA's dual mandate, limiting its primary mission to airline safety. The FAA made its decision to ground the ValuJet fleet, the first ever shutdown of a major U.S. airline. By November 1996 the FAA reversed its earlier position and issued a statement saying it intends to mandate the installation of fire-detection devices in the cargo holds of airlines.[83]

ADVISORY COMMISSIONS.   To avoid the pitfalls of bureaucratic inertia, sometimes presidents turn to task forces and presidential advisory commissions or outside consultants to study issues and obtain more information and policy options. An extensive analysis of presidential advisory commissions from Truman to Nixon indicated that such ad hoc advisory forums perform five functions.[84] Most study a specific problem, assess existing efforts to solve it, and recommend remedial action. The findings of the President's Commission on Law Enforcement and Administration of Justice (1965–1967), for example, led to congressional enactment of the Omnibus Crime Control and Safe Streets Act of 1968. Other advisory commissions serve the purpose of window dressing to persuade Congress, the bureaucracy, and the general public to back a proposal that already has presidential support.

Appointing a commission may highlight an aspect of the domestic agenda or a presidential commitment made in the State of the Union Address, or it can be a diversionary tactic for presidents to avoid taking meaningful action. George Bush mentioned "a thousand points of light" to refer to America's volunteer efforts in community service, and later he created the President's Advisory Committee on the Points of Light Initiative Foundation; Clinton, rather than immediately responding to the Social Security problem, appointed an advisory commission to find ways to keep the pension system solvent. The commission ultimately split into factions over whether Social Security contributions should be invested in the private stock market. Those members aligned with organized labor were most opposed, and the others were divided on how aggressively to allow individual retirees to manage their own investment portfolios. No one solution to the problem emerged from that panel, but the majority generally favored moving away from a solely tax-based Social Security system in favor of some kind of free-market investment strategy.

CRISIS

Domestic crisis augments presidential power because the "executive power" clause and the "take care" clause of Article II of the Constitution make the president the chief law enforcer. The use of force is supported by Article IV of the Constitution, which directs the national government to protect every state "against Invasion . . . and against domestic Violence." Federal intervention may be requested by a governor or state legislature, although the president can refuse to send assistance. Or a president might intervene in local disturbances when he believes the state and local authorities are not enforcing federal laws. The military, the "federalized" Arkansas National Guard, and U.S. marshals were dispatched without state consent when President Eisenhower desegregated Little Rock High School in 1957. More recently, on May 1, 1992, George Bush deployed some 4,000 marine and army personnel and federalized 6,000 national guard to help restore order in riot-torn Los Angeles,[85] after California governor Pete Wilson had called up 4,000 national guard troops to stop the two days of rioting.

Congress delegates extraordinary authority to the chief executive to deal with domestic crises whenever they can be anticipated, or sometimes the president extends the language of a law beyond its original purpose to deal with an emergency. In 1933 Franklin Roosevelt resurrected a 1917 law (Trading with the Enemy Act) to justify his declaring a bank holiday to stem massive withdrawals of funds from those financial institutions until public confidence could be restored.

There is a long history of presidential intervention to resolve labor/management disputes that disrupt the national economy. In the famous Pullman strike, President Grover Cleveland, over the objections of the governor of Illinois, dispatched federal troops to Chicago to protect U.S. property and the distribution of the mails. When the nation was threatened by an anthracite coal strike as winter approached in 1902, Theodore Roosevelt intervened in that dispute. After an investigation, he forced the union and management to submit their disagreement to an arbitration commission; had this plan failed, Roosevelt was ready to use the army to "dispossess the operators and run the mines as a receiver."[86]

To curb labor strikes that threaten the national interest today, the Taft-Hartley Act of 1947 permits the president to issue a temporary injunction to impose an eighty-day cooling-off period during which labor/managment negotiations would continue. As we described earlier, President Clinton in February 1997 faced mounting pressure to avoid a strike by the nine thousand American Airlines pilots that would have cost millions of dollars, according to official figures, and inconvenienced thousands of travelers. He was able to use presidential emergency powers granted to him under the 1926 Railway Labor Act. That act authorizes the president, at the recommendation of the National Mediation Board, to postpone a strike that will seriously disrupt interstate commerce by naming a three-member board to recommend a nonbinding resolution of the dispute. The panel has thirty days to devise recommendations after which labor and management have another thirty days to consider them, and during that period no work stoppage can take place.[87]

THE PATCO STRIKE.   During the air traffic controllers strike of 1981, President Reagan essentially destroyed a union to resolve what he viewed as a serious threat to the national economy and his own authority. The Professional Air Traffic Controllers Organization (PATCO) represented 85 percent of the 17,500 federal employees who direct the country's air traffic. After 2½ months of bargaining with the government, PATCO's president stated in May 1981 that his members would strike one month later unless an acceptable offer was made by their employer, the Federal Aviation Administration (FAA).

The settlement, however, was rejected by 95 percent of the PATCO membership, and the strike action began. The Reagan administration reacted with a hard-line position and threatened the striking employees with termination. Because only about 1,200 PATCO workers voluntarily returned to their jobs, more than 11,000 striking air controllers were dismissed.

PATCO was officially abolished when, at the end of October, the Federal Labor Relations Authority revoked its authority to represent traffic controllers. Reagan's action was the first time a union representing federal employees had been literally abrogated.[88]

SUMMARY

The location of chief executive at the midpoint along our continuum of presidential roles means that both authority and influence are relevant to his leadership. Congress understands that the president is responsible for the day-to-day management of government, but it is not willing to abdicate its power of oversight on behalf of clientele groups. Public opinion is mostly benign because Americans are not easily mobilized unless a scandal or bureaucratic blunder dramatizes the need for organizational change.

Each president arranges his own advisory system and structures a relationship between the Executive Office of the President, particularly the White House Office, and the cabinet. The institutionalized presidency was designed to help him supervise the permanent bureaucracy, yet no president has mastered the bureaucracy entirely for his own policy ends. Nixon failed in his attempt; arguably Reagan came closest to succeeding.

When crises affect the domestic economy Congress is willing to delegate authority to the chief executive, but crisis leadership is not the normal state of affairs. As political scientist Louis Koenig once observed, the bottom line is that any president would be envious of the authority available to the typical business executive in the United States.[89]

NOTES

1. James MacGregor Burns, "Our Super-Government—Can We Control It?" *New York Times* (April 24, 1949), p. 32.

2. Quoted in Burns, "Our Super-Government—Can We Control It?" p. 30.

3. See *Congressional Quarterly's: Guide to the Presidency* (Washington, DC: Congressional Quarterly, 1989), p. 260.

4. Richard M. Pious, *The American Presidency* (New York: Basic Books, 1979), p. 218.

5. This pattern may be changing,however. Calvin MacKenzie determined that only eleven major presidential nominations were rejected by the Senate from 1961 to 1973, whereas almost three times as many rejections occurred in 1974 (six), 1975 (seven), 1976 (ten), and 1977 (six). These data imply that the Congress may be scrutinizing the president's nominees more carefully in the post-Watergate era. See Calvin MacKenzie, *The Politics of Presidential Appointments* (New York: Free Press, 1981), p. 177.

6. For the account on Kimba Wood see the following articles: "Illegal-Alien Thorn Again Stings Clinton," *Salt Lake Tribune* (Feb. 6, 1993), pp. A1, Richard L. Berke, "2 Down: Another Cabinet Hopeful Withdraws," *Deseret News* (Feb. 6, 1993), pp. A1–A2, and Richard L. Berke, "Judge Wood Backs White House Stand on What She Told," *New York Times* (Feb. 8, 1993), pp. A1, C9.

7. Yet a third person who was being considered for the position had a similar problem. Charles F. C. Ruff, a Washington attorney, was quickly taken off the list after it was discovered he had hired a maid and had failed to pay her Social Security taxes until the Baird affair had become public knowledge. At that time he did pay $3,300 in back taxes. Richard L. Berke, "The White House's Side: Easy Confirmation Is Goal in Search for New Nominee," *New York Times* (Feb. 7, 1993), p. 16.

8. One of her Republican critics even referred to her as a "high priestess of political correctness" because of her close association with NOW. Larry Rohter, "Tough 'Front-line Warrior'," *New York Times* (Feb. 12, 1993), p. A10.

9. M. Glenn Abernathy, Dilys M. Hill and Phil Williams, *The Carter Years: The President and Policy Making* (London: Frances Pinter, 1984), pp. 106–108; also see Herbert D. Rosenbaum and Alexej Ugrinsky, eds., *The Presidency and Domestic Policies of Jimmy Carter* (Westport, CT: Greenwood, 1994), p. 739; and John Dumbrell, *The Carter Presidency: A Re-Evaluation* (Manchester: Manchester University Press, 1993), p. 77.

10. Carl Rowan, "President Did Federal Bench a Disservice," *Salt Lake Tribune,* (April 5, 1996), p. A29.

11. Jeffrey Rosen, "Mediocrity on the Bench," *New York Times,* (March 17, 1995), p. A15.

12. Rowan, "President Did Federal Bench a Disservice," p. A29.

13. Angie Cannon,"Clinton Changing the Face of Federal Bench," *Salt Lake Tribune* (Oct. 14, 1994), p. A8.

14. Joan Biskupic, "Bush Lags in Appointments to the Federal Judiciary," *Congressional Quarterly Weekly Report,* (Jan. 6, 1990), p. 39.

15. See Gregory A. Caldeira, "Public Opinion and the U.S. Supreme Court: FDR's Court-Packing Plan," *American Political Science Review* 81 (Dec. 1987), pp. 1139–1153; Franklin D. Roosevelt, "The President Presents a Plan for the Reorganization of the Judicial Branch of the Government," February 5, 1937, *The Public Papers and Addresses of Franklin D. Roosevelt* (New York: Russell & Russell, 1937), vol. 6, pp. 51–59; Franklin D. Roosevelt, "A 'Fireside Chat' Discussing the Plan for Reorganization of the Judiciary," March 9, 1937, *The Public Papers and Addresses of Franklin D. Roosevelt* (New York: Russell & Russell, 1937), vol. 6, pp. 122–133.

16. See Henry J. Abraham, *Justices and Presidents: A Political History of Appointments to the Supreme Court,* 3rd. ed. (New York: Oxford University Press, 1992), p. 211.

17. David M. O'Brien, *Storm Center: The Supreme Court in American Politics,* 2nd ed. (New York: Norton, 1990), pp. 94–95.

18. O'Brien, *Storm Center*, pp. 62-63.
19. "Remarks to the National Association of Evangelicals in Chicago, Illinois—March 3, 1992, "*Public Papers of the Presidents of the United States: Administration of George Bush, 1992, March 3, 1992* (Washington, DC: U.S. Government Printing Office, 1993), p. 368.
20. Henry J. Abraham, *Justices and Presidents*, p. 329; Stephen E. Ambrose, *Nixon*, vol.2: *The Triumph of a Politician, 1962–1972* (New York: Simon & Schuster, 1987), p. 469.
21. Henry J. Abraham, *Justices and Presidents*, p. 338.
22. Lawrence Baum, *The Supreme Court*, 5th ed. (Washington DC: Congressional Quarterly, 1995), p. 34.
23. Al Kamen, "Close, but No Confirmation: Despite a Flurry of Senate Votes, Clinton's Judicial Nominees Are still in Limbo," *Washington Post National Weekly Edition*, (Aug. 12-18, 1996), p. 14.
24. See David O'Brien, *Storm Center*, pp. 115-118.
25. See Gunter Bischof and Stephen E. Ambrose, eds., *Eisenhower: A Centenary Assessment*, p. 89; Hunter R. Clark, *Justice Brennan: The Great Conciliator* (Secaucus, N.J.: Carol, 1995), p. 79; Michael A. Kahn, "Shattering the Myth about President Eisenhower's Supreme Court Appointments," *Presidential Studies Quarterly*, 22 (Winter 1992) p. 52; and Henry J. Abraham, *Justices and Presidents*, pp. 256-258.
26. Bernard Schwartz, *Super Chief: Earl Warren and His Supreme Court—a Judicial Biography* (New York: New York University, 1983), pp. 2–3; and G. Edward White, *Earl Warren: A Public Life* (New York: Oxford University Press, 1982), p. 151.
27. Recently coming from the Nixon Justice Department, Rehnquist was the only Nixon appointee who did not vote against Nixon, but chose not to participate in the case fearing a conflict of interest.
28. These cases involving the president's removal power are cited in the discussion to follow: *U.S. v. Perkins*, U.S. 483, 485 (1886); *Parsons v. U.S.*, 167 U.S. 324, 343 (1897); *Shurtleff v. U.S.*, 189 U.S. 311, 317 (1903); *Wallace v. U.S.*, 257 US 541, 545–46 (1922); *Myers, Administratrix v. U.S.*, 272 U.S. 52 (1926); *Humphrey's Executor (Rathbun) v. U.S.*, 295 U.S. 602 (1935).
29. These cases are discussed in this section: *Wiener v. U.S.*, 357 U.S. 349 (1958); and *Carlucci, Secretary of Defense et al. v. Doe*, 488 U.S. 93 (1988).
30. See *Carlucci, Secretary of Defense et al. v. Doe*, 488 U.S. 99 (1988).
31. See *Humphrey's Executor (Rathbun) v. U.S.*, 295 U.S. 602 (1935).
32. The Senate's resolution stated "*Resolved*, That the President, in the late Executive proceeding in relation to the public revenue, has assumed upon himself authority and power not conferred by the Constitution and laws, but in derogation of both." See James D. Richardson, *A Compilation of the Messages and Papers of the Presidents, 1789–1887* (Washington, DC: U.S. Government Printing Office, 1896), vol. 3, p. 69.
33. Burt Solomon, "A Cabinet Member Gets the Boot . . . and More Turnover Seems Likely," *National Journal* (Dec. 22, 1990), p. 3098.
34. Paul F. Horvitz, "Aspin to Step Down as Defense Secretary," *International Herald Tribune*, (Dec. 16, 1993), News section, Information Bank Abstracts.
35. See Robert E. DiClerico, *The American President*, 3rd ed. (Englewood Cliffs, NJ: Prentice Hall, 1990), p. 164.
36. Discussion of the Reagan years and the civil service is primarily taken from Charles H. Levine, "The Federal Government in the Year 2000: Administrative Legacies of the Reagan Years," *Public Administration Review*, 46 (May/June 1986), pp. 195–206.
37. Ibid., p. 201.
38. Joel D. Aberbach and Bert A. Rockman, "Clashing Beliefs within the Executive Branch: The Nixon Administration Bureaucracy," *American Political Science Review 70* (June 1976), pp. 456–468.
39. Joel D. Aberbach and Bert A. Rockman, with Robert Copeland, "From Nixon's *Problem* to Reagan's *Achievement*—The Federal Executive Reexamined," in Larry Berman, ed., *Looking Back on the Reagan Presidency* (Baltimore: John Hopkins University Press, 1990), p. 182.
40. See Robert Maranto and David Schultz, *A Short History of the United States Civil Service* (Lanham, MD: University Press of America, 1991), p. 168.
41. "Hatch Act Veto," *Congress and the Nation* VIII (Washington, DC: Congressional Quarterly, 1993), pp. 859–861, 886–887; "Hatch Act Revisions Revised," *1993 Congressional Quarterly Almanac* XLIX (Washington, DC: Congressional Quarterly, 1994), pp. 201–204.
42. William F. Mullen, *Presidential Power and Politics* (New York: St. Martin's Press, 1978), p. 67.

43. See, for example, *Train v. City of New York*, 420 U.S. 35 (1975).
44. The report, entitled *From Red Tape to Results: Creating a Government That Works Better and Costs Less* was made public on September 8, 1993. See Ann Devroy and Stephen Barr, "Clinton Offers Plan to Fix 'Broken' Government," *Washington Post* (Sept. 8, 1993), pp. A1, A6. Also see Stephen Barr, "Gore Report Targets 252,000 Federal Jobs," *Washington Post* (Sept. 5, 1993), pp. A1, A18; and Stephen Barr, "Beyond Numbers: The Spirit of the Gore Report," *Washington Post* (Sept. 14, 1993), p. A19; Harold C. Relyea, *CRS Report for Congress: Reinventing Government and the 103d Congress: A Brief Overview* (Washington DC: Congressional Research Service, 1993), as well as National Performance Review, *Report: Creating a Government That Works Better and Costs Less*, (Washington, DC: (Sept. 7, 1993).
45. Jon Healey, "Reinventing Government Bit by Bit," *Congressional Quarterly Weekly Report* (Oct. 8, 1994), p. 2872.
46. John Hart, *The Presidential Branch: From Washington to Clinton*, 2nd ed. (Chatham, NJ: Chatham House, 1995), p. 149. Also see Morris S. Ogul, *Congress Oversees the Bureaucracy* (Pittsburgh: University of Pittsburgh Press, 1976), p. 181.
47. *INS v. Chadha*, 462 U.S. 919 (1983).
48. See Robert Rothman, "Despite High Court Ruling, Legislative Vetoes Abound," *Congressional Quarterly Weekly Report*, 42 (1984), p. 1797.
49. See Louis Fisher, "Judicial Misjudgments about the Law Making Process: The Legislative Veto Case," *Public Administration Review* 45 (Nov. 1985), p. 708.
50. Several options are discussed in Fisher, "Judicial Misjudgments, pp. 705–711; and Daniel Paul Franklin, "Why the Legislative Veto Isn't Dead," *Presidential Studies Quarterly*, 16 (Summer 1986), pp. 491–502.
51. Thomas Emerson, "The FBI as Political Police," in Pat Watters and Stephan Gillers, eds., *Investigating the FBI* (New York: Doubleday, 1973), pp. 239–254.
52. The latest breakdown of government units is from 1987. See Harold W. Stanley and Richard G. Niemi, *Vital Statistics on American Politics* (Washington, DC: Congressional Quarterly, 1990), p. 291.
53. Presidents like Ronald Reagan have further expanded the cabinet by allocating cabinet status to the vice president, UN ambassador, and such advisors as his White House counsel, the U.S. trade representative, CIA director, and the director of the Office of Management and Budget. DiClerico, *The American President*, p. 196.
54. Pious, *The American Presidency*, p. 240.
55. See John Hart, *The Presidential Branch: From Washington to Clinton*, 2nd ed. (Chatham, NJ: Chatham House, 1995), 137.
56. See Richard M. Pious, *The Presidency* (Boston: Allyn & Bacon, 1996), p. 69.
57. See Diana Dixon Healy, *America's Vice-Presidents* (New York: Atheneum, 1984), p. 8 for the John Adams's quotation and pp. 172–173 for Garner's comment.
58. See Robert E. DiClerico, *The American President*, 4th ed. (Englewood Cliffs, NJ: Prentice Hall, 1995), 378–379.
59. Ibid., p. 379.
60. Quoted in Herman Finer, *The Presidency: Crisis and Regeneration* (Chicago: University of Chicago Press, 1968), pp. 186–187.
61. Rich Jaroslovsky,"Washington Wire: A Special Weekly Report from the Wall Street Journal's Capital Bureau," *Wall Street Journal*, (Feb. 26, 1993), p. A1.
62. Humphrey Taylor, "Public Divided about Hillary Rodham Clinton: Slender Majority Gives Her Negative Rating but Majorities Believe She Did Not Commit Any Crime and Has Generally Told the Truth," *The Harris Poll* 7 (Jan. 31, 1996), pp. 1–2.
63. Cited in Edward N. Kearny, *Dimensions of the Modern Presidency* (St. Louis: Forum Press, 1981), p. 142.
64. John Hart, *The Presidential Branch: Executive Office of the President from Washington to Clinton* (Chatham, NJ: Chatham House Press, 1995).
65. Richard E. Neustadt, "Presidency and Legislation: The Growth of Central Clearance," in Aaron Wildavsky, ed., *The Presidency* (Boston: Little, Brown, 1969).
66. Hugh Heclo, "OMB and the Presidency—the Problem of 'Neutral Competence'," *The Public Interest* (Winter 1975), p. 89.
67. Richard P. Nathan, *The Administrative Presidency* (New York: Wiley, 1983); Terry M. Moe, "The Politicized Presidency," in J. Chubb and Paul Peterson, eds., *The New Direction in American Politics* (Washington, DC: The Brookings Institution, 1985).
68. Exempt from this are the actions of Independent Regulatory Commissions like the Federal Communications Commission.
69. See Joseph Cooper and William F. West, "Presidential Power and Republican Gov-

ernment: The Theory and Practice of OMB Review of Agency Rules," *Journal of Politics* 50 (November 1988), pp. 874–875.

70. Shirley Anne Warshaw, *The Domestic Presidency* (Boston: Allyn & Bacon, 1997), p. 218.

71. See "Excerpts from Clinton's Announcement of Appointments to Economic Posts," *New York Times*, (Dec. 11, 1992), p. A16. See also John Hart's detailed chapter 3 on "The Development of the Executive Office of the President" in his *The Presidential Branch: From Washington to Clinton*, 2nd ed. (Chatham, NJ: Chatham House, 1995), pp. 38–110.

72. See John Hart, *The Presidential Branch: From Washington to Clinton*, 2nd ed. (Chatham, NJ: Chatham House, 1995), p. 112.

73. John Burke, *The Institutional Presidency* (Baltimore: Johns Hopkins University Press, 1992), p.63.

74. Stephen Hess, *Organizing the Presidency* (Washington, DC : The Brookings Institution, 1976), p. 65.

75. Arthur M. Schlesinger, Jr., *A Thousand Days* (Boston: Houghton Mifflin, 1965), p. 688.

76. Shirley Anne Warshaw, *Powersharing: White House-Cabinet Relations in the Modern Presidency* (Albany, NY: SUNY Press, 1996), p. 228.

77. Ibid., p. 229.

78. The actual question was "I want to ask you about certain words that we hear a lot in political talk. For each one would you tell me whether it has a favorable connotation to you, or a negative meaning to you, or is just descriptive without either a favorable or unfavorable association? . . . A Bureaucrat. Roper Center for Public Opinion Research, Question ID: USROPER. 090886 R15E, Survey release date, Sept. 8, 1986.

79. Roger G. Noll, *Reforming Regulation* (Washington, DC: The Brooking Institution, 1971), p. 43.

80. Murray Edelman, *The Symbolic Uses of Politics* (Urbana: University of Illinois Press, 1970), chap. 3.

81. See Adam Bryant, "Maybe a Strike Wouldn't Have Cost That Much,"*New York Times*, (Feb. 23, 1997), p. E4.

82. See James S. Turner, *The Chemical Feast* (New York: Grossman, 1970), and Robert Fellmeth, *The Interstate Commerce Omission* (New York: Grossman, 1970).

83. Peter Grier, "Federal Inspectors Come under Fire over Airline Safety," *Christian Science Monitor* (May 16, 1996), p.1; Faye Bowers, "Fact vs. Guesswork in ValuJet Tragedy," *Christian Science Monitor* (May 24, 1996), p. 1; Faye Bowers, "Does ValuJet Shutdown Signal a Tougher FAA?" *Christian Science Monitor* (June 19, 1996), p.3; Faye Bowers, "A Call for FAA to Change, from Ground Up," *Christian Science Monitor* (June 20, 1996), p. 1; "Questions for the FAA," [Editorial], *Christian Science Monitor* (June 24, 1996), p. 20; Faye Bowers, "Value-Jet Investigation Escalates Tug of War over Airline Safety," *Christian Science Monitor* (November 21, 1996), p. 1.
   Note: These were all from the Web and can be located at: http://www.csmonitor.com/plweb-cgi...chives+archives++valujet%26tragedy.

84. Thomas R. Wolanin, *Presidential Advisory Commissions* (Madison: University of Wisconsin Press, 1975), chap. 2.

85. See Douglas Jehl and John M. Broder, "Bush Pledges Enough Force to Quell Riots," *Los Angeles Times*, May 2, 1992, p. 1.

86. Louis W. Koenig, *The Chief Executive,* 2nd ed. (New York: Harcourt Brace and World, 1968), p. 288.

87. See James Bennet, "White House Acts to Stop Strike by Airline Pilots," *New York Times*, February 15, 1997 @ http://search.nytimes.com/library/financial/0215american-pilots.html.

88. The White House announced on February 3, 1993, that 12 years after President Reagan had fired air traffic controllers who were members of PATCO, Bill Clinton was seriously thinking of lifting the ban and rehiring those who would like to become air traffic controllers again. Some 3,000 former members of PATCO indicated they would like to again become involved in the airline industry. President Clinton suggested he would like to change the relationship between the federal government and labor and lifting the ban would change the "tone" of the relationship. On August 13, 1993, President Clinton did just this through an executive order. See "Clinton May Lift Bar to Rehiring Controllers," *New York Times* (Feb. 4, 1993), p. A8, and "Testimony April 25, 1994 Public Employee Department, AFL-CIO House Appropriations/Transportation Appropriations," April 25, 1994, Federal Document Clearing House Congressional Testimony.

89. Louis W. Koenig, *The Chief Executive*, p. 155.

10

Insight on Chief Executive: Clinton's "Don't Ask, Don't Tell" Policy on Gays in the Military

In 1982 the Department of Defense issued a directive that prohibited homosexuals from serving in the military. Ten years later, as one of his campaign promises, Bill Clinton assured the gay voting bloc that he would sign an executive order to lift that ban. Moreover he assured them that it would be one of the first actions he would take as chief executive if elected. True to his campaign promise, Clinton moved forward and put in motion the process to remove the service ban for gays and lesbians. Beyond the political reaction of gays and the military establishment, however, the issue has drawn considerable interest among students of the presidency. It shows how difficult it is for the chief executive to overcome entrenched bureaucratic interests, congressional opposition, and adverse public opinion in order to make sweeping changes in the implementation of public policy.[1]

For the newly elected president, Clinton's promise to the gay community became a test case of his powers over the military establishment and his personal flexibility as the chief executive. In a sense, President Clinton found himself in "trench warfare" that set a negative tone for the remainder of his first term.[2]

The existing fifty-year ban on homosexuals in the military, which was implemented during World War II but became codified during the Reagan administration, has slowly been giving way (Table 10–1). Before World War II, homosexuals were allowed to serve in the military and, even though restrictions were created on a service-by-service basis, it was not until 1982 that a formal policy was established. During World War II homosexuality was treated as a mental illness, resulting in a dishonorable discharge if the treatment provided failed to change the individual's sexual orientation. Psychiatric treatment was halted in 1982 when the new policy, which Clinton sought to overturn, stated that "homosexuality is incompatible with military service."[3]

Table 10–1. Gays in the Military

Before World War I: No regulations barred gays. Commanding officers were permitted to assign homosexuals to noncombat jobs, but few gay soldiers were discharged.

During World War 2: Military psychiatrists labeled homosexuality a mental illness and tried to treat it. Those who failed to "improve" often were discharged for "ineptness or undesirable habits."

In the Late 1940s: As the Cold War intensified, gays were denied security clearances—ostensibly because they were vulnerable to blackmail. In 1947 the military began discharging soldiers deemed to have "homosexual tendencies." Those who committed homosexual acts were subject to court-martial or administrative discharge.

In 1951: The new Uniform Code of Military Justice made sodomy a criminal offense. The army began discharging homosexuals.

In 1966: The army required gay soldiers to undergo psychiatric examinations before separation from the service.

In the Late 1970s: In the face of growing court challenges to its practices, the military began reviewing its policies but did not necessarily rule in favor of homosexuals' rights.

In the Early 1980s: A landmark Pentagon study recommended lifting the ban on homosexuals. The document reviewed dozens of cases in which military personnel had compromised military secrets, and found that none of those who had been caught doing so was gay.

Since Then: The courts have been chipping away at the ban. On January 28, 1993, a U.S. District Court judge declared the ban on gays to be unconstitutional. President Clinton on January 29, 1993, partially lifted the ban, delaying full repeal for at least six months during which time Congress holds lengthy hearing on the issue.

Source: Data comes from Senate Armed Services Committee, Congressional Research Service, as it appeared in the *Los Angeles Times* (Jan. 31, 1993), p. A28.

Shortly after his election, Clinton announced that he would honor his campaign pledge and lift the ban entirely.[4] The move was no doubt meant to make him look decisive and to pay back 10 percent of the electorate who had rejected the GOP platform of George Bush that maintained the 1982 ban.[5] Once in the Oval Office, however, it was apparent that Clinton had underestimated the resistance the policy change would encounter from the military and the public. The resistance was so vociferous that, when the president signed an executive order lifting a Reagan-imposed gag rule banning abortion counseling at federally funded clinics, it was all but unnoticed, suggesting to some people that abortion, the social issue of the 1980s, was giving way to gay and lesbian rights in the 1990s.[6] Thus, not only was the change in policy toward gays viewed as a test of presidential power, but it also may determine the way in which sexual orientation and preferences will be defined in the future.[7]

The traditions and biases of the status quo can hamper the efforts of the president, effectively neutralizing his power. From one perspective, Clinton's decision to put the homosexual ban at the top of his policy agenda was theoretically sound.[8] A president enters the White House with a finite amount of goodwill that will quickly disappear if it is not taken advantage of.[9] Time will catch up with him and his initial political capital will have vanished, an especially telling point for a president who won the 1992 election with only 43 percent of the popular vote.

Clinton did not have a clear mandate other than to repair an ailing economy, which seemingly did not extend to public support for gays in the military. So the controversy over gays in the armed services had dire consequences for Clinton vis-à-vis other issues including the economy, the centerpiece of his campaign. As one report noted, much of the controversy over the gay issue probably would have been avoided if Clinton, as promised, had his economic policy ready for Congress when he was sworn in.[10] Instead, the gay issue dominated the media coverage of the new administration.

With respect to his *authority* as chief executive, one question asked by commentators at the time was why Clinton did not simply order the reversal of the ban by the stroke of the pen, using an executive order. Observers drew the analogy with President Truman's 1948 Executive Order Number 9981, which required races to be treated equally in the military, an order that displeased General Omar Bradley who stated, "The Army is not out to make social reform."[11] Although Clinton might have followed Truman's example, legislation could be enacted to override any executive order allowing homosexuals in the military services, and it did not appear that Clinton had the needed support.[12]

Clinton did have a measure of authority derived from his election victory but, as one scholar notes, an "electoral coalition even when it wins is not the same as a governing coalition."[13] The gay ban, in a sense, became a test of Clinton's moral authority and the political support he had in and out of Congress during the honeymoon period of his administration.[14]

Although Clinton never signed an executive order to repeal the ban, he did send his proposal to the Department of Defense for review and recommendations. Clinton would change the policy in a two-step approach. First, the president called for an immediate restriction on asking recruits about their sexual preferences as well as a halt to all discharges of homosexual personnel in the services. The second step was a six-month delay—until July 1993—to allow time to formulate a formal code of conduct on homosexual behavior, detailing what gays could and could not do in the military services. Clinton then would put it into the form of an executive order but with Department of Defense support. [15]

The president's formal authority does provide him with some degree of deferential treatment from his subordinates in the vast federal bureaucracy. Many members of the armed forces would have loved to fight any review of the gay ban policy but, as one army official noted, "we can't fight it openly."[16] Thus Clinton's military adversaries adopted a "cordial, honest and respectful" tone and quietly assisted opponents in Congress to maintain the present policy rather than openly defy the president.[17]

Bill Clinton's relationship with the military was already quite tenuous because of his past record as a student who protested the Vietnam War and evaded military service, and now as a president who anticipated a reduction in military forces as a consequence of the close of the Cold War.[18]

The *decision-making* process expanded the scope of conflict over gays in the military. Clinton's decision to act based on his executive authority met with Senate opposition and outrage among conservatives in and out of office. To contend with the political uproar, Clinton postponed any outright repeal until the Joint Chiefs of Staff could develop an acceptable policy for the combined services. Nonetheless, the president set a timetable for a response from the Department of Defense, instead of allowing an open-ended policy development that could move through the Pentagon bureaucracy at glacial speed. By this approach, Clinton hoped the defense establishment would work in good faith to determine if a new policy could be fashioned. It also gave President Clinton the time needed to try and enhance his tarnished image with the military.[19] Because Congress had the potential to block Clinton's executive initiatives, he had to devise a decision-making strategy to deal with that contingency. Clinton's timetable allowed Senate Armed Services Committee chairman Sam Nunn to open hearings into the proposed policy change, thereby circumventing the White House.

Openly challenging the president's authority were members of Congress, most notably Sam Nunn (D–Ga.), who contended the decision on gays was "not simply a presidential prerogative," but that changes to military law and personnel policy belong to the Congress.[20] He could point to Section 8 of Article I, which grants powers to Congress "[t]o raise and support Armies" and "[t]o make Rules for the Government and Regulations of the land and naval forces" of the United States. Nunn's committee took the lead in opposing the president, a step that had an important impact on the newly elected president who found himself challenged by a member of his own party in Congress.

For Bill Clinton, the gay ban was linked to the larger question of civil rights, and he called the policy shift a "dramatic step forward" in the "history of civil rights advancements."[21] He also believed other segments of society had confronted the question of homosexuality and the military establishment had lagged behind in integrating gays into its structure.[22] But despite the strength of Clinton's personal convictions, his personal decision-making style appeared less rigid. His record as governor of Arkansas had reflected a willingness to compromise, which some critics viewed as weakness, and a preference to offend as few individuals and factions as possible.[23]

Finding a workable middle ground commenced in early spring when the idea of separating troops by sexual preferences was proposed. But this trial balloon backfired, and President Clinton had to fend off open criticism from both the military and the gay community. He backed away from that proposal.[24] Yet despite strong resistance from the military, in February 1993 the Pentagon did issue Clinton's "don't ask, don't tell" option to its ten thousand recruiters.[25] But the relationship between the White House and the Pentagon remained strained, with rumors the military was intent on undermining any executive order that might be handed down.[26] Even Clinton's attempts to look and act like a commander in chief during trips to Japan and to U.S. troops stationed in Korea failed to lessen the tension between the White House and the armed forces.

In the final analysis, the number of decision-makers involved with the gays in the military controversy will surely extend to the federal judiciary as suits are filed based on this new policy.[27] The gays' legal case was strengthened by a prior ruling of a California judge that declared the exclusion of homosexuals in the armed services was unconstitutional.[28] Another case reinforced this when a federal judge ordered the navy to reinstate a sailor discharged after he revealed he was homosexual on national television, stating that "the rule of law applies to the military."[29] In 1996 the Connecticut Supreme Court handed down another decision that supported a ban on military recruiters at the Law School of the University of Connecticut because the judges felt the Pentagon's policy on homosexuals violated the state law on gay rights that bars discrimination.[30]

The federal courts historically have given the military considerable latitude, however, unless the question is presented strictly as an issue of civil rights and liberties. Until then, as one analyst suggested, perhaps an even more repressive climate will develop for homosexuals as the military perpetuates the ban.[31] Former strong supporters of Clinton's original campaign pledge, such as Representative Patricia Schroeder (D–Colo.), came to agree with the view of Attorney General Janet Reno that violations of individual rights will result from the compromise policy.[32]

The one reliable *public input* was the gay community itself, although Clinton's vacillation frustrated his homosexual backers. The gay movement was a critical voting bloc in California that Clinton was able to forge into a winning electoral coalition. Yet they felt betrayed by the president's reluctance to act boldly and remove the ban without seeking compromise with Congress on both his interim and final policy.[33] During the course of the policy debate, moreover, gay supporters viewed the level of opposition as a "scary thing" captured by "emotionalism"[34] and lacking reasoned debate. As a consequence, any potential supporters among civil rights and human rights groups were cautious, and other rights activists remained on the sidelines rather than jeopardize their own constituency interests.[35] The failure to acknowledge publicly the outstanding records of those gays discharged by the military raised many concerns, especially among the heavily decorated and careerists who only recently felt comfortable enough to "come out of the closet."[36] Records of harassment, sacrifices, and efforts to live a secluded unnoticed life were chronicled in the running commentary about the gays who served their country, helping to galvanize those who were concerned about rights and equal protection under the law.[37]

The contours of public opinion on this issue have remained unchanged for several decades, falling between the most conservative position that homosexuality is deviant behavior to the liberal end of the political spectrum that views homosexuals as an oppressed minority in need of protection. Both extremes do not represent the mainstream and, as one public opinion expert points out, "among most Americans, you don't see any great desire to condemn, but neither is there any desire to support."[38]

Public opinion appeared dampened by poll results collected as the issue unfolded during the first six months of Clinton's administration. In January, shortly after Clinton took office and announced his decision to abide by his campaign pledge, 72 percent of those surveyed believed that homosexuals could effectively serve in the armed forces, although 53 percent did not support Clinton's proposal to lift the ban.[39] By May 60 percent did not support the president's position,[40] and within the armed forces opposition among the rank and file increased to 74 percent. In addition, 81 percent believed that violent acts against homosexuals in the military would occur.[41] Reflecting this hostility in the armed services, veterans' groups besieged the White House and Congress, making it clear to the administration that more veterans than gays vote.[42]

As one analyst put it, "no one should underestimate the political importance of this shift in political imagery . . . America now sees a Democratic President sympathetic to the gay cause, but an undercurrent suggests silent opposition."[43] Both sides in the struggle tried to shape public opinion with symbolic appeals, including the use of competing videos illustrating their positions. Gestures by supporters at key military and veteran facilities, drawing parallels to the rights of blacks and women, were in opposition to videos that argued that lifting the ban would lead to the demasculization of the military in battle.[44]

The public's perception of Clinton during his brief honeymoon period was heavily influenced by the issue of gays in the military. It was perhaps *the* reason why Clinton's approval ratings suggested he was the most unpopular president in history at that point in his term. The president was not prepared for an opposition that was better organized, more experienced, and more focused than his administration. Clinton appeared weak, indecisive, and "not ready for prime time."[45]

One fascinating aspect of the public debate was the type of evidence and *expertise* employed by the adversaries in the policy process. Advocates claimed that no clear evidence indicates homosexuals have a negative effect on the armed forces. Congressional investigators, who were charged with the task of looking at policies on homosexual membership in the military forces of other countries, determined that in Australia and Canada, the two countries which most recently lifted their bans on homosexuals, no morale problems exist. Similarly, in Germany and Sweden, countries that opened their doors some time ago to homosexuals in the armed forces, no evidence was found of a decline in effectiveness or morale. Denmark and the Netherlands also allow homosexuals in the military, and the Netherlands went so far as to establish a union for gay soldiers.[46] Israel, another example, has integrated its armed services since inception in 1948.[47]

What underscores the use of expertise as a power source in this struggle between the chief executive and the military establishment are the unique organizational characteristics of the military. No other bureaucracy has the same rigid hierarchy and tradition of heroics, which the military establishment used to gain leverage primarily through the auspices of Congress. Most notably Senator Sam Nunn (D–Ga.), as chairman of the Senate Armed Services Committee, had tremendous respect from his colleagues and the Washington establishment in the area of military affairs.

By taking the lead in opposing Clinton on the issue, Nunn used his position to head off the proposed executive order. Nunn, knowing the president would not risk suffering a major defeat in Congress so early in his tenure, was able to neutralize the president by making Clinton unsure of how to proceed and by making him appear weak in the opening months of his new administration in the eyes of the critics.[48] More than simply a test of presidential power, Senator Nunn saw it as a demonstration of his own political strength and possibly as an opportunity to upstage Les Aspin, Clinton's pick for secretary of defense, chosen instead of Nunn. In the end, Nunn's experience and stature as chairman and military affairs expert was more than a match for the less experienced president.[49]

Secretary of Defense Les Aspin seemed an odd choice to act as point man for the military because as a member of the House of Representatives he had been at odds with the Pentagon quite frequently. Aspin's presence did not do much to erode the relationships between the career military and political appointees that developed during the previous twelve years of Republican administrations.[50] Moreover, Aspin worked slowly. He chose a working group that would take six months, until July 1993, to develop an acceptable policy that incorporated Clinton's concessions to Nunn, in order to sidetrack Republican attempts to enact into law a total ban.[51]

Another key player in the congressional debate was Representative Barney Frank (D–Mass.), an openly gay member of Congress who advocated that gay military personnel should be protected, especially when they are off duty. His view contrasted with Senator Nunn's argument that gays in the armed services would undermine military cohesiveness and effectiveness. Yet another voice was heard from an unexpected source. Well-known conservative and former senator Barry Goldwater(R–Ariz.) sided with President Clinton based on his own career as a reservist in the Air Force. In Goldwater's words, " You don't need to be straight to fight and die for your country. You just need to shoot straight."[52] He argued that Clinton was correct on the issue and that Americans needed to move regardless of political party into a bipartisan mode.[53] Both Barney Frank and Barry Goldwater noted that no evidence supports the position that gays would affect the efficiency of the military or cohesiveness within the ranks.[54] This same conclusion was drawn by a $1.3 million study completed by the Rand Corporation for the Pentagon, but was kept secret until after President Clinton had announced his policy. Congressman Frank criticized Clinton's compromise as selling short his campaign promise to the gay and lesbian community, although he was cognizant that "sentiment in Congress (was) running strongly against Mr. Clinton and the gay rights movement."[55]

Lawrence Korb, who served as the top civilian for military personnel during the Reagan era, testified before the Senate Armed Services Committee that no evidence existed to suggest homosexuals would impair a fighting unit's cohesion and that "condoning prejudice is an appalling means to obtain unit cohesion."[56] Meanwhile, other proponents, including retired military officers who had to hide their homosexuality during their careers, pointed out that "sexual orientation does not equal sexual misconduct" and further argued that the biggest scandal in the military in the 1990s was the heterosexual misconduct among naval officers at a convention in Las Vegas.[57] During a period of great concern about the cost of the military establishment, they also pointed out, the Pentagon was spending at least $27 million a year to perpetuate a policy unsupported by scientific evidence.[58]

But Senator Nunn garnered the support of General Colin Powell, chairman of the Joint Chiefs of Staff.[59] Nunn equated the hands-off policy proposed by the president to the disastrous, short-lived drug policy that the military implemented during the 1970s, which cast a blind eye on casual, nonperformance drug use by members of the armed services.[60] In the end, as Clinton's self-imposed deadline approached in midsummer, Nunn was able to move Frank, Les Aspin, the Joint Chiefs, and the president into the compromise position of "don't ask, and don't tell."

Committee hearings were used by Senator Nunn to call on expert witnesses who praised the traditions of the military and claimed that special consideration should be given to the preferences of military commanders. Those testifying favored Nunn's position over the president's and showed that the military subgovernment had considerable political muscle.[61] Despite General Colin Powell's remark that he was committed to taking his instructions "from the President . . . and once we receive those instructions we will execute them,"[62] he also stated unequivocally that gays were "prejudicial to the good order and discipline" of the military[63] and, moreover, that the issue did not belong in the White House but rather should be dealt with by the military culture. In one sense, General Powell gave the president some political cover for him to refer the policy back to the Department of Defense.[64]

Although President Clinton's first months in office showed a White House in disarray, with his approval ratings falling, amid a series of administrative blunders and the controversy over gays in the military, in no sense did a *crisis* develop around this issue. The perception among congressional opponents—even his supporters—and the general public was that Clinton was simply trying to make a payoff to a voter bloc. There was no sense of urgency that gays in the military demanded a quick policy response, indeed, Clinton allowed the policy process to evolve over several

months. So although a widely perceived crisis may help the chief executive mobilize his bureaucratic subordinates, public opinion, and the legislative branch around presidential leadership, this variable was a non-
event during the controversy over homosexuals in the armed services.

The final policy on homosexuals that passed the House and Senate in the
early fall of 1993 put strict limits on sexual orientation and noted that "homosexuality is incompatible with military service." Although recruits cannot
be asked about their sexual orientation, the policy states that "homosexual
conduct will be grounds for separation from the military services."[65] Had the
president vetoed this legislation to meet his campaign pledge, most likely it
would not have survived a congressional override. So it appears that, although this policy outcome was not a complete defeat for the chief executive,
it was clearly not the outcome Clinton would have preferred. The enormous
imbalance between Clinton's policy objectives and his power base as chief executive showed he was unable to redeem his pledge to the gay community.

NOTES

1. Eric Schmitt, "Clinton Set to End Ban on Gay Troops," *New York Times* (Jan. 21, 1993), pp. A1, A17.
2. Art Pine, "Gays in Armed Forces Would Still Confront Minefield of Regulations," *Los Angeles Times* (Jan. 31, 1993), p. A23.
3. Eric Schmitt, "Military's Ban on Homosexuals Has Not Always Been Policy," *New York Times* (Jan. 26, 1993), p. A12.
4. Eric Schmitt, "Challenging the Military," *New York Times* (Nov. 11, 1992), pp. A1, A9.
5. Scott Pendleton, Homosexuals Say GOP Platform Left Them Out," *Christian Science Monitor* (Aug. 18, 1992), p. 8.
6. Peter Grier, "Clinton Forges Ahead on Gays-in-Military Front," *Christian Science Monitor* (Jan. 29, 1993), p. 3.
7. Brad Knickerbocker, "Gay Rights May Be Social Issue of the 1990s," *Christian Science Monitor* (Feb. 11, 1993), pp. 1–4.
8. Tony Kushner, "Gays in the Military: The Pursuit of Social Justice," *Los Angeles Times* (Jan. 31, 1993), pp. M1, M6.
9. Richard J. Cattani, "Inauguration and First Thoughts," *Christian Science Monitor* (Jan. 20, 1993), p. 18.
10. Dan Balz and Ann Devroy, "Clinton's School of Hard Knocks," *Washington Post National Weekly Edition* (Feb. 8–14, 1993), p. 13.
11. Lucian K. Truscott, IV, "Truman's Legacy to Clinton," *New York Times* (Feb. 1, 1993), p. A13; Art Pine, "Gay Issue Quietly Spreads Rifts through Civil Rights Groups," *Los Angeles Times* (Jan. 29, 1993), p. A20; Maurice McGregor, *The Integration of the Armed Forces: 1940–1965.* Washington, DC: Center for Military History, United States Army, 1981; Bernard Naulty, *Strength for the Fight: The History of Black Americans in the Military.* New York: Free Press, 1986; Allan Berube, *Coming Out under Fire: The History of Gay Men and Women in World War II* (New York: Free Press), 1990.
12. Peter Grier, "Clinton Faces Early Showdown on Ban on Gays," *Christian Science Monitor* (Jan. 27, 1993), pp. 1, 4.
13. Clarence N. Stone, *Regime Politics: Governing Atlanta, 1946–1988.* Lawrence: University of Kansas Press, 1989, p. xi.
14. Michael Weisskopf, "The Gay and Lesbian Lobby Is Put to the Test," *Washington Post National Weekly Edition* (Feb. 1–7, 1993), p. 14.
15. Grier, "Clinton Forges Ahead on Gays in Military Front," pp. 1, 4.
16. Eric Schmitt, "Months after Order on Gay Ban, Military is Still Resisting Clinton," *New York Times* (March 23, 1993), pp. A1, A5.
17. Mark Thompson, "Clinton Aims to End Troop Ban on Gays," *Las Vegas Review Journal* (Jan. 26, 1993), pp. 1A, 3A.

Some evidence suggests there has been a backlash in the military since the policy was enacted, given the increasing number of military discharges from each of the services in 1997 for homosexuality. A recent study by the Servicemembers Legal Defense Network indicated that 850 men and women were so discharged in 1996–1997, an 18 percent increase over the 1995–1996 period and a 42 percent increase from 1994, the year the policy went into effect. See Philip Shenon, "New Study Faults Pentagon's Gay Policy," *New York Times*, (Feb. 26, 1997), p. A8.

18. Barton Gellman, "For Clinton and the Military, A Time of Testing," *Washington Post National Weekly Edition*, (April 12–18, 1993), p. 32; Peter Grier, "White House and Military Are Not In-Step, So Far," *Christian Science Monitor* (Feb. 17, 1993), pp. 1, 4.

19. David Lauter, "Clinton Strikes Deal with Military on Gays," *Los Angeles Times* (Jan. 29, 1993), pp. A1, A20.

20. Thompson, "Clinton Aims to End Troop Ban on Gays," pp. 1A, 3A.

21. David Lauter, "Clinton Compromises, Partially Lifts Gay Ban," *Los Angeles Times* (Jan. 30, 1993), pp. A1, A18.

22. Alan C. Miller, "Disruption Rare as Gays Have Been Integrated," *Los Angeles Times* (Jan. 30, 1993), pp. A1, A20.

23. Mary McGrory, "Hail All Hail 'William the Procrastinator'," *Washington Post National Weekly Edition* (May 31–June 6, 1993), p. 25.

24. Richard L. Berke, "Clinton Says He'd Consider Separating Gay Troops," *New York Times* (March 24, 1993), pp. A1, A8; Eric Schmitt, "Clinton Tries to Counter View He'd Place Gay Troops Apart," *New York Times* (March 26, 1993), pp. A1, A9; Richard L. Berke, "White House Gets a Warning against Retreat on Gay Issue," *New York Times* (March 27, 1993), pp. A1, A8.

25. Sam Howe Verhovek, "Perplexed Recruiters Try to Sort Out Orders on Military's Homosexual Ban," *New York Times* (Feb. 4, 1993), p. A8.

26. Schmitt, "Months after Order on Gay Ban, Military Is Still Resisting Clinton," pp. A1, A5.

27. Stephen Labaton, "Homosexuals in Service Sue over Clinton's Compromise," *New York Times* (July 28, 1993), p. A10.

28. Thomas L. Friedman, "Compromise Near on Military's Ban on Homosexuals," *New York Times* (Jan. 29, 1993), p. A12.

29. Seth Mydans, "Navy Is Ordered to Return Job to a Gay Sailor," *New York Times* (Nov. 11, 1992), p. A8.

30. George Judson, "Military Recruiting Ban on a Campus Is Upheld," *New York Times* (March 20, 1996), p. B7.

31. Scott Shuger, "The Silencing of a Gay Sailor," *Washington Post National Weekly Edition* (March 22–28, 1993), p. 24. There may be some evidence of this as military discharges in 1995 increased 17 percent over 1994. Philip Shenon, "Word for Word: Military Gay Policy; When 'Don't Ask, Don't Tell' Means Do Ask and Do Tell All," *New York Times* (March 3, 1996), Sec. 4, p. 7.

32. Melissa Healey, "New Policy Will Allow Military to Expel Gays," *Los Angeles Times* (July 16, 1993), pp. A1, A19.

33. Labaton, "Homosexuals in Service Sue over Clinton's Compromise," p. A10.

34. Eric Schmitt, "Forum on Military's Gay Ban Starts, and Stays, Shrill," *New York Times* (March 25, 1993), p. A8.

35. Art Pine, "Gay Issue Quietly Spreads Rifts through Civil Rights Groups," *Los Angeles Times* (Jan. 29, 1993), p. A20.

36. Associated Press, "Army Discharges Gay 1992 Soldier of Year," *Las Vegas Review Journal* (May 11, 1993), p. B2; Seth Mydans, "Navy Is Ordered to return Job to a Gay Sailor," *New York Times* (Nov. 11, 1992), p. A8.

37. Eric Schmitt, "For Gay Soldiers, Worry and Hope in Ban Repeal," *The New York Times* (Nov. 16, 1992), p. A8.

38. Susan Baer, "Imagery a Weapon in Battle over Gay Rights," *Las Vegas Review Journal* (June 11, 1993), p. 14B.

39. Max Boot, "First Monday in Office: Clinton Picks Take Over," *Christian Science Monitor* (Jan. 25, 1993), p. 3.

40. Peter Grier, "Key Senators Push Compromise on Issue of Gays in Armed Forces," *Christian Science Monitor* (May 13, 1993), pp. 1, 4.

41. Melissa Healy, "74% of Military Enlistees Oppose Lifting Gay Ban," *Los Angeles Times* (Feb. 28, 1993), pp. 1A, A23.

42. Bernard E. Trainor and Eric L. Chase, "Keep Gays Out," *New York Times* (March 29, 1993), p. A13; Associated Press, "Retired Military Officers to Ask Congress to Legalize Homosexual Ban," *Las Vegas Review Journal* (May 4, 1993), p. 5A.

43. Kevin Phillips, "Getting America's Priorities All Wrong," *Washington Post National Weekly Edition* (Feb. 8–14, 1993), p. 23.

44. Max Boot, "Activists Make Last Pitch on Gay Ban," *Christian Science Monitor* (June 25, 1993), p. 7; *The Washington Post*, "Controversy Greets Powell," *Las Vegas Review Journal* (June 11, 1993), p. 5A.

45. Ann Devroy and Ruth Marcus, "The Clutch Seems to Be Slipping," *Washington Post National Weekly Edition* (June 14–20, 1993), p. 12.

46. Eric Schmitt, "Gay Soldiers Elsewhere: No Problems, Panel Told," *The New York Times* (April 30, 1993), p. A9.

47. Miller, "Disruption Rare as Gays Have Been Integrated," pp. A1, A20.

48. Peter Grier, "Nunn to Open Hearings on Military's Gay Ban," *Christian Science Monitor* (March 29, 1993), p. 2.

49. David Lauter, "Clash with Nunn Becomes Test of Power for Clinton," *Los Angeles Times* (Jan. 28, 1993), pp. A1, A16.

50. Barton Gellman, "Pin Stripes Clash with Stars and Bars," *Washington Post National Weekly Edition* (June 28–July 4, 1993), p. 31.

51. Eric Schmitt, "Pentagon Aides to Study Option of the Segregation of Gay Troops, *New York Times* (Jan. 31, 1993), pp. A1, A14; Clifford Krauss, "Agreement Is Setback for Republican Amendment," *New York Times* (Jan. 31, 1993), A14.

52. Barry M. Goldwater, "The Gay Ban: Just Plain Un-American," *The Washington Post National Weekly Edition* (June 21–27, 1993), p. 28.

53. Ibid.

54. Barry M. Goldwater, "The Gay Ban: Just Plain Un-American," *The Washington Post National Weekly Edition*, June 21–27, 1993, p. 28.

55. Peter Grier, "Competing Compromises on Gays in the Military," *Christian Science Monitor* (May 24, 1993), p. 3.

56. Newsday, "Ex-Defense Boss Backs Military Gays," *Las Vegas Review-Journal* (April 1, 1993), p. 4A.

57. Peter Grier, "Key Senators Push Compromise on Issue of Gays in Armed Forces," *Christian Science Monitor* (May 13, 1993), pp. 1, 4.

58. Eric Schmitt, "Barring Homosexuals Called Costly to Military," *New York Times* (June 19, 1993), p. A10.

59. Michael R. Gordon, "Senate Panel Chief Backs Compromise on Gay-Troop Ban," *New York Times* (March 30, 1993), pp. A1, A13; The Washington Post, "Controversy Greets Powell," *Las Vegas Review Journal* (June 11, 1993), p. 5A.

60. Associated Press, "Nunn, Frank Exchange Barbs on Gays in Military, *Las Vegas Review Journal*, (May 31, 1993), p. 5A.

61. Gordon, "Senate Panel Chief Backs Compromise on Gay-Troop Ban," pp. A1, A13.

62. Eric Schmitt, "Top Generals Ease Stance on Gay Ban," *New York Times* (Dec. 2, 1992), p. A10.

63. Peter Grier, "U.S. Military Faces Upheaval over Women and Gay Personnel," *Christian Science Monitor* (Nov. 17, 1992), pp. 1, 4.

64. Bob Woodward, "The Education of Les Aspin," *Washington Post National Weekly Edition* (March 1–7, 1993), pp. 6–9.

65. Healy, " New Policy Will Allow Military to Expel Gays," pp. A1, A19.

11

Chief Diplomat: The Primacy of Executive Authority

Foreign affairs is considered by most presidents to be more important than domestic policy, yet few presidents come into office with much experience in foreign affairs. Dwight Eisenhower and George Bush may have been the exceptions—Eisenhower because of his military experience and Bush as a result of his experience as CIA director and ambassador to China prior to becoming vice president.[1] Although foreign affairs does not give the president as much leverage with the Congress and may even create institutional hostility, as Bill Clinton found out in July 1995 when the Senate voted 69 to 29 to override the Clinton arms embargo policy in Bosnia,[2] arguably a president who comes into office as a result of a close election is much better off involved with foreign policy than with domestic policy.[3]

Although advocacy of foreign policy remains an attractive option for the president, the Bush presidency suggests that no president can afford to ignore domestic policy while carrying foreign affairs to excess. It seemed quite natural for George Bush to devote a good share of his time to foreign affairs given the changes that had taken place in the world from 1989 to 1991 (Table 11–1). When the public by 83 percent approved Bush's handling of foreign affairs in March 1991, for example, everyone including the leadership of the Democratic Party expected him to have no difficulty in winning reelection the next year.[4] But by October 1991, as the economy slipped into recession, the public began to view Bush's time spent on foreign affairs as a real disadvantage. Now 59 percent felt the president had ignored domestic affairs and 78 percent demanded he spend more time on the economy.[5] In June 1992 Bush lost on both fronts because his handling of foreign policy was approved by less than half the public.[6]

Bill Clinton followed quite a different path than Bush. He entered the presidency with an innovative domestic policy agenda: health care, gun control, welfare reform, abortion revisions, military and governmental reorganization, and what appeared to be little interest in foreign policy. Clinton did not want to "be pinned down by conflicts such as those in the Balkans, Somalia, Haiti, and parts of the former Soviet Union. He did not

Table 11–1. World Changes during the Bush Years

Date	Countries Involved	Result
August 1989–February 1990	Kuwait, Iraq, and UN	Iraq expelled from Kuwait in Persian Gulf
October 1989	Hungary	Hungary declared freedom from communist control
November 1989–October 1990	East and West Germany	Reunification of Germany
December 1990–February 1991	Baltic States and USSR	Baltic States declared independence from communism
December 1990	Romania	Communist government overthrown
December 1990	Panama	Panamanian leader General Noriega removed from power
January 1991	Bulgaria	Communism toppled: free elections held
June 1991	Czechoslovakia	Communism toppled: free elections held
June 1991–present	Croatia, Slovenia, Serbia, Bosnia-Herzegovina, Macedonia, Montenegro	Yugoslavian civil war
December 1991	Former Soviet Union (Armenia, Azerbaijan, Kazakhstan and Uzbekistan, Kyrgyzstan, Moldova, Russian Federation, Tajikistan, Turkmenistan, Ukraine, Uzebistan, Belarus)	Formation of Commonwealth of Independent States (C.I.S.)

Source: *The World Almanac and Book of Facts* (New York: Pharos Books, 1990–1992).

want to be a captive of foreign policy."[7] But world events would not allow his domestic focus at the exclusion of foreign affairs. Crises in Somalia, Bosnia, Russia, Rwanda, Haiti, and North Korea demanded and continued to demand his attention. Almost from the start Clinton received as much criticism for his foreign policy as Bush did for his inattention to domestic matters. This criticism was reflected in polls taken by the *New York Times*/CBS News on April 21–23, 1994, revealing a drop in support for the president since January of that year, with 41 percent of the respondents disapproving of Clinton's policies and 40 percent supporting them.[8] In his own defense, Clinton responded to his critics by explaining the main reason he had been elected: "My premise was that the American people were hungry for a president who showed that he knew that something had to be done here to address our problems at home that had been long neglected."[9]

Although one easily could interpret Clinton's defeat of Bush in this way, observers within and outside his administration were unhappy with his early foreign policy efforts. He was criticized for lacking focus on foreign policy, of being shallow,[10] of being hesitant to commit,[11] of turning "TR on his head by speaking loudly and carrying a small stick."[12] One of Clinton's first foreign policy problems surfaced when twelve Balkan experts within the State Department as well as UN ambassador Madeleine Albright labeled the administration's Balkan policy a failure.[13]

Clinton had also been criticized for relying too much on his subordinates and failing to use his presidency to define foreign policy goals. Although the president had indicated three prongs to his foreign policy—expanding democracy abroad, strengthening the economy at home, and reducing the professional military forces[14]—Clinton also talked about the need to protect human rights in other countries and, in doing so, "join with others to do what we can to relieve the suffering and restore peace."[15]

Part of this dissatisfaction with President Clinton's approach to foreign policy can no doubt be attributed to the disorder and uncertainty of the times since the close of the Cold War. Yet his hesitation to commit his administration to particular policies regardless of the reasons proved to be frustrating to some members of Congress. Senator Judd Gregg (R–N.H.) pointed to Clinton's indecision in foreign policy and suggested, "we appear to be stumbling in our approach to foreign policy, something like a bear coming out of hibernation, hitting this tree and that tree and not having a distinct direction on the issue of how we handle ourselves in the post-cold war period."[16] Instability in the world did not help the president. By one estimate 42 different conflicts were going on in 39 different countries in 1994.[17] Uncertainty about the U.S. role—whether and how to intervene—in this diplomatic turmoil complicated foreign policy.

TRENDS IN DIPLOMACY

Major trends in U.S. diplomacy can best be identified through the singular contributions of individual presidents (Table 11–2). George Washington articulated a clear commitment to isolationism in both his Neutrality Proclamation of 1793 and his Farewell Address in 1796. Theodore Roosevelt built the Panama Canal and stood firm in his dealings with Latin America; this policy was moderated through Franklin Roosevelt's Good Neighbor Policy that established new relations with countries of Central and South America. The Cold War was shaped by Harry Truman when he declared a containment policy directed toward the Soviet Union and its allies, whereas four decades later George Bush announced in 1990 a new world order to symbolize the democratization of communist Eastern Europe and the creation of the Commonwealth of Independent States (the former Soviet Union). His hope was that reordering political and economic relationships among nations would bring about a lasting peace.[18] But that reordering has brought about a great deal of tension and uncertainty as well.

The direction of U.S. foreign policy has not always been enlightened, successful, or well conceived. Presidency scholar Dorothy Buckton James

Table 11–2. Significant Historical Events in the Chief Diplomat Role

President	Historical Event or Decision
Washington	• Recognition of republican France • Asserted "executive privilege" over Jay Treaty • (Indian) treaty-making process • Neutrality Proclamation of 1793 based on inherent power • "Personal" agents in diplomacy • Farewell Address of 1796 (isolationism)
Monroe	• Monroe Doctrine of 1823 toward Western Hemisphere
T. Roosevelt	• Gunboat Diplomacy in Latin America • Build the Panama Canal
F.D. Roosevelt	• *U.S. v. Belmont* (1937) on executive agreements • *U.S. v. Curtiss-Wright Export Corp.* (1936) on inherent powers of chief diplomat • Good Neighbor Policy toward Latin America
Truman	• Marshall Plan to assist reconstruction of Europe • Truman Doctrine (containment of communism) and Cold War begins
Carter	• *Goldwater v. Carter* (1979) and treaty-ending power
Bush	• End of the Cold War

suggested that Franklin Roosevelt, for example, followed no real policy format, no established principles undergird his policy initiatives, and he generally made policy in an ad hoc way on a case-by-case basis.[19] Yet this haphazard style does not mean presidents cannot leave their imprints on foreign policy. It is difficult to recall a time after the Civil War when the president did not dominate decisions in foreign affairs.

As Alexander Hamilton and John Jay argued during the Federalist period, the president enjoys certain advantages in foreign affairs that Congress lacks. Because the president is a single person and is always in office—unlike Congress which adjourns from time to time—he can act quickly and maintain secrecy of communications. Furthermore, the role of chief diplomat has many legal and political resources. The conduct of foreign affairs, for example, is both a "plenary" and an "exclusive" power of the national government. It is plenary in that the United States is a sovereign nation within the international community of nations. Thus U.S. conduct of foreign policy is not limited in the same way that governmental power over domestic affairs is restricted.

AUTHORITY

To say that foreign policy is the domain of the national government does not fix authority in any one branch of government. If one branch was to dominate, its authority needed to be secured by custom, statutory law, and judicial decision. George Washington helped pave the way for the executive's predominance in foreign affairs by establishing a number of important precedents that became routine practices for presidents who followed. He received envoys from foreign countries and in so doing recognized their governments. Washington also refused to give the House of Representatives documents relating to the Jay Treaty—an unpopular agreement that made trade concessions to the English without safeguarding American shipping interests—beginning the practice of executive privilege. Washington further refused to allow the Senate to participate in the negotiating of treaties, limiting the Senate's right to "advice and consent" in treaty making.

Sole Organ of Diplomacy

Implicit in these actions of George Washington's was the president acting as sole organ in the conduct of foreign affairs. It was John Marshall, chief justice of the Supreme Court, who in 1800 argued that the president was the "sole organ" of the nation in its external affairs and its "sole representative" to foreign nations.

Alexander Hamilton and James Madison had very different ideas on what that meant, and eventually they debated this issue when President Washington issued his Proclamation of Neutrality of 1793 at the outbreak of war between France and Great Britain. Hamilton, writing under the pseudonym Pacificus, penned a series of articles for the Federalist-created *Gazette of the United States* in which he argued that the conduct of foreign affairs was inherently an executive function. He contended that the president was supposed to act as the "*organ* of intercourse between the nation and foreign nations; as the *interpreter* of the national treaties, in those cases in which the judiciary is not competent . . . as the *power* which is charged with the command and disposition of the public force." Hamilton concluded his defense by suggesting that the President is also the constitutional executor of the laws.

James Madison, at the urging of Thomas Jefferson, responded as Helvidius and wrote in the same newspaper. Madison charged that Hamilton was trying to give the president the "royal" prerogative of the English monarch. He maintained that Congress, from its authority to declare war, should make foreign policy. The president's role, he asserted, was merely instrumental to the ends set by Congress. Although Madison probably won this intellectual battle with Hamilton, history suggests that Hamilton won the war.[20]

Hamilton's view of inherent executive power over foreign affairs was validated in the Supreme Court's landmark decision in *United States v. Curtiss-Wright Export Corporation* (1936). Here the Court legitimized a very broad interpretation of the president as the sole organ of diplomacy. It said in part:

> [W]e are here dealing not alone with an authority vested in the President by an exertion of legislative power, but with such an authority plus the very delicate, plenary and exclusive power of the President as the sole organ of the Federal government in the field of international relations—a power which does not re-

quire as a basis for its exercise an act of Congress, but which . . . must be exercised in subordination to the applicable provisions of the Constitution.[21]

Treaties and Executive Agreements

Presidents enjoy a tremendous advantage when they negotiate international agreements. The Constitution grants the president the power to make treaties "by and with the advice and consent of the Senate," as long as "two-thirds of the Senators present concur." Although presidents are dominant at the beginning stages of treaty making, they usually consult with their own Senate party leadership and other key senators to assist in getting Senate ratification of treaties.

Virtually all of the Senate's involvement with treaty making comes at a point of ratification, although a president may modify a proposed treaty to accommodate its political sentiments. But few treaties are rejected outright. To date the Senate has refused to approve only about 1 percent of all treaties, and another 15 percent have been accepted by the Senate after it added "reservations" or amendments.

Executive agreements—among heads of state—were recognized by the Supreme Court in the cases of *U.S. v. Belmont* (1937) and *U.S. v. Pink* (1942) as having equal legal status with treaties.[22] Actually, presidents have increasingly relied on executive agreements in negotiations with foreign governments (Table 11–3). There are approximately seven times as many executive agreements as treaties. Historically they have been used for such minor purposes as defining fishing rights between nations, settling boundary disputes involving the United States, and providing for annexation of territory, but more controversial was the use of executive agreements by Presidents Roosevelt (the Yalta Conference) and Truman (the Potsdam Conference) to finalize post–World War II spheres of influence between the Allies and the Soviet Union.

Since World War II the ratio between agreements and treaties has grown nearly twenty times. As a result of the wartime personal diplomacy of FDR and Truman—which conservatives attacked as capitulation to the Soviet Union—Congress debated the Bricker Amendment, introduced by Senator John Bricker (R–Ohio) in September 1951. This proviso was "an expression of intense disapprobation of Roosevelt's and Truman's personal diplomacy of the conviction that agreements made at the various wartime conferences were responsible for the cold war."[23] It also posed a challenge to internationalism, America's leadership role of the free world, and particularly the presidential role in diplomatic negotiations.[24]

By 1953 the Bricker Amendment was endorsed by sixty-two senators of both political parties. Among the several versions considered, its final language prevented the president from negotiating a treaty or agreement that would conflict with the Constitution and, furthermore, provided that a treaty could not become law without passage of federal- or state-enabling legislation.

The Senate narrowly defeated the Bricker Amendment in 1954, but the same issue resurfaced during the Vietnam War. In 1969 the Senate

Table 11–3. Treaties versus Executive Agreements, 1789–1990

Years	President	Executive Agreements*	Treaties	Ratio of Agreements to Treaties	Fast Track (trade)
1789–1839	—	27	60	1.0 : 2.2	—
1839–1889	—	238	215	1.1 : 1	—
1889–1929	—	763	382	2.0 : 1	—
1930–1932	Hoover	41	49	1.0 : 1.2	—
1933–1944	Roosevelt	369	131	2.8 : 1	—
1945–1952	Truman	1,324	132	10.0 : 1	—
1953–1960	Eisenhower	1,834	89	20.6 : 1	—
1961–1962	Kennedy	813	36	22.6 : 1	—
1963–1968	Johnson	1,083	67	16.2 : 1	—
1969–1974	Nixon	1,317	93	13.6 : 1	—
1975–1976	Ford	666	26	25.6 : 1	—
1977–1980	Carter	1,476	79	18.7 : 1	—
1981–1988	Reagan	2,837	117	24.3 : 1	2
1989–1992	Bush	1,344	67	20.1 : 1	1
1993–1995	Clinton	894	58	15.4 : 1	2
Totals		15,026	1,601	9.4 : 1	5

*Varying definitions of what comprises an executive agreement and their entry-into-force dates make all numbers approximate.

Sources: Harold W. Stanley and Richard G. Niemi, *Vital Statistics on American Politics* (Washington, D.C.: Congressional Quarterly, 1990), p. 255; *Congressional Quarterly's Guide to Congress* (Washington, D.C.: Congressional Quarterly, 1991), p. 182; United States Congress, Senate Foreign Relations Committee, *Treaties and Other International Agreements: The Role of the United States Senate.* Report prepared by the Congressional Research Service. 103rd Cong., 1st sess., 1993, Committee Print 14; Clinton data from the Office of the Assistant Legal Advisor for Treaty Affairs, U.S. Department of State; fast track information from the Office of the U.S. Trade Representative, General Council.

Foreign Relations Committee sponsored a "National Commitments Resolution" that would allow financial assistance or military forces to assist other nations only after a treaty, statute, or concurrent resolution was drawn up with the agreement of the president and both houses of Congress.[25] President Nixon ignored this resolution and in 1970 negotiated a military base agreement with Spain, which included security guarantees. Nixon's action prompted the Senate to pass a resolution stating that his agreement with Spain did not constitute a U.S. commitment.[26]

By 1972 Congress was frustrated enough to pass legislation instructing the secretary of state to "transmit to the Congress the text of any international agreement, other than a treaty, to which the United States is a party as soon as possible after such agreement has entered into force with respect to the United States, but in no event later than sixty days thereafter."[27] Although the law seemed clear in its language, it made no attempt to define the exact nature of an "executive agreement," so a president could simply assert his negotiations were not an "executive agreement," which did not have to be reported to Congress. In 1975 Congressman Les Aspin (D–Wisc.)

calculated that between 400 and 600 agreements with other nations had gone unreported to Congress since passage of this law in 1972.[28]

Treaty Breaking

Although the presidential role in treaty making now seems clear, it is not so obvious whether the president can terminate a treaty unilaterally. This question arose when President Carter announced he was ending a 1958 mutual defense treaty with Taiwan (an island off the coast of mainland China) pursuant to his establishing full diplomatic relations with the People's Republic of China. As justification he cited a provision of that treaty allowing its termination after one year's notice. The defense treaty with Taiwan did not specifically require Senate approval for its termination, and the Constitution made no mention of the Senate role in ending treaties.

Senator Barry Goldwater (R–Ariz.) and other senators, however, understood the situation quite differently. Believing that Carter needed Senate approval, they got the Senate to pass a resolution to that effect, whereupon Goldwater and his allies took Carter to court. In the case of *Goldwater v. Carter* (1979) the Supreme Court gave the president a "political" victory, although technically it sided with neither branch of government on the merits of the case.[29] The Court judged the controversy premature, withheld judgment, and dismissed the complaint.

Executive Privilege

Another precedent established by George Washington was executive privilege. In 1796 Washington became the first president to refuse to comply with a request from the House of Representatives to turn over documents pertaining to the negotiations of the Jay Treaty. Washington refused to comply with the House's request because the lower chamber was not a partner to the treaty-making process and, moreover, because the papers involved secret diplomatic negotiations. It was then that the tradition of executive privilege was established.

Its use has since been extended by presidents to justify their refusal to supply information to both the House and Senate on a variety of matters. Executive privilege was used by Presidents John Adams, Jefferson, Monroe, Jackson, and Buchanan relative to information affecting military or foreign policy. Since World War II executive privilege has been used to protect all types of interagency communications, records, files, reports, advice by staff to a president, and information or testimony by a president's subordinates. A broad claim of executive privilege was given legitimacy by Dwight Eisenhower when he refused to give personnel records of military officers to Senator Joseph McCarthy (R–Wisc.) during the infamous Red Scare of the early 1950s, and neither Congress nor the federal judiciary challenged his authority.

But it was Richard Nixon who became most involved with the doctrine of executive privilege in the Watergate scandal and broadened its coverage. Nixon announced he would use executive privilege to protect not only those in his administration at the time but also all those who had ever worked with his administration. In the case of *U.S. v. Nixon*,[30] however, the Supreme Court required him to release the Watergate tapes, although the legality of executive privilege was upheld where national security interests were at stake. So much did Nixon discredit executive privilege that well-known conservative scholars argued there was absolutely no basis in the Constitution for the doctrine,[31] although a more recent and dispassionate analysis by Mark Rozell argues that "executive privilege is a legitimate constitutional doctrine validated by the writings of the constitutional Fathers, broad residual executive powers contained in Article II of the Constitution, historical exercise, congressional acceptance, and judicial opinion."[32]

Recognition

The Constitution empowers the president to receive ambassadors, an action tantamount to recognizing foreign governments. George Washington was the first president to use this authority when he recognized the new French Republic established after the bloody French Revolution. This power is fully executive in nature and not shared with Congress. The president can use it to affect international events or to set the tone of foreign policy, for example when President Bush recognized the independence of Slovenia and Croatia in the 1990s. It marked an end to U.S. recognition of Yugoslavia as one unified country and began an entirely new relationship between the United States and the individual Balkan countries.

Ambassadors and Special Agents

The Constitution states that the president "shall nominate, and by and with the Advice and Consent of the Senate, shall appoint Ambassadors, other public ministers and Consuls." This power is somewhat limited by the fact that the entire diplomatic and consular establishment is organized in detail by statute in terms of grades, salaries, appointments, promotions, and duties. Moreover, ambassadorial appointees may be political friends with little or no foreign affairs experience. Clinton was criticized for his first year ambassadorial appointments because 40 percent were political appointees, a relatively high percentage compared to Bush's 23 percent political appointments.[33]

The importance of the ambassador sometimes is superseded by the president's use of "personal agents" to conduct diplomacy because they can be appointed *without* Senate confirmation. Their use, although not explicitly authorized by the Constitution, is another manifestation of Alexander Hamilton's view of executive power. Special agents often are used to assure the president direct control over diplomatic missions, and they usually enjoy the full confidence of the executive. In 1982, after Israeli troops had trapped Palestine Liberation Organization (PLO) forces in Beirut, Lebanon, President Reagan dispatched Philip Habib to the Middle East to resolve the stalemate. His delicate negotiations with all parties, including the PLO, Israel, and Lebanon, led to the eventual (peaceful) evacuation of the PLO troops from Beirut.

Presidents also have delegated diplomatic duties to cabinet members that are unrelated to their departmental responsibilities. Jimmy Carter asked Treasury Secretary Michael Blumenthal to begin negotiations with the People's Republic of China before the president formalized U.S. relations with China;[34] President Bush relied on Secretary of State James A. Baker to arrange talks between the Israelis and the Palestinians.

DECISION MAKING

In conducting diplomacy the president can rely on his secretary of state—an office dating back to George Washington's cabinet—the Department of State, and his secretary of defense and the Defense Department as well as others in his advisory system including the national security advisor, chair of the Joint Chiefs of Staff, and the Central Intelligence Agency. Presidents may also utilize other department heads as Bush did when he called on the secretary of the treasury and the attorney general.

In the diplomatic arena, the most heated exchanges and clashes occur between the secretary of state and the national security advisor. Serious institutional rivalries developed throughout the presidency of Jimmy Carter and during the early months of the Reagan administration when Reagan's first secretary of state, (former army general) Alexander Haig, Jr., moved to consolidate his dominance over foreign policymaking. Haig soon confronted other decision-makers who shared jurisdiction including National Security Advisor Richard Allen and his successor William Clark, Defense Secretary Caspar Weinberger, and UN Ambassador Jeane Kirkpatrick. Haig and Weinberger disagreed about U.S. policy in the Middle East and, after the imposition of martial law in Poland, Weinberger encouraged Reagan, much to Haig's dismay, to impose sanctions on the Soviet Union. Haig also had differences of opinion with UN Ambassador Kirkpatrick over the Falkland Islands War between Argentina and Britain. Haig felt slighted because he was not consulted when Reagan selected Philip C. Habib as the Middle East emissary to persuade Israel to withdraw from Beirut. Haig was an outsider rather than one of Reagan's inner circle, and eventually he lost control over foreign policy at the hands of the secretary of defense, the NSC, and White House advisors James Baker, Edwin Meese, and Michael Deaver, a group Haig referred to as "the three-headed monster."[35] When Haig finally resigned on June 26, 1982, no one was surprised. George Schultz, the new secretary of state, became more of a Reagan loyalist and so-called team player.

Secretary of State

As Haig's troubles in the Reagan administration certainly suggest, the secretary of state is influential only so long as the president allows him to control foreign policy. John Foster Dulles served Dwight D. Eisenhower as secretary of state and was his closest foreign policy advisor. So visible was Dulles that former senator William Fulbright (D–Ark.) once observed that he "seemed at times to be exercising those 'delicate, plenary, and exclusive powers' which are supposed to be vested in the President."[36] Henry Kissinger, first appointed by Nixon as his national security advisor, and later as secretary of state, used his style of shuttle diplomacy by repeatedly traveling to the Middle East, to India, to the Soviet Union and to Vietnam. His negotiations with the Vietnamese resulted in the January 23, 1973 Paris Peace Accord that brought an end to the Vietnam conflict. James A. Baker, George Bush's secretary of state until 1992, became a very active participant in foreign affairs and was instrumental in the reunification of Germany, negotiations with Moscow on arms limitations, and the organization of the Arab-Israeli peace talks of 1992.

Bill Clinton's first secretary of state, Warren Christopher, in contrast, was criticized for not being assertive enough when engaging foreign leaders. When Christopher visited the People's Republic of China (PRC) in 1994 to urge foreign minister Qian Qichen to improve China's human rights record if it expected the United States to grant China a most-favored-nation (MFN) status on trade,[37] the Chinese responded by threatening trade reprisals against the United States. A *New York Times* columnist called Christopher's approach a "diplomatic mugging"[38] and Christopher left China with little to show for his efforts.

Looking back over recent history, few secretaries of state have been selected for their diplomatic experience.[39] Most lacked experience in foreign affairs and, therefore, were minor advisors who were eclipsed by the national security advisor. This happened under Nixon when he appointed William Rogers, a lawyer with little diplomatic experience, as secretary of state. It was Henry Kissinger, then Nixon's national security advisor, who worked closely with Nixon as the chief architect of U.S. foreign policy long before he became secretary of state.

Department of State

One complication for the secretary of state is the reputation the State Department, which has been perceived as too cautious in problem solving, too rigid in bureaucratic procedures, and too biased in its perception of world events. Moreover, the Department of State has no domestic clientele or political constituency like the Department of Defense—with its military contractors—that can be aroused to defend the department when necessary. Organizations of intellectuals and specialists focus on foreign policy, such as the Council on Foreign Relations, but they do not carry the political clout available to economically based interests. Also the American public does not always appreciate the department's obligation to represent the views of foreign governments to U.S. leaders.

Presidents must shoulder some blame for the poor image of the Department of State. For example, consider the relationship between Presi-

dent Kennedy and his hand-picked ambassador to India, Harvard economist John Kenneth Galbraith. Rather than communicate with Galbraith
through the secretary of state, Kennedy contacted him directly, which was
particularly damaging to department morale because it was Galbraith
who once said about the Department of State, "You'll find that it's the kind
of organization which, though it does big things badly, [it] does small
things badly too."[40]

NSC and the National Security Advisor

The role of the National Security Council (NSC) is pivotal to foreign
policymaking. As Thomas Mann of The Brookings Institution observed,
"[i]n most recent administrations the National Security Council staff has
eclipsed the State Department, and the antipathy of the president's political advisers toward the foreign service and other parts of the bureaucracy
has been exacerbated."[41]

President Truman in 1945 requested Congress to unify the military
establishment and to create "an advisory board of chiefs of staff and service commanders and . . . a national defense council."[42] The NSC was thus
established by the National Security Act of 1947 to integrate domestic, foreign, and military policies as related to national security. As originally
structured the NSC included the president, vice president, secretary of
state, and secretary of defense as permanent members, with the chairman
of the Joint Chiefs of Staff, head of the Arms Control and Disarmament
Agency, and the CIA director as staff advisors to the NSC.

But the NSC began slowly as an advisor to the White House because,
prior to the Korean War, Harry Truman attended only 11 of the 56 scheduled
meetings, and he did not appear enthusiastic about its potential. Instead, Truman relied on his newly appointed secretary of state, World War II general
George C. Marshall.[43] After the Korean War began, however, Truman made
greater use of the NSC as a forum and sounding board for policy options.

It was Eisenhower, Supreme Allied Commander in World War II, who
institutionalized and expanded the NSC. Now the NSC met on a regular
basis. During the first three years of the Eisenhower administration the
NSC met 145 times and took 829 policy actions as compared with 128 meetings and 699 policy actions during its five years under Harry Truman.[44]

The NSC changed again under John Kennedy, who preferred a loose,
flexible, and pragmatic advisory arrangement. The size of the NSC was
limited to its statutory membership, although others were consulted as
necessary, but more importantly the NSC was only one of many advisory
forums Kennedy used to make foreign policy. For one, the position of special assistant for national security affairs gained new prominence under
Kennedy. This office was created by Eisenhower, who wanted a low-
profile staffer to assist the president with national security matters. But
Kennedy appointed the highly visible and influential McGeorge Bundy,
who monitored proposals from the departments and strengthened the
president's control over the implementation of foreign policy.

President Nixon wanted to combine Eisenhower's structure and Kennedy's personalized style to maximize White House control over foreign policy. He achieved this objective through National Security Advisor Henry Kissinger, who also chaired various committees of the NSC. In 1973 Kissinger consolidated his power over diplomacy by being appointed secretary of state while retaining his former job as special assistant.

Carter tried to separate the NSC from the State Department but failed to prevent personality conflicts among his national security advisors. He appointed Columbia University political scientist Zbigniew Brzezinski as his national security advisor, thinking he would be a subordinate to Secretary of State Cyrus Vance. Brzezinski was unwilling to take a lesser role than Vance, however, which encouraged many clashes of views between these men.[45] Vance was considered a foreign policy professional among his peers,[46] but his more reserved and cautious personality came into conflict with Brzezinski's assertive style; this discord eventually led to Vance's resignation in April 1980.[47]

To avoid similar conflict in their own administrations, both Reagan and Bush made their secretary of state the dominant figure in foreign policy. President Bush selected a longtime political associate, James A. Baker, III, to be his secretary of state and General Brent Scowcroft to be his national security advisor. Scowcroft was no egomaniac, seeing himself as a team player who avoided the publicity that surrounded Jim Baker.

During his first term President Clinton witnessed some infighting between National Security Advisor Anthony Lake and Secretary of State Warren Christopher, despite their efforts to remain harmonious in public. Clinton may have contributed to weakening Christopher's position when he upstaged the secretary in asking former president Jimmy Carter, Senator Sam Nunn (D–Ga.), and JCS chairman General Colin Powell to go to Haiti to negotiate the peaceful exit of the military junta that ruled the island.[48]

Role of Congress

A potentially contentious element of foreign policymaking is the relationship between the president and Congress. We have updated an older study of the decision-making process in 22 foreign policy actions from 1930 to 1961[49] through 1996 to include 41 more foreign policy actions (see Appendix 1). Each decision is evaluated according to whether Congress or the president *initiated* the action and then proceeds to analyze key interrelationships, which are summarized (Table 11-4). Many important foreign policy events are included in this sample of 63 cases, although they are likely biased in favor of so-called successful foreign policy decisions. Despite that word of caution, our findings regarding the years 1962 to 1992 parallel the earlier study.

The overwhelming advantage goes to the president, relative to Congress, in managing foreign affairs. The chief diplomat was the predominant influence in 77 percent of the episodes from 1930 to 1961 and in 88 percent from 1962 to 1992. This is impressive because most foreign policy decisions provided the opportunity for Congress to assert its prerogatives. The time frame involved in making these decisions was relatively long in over two-thirds of the cases during both historical periods, so most episodes did not involve crises. Also Congress had enacted resolutions or statutes to support its policy preferences in two-thirds of the decisions from 1930 to 1961 and in two-fifths of the cases since then. In summary, although Congress passed legislation and had adequate time to judge presidential foreign policy initiatives, the White House still predominated in a majority of decisions across the entire 1930 to 1992 period. The ability to initiate foreign policy largely determines why the president prevails over Congress in the decision-making process.

CONGRESSIONAL OVERSIGHT.   Congress tries to oversee the conduct of foreign affairs in other ways including its power over the purse. It can require the president to issue periodic reports on various programs, give Congress advance warning about actions taken pursuant to legislation, or use committee hearings to publicize administrative blunders in foreign policy.

As a backlash against presidential deceit during the Vietnam War, Congress attempted to exercise oversight over arms shipments. At first the

Table 11–4. Legislative-Executive Relationships in Major Foreign Policy Decisions, 1930–1996

		1930–1961*	1962–1992†
Number of Cases		22	41
Degree of Congressional Involvement	High	16(2)‡	24(12)‡
	Low	4(3)	10(9)
	None	2(2)	7(5)
Initiator of Decision	Executive	19(7)	35(24)
	Congress	3(0)	6(2)
Predominant Influence in Decision	Executive	16(6)	32(24)
	Congress	6(1)	9(2)
Formal Legislation or Resolution	Yes	17(3)	22(14)
	No	5(4)	19(12)
Decision-making Time Available	Long	20(5)	28(16)
	Short	2(2)	13(10)

*This analysis is based on documentation supplied by James A. Robinson in *Congress and Foreign Policy-making* (Homewood, IL: Dorsey Press, 1962), pp. 64–69.
†This analysis is based on our classification of policy decisions found in Appendix 1.
‡The cases in parentheses involved violence or the threat of violence.

law simply required the secretary of state to report semiannually to Congress on any significant arms sales, but this procedure was changed in 1974 to mandate that the president give Congress a detailed description of any weapons sale involving $25 million or more. Within thirty days an arms sale could be stopped by a two-chamber legislative veto unless the president stipulated it was an emergency. During the five years following 1974 no arms sale was vetoed by Congress, but there were occasions when presidents modified their proposals to obtain legislative approval.

In 1975, for example, the Ford administration wanted to sell fourteen Hawk missile batteries to Jordan; the deal had been arranged secretly to minimize the time available for Israeli lobbyists to oppose the sale. When Congress was informed, a controversy erupted, and Jordan's King Hussein had to come to the United States to persuade key members of Congress to support Jordan. In the end the Hawk missile was modified to assure its defensive rather than offensive use, and the sale was finalized.

Congressional oversight of U.S. intelligence activities has been a thorny issue between the legislative and executive branches, especially regarding covert actions abroad. More often than not the White House is reluctant to reveal such information to Congress. The Iran-contra affair of 1985–1987 illustrates how an assertive President Reagan could resist sharing information about that covert operation with the Congress.[50]

PUBLIC INPUTS

Presidents often legitimize their domestic and foreign policies by referring to their election mandate from the people, but elections are very imprecise barometers of public opinion, especially on foreign policy. Most presidential elections are shaped by domestic issues, notably the health of the economy, rather than foreign affairs.

Communism, Korea, and corruption in the Truman administration was a GOP campaign slogan in 1952. In 1960 John Kennedy pointed to the "missile gap" as evidence of falling behind the Soviets, and in 1968 and 1972 the Vietnam War was highly salient to voters. The Carter-Reagan contest in 1980 saw the Republicans using the Iran-hostage crisis and the Russian occupation of Afghanistan to prove that Democrats were soft on military preparedness. However, even these elections were not purely contests over foreign policy because two recessions during the late 1950s badly hurt Nixon's chances in 1960, and in 1980 Jimmy Carter was faced with explaining away double-digit inflation. The more relevant question, therefore, is whether public opinion acts to constrain the chief diplomat during the course of foreign policymaking.

Public Opinion

The impact of public opinion is a very complicated issue to unravel, and over time analysts have offered various interpretations. Earlier in this century some commentators believed different public "moods" toward foreign affairs characterized different historical periods and they were "volatile and irrational" in nature.[51] Before World War I the United States had strong isolationist sentiments but, once America entered that war, Americans wanted to win a total victory. Public vacillation between isolationism and internationalism has been linked to the fact that public opinion is greatly influenced by world events.[52] Pearl Harbor ended U.S. isolationism, and the close of World War II saw public opinion shift decidedly toward internationalism and an optimistic view that the United States should help achieve a lasting world peace. Yet the advent of the Cold War and the rise of McCarthyism in the early 1950s yielded to greater pessimism that somehow the United States was betrayed by its political leaders.[53]

With regard to high-stake issues in foreign policy, some observers argue that public opinion defines the permissible boundaries within which the White House must operate,[54] and presidency scholar Erwin Hargrove once rhetorically asked, for example, whether John F. Kennedy could have survived politically had he allowed the Soviets to establish a missile base in Cuba, 90 miles from Florida. For that reason, an effective chief diplomat who seeks to make a fundamental shift in American foreign policy must try to educate the American people. Richard Nixon visited Communist China to pave the way for a softening of U.S.-Chinese diplomatic relations, yet it would have been premature for Nixon to grant China full diplomatic recognition. By his opening the dialogue with China, however, Nixon prepared public opinion for the decision by President Carter to end the U.S. nonrecognition policy toward mainland China.

The Panama Canals were constructed during the presidency of Theodore Roosevelt, who helped orchestrate a coup d'état against Columbia in order to gain political influence over Panama. Many people including key members of Congress viewed the Panama Canal Zone as American as any of the fifty states, so the decision by Jimmy Carter to return sovereignty over the canal to the Republic of Panama required substantial efforts to educate public opinion. The Carter administration sent spokespersons across the country to encourage support for the Panama Canal Treaties and State Department officials made about 800 speaking engagements, appeared on TV talk shows, and gave interviews. President Carter used a fireside chat to rally public support for the treaties and, to focus specifically on opinion leaders, a White House conference was held in January 1978. All these public relations activities paid off because the treaties were ratified, albeit with certain Senate "reservations" attached.

Of course, presidents are not enslaved by public opinion and may choose to ignore it. Most likely this strategy works with national security matters that do not directly affect the United States or its domestic society. When President Reagan intervened in the Falklands War between Great Britain and Argentina, for example, lukewarm public opinion did not deter him from taking a strong stand behind Britain. It occurred in 1982 when public approval for Reagan's foreign policy was declining. Argentina had landed troops on the Falkland Islands, off its coast, even though that territory was under British rule, and Prime Minister Margaret Thatcher ordered a naval task force to sail to the Falklands. U.S. attempts to resolve the conflict failed, so Reagan proceeded to offer Great Britain war supplies, repair facilities for its fleet, and intelligence data on Argentine troop movements and the location of Soviet naval vessels.

There is a partisan angle to foreign affairs. Going back to the era when communism engulfed Eastern Europe and China, and during the Red Scare of the 1950s, polls consistently indicated that the Republican Party was perceived as more able to safeguard national security (whereas Democrats were viewed as the better guardians of domestic prosperity). Yet the specific issue or condition of the country, along with the general images of each political party, may be less relevant than how the public evaluates the actions or inactions of specific Republican or Democratic presidents.

No Republican president can focus on foreign affairs at the expense of domestic policy when domestic problems are salient. Although the economy in 1992 was the most important concern of voters during that election campaign, an April 1992 survey found that 60 percent of the public approved of the way George Bush was handling foreign affairs, whereas only 22 percent endorsed his handling of the economy.[55] Neither can a Democratic president neglect foreign policy entirely, as Clinton learned to his chagrin. Clinton won the 1992 election largely because of the economic recession, yet once in office the public began to judge Clinton as too weak in his response to foreign affairs. Two polls taken in April 1994 showed that only about 40 percent of respondents approved of his handling of foreign affairs.[56]

Rally round the Flag

Actions associated with foreign affairs do not always translate into higher approval ratings for the president. One researcher indicated that meeting with foreign leaders in summit conferences during the period 1952 to 1972 almost always improved presidential ratings, but during the decade of the 1960s those high-level diplomatic meetings rarely had a positive effect on presidential popularity.[57] Similarly, Brace and Hinckley show empirically that "the conduct of foreign affairs has weakly negative effects [on popularity]. After presidents announce treaties or send foreign policy messages to Congress, their approval will fall slightly."[58] What really matters in foreign affairs is an international crisis in which military force is threatened or used. Those episodes cause the public to rally round the flag and bolster presidential approval because the president symbolizes the nation and the need for decisive action is recognized.[59] This primordial response to crisis by public opinion is unrelated to success or failure, as political scientist Nelson Polsby observed: "Invariably, the popular response to a President during international crisis is favorable regardless of the wisdom of the policies he pursues."[60] Indeed, the pattern is for presidential approval to increase even when the chief diplomat has failed to accomplish his objectives or to defend American interests abroad (Table 11-5).

Despite President Kennedy's involvement in the disastrous Bay of Pigs invasion, when U.S.-backed Cuban freedom fighters were defeated by the Communist forces of Fidel Castro, his popularity rallied by ten percentage points. The seizure of American hostages by Iran in 1979 was not the high point of Carter diplomacy, but after it happened Carter's approval rating soared from 32 to 61 percent within one month. In 1983 a terrorist bomb exploded in Beirut, Lebanon, killing a few hundred U.S. marines, but the Reagan approval rating nevertheless rose from 48 to 56 percent. One "failure" in foreign affairs did result in a loss of public support for President Clinton. It involved the killings of eighteen American servicemen on October 3, 1993, in Somalia. They were sent to the African nation by President Bush to provide humanitarian aid but soon got bogged down in a civil war between rival gangs of thugs. American newscasts televised the bodies of dead Americans being dragged through the streets of the capital city, and this public humiliation of the U.S. armed services undoubtedly caused Clinton's popularity to fall six points to 50 percent approval.

Economic Interests

International trade and finance is one policy area in which foreign affairs and domestic politics interact, with the consequence which economic interests which normally ignore foreign policy become mobilized to defend their narrow self-interest. Throughout the nineteenth and early twentieth centuries trade policy was controlled by Congress, not the executive, and its objective was to erect barriers to imports through the use of tariffs and quotas in order to protect domestic industries and jobs from foreign competition. But then, beginning with the Reciprocal Trade Agreements Act of 1934, the United States embarked on a long-term policy of "free trade" by negotiating the mutual lowering of trade barriers among nations to allow the open exchange of goods, services, and capital.

The emerging consensus on free trade was so powerful that Congress, through the Trade Act of 1974, acceded greater authority to the president under a "fast-track" procedure. Fast-tracking allows the president and the U.S. trade representative to negotiate trade agreements and write an implementing bill that is presented to Congress. Congress has a difficult time in altering the measure under fast tracking because it only has ninety days in which to approve or disapprove it.[61]

Businesses favoring trade liberalization often speak through the Emergency Committee for American Trade (ECAT). In 1974, when the Trade Reform Act was debated, ECAT helped organize about twelve hundred corporate executives to lobby for its passage. The American Iron and Steel Institute, in contrast, tends to pressure Congress for trade protection, and its arguments are often supported by the United Steelworkers of America.

The political conflict between big business and organized labor attracted attention in 1993 when Congress had to enact legislation to implement the North American Free Trade Agreement (NAFTA), which was

Table 11–5. Presidential Popularity and Foreign Policy "Failures"

Foreign Policy "Failure"	Percentage Approval	
	Before	After
American U-2 spy plan downed in Soviet territory, 1960	62	65
Bay of Pigs invasion by exiled Cubans from the United States ends in failure, 1961	73	83
Iran militants Seize U.S. embassy and take hostages, 1979	32	61
U.S. marines killed in terrorist bombing in Beirut, Lebanon, 1983	48	56
Cruise missiles attack Iraqi intelligence headquarters but Saddam Hussein escapes harm, 1993	39	50
U.S. troops on humanitarian mission to Somalia are killed and their bodies dragged through streets of capital, 1993	56	50

Sources: Data on 1960 episode from Jong R. Lee, "Rallying around the Flag: Foreign Policy Events and Presidential Popularity," *Presidential Studies Quarterly* 7 (Fall 1977), pp. 254–255; data on 1961, 1979, 1983, and 1993 Iraqi episodes are from the 1st edition, and the 1993 Somalia episode is from the 2nd edition of Theodore J. Lowi and Benjamin Ginsberg, *American Government* (New York: W.W. Norton, 1990 and 1996), pp. 288 and 258. The Somalia data comes from C. Gray Wheeler and David W. Moore, "Clinton's Foreign Policy Ratings Plunge," *The Gallup Poll Monthly* 337 (Oct. 1993), p. 25.

negotiated by the Bush administration, President Carlos Salinas de Gortari of Mexico, and Prime Minister Brian Mulroney of Canada. NAFTA was negotiated by President Bush but to President Clinton fell the responsibility of obtaining congressional approval. During the 1992 presidential campaign Clinton was ambivalent about NAFTA, stating that side agreements had to be negotiated to assure humane working conditions and environmental safeguards, but independent presidential candidate Ross Perot was so opposed to NAFTA that he made it a major campaign issue. Perot warned audiences of American workers that the huge "sucking sound" that can be heard from NAFTA will be the tremendous loss of U.S. jobs to cheap Mexican laborers.

Clinton ultimately betrayed his supporters in organized labor as well as the Democratic leadership in Congress and embraced NAFTA. He was joined by every ex-president, Democrat and Republican, and backed by a phalanx of lobbyists from corporate America. The labor unions were allied with environmentalists and some civil rights groups, but their coalition was unable to prevent Congress from enacting the necessary legislation.

On the final vote, the majority of Democrats in the House and the Senate opposed NAFTA, but the old conservative coalition of Republicans and southern Democrats passed the bill. The outcome showed the political power of the Sun Belt over the Frost Belt: southerners and westerners looked forward to increased trade opportunities with Mexico, whereas blue-collar workers in the aging manufacturing industries in the North and Midwest feared for their economic survival. Almost every northern Democrat in the House of Representatives voted with labor against their president and they were joined by a small group of Republicans. An empirical analysis by Holian, Krebs, and Walsh found that, even though the GOP strongly favored the trade pact, those Republican members of Congress who themselves won election by narrow margins and whose constituents cast disproportionate votes for Ross Perot for president also voted against NAFTA on final passage.[62]

Multinational corporations are also an important political force in world affairs, and since 1945 American businesses have developed about eight thousand overseas subsidiaries. Because mergers, licensing requirements, and equipment sales take place across national boundaries, no one government is equal to the task of monitoring those transactions. Huge corporate conglomerates have more resources than some governments in the developing nations, and there are surely occasions when they attempt to intervene in the domestic affairs of another nation with or without the tacit approval of the U.S. government.

Perhaps the most outlandish example in recent decades was the International Telephone and Telegraph (ITT) involvement in Chile in 1970–1971. What prompted ITT's concern was the prospect that the ruling conservative party would lose a national election to the Marxists, thus allowing the leftist party under Salvador Allende to seize foreign capital and undercut ITT profits. To head off that development, ITT made substantial election contributions to conservative presidential candidate Jorge Alessandri Rodriquez hoping to help him defeat Allende. In September 1970 ITT even offered a grant of $1 million to the State Department, national security advisor Henry Kissinger, or to the CIA if any of them would develop a plan to protect American private investment in Chile. That money, ITT reasoned, could be used to unify the opposition to Allende, bring about economic turmoil in the country, or even promote a military coup d'état.[63] Although U.S. foreign policy was not changed because of the ITT-CIA discussions, nor was there a conspiracy of American multinational corporations to undermine Allende's position, the entire ITT-CIA scheme proceeded without the explicit approval of the State Department or President Nixon. This episode clearly points out how difficult it is for the chief diplomat to control such intrigues by American companies on foreign soil.

Ethnic Groups

Immigration policy and foreign aid programs may cause heightened political lobbying by ethnic groups in behalf of their homelands. The efforts by the American Jewish community in behalf of Israel are long standing but have become more publicized as the United States plays a leading role in Middle East peace negotiations. The Israeli lobby in the United States has always overpowered the Arab lobby,[64] and there is a vast difference in their political strategies. Arab countries tend to lobby Congress directly for military sales, whereas Israel refrains from such activities and instead relies on the American Jewish community to promote its interests indirectly. The American Israel Public Affairs Committee (AIPAC) has been called "the most effective citizen-ethnic lobby" in America.[65] AIPAC speaks for all major Jewish organizations in the United States and is an effective voice because its professional staff provides well-documented, expert opinion on Israeli issues and is also able to mobilize grassroots opinion behind its objectives.

Most Americans are sympathetic toward Israel in its dealings with the Arab countries, whereas public opinion is less favorably disposed toward the Arab states. In 1991, when the United States was waging the Persian Gulf War, Arab Americans felt this antagonism from both private and governmental sources. The FBI began questioning some Arab Americans concerning their political sympathies and affiliations; Pan American World Airways stopped people with Iraqi passports from flying on its airlines; and Iraqi American citizens were held at airports for questioning about terrorist activities.[66] Jamin Raskin called Arab Americans the "Japanese of 1991" and asked whether they need fear being "rounded up" much as the Japanese Americans were in the 1940s.[67]

Cubans and Castro

Ever since middle-class and professional Cubans fled Cuba and landed in Miami in the late 1950s after the takeover by communist revolutionary Fidel Castro, the United States has refused to recognize its government and placed an embargo on a commercial relationship between the two countries. Cuban exiles in Florida are determined to see the day when Castro's regime is toppled, and their fervent anticommunism has aligned them with the national Republican Party.

Angered by the February 24, 1996, Cuban fighter plane firings on two U.S. civilian airplanes that allegedly entered Cuban air space and ended up killing four Americans, Congress passed a law penalizing foreign companies and countries that do business with Cuba. The bill, co-authored by Senator Jesse Helms (R–N.C.) and Representative Dan Burton (R–Ind.) and commonly known as the Helms-Burton Act (PL 104–114), was signed by President Clinton on March 12. To assure that Clinton would sign the bill, despite opposition from businesses and allies abroad, Congress included a mechanism allowing the chief diplomat to delay implementation or prevent any legal actions pursuant to that legislation.[68] The bill also made permanent other sanctions against Cuba including the trade embargo.[69]

Reaction to the bill from U.S. allies, particularly Canada and Mexico, was quick.[70] The European Union was opposed, claiming that the impact of this bill could be compared to the "sword of Damocles."[71] But some Cuban American members of Congress criticized President Clinton for his hesitation in implementing the bill. Congressman Lincoln Diaz-Balart (R–Fla.) accused Clinton of having a "[c]haracter of Jell-O, backbone of Jell-O,"[72] and Democratic Representative Robert Menendez (D–N.J.) believed Clinton might be able to change the minds of Cuban Americans, who usually vote Republican, if he would implement the lawsuit provision. Said

Menendez, "If he does that, he has every possibility of galvanizing his support [among Cuban Americans] and bringing it home in November."[73]

In light of the criticism from American businesses and North American and European allies, Clinton decided to delay for six months implementation of the legislation, thus deferring any likely lawsuits against violators. His action, of course, drew criticism from Republicans like presidential contender Bob Dole, who indicated that "President Clinton's continued indecision until the last possible moment demonstrates, once again, that this President is rudderless when it comes to standing up for American principles around the world."[74]

Caught in a bind between diplomatic reality and domestic politics, Clinton tried to placate foreign business and political leaders. But the law also barred anyone found guilty of violating Helms-Burton from entering the United States, as the officers and shareholders of a Canadian mining firm, Sherritt International Corporation, learned in July 1996.[75] The prospect that large multinational corporations could be penalized sent rippling effects throughout Latin America and Europe and caused some second thoughts by Clinton's closest advisors. As Secretary of the Treasury Robert Rubin explained, "I have some real concerns about the extra-territorial application of American law . . . [b]ut you have to balance that with our interests in bringing pressure to bear on countries like Cuba and Iran."[76]

EXPERTISE

One major advantage enjoyed by the chief diplomat is the ability to maintain secrecy and personal control over information vital to diplomatic initiatives. Sometimes presidents can utilize privileged lines of communication to ensure the confidentiality of their instructions to diplomatic agents. President John F. Kennedy in 1963 used such methods to communicate directly with Averill Harriman who was negotiating a test-ban treaty with the Soviet Union. Only six persons in the Kennedy administration had access to that information so those delicate negotiations would not be revealed to the Department of Defense or to the Joint Chiefs of Staff.

Congress clearly faces tremendous difficulties in trying to oversee the conduct of foreign affairs as presidential diplomatic initiatives are taking place. It is more likely that Congress must wait until those actions are completed before being fully appraised of their implications. Also, presidents make secret commitments to other nations that are not easily reversed. After Egypt and Israel signed the second Sinai disengagement agreement in the early 1970s, Congress learned that Secretary of State Henry Kissinger had made commitments to both countries which, although secret, involved the United States. One caveat bound the United States to support and assist Israel even though Congress was totally uninformed.[77]

Bosnian Arms Embargo

Although not all the details about secret arms shipments to the Bosnian Muslims during their civil war against the Bosnian Serbs in Yugoslavia have yet been revealed, what is known points to deception by Clinton's foreign policy team and a deliberate effort to keep Congress uninformed. During 1994 it was unclear what kind of policy the Clinton administration supported. At first the White House backed the idea of air strikes by UN forces against Serbian positions in Bosnia but later supported a less aggressive approach, favored by U.S. NATO allies, that stressed diplomacy.

At this time Congress also was conflicted about what policy to pursue in Bosnia. Some members advocated decisive military action and favored UN bombing raids against Serbian positions, while also lifting an arms embargo which prevented the Bosnian Muslims from getting the weapons and armaments they needed to defend themselves against the heavily armed Serbian forces. Other legislators were more cautious. Eventually the Senate in January 1994 attached a "nonbinding" amendment to the Department of State authorization act that urged the Clinton administration to arm the Bosnian Muslims.

The Clinton administration in 1994 firmly supported the UN arms embargo that prevented the Bosnian Muslims from taking the offensive against the Serbs. At the same time, however, the Clinton administration, unbeknownst to Congress, which was against the embargo, was supporting a Croatian plan to allow Iranian weapons to come to the Bosnian Muslims through Croatia. U.S. diplomats were told to indicate to Croatian president Franjo Tudjman that the United States would not oppose such a move.[78]

When the *Los Angeles Times* in April 1996 broke the story, members of Congress who had been pressing the administration to lift the embargo were irritated for a number of reasons. To begin with, they could not understand how the administration could maintain a public position against arming the Bosnian Muslims, veto legislation that had been passed in the summer of 1995 to require the president to end the arms embargo, and at the same time allow a supply line of arms to come to the Muslims from Iran. Moreover, they charged that the president and his foreign policy team had failed to report this "covert" operation to the Congress, as the law requires. Finally, congressional Republicans were opposed to Iran being drawn into the political turmoil of Bosnia.

As Congressman Henry J. Hyde (R–Ill.), chairman of the special committee investigation of the Bosnian arms operation said, "What we are concerned about is the wisdom, the propriety, the common sense of standing by while the most terrorist nation on earth comes into the bosom of the most volatile place on earth."[79] Senator Robert Dole (R–Kans.), who would oppose Clinton as the GOP presidential candidate and had fought hard to reverse the embargo, expressed the outrage of congressional Republicans when he declared, "This duplicitous policy has seriously damaged our credibility with our allies" and added that having Iranian military troops in Bosnia produced "one of the most serious threats to our military forces in Bosnia."[80]

Although they did not wish U.S. arms to go to the Bosnian Muslims, the Clinton administration defended itself by suggesting they were willing to allow Iranian arms to be supplied to them. The White House also contended that the plan was not a covert operation because people knew it was taking place, no U.S. funds were being used for the operation, and nobody was acting for or on behalf of the United States. Thus the Clinton administration argued it was under no legal obligation to report the matter to Congress.

Eventually this stated position came back to haunt the administration because Anthony Lake, national security advisor during Clinton's first term, was nominated by the president to become the CIA director in his second term.[81] Senate Republicans planned to use the confirmation hearings on Lake to probe deeply into his involvement with the Bosnian arms shipments. As this instance illustrates, Congress once again attempted to hold the executive branch accountable for its foreign policy mistakes after the fact because the White House was able to prevent Congress from knowing anything about its decision to support covert Bosnian arms shipments at the time that policy was implemented.

An organizational problem that has undercut congressional oversight of foreign affairs is its fragmented committee system. Neither the House Committee on International Relations (formerly Foreign Affairs) nor the Senate Committee on Foreign Relations have complete jurisdiction over foreign policy. In the House, for example, foreign trade is reviewed by the Ways and Means Committee, international finance and currency is examined by the Committee on Banking and Financial Services, shipping is looked at by the Committee on Transportation and Infrastructure, and fisheries is studied by the Resources Committee.

CRISIS

Crises rally public opinion behind the president's leadership in foreign affairs, but more significant is the qualitative change in executive-legislative relations during dramatic foreign events that greatly reduces congressional influence in foreign policy. In general, as we argued previously, foreign policy is normally shaped by the president and his advisors and sometimes Congress in its constitutional role. When the president confronts a crisis in foreign affairs, however, the pattern of decision making is analogous to what is exhibited by the commander in chief: only the president and his key advisors are privy to those decisions. When Ripley and Franklin analyzed the policy process, they noted that crises were uniquely the purview of:

> ... the President and whomever he chooses to consult. Mostly he will choose to consult only a few of his top advisors; sometimes he will bring in leading individual members of Congress or occasionally "peak association" leaders. The issues are defined quickly, debated in private by the executive actors, and responded to quickly in a highly centralized fashion through executive (presidential) action. Of course, the decisions may provoke considerable public debate after they are announced.[82]

Therefore crisis decisions in foreign affairs are analogous to military actions taken by the commander in chief: both tend to consolidate power in the hands of the president.[83] This pattern is illustrated by cases of decision making in foreign affairs (see Table 11-4).

The sample of 22 pre-1962 and 32 post-1962 foreign policy decisions were differentiated by whether or not there was an imminent threat of violence. In the early period, the president dominated over Congress in 16 of the total of 22 cases (73 percent) but in six of seven (86 percent) where violence was threatened. Since 1962 presidential dominance has occurred in 23 of 32 cases overall (72 percent) but again increased to 15 of 17 (88 percent) cases where the prospect of violent confrontations existed. *Violence* is the key variable that draws the line between the spheres of diplomacy and warfare. Today the term national security denotes the interaction between the chief diplomat and the commander-in-chief roles, but the use of military force usually follows after any efforts at peaceful negotiations between nations have broken down. Thus the prospects of crisis in the chief diplomat role suggests that violence is an imminent threat, and therefore these episodes take on the attributes of the president acting as commander in chief.

SUMMARY

The constitutional basis for presidential power in foreign affairs has been greatly strengthened by customary practice and historic abdication by Congress of its responsibility. Yet no president can totally ignore the legislature given its power over the purse.

Congress reasserted its role over diplomacy during the 1970s, but that reaction to Vietnam did not survive into the 1980s and 1990s. On certain issues, like aid to the Nicaraguan contras in the 1980s and NAFTA in the 1990s, Congress becomes aroused and tries to block presidential initiatives. For the most part, however, the White House still dominates foreign policy. Presidents dominate because Congress lacks the ability to stop his foreign policy *initiatives,* which are the fundamental source of presidential power. Presidents deal personally with the leaders of other nations or delegate sensitive negotiations to ambassadors or, more likely, special diplomatic agents who answer only to the chief diplomat. Public opinion worries less about foreign affairs than domestic policy, usually defers to presidential leadership in times of international crisis, and White House policy options are usually not constrained by public opinion or organized interests.

NOTES

1. Refer to Richard Rose and Robert Thompson's fine article, "The President in a Changing International System," *Presidential Studies Quarterly* 21 (4) (Fall 1991), p. 760.

2. Elaine Sciolino, "Defiant Senators Vote to Override Bosnian Arms Ban," *New York Times* (July 27, 1995), p. A1.

3. Renka and Jones convincingly argue the "two presidencies" thesis, first advocated by Aaron Wildavsky in 1966, which argues that presidents consistently do better in getting their foreign policies and defense policies through Congress than their domestic policies. This, of course, became much more difficult given the growing independence and strength of the Congress in the 1970s and 1980s. See the original Wildavsky article in "The Two Presidencies," *Trans-Action* 4 (Dec. 1966), pp. 7–14. See the Renka and Jones article, "The 'Two Presidencies' Thesis and the Reagan Administration," *Congress and the Presidency* 18 (1) (Spring 1991), pp. 17–35. Also see George C. Edwards, III, *At the Margins: Presidential Leadership of Congress* (New Haven, CT: Yale University Press, 1989) whose conclusions support the argument made by Renka and Jones.

4. See Maureen Dowd, "Unable to Out-Hero Bush, Democrats Just Join Him," *New York Times* (March 8, 1991), p. A1.

5. See R. W. Apple, Jr., "Majority in a Poll Fault Bush for Foreign Focus," *New York Times* (Oct. 11, 1991), p. A6.

6. The *New York Times*/CBS News Poll showed approximately 46 percent of the public approved the way George Bush was handling foreign policy. See Thomas L. Friedman, "Bush's Roles on World Stage: Triumphs, but Troubles, Too," *New York Times* (June 26, 1992), p. A12.

7. Bert A. Rockman, "Leadership Style and the Clinton Presidency," in Colin Campbell and Bert A. Rockman, eds., *The Clinton Presidency: First Appraisals* (Chatham, NJ: Chatham House, 1996), p. 341.

8. Gwen Ifill, "Clinton Defends Foreign Policy Record," *New York Times* (May 4, 1994), p. A4.

9. Ann Devroy and R. Jeffrey Smith, "Clinton Reexamines a Foreign Policy under Siege," *Washington Post* (Oct. 17, 1993), p. A28.

10. See Anthony Lewis, "Whistling past Weimar," *New York Times* (Jan. 28, 1994), p. A17.

11. R. W. Apple, Jr., "Clinton Looks Homeward," *New York Times* (Jan. 13, 1994), p. A1.

12. This statement, attributed to Bruce Jentleson, formerly of Clinton's State Department, appeared in Larry Berman and Emily O. Goldman, "Clinton's Foreign Policy at Midterm," in Campbell and Rockman, *The Clinton Presidency: First Appraisals*, p. 300.

13. Michael R. Gordon, "12 in State Dept. Ask Military Move against the Serbs," *New York Times* (April 12, 1993), p. A1.

14. See Daniel Williams and Ann Devroy, "Defining Clinton's Foreign Policy," *Washington Post* (Sept. 20, 1993), p. A16.

15. Gwen Ifill, "Clinton Defends Foreign Policy Record," *New York Times* (May 4, 1994), p. A4.

16. "Bankruptcy Amendments Act of 1993," *Congressional Record—Senate*, 103rd Congress, 2nd session, April 21, 1994, S4641.

17. "Bankruptcy Amendments Act of 1993," *Congressional Record—Senate*, 103rd Congress, 2nd session, April 21, 1994, S4642.

18. Although the term *new world order* was born out of a conversation between Brent Scowcroft and several White House press aides in August 1990 (See Thomas L. Friedman, "Bush's Roles on World Stage: Triumphs, but Troubles, Too," *New York Times* (June 26, 1992, p. A12), others have given substance to the idea and at least one, Senator Joseph R. Biden, Jr. (D–Del.), suggested it was a concept that needed elaboration and had "immense potential . . . for American foreign policy in the 1990s and beyond." "The Threshold of the New World Order: The Wilsonian Vision and American Foreign Policy in the 1990s and Beyond," *Congressional Record—Senate*, 102nd Congress, 2nd session, June 29, 1992, S9098.

19. See Dorothy Buckton James, *The Contemporary Presidency*, 2nd ed. (Indianapolis: Pegasus, 1974), pp. 248–249; also see Sidney M. Milkis and Michael Nelson, *The American Presidency: Origins and Development 1776–1993* (Washington, DC: Congressional Quarterly, 1994), 291–294.

20. For the complete series of "Pacificus" essays see John C. Hamilton, ed., *The Works of Alexander Hamilton*, vol. 7 (New York: Charles S. Francis, 1851), pp. 76–117; for the complete series of "Helvidius" essays see Thomas A. Mason, Robert A. Rutland, and Jeanne K. Sisson, eds., *The Papers of James Madison*, vol. 15 (Charlottesville: University Press of Virginia, 1985), pp. 64–120.

21. *United States v. Curtiss-Wright Export Corporation*, 299 U.S. 304 (1936).

22. *U.S. v. Belmont*, 57 S. Ct. 758–764 (1937); and *U.S. v. Pink*, 315 U.S. 203 (1942).

23. See Sidney Warren, *The President as World Leader* (New York: McGraw-Hill, 1964), p. 379.

24. See Cathal J. Nolan, "The Last Hurrah of Conservative Isolationism: Eisenhower, Congress, and the Bricker Amendment," *Presidential Studies Quarterly* 22 (2) (Spring 1992), pp. 337–349.

25. Senate Resolution 85, *Congressional Record*, 91st Congress, 1st Session, June 25, 1969, 17245.

26. Senate Resolution 469, *Congressional Record*, 91st Congress, 2nd Session, December 11, 1970, 41167.

27. Public Law 92–404.

28. See Leslie Gelb, "Ford-Congress Rift Grows on Executive Agreements," *New York Times* (Aug. 15, 1975), p. 2.

29. *Goldwater v. Carter*, 444 U.S. 996 (1979).

30. *United States v. Nixon*, 418 U.S. 683 (1974).

31. Raoul Berger, *Executive Privilege: A Constitutional Myth* (Cambridge, MA: Harvard University Press, 1974).

32. Mark J. Rozell, *Executive Privilege* (Baltimore: Johns Hopkins University Press, 1994), p. 143.

33. Steven Greenhouse, "Clinton Envoy Choices Are Faulted as Political," *New York Times* (April 13, 1994), p. A6.

34. See Edward Cowan, "China Will Pay 41 Cents on Dollar for American Assets Seized in '49," *New York Times* (March 2, 1979), pp. A1, A5.

35. See David M. Alpern, et al., "The Resignation That Took," *Newsweek* (July 5, 1982), p. 18.

36. See Louis W. Koenig, *The Chief Executive*, 3rd ed. (New York: Harcourt Brace Jovanovich, 1975), p. 223.

37. Elaine Sciolino, "Christopher Is Drawing Fire in Washington on China Visit," *New York Times* (March 18, 1994), p. A1.

38. Patrick E. Tyler, "Chinese Puzzle," *New York Times* (March 14, 1994), p. A1.

39. Exceptions were Dean Acheson, Henry Kissinger, John Foster Dulles, and Cyrus Vance.

40. Richard M. Pious, *The American Presidency* (New York: Basic Books, 1979), p. 359.

41. See Thomas E. Mann, ed., *A Question of Balance: The President, the Congress, and Foreign Policy* (Washington,DC: The Brookings Institution, 1990), p. 16.

42. See John Prados, *Keepers of the Keys: A History of the National Security Council from Truman to Bush* (New York: William Morrow, 1991), p. 29.

43. Stanley L. Falk, "The National Security Council under Truman, Eisenhower, and Kennedy," in Aaron Wildavsky, ed., *The Presidency* (Boston: Little, Brown, 1969), p. 673.

44. Ibid., p. 685.

45. See Prados, *Keepers of the Keys*, p. 444.

46. See I.M. Destler, "National Security II: The Rise of the Assistant," in Hugh Heclo and Lester M. Salamon, eds., *Illusion of Presidential Government* (Boulder, CO: Westview Press, 1981), p. 272.

47. See Kevin V. Mulcahy, "The Secretary of State and the National Security Adviser: Foreign Policymaking in the Carter and Reagan Administration," *Presidential Studies Quarterly* 16 (2) (Spring 1986), pp. 280–299; as well as Dick Kirschten, "Beyond the Vance-Brzezinski Clash Lurks an NSC under Fire," *National Journal* (May 17, 1980), pp. 814–818, for a fine treatment of this clash between Brzezinski and Vance.

48. See Elaine Sciolino, "Christopher and Lake Vying for Control of Foreign Policy,"*New York Times* (Sept. 23, 1994), pp. A1, A5.

49. James A. Robinson, *Congress and Foreign Policy-Making* (Homewood, IL: Dorsey Press, 1962), pp. 64–69.

50. See Gregory F. Treverton, "Intelligence: Welcome to the American Government," in Thomas E. Mann, ed., *A Question of Balance: The President, the Congress, and Foreign Policy* (Washington,DC: The Brookings Institution, 1990), pp. 70–108.

51. See Walter Lippmann, *The Public Philosophy* (Boston: Little, Brown, 1950).

52. Gabriel Almond, *The American People and Foreign Policy* (New York: Praeger, 1960). Also see William Caspary, "The 'Mood Theory': A Study of Public Opinion and Foreign Policy," *American Political Science Review* (June 1970), pp. 536–547.

53. In this context, Theodore Lowi suggests that political intolerance usually follows in the aftermath of war, mainly because the citizenry is not easily calmed after being emotionally aroused and seeks scapegoats. See "Postwar Panic and the Chilling of Dissent," in Theodore J. Lowi, *The Politics of Disorder* (New York: Basic Books, 1971), pp. 102–119.

54. See Erwin C. Hargrove, *The Power of the Modern Presidency* (New York: Knopf, 1974), pp. 114–118.

55. See"Bush Job Performance—Trend," *The Gallup Poll Monthly* (April 1992), pp. 19, 24–25.

56. Richard Benedetto, "Economic Concerns Drop Clinton Ratings Below 50%" *USA*

Today (April 27, 1994), p. 5A; Gwen Ifill, "Clinton Defends Foreign Policy Record," *New York Times* (May 4, 1994), p. A4.

57. See Elmer Plischke, "The President's Image as Diplomat in Chief," *The Review of Politics* 47 (Oct. 1985), p. 558.

58. Paul Brace and Barbara Hinckley, *Follow the Leader* (New York: Basic Books, 1992), p. 109.

59. John E. Mueller, "Presidential Popularity from Truman to Johnson," *American Political Science Review* 64, (March 1970), pp. 18–34.

60. Nelson Polsby, *Congress and the Presidency* (Englewood Cliffs, NJ: Prentice-Hall, 1964), p. 25.

61. Byron W. Daynes and Glen Sussman, "Trade Politics and the Fast Track: Impact on Congressional-Presidential Relations," *American Review of Politics* 15 (Spring 1994), pp. 73–87.

62. David B. Holian, Timothy B. Krebs, and Michael H. Walsh, "Constituency Opinion, Ross Perot, and Roll-Call Behavior in the U.S. House: The Case of the North American Free Trade Agreement," *Legislative Studies Quarterly* (August 1997). [forthcoming].

63. Hearings, March-April 1973, Before the Subcommittee on Multinational Corporations of the Committee on Foreign Relations, U.S. Senate, 93rd Congress, part 1 (Washington,DC: U.S. Government Printing Office, 1973), p. 77.

64. See Sanford J. Unger, "Washington: Jewish and Arab Lobbyists," *The Atlantic* (March 1978), p. 6.

65. Richard Franck and Edward Weisband, eds., *Secrecy and Foreign Policy* (New York: Oxford University Press, 1974), p. 186.

66. See Nancy Gibbs, "Walking a Tightrope," *Time* (Feb. 4, 1991), pp. 42–43.

67. See Jamin B. Raskin, "Remember Korematsu: A Precedent for Arab-Americans?" *Nation* (Feb. 4, 1991), pp. 117–119.

68. "Issue: Cuban Sanctions," *Congressional Quarterly Weekly Report* (Aug. 31, 1996), p. 24564.

69. Carroll J. Doherty, "Cuba: Planes' Downing Forces Clinton to Compromise on Sanctions," *Congressional Quarterly Weekly Report* (March 2, 1996), p. 565.

70. Carroll J. Doherty, "Congress Ignores Objections in Push to Punish Cuba," *Congressional Quarterly Weekly Report* (March 9, 1996), p. 632.

71. Carroll J. Doherty, "Clinton Delays but Allows Suits over Confiscated Property," *Congressional Quarterly Weekly Report* (July 20, 1996), p. 2063.

72. Ibid.

73. Carroll J. Doherty, "Clinton Fires Warning Shot in Cuban Trade Crackdown," *Congressional Quarterly Weekly Report* (July 13, 1996), p. 1983.

74. David E. Sanger, "Clinton Grants, Then Suspends, Right to Sue Foreigners on Cuba," *New York Times* (July 7, 1997), pp. A1, A4.

75. David E. Sanger, "U.S. Will Penalize Canadian Company for Cuba Dealings," *New York Times* (July 11, 1996), p. A1.

76. Ibid., p. A5.

77. U.S. Senate, *Congressional Record* (Oct. 9, 1975), pp. S17957–S17965.

78. Pat Towell, "Clinton's Pick of Lake for CIA Raises Senate GOP Hackles," *Congressional Quarterly Weekly Report* (Dec. 21, 1996), p. 3442.

79. Carroll J. Doherty, "White House Walks Fine Line on Policy toward Iran," *Congressional Quarterly Weekly Report* (May 25, 1996), p. 1474.

80. Carroll J. Doherty, "GOP Seeks White House Report on Iran's Arms Shipments," *Congressional Quarterly Weekly Report* (April 20, 1996), p. 1059.

81. Pat Towell, "Clinton's Pick of Lake for CIA Raises Senate GOP Hackles," *Congressional Quarterly Weekly Report* (Dec. 21, 1996), p. 3442.

82. Ripley and Franklin, *Congress, the Bureaucracy, and Public Policy*, pp. 143–144.

83. James Robinson in his study indicated the same thing. He differentiated between seven foreign or military policy decisions that involved the potential for violence and those that did not. His data shows that the executive both initiated and had predominant influence in such policies as Lend-Lease, Berlin Airlift, Korean War, Indochina in 1954, the Formosan resolution of 1955, and the Bay of Pigs invasion. See James A. Robinson in *Congress and Foreign Policy-Making* (Homewood, IL: Dorsey Press, 1962), pp. 64–69.

12

Insight on Chief Diplomat: Jimmy Carter and the Quest for Peace in the Middle East

Prior to the 1967 Arab-Israeli War, U.S. interests in the Middle East, although important, were relatively minor when compared to those of Europe and Asia. The crushing defeat of the Arabs fundamentally changed the political balance of power in the Middle East. When viewed in combination with the series of events Americans have come to call the energy crisis of the 1970s, the Middle East preempted other areas of the world for the president in his role as chief diplomat. Today the events of the Middle East have an equal place on the U.S. foreign policy agenda and often take precedence over other parts of the world. In one generation, presidents have had to send troops or use armed forces no less than a half a dozen times when the role of diplomacy seemingly failed to protect the nation's interests.

This Insight looks at the Camp David Accords of 1978, in which Jimmy Carter negotiated an historic opening of lines of communication and mutual recognition between longtime political adversaries in the Middle East.[1] Egypt was represented in the negotiations by Anwar Sadat and Israel by Menachem Begin, and they demonstrated that under the right circumstances diplomacy can shift aggression and confrontation to political accommodation and cooperation. Jimmy Carter was nominated for the Nobel Peace Prize for his efforts in bringing these two adversaries together for meetings that led to the recognition of Israel as a sovereign state after thirty years of "unremitting hostility."[2]

Given Carter's relative lack of experience in foreign affairs, compared to George Bush or Richard Nixon, how was he able to put together one of the diplomatic successes of the twentieth century? Why, after the successive attempts of every president since Eisenhower—who had proclaimed the United States would come to the aid of any Middle East country threatened by "international communism"[3]—was Carter able to coordinate what has been referred to as a "remarkable breakthrough in more than

thirty years of hostility"?[4] From another perspective, the Carter administration's "preoccupation" with the substantive domestic problems of the
late 1970s[5], perhaps resembling the difficulties of the Clinton administration, makes it even more interesting to look at the role Jimmy Carter
played at Camp David in the late summer of 1978.

Carter's interest in foreign affairs was far removed from the Middle
East at the beginning of his administration. Had he been given a choice,
he would have focused on broader global issues such as human rights. But
circumstances forced him to contend with bipolar strategic concerns such
as arms control and those issues he put forth in his campaign, such as the
transfer of the Panama Canal back to Panama. Added to this was the
hostage crisis in Iran, which proved to be his ultimate undoing, as well as
the Soviet invasion of Afghanistan in November 1979 causing world unrest. The United States found it could do nothing in either case, which led
to Carter's relatively low overall rating as chief diplomat. Thus the success
of the Camp David Accords is of even greater interest when we consider
that it was concluded by a president with relatively little interest in the
Middle East and one without expertise in foreign policy.

The Arab-Israeli conflict, underscoring relationships in the Middle
East, has existed since the United Nations first considered the so-called
Palestine problem in 1947. In essence, the conflict ensued after the British
declared they could no longer maintain their presence in the Middle East
and turned control of the area over to the United Nations. The UN created
the United Nations Special Committee on Palestine, which recommended
in its majority opinion that Palestine be partitioned into an Arab state and
a Jewish state bound through economic union. The minority opinion favored two independent states in the region.[6] Thus in 1947 UN members
voted to split Palestine into Arab and Jewish states. Despite Arab protests,
the Palestinian Jews, on the eve of the final British withdrawal in May
1948, declared the creation of the state of Israel, which was to be made up
of over half of the territory of Palestine. The failure of the partition plan
set the stage for the 1948 Arab-Israeli war, and an Israeli victory, which resulted in a continuing series of conflicts and numerous peace proposals
put forth over three decades.[7] In addition, nearly 750,000 Arab Palestinian
refugees where left without a homeland.

American presidents attempted to respond to the situation and test
their skills in the diplomatic waters of the Middle East. Dwight Eisenhower sent an emissary to improve economic and social conditions in the
region and undertake discussions concerning the development of the Jordan River in order to enhance the quality of life among those residing in
the transnational watershed.[8] Secretary of State John Foster Dulles suggested a multifaceted approach to the problems of refugees caused by the
lack of permanent political boundaries in the region, with no evidence of
success.[9]

President John Kennedy appointed a special representative to assist in
the attempt to lessen Arab-Israeli tensions. However, the proposals developed were also deemed politically unacceptable to one or both parties.[10]

The 1967 war significantly changed the political climate in the region as well as proving to be a test of American foreign policy. Lyndon Johnson created a five-point plan for a negotiated settlement, resulting in UN Security Council Resolution 242, the resolution that would lay the groundwork for all peace efforts until the summit meeting at Camp David. The resolution called for a "just and lasting peace" and a set of principles for developing a settlement to the conflict between Israel and Arab states.[11]

Following Johnson, the Nixon administration likewise called for a "just and lasting peace," but Secretary of State William Rogers's proposals were summarily dismissed by political leaders in the Middle East, and the Nixon administration's efforts were diverted to Southeast Asia and détente with the Soviet Union. Suspicion that the United States was decidedly pro-Israel also made any overtures from Washington largely cosmetic. Even though Secretary of State Henry Kissinger, Rogers's successor, made some inroads as a result of his shuttle diplomacy, lasting peace was far away.

Jimmy Carter was engaged in Middle East politics from the beginning of his administration. Initially the Carter foreign policy team set a goal of bringing the two major parties—Israel and Egypt—together for negotiations. The plan was to use a set of basic principles to direct the negotiations instead of the step-by-step process that in the past had allowed for roadblocks at nearly every juncture. Carter's three principles, in retrospect, are admirable for their elegance and served as goals to be achieved regardless of the political mechanisms. First was the definition of and assurance of a permanent peace, which Carter saw as a "termination of belligerence toward Israel by her neighbors, recognition of Israel's right to exist, the right to exist in peace, the opening of borders with free trade, tourist travel, cultural exchange between Israel and her neighbors."[12] Second was the recognition of borders critical to assuring and maintaining national sovereignty. Third was the most volatile, the Palestinian issue. Carter, unlike his predecessors, believed there should be a Palestinian homeland and that an effective solution required participation of the Palestinians, which would result in a de facto recognition of a people without a country.

The initial Carter effort was overshadowed by the surprise visit of Egyptian president Anwar Sadat to Jerusalem and his announcement that the Israelis and Egyptians would sit down voluntarily at the negotiating table. Yet Sadat and Begin quickly learned that their respective plans were very different and, for all intent and purposes, incompatible. Thus the appearance of good intentions by the two lifetime political rivals, now heads of state, provided a window of opportunity for Jimmy Carter as chief diplomat. By some accounts, the Carter effort was "schizophrenic policy,"[13] suggesting it was motivated by Sadat's Jerusalem sojourn and encouraged the United States to accept any reasonable effort to bring about a Egyptian-Israeli peace plan, even to the point of having President Carter serve as mediator, which at the time seemed very risky. As history bears out, however, this was perhaps the key to the success of the talks. The president of the United States, serving in his capacity as chief diplomat, was able to use all the powers and prestige of the office at his disposal to forge regional stability from the remnants of a generation of war.

Authority for the Camp David talks was generated in the form of support from Congress. Carter notified congressional leaders and ex-presidents Ford and Nixon of the impending talks. He recalls that everyone on the Hill was supportive of the concept, with the exception of Senator Howard Baker (R–Tenn.), who was "cautious," and Senator Jackson (D–Wash.), who was "very critical."[14] Outside of Congress, Carter enhanced his position by garnering support from other world leaders, asking for their support, or at least asking them to withhold criticism.

What makes authority problematic in the international domain is the legal, if not political, equality accorded to heads of state. Carter was not leading a meeting of those subservient to him or deferential to the office. Instead, he was acting as the liaison between two world leaders, and even though they represented sovereign powers that were not superpowers like the United States, they were respected global leaders in their own right. Anwar Sadat was cognizant of the "mantle of authority from the great pharaohs" that lay on the shoulders of the leader of Egypt. As such he felt destined to do something on a grand scale, to ensure his place in his nation's history. Thus Sadat brought the prestige and power of his own office, which not only enhanced the meaning of the negotiations, but helped Jimmy Carter's position as well.[15] Menachem Begin also saw himself as a man of destiny. His position was nearly biblical as he held the charge of "God's chosen people." Inasmuch as over two thousand years had passed in the Middle East without an agreement between a Jewish state and Egypt, Carter was in a high-risk position, but one that would play itself out, testing and in turn enhancing his prestige through the course of the negotiations.

As leader of the Western world, Carter was able to generate and sustain his authority in order to keep the sensitive and often tenuous negotiations moving forward. The stature brought to the talks by the participants and the course of world events must be recognized as a window of opportunity for Carter. The president's authority allowed him to take a senior position at times, a position unique in international negotiations among sovereigns, and one perhaps even more unusual given Carter's lack of foreign policy experience, which he alludes to in his memoirs.[16]

The Camp David Accords followed in the wake of a series of *crises* in the Middle East after the establishment of Israel in 1948. American presidents had dealt with Lebanon in 1958, the Syrian-Jordan War of 1970, the Yom Kippur War of 1973, and the aftermath of the oil crisis. These crises were different from many other foreign policy forays because of the lack of control by the United States over events in the Middle East. Thus, although foreign policy has historically been a device to enhance domestic support, the Middle East had not been the arena of choice among presidents. For Carter, the overtures leading to and the culmination of peace talks was not a high-profile media event. Rather it was narrow in focus, based on substantive issues and details, exactly the format he preferred. It allowed him to combine his own personal characteristics and the powers of the president to his advantage.

The format reflected to a large degree the foreign policy apparatus under the direction of National Security Advisor Zbigniew Brzezinski. It was attempting to develop consultative *decision making* between the National Security Council and the cabinet-level foreign policy actors, namely the State Department. The success of the reconfiguration engineered during the Carter years is debatable. But note that one of the cabinet secretaries was invited to chair the Policy Review Committee that did the early work for the president in assessing Arab-Israeli relations, work that would become important in preparing Carter for the summit. Consultative decision making provided Carter with a broader set of background characteristics to consider than had he relied exclusively on one cabinet department.

Although the decision to host the meeting was very risky, it was consistent with Carter's expansionist agenda.[17] The decision was hailed as a "bold stroke in spite of the chilly negotiating atmosphere and the relative absence of diplomatic preparation."[18] In addition, Carter's ability to work with both Sadat and Begin reflected the personal chemistry he was able to generate with the other two, which broke down some of the barriers of the more typical structured atmosphere of summit diplomacy.[19]

From another perspective, Carter might be seen as following the same path as all presidents since World War II, contending that Israel must exist and the Arabs "must" agree to peace.[20] Thus Carter's approach may not have been novel, but his implementation of the negotiations and his acting as the de facto secretary of state and primary representative of the United Nations set an unprecedented tone for the talks. Perhaps his relative newness to the arena of foreign policy and Middle East politics made him less linked intellectually to a predisposed position, or perhaps his ability to bring these rivals together was a function of the man himself.

The decision to host the talks appears to have been quickly implemented, but the record indicates that the Carter administration had been involved in shuttle diplomacy for over a year prior to the talks. Secretary of State Cyrus Vance was in the Middle East routinely in the summer of 1977 and at each stop discussed ideas for a summit meeting and a transitional regime.[21] One purpose for the trips by Secretary Vance was to set up a summit in Geneva, Switzerland, not Camp David. A second goal was to assess Egypt's receptivity to an Israeli draft treaty in order "to get the parties to engage in the negotiating process."[22] As a decision tool, this was a conscious effort to see what Sadat's position might be, an inquiry that proved most fortunate when it was discovered Sadat was willing and ready to move forward. Sadat was also important because he encouraged the Carter administration to act as the initial intermediary in much the same way as Kissinger had done during the first disengagement agreement earlier in the decade.[23] Sadat was ready to meet with Begin and had provided Vance with a draft treaty, which, he noted, "Egypt would be prepared to sign." The decision to move forward may be viewed as less of a U.S. initiative than a recognition by leaders in the Middle East that the status quo was threatened and no longer a workable alternative.[24]

Thus the stage was set for what most thought would be a three-day summit with slim chances of a resolution to the years of conflict.[25] But the summit was prolonged, lasting twelve days. The success of the meetings has in part been linked to the tight security and media blackout of the daily activities. The window of opportunity was beginning to close because the more radical elements in the Middle East were intent on increasing their pressure on the summit. In essence, this added a sense of crisis to the proceedings.[26] The Carter team also benefited from the inroads made by the previous secretary of state, Henry Kissinger, who had developed an incremental, step-by-step approach. Carter combined Kissinger's approach with his own optimism, believing all problems could be solved, an intuitive hunch no doubt a result of his training as an engineer.

Carter moved forward with hopes of a peace in the Middle East through a balanced comprehensive plan. He believed in human goodness and based his hopes on this belief, bringing everyone to the table with the assumption that peace was a common goal. Henry Kissinger had previously referred to an approach nearly identical to Carter's as "constructive confrontation."[27] The volatility of the Middle East was clearly evidenced by the fall of the shah in Iran. Given the other Middle East hot spots in Turkey and Afghanistan, there was little choice but to focus on accords between Egypt and Israel. The region on the whole was pushed aside in hopes of getting two key states to settle their differences. The effort ideally would spill over to the other problem areas of the region.

In retrospect, the Carter administration may have taken a position in 1976–1977 that hampered the accords. By ensuring military aid to Israel over the objections of the Arab world, and in criticizing Israeli settlements in the West Bank at the same time, it had no diplomatic capital on which to move the prospects of the talks forward. Only the genuine interest in peace could have led to the conditions at Camp David, especially when proposed talks among all Middle East states in Geneva failed to materialize, which again placed the burden on Egypt and Israel with the United States as mediator. The role thrust on Carter was even more pronounced when Anwar Sadat, in a speech to the Egyptian assembly, said he would go anywhere to secure peace, making talks at Geneva irrelevant and keeping the window of opportunity open for Carter, who initially favored Switzerland as the site for the multilateral talks, before consenting to the United States.[28]

Carter knew no more about the Middle East than any former governor might be expected to know. His *expertise* came from his staff, most notably Brzezinski, although the national security advisor was not a

Middle East scholar. Carter's indoctrination depended on Brzezinski, who served as a tutor to the president, and his love of details made him a good student.[29] Secretary of State Vance, who gained and and then lost power to Brzezinski, served to balance Carter's penchant for detail by placing events within the larger context of the Middle East and global politics.[30]

Carter was able to immerse himself in the intricacies of the negotiations without losing focus. This character trait, that some contend led to his downfall, allowed him to keep the talks at Camp David alive.[31] He had enhanced his knowledge during a vacation in late August in the Grand Tetons and demonstrated he was a quick and able student. He did not rely exclusively on his learning skills, however, but brought in U.S. ambassadors from Cairo and Jerusalem to brief him on those participating in the talks and on the political atmosphere in the Middle East.[32] During the negotiations, Carter's ability to grasp numerous details and take copious notes, which were transcribed on the spot, allowed him to double-check what had been said by Sadat and Begin and keep them focused as well.[33]

The meetings (September 5–17, 1978) required quick thinking and action on Carter's part. Phrasing and rephrasing of memorandum and constant repositioning by both Egypt and Israel when agreement seemed to have been achieved challenged the president throughout the negotiations. Carter worked one on one and had to cope with at least seven major potential breakdowns, including Sadat ordering a helicopter and saying farewell after Israeli negotiators had informed him they would not sign any agreement.[34] Carter took control and used his expertise as a negotiator and believer in doing what was right to get Egypt and Israel to negotiate and "press for peace." As Brzezinski recalled, "the outcome was a triumph of Carter's determined mastery of enormous detail and of his perseverance in sometimes angry and always complex negotiations. He showed himself to be a skillful debater, a master psychologist, and a very effective mediator. Without him, there would have been no agreement."[35] The Camp David negotiations set the framework for peace negotiations that continued through 1979 but were ignored by the Reagan administration two years later.[36] Yet, as King Hassan of Morocco noted, Camp David was irreversible.

In his memoirs, Carter notes a "curious fatalism" and the real potential for failure prior to the start of the talks.[37] He recalls wishing for a little luck as the talks began, and provides no evidence even in his own writings that he was confident or an experienced chief diplomat. This factor aside, Carter did have a competent foreign policy advisory staff and enjoyed the support of the general public, who lent broad approval to foreign policy activities of the president.

Carter's decision to limit the role of the press may be seen as a key strategic move critical to the success of the talks. Because limiting the access the press would have to the summit contradicted the advice given him by his own staff,[38] it was somewhat surprising that Carter insisted on it. Allowing the world's press to speculate on the context and meaning of the negotiation's components might have detracted seriously from the meetings and led to an early and most likely unsuccessful conclusion. Carter's decision to limit the press allowed the three world leaders to work through the process of negotiation without media fanfare. Although this decision may have hurt Carter's public image, it enhanced his powers within the controlled environment of Camp David. This environment established a comfortable setting within which progress might be achieved without having to respond to the media at each juncture.[39]

Camp David, as one scholar noted, "did miracles for the Carter presidency." Prior to the summit Carter had suffered in the polls, but Camp David made him "a hero and statesman."[40] The peace accords did result in an eleven-point jump in Carter's approval ratings. A short-lived jump in approval, given the historical pattern of increased support for the president, can be expected as a result of foreign policy actions. It can be argued, however, that overall, Carter had less support from various *public inputs* than he might have been able to generate had the Camp David talks been orchestrated into a media event. The decision to have a near media blackout, combined with a printing strike in New York City, kept public interest low.

A foreign policy event occurring on American soil is less dramatic than a summit abroad. For the American public, the Maryland countryside does not carry the same romance as Moscow, Cairo, or Hong Kong. As Darcy and Richman point out, "Presidential visits abroad, while perhaps diplomatically dysfunctional, have long been thought to enhance domestic support for the President."[41] High public approval ratings may enhance the president's relative power, but they do not represent his competence as chief diplomat.[42] Thus Carter, less concerned about the polls that would become a harbinger of his single term more than a year later, did not see the summit as a way to increase his approval with the electorate.

Carter was aware that public opinion supporting the Israeli position was effectively limiting him in the foreign policy arena.[43] Most notably this was lodged among American Jewish organizations that backed the Begin government and had close ties with members of the U.S. Congress. This aspect of public opinion may have constrained his powers vis-à-vis Congress and in his own mind. Thus the public input factor prior to the summit did not add significantly to the powers of the president.

Camp David illustrates how the role of the president as chief diplomat can be used as arbitrator and negotiator over sensitive global issues. It demonstrates how a president is able to use his position as chief diplomat to move two hostile nations beyond their rigid positions toward a workable outcome even if it takes twenty-three drafts of a treaty.[44] Carter also proved adept at both defending each leader as well as criticizing them when necessary.

The Camp David Accords were negotiated in an atmosphere of a pending Middle East Crisis, the likelihood that new Israeli-Arab hostilities would erupt if the talks did not succeed.[45] Later scholars suggested the Camp David talks were a noncrisis because no immediate national security threat actually existed for the United States.[46] Even though it may not have fit the traditional notion of a national security crisis, in light of the time, the Middle East was a political and diplomatic hot spot vital to U.S. strategic interests.

Indeed, the Middle East may be characterized as a region of recurring crises, where American foreign policy success had been minimal. Potential failure thus was always possible during the talks, a potential made more politically interesting by the hands-on effort of the president of the United States as a broker in Middle East politics.[47] One possible reason for failure, alluded to in the documentation and memoirs pertaining to the talks, involved exhaustion and fatigue.[48] Many times Carter believed the talks would fail. He even went as far as to make plans to terminate the summit in its eleventh day, which he recalls as "a terrible moment" reflecting crisis emotions.[49]

The success of Camp David is difficult to define, but the "Jimmy Carter Conference," as Sadat termed it, was largely successful only because Carter had worked so hard to reach an agreement. One wonders if any other leader in the world could have brought two such adversaries together and held them together during sensitive negotiations. It was a very personal commitment for President Carter, and no other president made a comparable personal effort, as Brzezinski points out.[50] Jimmy Carter's search for compromise, an understanding of the psychological and historical barriers to any reduction of hostilities in the Middle East, and his personal style placed him in the decisive role. In combination with the powers of the chief diplomat, Carter, who spent roughly 75 percent of his time on domestic issues, left his mark in the area of foreign policy.[51] As time goes by, one scholar notes, the further back we look at Carter's policy, "the better it may look in the future."[52]

In summation, what were the ingredients for Carter's success in negotiating the Camp David Accords? President Carter had the constitutional authority to attempt those negotiations and he, alone, was perhaps the crucial decision-maker who made possible the final outcome. Moreover, Congress deferred to presidential leadership from the outset. Carter gave specific directives to his secretary of state when Cyrus Vance acted as an emissary for the White House and, although Carter was not an expert in the politics of the Middle East, he could draw on the resources of specialists in his administration. Although Carter was alert to constraints from segments of the population who are deeply concerned about the security of Israel, public opinion as such was not an obstacle to his initiatives. Even though no imminent crisis was apparent in the region, the Congress, opinion leaders, the Washington establishment, and many Americans were all too aware that relations between Israel and the Arab states could deteriorate easily into open warfare. The Middle East, with its oil reserves, was then and remains today a political tinderbox for U.S. diplomacy.

NOTES

1. This Insight differs from the others because we have Carter's memoirs from the meetings at Camp David. As a result, there are two perspectives, one based on the historical record and the other on the diary and interpretations of the chief diplomat during the course of the negotiations.

2 Amos A. Jordan and William J. Taylor, Jr., *American National Security: Policy and Process* (Baltimore: Johns Hopkins University Press, 1981).

3. Tareq Y. Ismael, *The Middle East in World Politics* (Syracuse, NY: Syracuse University Press, 1974), pp. 124–127.

4. Elihu Bergman, "A Global Perspective on United States Energy Policymaking," *Middle East Review* 13 (Winter 1980/1981), p. 10.

5. Robert A. Strong, "Recapturing Leadership: The Carter Administration and the Crisis of Confidence," *Presidential Studies Quarterly* 16 (1986), p. 641.

6. Bernard Reich and Elizabeth L. Conroy, "Peace Plans and Proposals for the Arab-Israeli Conflict: 1947–1977," *Middle East Review* 10 (Winter 1977/1978), p. 7.

7. See, for example, Bernard Reich, *Quest for Peace: United States-Israel Relations and the Arab-Israeli Conflict* (New Brunswick, NJ: Transaction Books, 1977).

8. Dwight David Eisenhower, *Waging Peace: The White House Years, 1956–1961* (Garden City, NY: Doubleday, 1965).

9. Reich and Conroy, "Peace Plans and Proposals for the Arab-Israeli Conflict," p. 10.

10. Ibid.

11. For a fuller elaboration see U.S. Department of State, *Department of State Bulletin,* July 10, 1967; and Reich, *Quest for Peace.*

12. Cited in Reich and Conroy, "Peace Plans and Proposals for the Arab-Israeli Conflict," p. 14.

13. Steven L. Spiegel, "The Philosophy behind Recent American Policy in the Middle East," *Middle East Review* 13 (Winter 1980/1981), p. 6.

14. Jimmy Carter, *Keeping Faith: Memoirs of a President* (New York: Bantam Books, 1983), pp. 316–317.

15. Ibid., p. 328.

16. Ibid., pp. 319–404.

17. Louis W. Koenig, *The Chief Executive* (New York: Harcourt, Brace and Jovanovich, 1981), p. 336; and Adam Clymer, "Carter's Vision of America," *New York Times Magazine* (July 27, 1980), pp. 16–18.

18. Hedrick Smith, "A New Gamble on Mideast," *New York Times,* (Aug. 9, 1978), p. A1.

19. Terrence Smith, "Carter to Meet Begin and Sadat in the U.S. Sept. 5," *New York Times* (Aug. 9, 1978), pp. A1, A4.

20. Stephen Oren, "The Carter Administration and the Middle East," *Middle East Review* 10 (Fall 1977), p. 14.

21. Richard C. Thornton, *The Carter Years* (New York: Paragon House, 1991), p. 154.

22. Zbigniew Brzezinski, *Power and Principle* (New York: Farrar, Straus, Giroux, 1983), p. 121.

23. William B. Quandt, *Camp David: Peacemaking and Politics* (Washington, DC: The Brookings Institution, 1986), pp. 292–295.

24. Carter, *Keeping Faith,* p. 296; Quandt, *Camp David,* pp. 88–90.

25. Dave Binder, August 16, 1978, *New York Times News Service,* pp. 31–32. (The *New York Times* was not published from August 10, 1978, until October of the same year because of a pressman strike in New York City. The Times News Service still prepared and released stories from which this and other documents under the News Service title are culled.)

26. Oren, "The Carter Administration and the Middle East," p. 18.

27. Abraham Ben-Zvi, "Full Circle on the Road to Peace? American Preconceptions of Peace in the Middle East: 1973–1978," *Middle East Review* 11 (Winter 1978/1979), p. 54.

28. Thornton, *The Carter Years,* p. 162. Studying the year leading up to the talks is an excellent way to learn about the Middle East and diplomacy. Thornton, Brzezinski, and Carter all have chapters in their books on the period.

29. Oren, "The Carter Administration and the Middle East," p. 14.

30. Thornton, *The Carter Years,* p. 196.

31. James David Barber, *The Presidential Character* (Englewood Cliffs, NJ: Prentice-Hall, 1977), pp. 524–536.

32. Carter, *Keeping Faith,* pp. 320–321.

33. Ibid., 327.

34. Ibid., p. 392–393.

35. Brzezinski, *Power and Principle,* p. 273.

36. John Marks, "Bill Clinton's Opportunity in the Middle East," *The Christian Science Monitor* (Nov. 20, 1992), p. 18.

37. Ibid., pp. 322–324.

38. Carter, *Keeping Faith,* p. 317.

39. Ibid., p. 318.

40. Betty Glad, *Jimmy Carter: In Search of the Great White House* (New York: Norton, 1980), p. 433.

41. Robert E. Darcy and Alvin Richman, "Presidential Travel and Public Opinion," *Presidential Studies Quarterly* 18 (1988), p. 85.

42. Elmer Pilschke, "Rating Presidents and Diplomats in Chief," *Presidential Studies Quarterly* 15 (1985), p. 727.

43. Thornton, *The Carter Years,* p. 158.

44. Ibid., p. 344.

45. Terrence Smith, "Carter to Meet Begin and Sadat in the U.S. Sept. 5," p. A5.

46. Ryan J. Barilleaux, "Evaluating Presidential Performance in Foreign Affairs," in George C. Edwards, III, Steven A. Shull, and Norman C. Thomas, eds., *The Presidency and Public Policy Making* (Pittsburgh: University of Pittsburgh Press, 1985), p. 119.

47. Thornton, *The Carter Years,* p. 208.

48. Carter, *Keeping Faith,* p. 370.

49. Ibid., pp. 383–390.

50. Brzezinski, *Power and Principle,* p. 288.

51. Hamilton Jordan, *Crisis: The Last Year of the Carter Presidency* (New York: G.P. Putnam's Sons, 1983), pp. 46–47.

52. M. Glenn Abernathy, Dils M. Hill, and Phil Williams, *The Carter Years* (New York: St. Martin's Press, 1984), p. 76.

13

Commander in Chief: Can the Constitutional Dictator Be Checked?

The commander-in-chief role is the most visible of the president's roles, the one in which presidents exhibit maximum strength. It commands the most respect from the other institutions of government, receives the greatest attention from the media, and is of great concern to students of civil liberties because it poses the biggest potential threat to democratic government. This role has been defined and expanded by presidents beginning with George Washington, who accompanied state militiamen into western Pennsylvania to restore order during the Whiskey Rebellion of 1793 (see Table 13-1). The sage comment by political scientist Sidney Hyman many years ago is equally relevant today, namely that a president can commit the nation to war because "the decisions of any President have held this same potential since 1790: the cause lies in the functions the Constitution allocates to the presidency."[1]

AUTHORITY

It was *not* the Framers' intent that the commander-in-chief role be as powerful as it has become today. The commander in chief was to be little more than a military title, similar to that given to General George Washington in 1783 by the Continental Congress. Members of the Constitutional Convention of 1787 wrote Article II, Section 2, of the Constitution in direct and clear language: the president was to be "Commander in chief of the army and navy of the United States, and of the militia of the several states, when called into the actual service of the United States." Yet the meaning was still ambiguous because it was not spelled out what a commander in chief could do in times of war and peace.

This role was transformed from a rather innocuous power to one that Supreme Court Justice Robert Jackson once termed "the most dangerous one to free government in the whole catalogue of powers."[2] A commander in chief today can decide if and when troops are deployed in a crisis

Table 13–1. Significant Historical Developments in the Commander in Chief
Role

President	Historical Event or Decision
Washington	• Whiskey Rebellion of 1793: Washington led militiamen into western Pennsylvania
Jefferson	• Barbary Pirates War of 1801–1805 was first use of military forces (navy) abroad
Madison	• War of 1812 (first declared war)
Polk	• Mexican War of 1846–1847 (second declared war); • Polk chose generals and made military strategy
Lincoln	• Emergency "war" powers during Civil War fused from "commander-in-chief" and "take care" clauses
McKinley	• Spanish-American War of 1898 (third declared war)
Wilson	• World War I (fourth declared war)
Roosevelt	• World War II (fifth declared war)
Truman	• Authorized dropping of two atomic bombs on Japan • North Atlantic Treaty Organization (NATO) • Korean War of 1950–1953 (undeclared war based partly on UN authorization); • Affirmed principle of "civilian control" by firing Korean War general Douglas MacArthur
Kennedy	• Cuban missile crisis; Cuban Bay of Pigs invasion
Johnson	• Vietnam War of 1965–1973 (undeclared)
Nixon	• Bombed "neutral" Cambodia in 1970 during Vietnam War
Bush	• Persian Gulf War of 1990 (undeclared)
Clinton	• Sent U.S. troops as UN peacekeeping force into Bosnia without formal approval by Congress • Somalia, protecting humanitarian relief, 1993 • Haiti military effort to reinstate democratic government

and determine troop strength, call up reservists and the National Guard, formulate air, sea, and ground strategies for war, commit U.S. troops to battle for whatever duration, and specify when the war will end—all without a declaration of war. As Justice Jackson added, the authority of the commander in chief essentially is the power to "do anything, anywhere, that can be done with an army or navy."[3]

The meaning of war has changed. Few have questioned the power of a president to respond to insurrection or invasion, but are there limits in terms of what a president can do without a congressional declaration of war? The traditional understanding is that the Framers granted Congress the authority to "declare" war instead of the president so the legislature would control both international and domestic concerns of war. "Making war," however, was considered an executive power that would allow the president to repel an invasion without a formal declaration of war.[4] This power was never meant to be an "inherent" or "prerogative" power for a president to *initiate* offensive military engagements,[5] contrary to what is often heard from twentieth-century presidents (see Appendix 1 for a listing of undeclared wars).

Congressional Response

Since the beginning Congress has been both sympathetic to and suspicious of a strong commander in chief. As early as 1791 Congress granted George Washington authority to enlist additional troops to engage Indian tribes; a year later Congress gave Washington the authority to organize the militia. By 1795 Congress had given Washington the power, under the Militia Act, to call up the militia if the country was invaded or whenever it appeared it was in danger of being invaded.

A recent attempt by Congress to restrain the commander in chief occurred in 1993 when President Bill Clinton wanted to deploy troops to Haiti. Senate Minority Leader Robert Dole (R–Kans.) strongly objected and attempted to require an authorization from Congress before Clinton could commit troops. In the Dole measure there were exceptions to congressional restrictions. If, for example, the safety of U.S. troops was in question, U.S. citizens were being evacuated, or it was necessary to maintain national security, a president's acts would not be questioned. Another Republican effort to limit the president was initiated by Senator Don Nickles (R–Okla.), who proposed an amendment to the troop deployment act that would have required a president to first obtain congressional approval for any commitment of U.S. troops for any peacekeeping operation under the authority of the United Nations.[6] Clinton viewed both measures as interfering with his constitutionally sanctioned role as commander in chief.

Both were eventually defeated and a nonbinding substitute was introduced in the Senate requesting the president to first consult with Congress before U.S. troops are put under any foreign command.[7] Under this measure, passed by a vote of 96 to 2, consultation would take place within a 48-hour period after troops are deployed. A second Senate nonbinding resolution was passed relating to both Bosnia and Haiti by a 99 to 1 vote to urge the president again to consult with Congress before troops are deployed to those countries.[8] In this series of votes, the message was clear: the Senate did not wish to be ignored in the decision to deploy troops, but Congress was unable to limit effectively the commander in chief powers of President Clinton.

Post–Cold War Presidency

What the Congress neglected to do in trying to restrict a president in this role, conditions of the post–Cold War era may accomplish instead. Presidency scholar Richard Rose argues that changing world conditions— the end of the Cold War between the United States and the Soviet Union and the rise of Japan and Germany as economic competitors to the United

States—have helped to create a new "postmodern president" who finds that he has insufficient resources to meet international challenges and, therefore, is forced into an interdependent relationship with other nations.[9] Bill Clinton fits this description quite well. In Bosnia, for example, Clinton in 1994 found it necessary to share his control over the U.S. military with NATO and the United Nations, which put him in a position of having to comply with decisions made by British lieutenant general Sir Michael Rose, the UN commander. When on April 10, 1994, NATO called for U.S. war planes to bomb Serbian positions in Bosnia to protect UN ground forces, President Clinton defended his willingness to comply in this way: "This [bombing] is a clear expression of the will of NATO and the will of the United Nations. . . . We have said we would act if we were requested to do so. We have now done so and we will do so again if we are requested."[10]

Not all who heard Clinton's argument were sympathetic. A *New York Times* columnist was critical of Clinton: "I think the Clinton team made a mistake getting the U.S. into a situation where foreign generals and foreign governments can decide when American bombers take off. There is the American President telling us it was not really his decision. Are we hearing right?"[11] Senator Judd Gregg (R–N.H.), also saw the potential for weakened presidential control in Bosnia under this plan of shared responsibility. He stated that "[w]hen American lives are put at risk, it should be because an American commander has received a directive from an American President or an authoritarian figure below the Presidency in the American chain of command. We should never abrogate that authority to another institution, as has already occurred in the Bosnian situation."[12]

On May 5, 1994, Bill Clinton announced a new policy, to succeed his August 1993 directive (PDD 13), which indicated that the primary goal of the United Nations should be the maintenance of peace and that the United States would play a role by submitting the U.S. military to UN authority.[13] The 1994 order—Presidential Decision Directive 25 (PDD 25)—tried to blunt the criticism Clinton had received from his earlier policy.[14] The new 1994 order stated that, before the United States again becomes involved in a peacekeeping operation, the following conditions must be met:

> The crisis must represent a threat to international peace and security (specifically, threatened access to starving civilians), gross abuses of human rights, or a violent overthrow of a democratically elected government. Any intervention must involve clear objectives, and, most important, consent of the parties and a realistic exit strategy.[15]

Checking the President

Any time Congress tries to restrict a president, as in Clinton's case, there is a political risk for the lawmakers. No representative wants to face constituents if the public perceives the legislative branch has attempted to cripple the president's ability to protect American forces under combat conditions. From 1789 to 1950, in fact, every president sought congressional authorization for war-making before commiting the nation to combat. Harry Truman was the first president in 161 years to fail to do this.[16]

After World War II President Truman stationed troops in Europe for an indefinite period because he anticipated that armed conflict with the Russians might begin. Those troops were committed without any consultation or authorization from the Congress, and Truman's justification was the North Atlantic Treaty Organization (NATO) obligations insisting that the United States interpret any attack on any country in Europe as a direct attack on the United States.[17] Here Truman became the forerunner of modern presidents who would interpret Article II powers more flexibly. Moreover, in sending thousands of troops into the Korean War, Truman claimed an "inherent" right of the presidency to commit troops to serve foreign policy objectives, going beyond the traditional presidential military justification of protecting the country or U.S. citizens abroad. Truman also established an important precedent by referring to the war as a UN "police action," which he was waging under the legal auspices of resolutions adopted by the Security Council. This basis for presidential warmaking was repeated by President Bush when he committed troops to the Persian Gulf War.

Treaties give a president another source of legal authority besides the Constitution to rationalize his military actions. Lyndon Johnson, for example, in addition to his commander-in-chief authority, relied on the Southeast Asia Treaty Organization (SEATO) mutual security provisions to justify his involvement in South Vietnam.[18]

International organizations like the United Nations can legitimate presidential leadership in war. In 1991 President Bush involved the United States in the Persian Gulf War based on UN Security Council sanctions granting the Allied forces "all necessary means" to force Iraq out of Kuwait. Throughout the war those sanctions remained Bush's primary justification for action, yet even with this authorization, he felt it was necessary to win explicit congressional approval.

Undeclared War-making

Since 1789 the United States has been involved in approximately 253 conflicts or potential conflicts that required troops to be sent abroad to protect lives, property, or other U.S. interests. Of these, *five* have been declared wars—War of 1918, Mexican War, Spanish-American War, World War I, World War II—and most presidents regardless of political party have been involved in at least one undeclared military action (Table 13-2).

Early commanders in chief used their power to confront pirates, to dispatch troops to protect property and civil rights, and to pursue bandits across U.S. borders. There were only two declarations of war during the

Table 13–2. Number of Undeclared Hostilities Where U.S. Troops Have Been Committed Abroad to Conflict or Potential Conflict, by President, 1789–1994

President	Number	President	Number	President	Number
Washington	0	Buchanan	13	Harding	3
J. Adams	1	Lincoln	3	Coolidge	8
Jefferson	3	A. Johnson	8	Hoover	1
Madison	10	Grant	9	F. Roosevelt	9
Monroe	7	Hayes	0	Truman	10
J.Q. Adams	3	Garfield	0	Eisenhower	10
Jackson	7	Arthur	2	Kennedy	6
Van Buren	3	Cleveland	4	L. Johnson	6
W. Harrison	0	B. Harrison	6	Nixon	3
J. Tyler	7	Cleveland	8	Ford	7
Polk	1	McKinley	7	Carter	2
Taylor	2	T. Roosevelt	16	Reagan	17
Fillmore	3	Taft	9	Bush	5
Pierce	13	Wilson	21	Clinton	6

Source: "Instances of the Use of United States Armed Forces Abroad,1798–1989," *Congressional Record—Senate* 137(1), 102nd Congress, 1st Session (Jan. 3, 1991), pp. S14–S19; "War without Declaration," *Congressional Record—Senate* 119, part 20, 93rd Congress, 1st Session (July 20, 1973), pp. 25066–25077; and the Reagan conflicts came from Amicus Brief of Cong. Howard Berman for *Lowry v. Reagan*, U.S. District Court (DC), civil action no. 87–2196, in "The War Power after 200 Years: Congress and the President at a Constitutional Impasse," Hearings before the Special Subcommittee on War Powers of the Committee on Foreign Relations, U. S. Senate, 100th Congress, 1st Session (July 13,14; August 5; September 7, 15, 16, 20, 23, and 29, 1988), pp. 1004–1005; "Senators Approve Troop Compromise," *Washington Post* (Oct. 21, 1993), p. A1; "Chronology of the Year's Events," *World Almanac and Book of Facts 1994*. Mahwah, NJ: Funk and Wagnalls, 1993, pp. 44–64 and 73–76; "Chronology of the Year's Events," *World Almanac and Book of Facts 1996*. Mahwah, NJ: Funk and Wagnalls, 1995, 42–71.

nineteenth century, the War of 1812 when President Madison was pressured into war against Great Britain by the "War Hawk" faction in Congress, and the Mexican War of 1846–1848 when President Polk sent troops into a disputed border area with Mexico in order to gain territory for the United States through a military provocation. Sixty-seven military engagements occurring before the Civil War had no declaration of war,[19] but thirty-three of them did have a congressional statute or a treaty as a legal source of authority. In the remainder, presidents relied exclusively on their authority as commander in chief.

Lincoln's Prerogative Power

It was Abraham Lincoln who brought the commander-in-chief role to its full potential. So broadly did he interpret Article II of the Constitution, in responding to the Civil War, that many of Lincoln's actions could reasonably be characterized as evidence of a "constitutional dictatorship."[20] During those eleven weeks at the start of the Civil War (when Congress was not in session), Lincoln called into service 75,000 troops, blockaded southern ports, suspended the writ of habeas corpus, recruited 22,714 additional army officers, increased the navy by 18,000 persons, and requested 42,034 military volunteers over a three-year period. He also demanded that a draft be instituted to recruit 300,000 militiamen and issued the famous Emancipation Proclamation freeing slaves in the South. Other actions of questionable legality included his closing the postal service to prevent treasonable correspondence, seizing telegraph lines, enforcing strict passport clearance for citizens, establishing military commissions, placing the entire state of Kentucky under martial law, and spending unappropriated funds from the U.S. Treasury to pay Union spies. In one of his last actions President Lincoln issued a proclamation of amnesty and reconstruction for all people in the South.

All this was done by executive proclamation, without legislative authorization, but when Congress later examined Lincoln's war activities, most were supported and a few were even ignored. Because the survival of the Union was at stake, members of Congress felt compelled to support Lincoln whether or not his actions were legal. The Supreme Court, in contrast, had few opportunities to test the legality of inherent commander-in-chief authority, but when it did, it generally supported broad executive power while at the same time limiting it in specific instances. In a pre-Civil War ruling, the Supreme Court in 1849 declared it would be improper for it to question a president's judgment of whether a military emergency existed.[21] One year later the Court, in *Fleming v. Page* (1850), defined the military power of the commander in chief as all but complete in times of war.

One of Lincoln's actions that *was* challenged in the Supreme Court was his suspension of the writ of habeas corpus. Justice Taney in *Ex Parte Merryman* (1861) argued that the president had no right or authority to suspend the writ against a civilian because there was no justifiable need to do so. In *The Prize Cases* (1862), however, the Supreme Court again supported a broad interpretation of the commander in chief powers indicating that, although a president could not begin a war or officially declare it, he was "bound to resist force by force." But the Supreme Court was highly critical of Lincoln's suspension of civilian courts in Indiana because there seemed to be no need for it. As Justice Davis stated in *Ex Parte Milligan* (1866),

> The Constitution of the United States is a law for rulers and people, equally in war and in peace. No doctrine, involving more pernicious consequences, was ever invented by the wit of man than that any of its provisions can be suspended during any of the great exigencies of government.

Such a doctrine leads directly to anarchy or despotism. As the Civil War came to an end, the Court had restricted the president after the fact from suspending portions of the Constitution by establishing military tribunals without cause.

The World Wars

During World War I President Woodrow Wilson relied on both his constitutional authority as commander in chief as well as a declaration of war from Congress. Wilson did not wait for the enactment of legislation, however, before taking action. For example, when he asked Congress for authority to arm merchant vessels with defensive weapons in the Atlantic, he was refused but went ahead anyway and issued weapons to the merchant marine.

Prior to the congressional declaration of World War II, President Roosevelt similarly took actions that inched the nation toward a military confrontation with the Axis powers. One example was the Neutrality Act of 1935, which imposed an embargo on shipping "arms, ammunition, or implements of war" to the belligerent nations (Britain and Germany) but also allowed the president to define what "implements of war" meant and stipulate when the embargo was to go into effect. This act also prevented American ships from transporting arms and machinery to those involved.[22] Despite those restrictions, FDR took several actions to assist the Allies including the supplying of aircraft to the French in 1938 when FDR increased U.S. aircraft production from 2,600 to 15,000 by assembling 5,000 of them in Canadian factories where the Neutrality Act would have no effect.[23]

In the famous "Fifty Destroyer Deal" of September 1940 Roosevelt sent Great Britain 50 formerly decommissioned ships that had been built during the First World War in exchange for 99-year leases on six naval bases in the Western Hemisphere.[24] In a final action FDR then formulated his Lend-Lease Program to circumvent the Neutrality Act. He proposed "lending" to Britain the needed arms and ships it needed as long as Britain would return those arms and ships at the end of the war. Roosevelt told Congress that he did not have any desire to repeal the Neutrality Acts and that Lend-Lease was not in violation of them. Aid short of war was not considered by FDR to violate the neutral position of the United States.

FDR's interpretation of his Article II powers was sometimes questionable. For example, he deployed troops to Greenland and Iceland in 1941 even though the 1940 Reserve Act and the Selective Service Act of 1940 prohibited it. Yet few of Roosevelt's prewar actions were ever challenged in court.

Vietnam

On August 2, 1964, the *Maddox*, a U.S. destroyer, was attacked by three Vietnamese PT boats in international waters. While sailing in the Gulf of Tonkin, off the coast of North Vietnam, the North Vietnamese boats were repelled. In reply the State Department sent a warning to the North Vietnamese government that any repeat of such attacks would result in serious consequences. Two days later North Vietnamese boats again shelled two U.S. destroyers—the *Maddox* and the *Turner Joy*—in the Gulf before retreating and being damaged themselves. That night President Lyndon Johnson in an address to the American people declared that the United States had responded with air raids against the gunboats and "certain supporting facilities of North Vietnam which have been used in these hostile operations."[25] Johnson also met on August 4 with congressional leaders and asked them to pass a resolution that would express a unified U.S. effort to defend freedom. The next day he sent a special message asking Congress to pass a resolution that would make clear the United States supported this action and would also give assistance to the other SEATO nations.

By August 7, H.J. Resolution 1145 was adopted by the House (414–0) and by the Senate (88–2), later to be signed by the president. In passing this legislation Congress had augmented Johnson's commander-in-chief authority by approving the Gulf of Tonkin Resolution.

President Nixon further extended the Vietnam War by bombing neutral Cambodia, without congressional authorization or consultation. As commander in chief Nixon argued that he had no choice but to defend U.S. troops through such an invasion. In reflecting on the Johnson and Nixon era of war-making, historian Arthur Schlesinger, Jr., stated,

> Both Johnson and Nixon had indulged in presidential war-making beyond the boldest dreams of their predecessors . . . in claiming that inherent and exclusive presidential authority, unaccompanied by emergencies threatening the life of the nation, unaccompanied by the authorization of Congress or the blessing of an international organization, permitted a President to order troops into battle at his unilateral pleasure.[26]

War Powers Resolution

After overriding Nixon's veto, Congress enacted into law the War Powers Resolution (PL 93–148) on November 7, 1973.[27] The resolution attempted to counteract presidential domination of Congress by requiring that Congress have an input in all decisions that involve U.S. troops in undeclared military conflicts.

Originally the legislation restricted the president from sending troops abroad in all but four instances: (1) if the United States was attacked; (2) if U.S. troops were attacked elsewhere; (3) if there was a need to protect U.S. citizens or U.S. property; or (4) to fulfill treaties.[28] This enactment also would have troops assigned to battle areas based on the "collective judgment" of the president and Congress and specified the president could exercise his commander-in-chief authority only where pursuant to a statute, if Congress had declared war, or where U.S. troops or the United States was under attack. Although the president retains leadership in foreign affairs, the resolution mandates that military involvement cannot go beyond sixty days (ninety days if troops are being withdrawn) without congressional consultation and approval or statutory authorization that extends the timetable. Virtually every president has resisted the resolution and questioned its constitutionality.

Perhaps the most controversial part of the resolution is Section 5b, concerning the sixty-day limit on troops staying in a hostile zone without congressional sanction. President Reagan, for example, delivered fourteen reports to Congress between 1982 and 1986, but all were worded in ways to avoid starting the sixty-day limitation on troop deployment.[29] Only once since the passage of the War Powers Resolution has a president submitted the type of a report that would begin the sixty-day "clock"; it was Gerald Ford who reported on the *Mayaquez* incident, although it was submitted only after the *Mayaquez* was safely again in U.S. possession.[30]

Political scientist Michael Mezey argues there are more incentives for presidents to avoid the resolution altogether by denying that hostilities even exist.[31] Ford, Carter, Reagan, and Bush all questioned the constitutionality of the War Powers Resolution, and Clinton was quite ambivalent when he reported to congressional leaders on October 20, 1993, regarding a U.S. peacekeeping force going to Haiti.[32]

Although many presidents have questioned the resolution, a number have at least partially complied with its requirements. In August 1982, for example, Ronald Reagan technically complied with the War Powers Resolution when he decided to keep twelve hundred marines in Beirut, Lebanon, as part of the multinational peacekeeping force. Reagan did so without consulting Congress, although he informed the Congress of his intentions "in accordance with [his] desire that the Congress be fully informed" and "consistent with"—not "pursuant to"—the War Powers Resolution. As troop casualties began mounting, a joint resolution was passed by Congress in 1983 and signed by the president. It recognized that U.S. troops were, in fact, involved in hostilities and, in order for troops to continue to stay, congressional authorization would be needed. By signing the joint resolution President Reagan recognized the War Powers Resolution but not before Congress also agreed—in advance—to authorize the troops to stay an additional eighteen months. After 241 marines were killed in a terrorist bomb attack, however, Reagan ordered an immediate troop withdrawal.

DECISION MAKING

Because the commander in chief has significant authority, decision making tends to be highly centralized and involve only the president and his key advisors. Presidents are likely to call on the National Security Council (NSC), the Joint Chiefs of Staff, selected cabinet members, White House staffers, or outside consultants. Congress does not participate in formulating military policy during crises although it serves to legitimize presidential actions afterward.

Joint Chiefs of Staff (JCS)

During wartime a primary advisory group is the Joint Chiefs of Staff, created in 1942 during World War II and institutionalized by the National Security Act of 1947. Included among the Joint Chiefs of Staff is the chief of staff of the army, the chief of naval operations, the chief of staff of the air force, and the commandant of the marine corps. A military chairman appointed by the president presides after confirmation by the Senate. The JCS is responsible for military planning and operations and advises the president on personnel, material requirements, and military strategy.

A 1986 law designated the chair of the Joint Chiefs to be the president's primary military advisor, giving him power independent of the other chiefs and its 1,600-member staff.[33] One who profited from this change in JCS structure was General Colin Powell, appointed by President Bush in 1989. As the youngest chairman and the first African American to occupy the position, Powell was highly visible and so politically astute that pundits speculated on whether (after his retirement from the JCS) he would seek the GOP presidential nomination for 1996.

National Security Council (NSC)

Since its establishment in 1947, the National Security Council has formulated much of the security planning that previously had been done by presidents and their personal staff. In 1949 the NSC was strengthened by mandating that the secretary of defense become the primary spokesperson for the Pentagon. During the 1991 Persian Gulf War, Defense Secretary Dick Cheney was the most assertive hawk favoring the war effort. The president, secretaries of state and defense, the chairman of the National Security Resources Board, and the vice president are the regular statutory members of the NSC, although presidents may add other officials as needed.

Other Advisors

The key members of the cabinet are usually the "inner four"—secretaries of state, defense, treasury, and attorney general. They are more likely to be advisors in times of crisis, whereas the cabinet as a collectivity has never been utilized. In World War I President Wilson never once met with his cabinet. Leaders of Congress rarely participate in the decision to use military force but are informed of the decision or about future options; that has been pattern in five of six undeclared wars since 1950 (Table 13-3). During the Korean War, for example, Truman's primary advisor was Secretary of State Dean Acheson.[34] Truman did not convene the National Security Council but instead relied on a dozen top-level advisors from the Departments of Defense and State and the JCS.

An entirely different set of decision-makers surrounded President

Table 13–3. Presidential Advisors in Selected Undeclared Wars—Decision Makers

Incidents	CIA	VP	NSC	Cabinet					Selected White House Staff	Ad Hoc Groups	Congressional Leaders
				Joint Chiefs	*Defense*	*Treasury*	*State*	*Attorney General*			
Korea (1950): Truman				X	X		(X)¹				
Bay of Pigs (1961): Kennedy	(X)			X	X		X		X	X	
Cuban Missile Crisis (1962): Kennedy			X	X	X	X	X	X		X	
Iranian Crisis (1980): Carter		X	X	(X)	X		X		X		
Grenada (1983): Reagan	X	X	X	X	X		(X)		X	X	
Persian Gulf (1991): Bush	X	X	X	(X)²	(X)		X		X		X³

¹(X) = primary advisers to the president

²In addition to General Colin Powell, head of the Joint Chiefs of Staff, General Norman Schwarzkopf, the commanding general in charge of Persian Gulf operations, was also an important advisor to the president.

³Although only playing a minor role, congressional leaders did advise the president on occasion.

Kennedy during the Cuban missile crisis.[35] Most important during this thirteen-day crisis was the Executive Committee of the National Security Council (EXCOM), comprised of fifteen high-ranking officials whom Kennedy personally selected. Included were Secretary of State Dean Rusk, Defense Secretary Robert McNamara, Attorney General Robert Kennedy, Treasury Secretary Douglas Dillon, National Security Advisor McGeorge Bundy, and General Maxwell Taylor, chairman of the Joint Chiefs of Staff. EXCOM was convened by the president three hours after he learned missiles were being sent to Cuba. Its major responsibility was to assess the risks involved with the various policy options under study. Although President Kennedy made greater use of his political advisors than he did of his military leadership, he made no use of members of Congress. He only consulted with the party leadership in Congress once EXCOM had prepared its policy response to the Soviets.

Iranian Crisis

In 1979 fifty-two Americans were taken hostage in the U.S. Embassy in Tehran for 444 days. President Carter met formally with the National Security Council but more important was the Special Coordinating Committee of the NSC chaired by National Security Advisor Zbigniew Brzezinski. Also advising Carter was Secretary of State Cyrus Vance, whose restrained views counterbalanced the hawkish approach of Brzezinski. Vance favored a diplomatic resolution to the problem; Brzezinski wanted a reconnaissance mission to rescue the hostages. Carter vacillated[36] because he wanted to hear many viewpoints before making any decision. On April 25, 1980, Carter finally decided on the aborted rescue mission, but this time he had conferred with only a few advisors including his military aides and Brzezinski. In protest, Cyrus Vance resigned as secretary of state because his advice had been ignored.[37]

Although it was the Joint Chiefs of Staff who planned the disastrous rescue mission that ended 200 miles from Teheran, with three of the eight helicopters rendered useless because of mechanical malfunctions, Carter admitted to the American people and to Congress that the rescue attempt had been his decision alone, and he took full responsibility for it.[38] As legal justification, the president mentioned his constitutional powers as chief executive and commander in chief and his authority under Article 51 of the UN Charter.[39]

Grenada

The Grenada invasion of October 1983 posed quite another challenge to a president.[40] To show a greater U.S. presence in the Caribbean and to counteract what he perceived as U.S. weakness from the Carter years, President Reagan increased military exercises in this area during 1982. Attention was paid to Grenada because several hundred U.S. medical students were being trained there. Those who defended the decision to invade the island pointed to the need to protect Americans who were on the island from both Soviet embassy personnel and Cuban military units stationed there.

A nonmilitary evacuation plan was referred for approval to an ad hoc group of advisors from the Department of Defense, the CIA, the JCS, and the Department of State. Several days later the NSC's Special Situation Group, headed by Vice President George Bush, supported military action and directed the Joint Chiefs to formulate a comprehensive evacuation plan of action. Reagan's most intimate advisors in this operation were Secretary of State George Schultz, Bush, National Security Affairs Advisor Robert McFarlane, Defense Secretary Casper Weinberger, Major General George B. Crist of the JCS, and Francis J. McNeil, a former ambassador to Costa Rica. A number of these advisors voiced concern, fearing the plan had the potential to be another failed (Iran) rescue mission. Reagan's advisors also met with Caribbean leaders before the invasion to encourage regional support and requested military assistance for the Grenada invasion from the Organization of Eastern Caribbean States. In final meetings, the president met with Attorney General Edwin Meese, Deputy Chief of Staff Michael Deaver, and Latin American experts from the NSC before approving the invasion plan. In the end it was Shultz and McFarlane who gave the go-ahead, whereas Casper Weinberger withheld his support, thinking the operation was too hastily prepared.

The military operation began on October 25, 1983, with a force of 1,900 U.S. marines and army forces and 500 troops from the other Caribbean nations. It was only after President Reagan issued the invasion order that congressional leaders were called in, as Senator Robert Byrd (D–W.Va.) recalled: "The Administration only tells the Senate after the Administration makes its decision. It informs us then that it is going to do this and that. It does not ask for advice of the Senate.[41] Critics complained that the invasion resembled nineteenth-century U.S. "gunboat" diplomacy, with no justification. Nonetheless a *New York Times*/CBS poll showed that 55 percent of the public backed the invasion and 31 percent disapproved.[42]

Persian Gulf War

President George Bush followed the Reagan example by relying on a small number of military and civilian advisors when he planned to wage war on Iraq in 1990 (see case study in chapter 14). Defense Secretary Dick Cheney, chairman of the JCS Colin Powell, Secretary of State James Baker, National Security Advisor Brent Scowcroft, and General Norman Schwarzkopf, who commanded the Persian Gulf forces, were the key decision-makers.[43] Others in attendance at the strategy meetings included White House Chief of Staff John Sununu, Robert Gates, deputy chief of the NSC, White House Press Secretary Marlin Fitzwater, Under-Secretary of State Robert M. Kimmitt, and Vice President Dan Quayle. As in previous military confrontations, although congressional leaders were consulted by the president from time to time, none were involved as advisors or strategists.

PUBLIC INPUTS

Whenever the United States goes to war, the nation usually supports the commander in chief, at least at the beginning of a military conflict. Because Americans want to win their wars relatively quickly, public support for the commander in chief will last only as long as victory seems possible.

Korea and Vietnam are examples of conflicts in which support for the commander in chief came into question. John Mueller points out that those wars became increasingly unpopular as the cost and casualties mounted.[44] The Korean invasion to stop Communist aggression initially was very popular. When Truman shipped troops to South Korea a Gallup poll in July 1950 indicated that 77 percent approved the war effort. After the Communist Chinese troops from the People's Republic of China entered the war, however, support for the Korean war dropped 25 percentage points. This loss of support was undoubtedly because of the tremendous cost of the war in American lives and, in addition, the widespread perception that the U.S. military offensive was stalemated. Sixty-six percent now favored pulling out troops by January 1951.

Support for the Vietnam War also was high in 1965 when Lyndon Johnson first committed 500,000 U.S. troops. Americans saw Vietnam as an American war, and 62.5 percent supported the intervention against Communist North Vietnam. But then support dropped off as the public saw evidence of an unstable and corrupt government in South Vietnam as well as heightened U.S. opposition to the war. The public began to lose confidence in Johnson's leadership as war casualties soared. After the Tet offensive against the United States by Communist forces in 1968, popular approval for LBJ gradually declined to a low point of 44 percent in March 1969.

By November 1969, when Richard Nixon succeeded to the presidency, public opinion again rallied and approved his handling of the war by 64 percent.[45] Despite this momentary rise in public approval, Gallup polls from 1965 to 1969 revealed a nearly steady growth in disillusionment with the war.

These shifting patterns of public support for the Korean and Vietnam wars differed markedly from the support given in World War II. World War II was a "popular war" and the people identified almost immediately with the war objectives of Franklin Roosevelt.[46]

Although strong isolationist sentiments characterized American thinking before U.S. entrance into World War II, once involved, the belief was widespread that America would win the war against Germany.[47] Eighty-two percent of those surveyed also supported Roosevelt's demand for Germany's "unconditional surrender" before the war ended. By 1945 an even higher percentage (84 percent) of the public wanted Japan's unconditional surrender two months before V-J Day. The popular consensus also backed President Truman's decision (85 percent) to drop the atomic bomb on Nagasaki and Hiroshima and end the war against Japan.

Although the unexpected attack by Japan on the U.S. fleet stationed at Pearl Harbor, Hawaii—which caused Congress to declare war on the Axis powers—could hardly be described a success for President Roosevelt, nonetheless his approval ratings jumped from 72 to 84 percent (Table 13-4). Sudden military confrontations rally Americans behind presidential leadership and if wars, declared or undeclared, and preemptive military strikes can be short, clean, and victorious, the president is always the winner in the polls. That seems to be the lesson from the history of warfare.

One example was the short-lived bombing of Baghdad, on June 26, 1993, when President Clinton retaliated against the plot to assassinate for-

Table 13–4. Presidential Popularity Rallies during Wartime

War Episode	Percentage Approval	
	Before	*After*
Japan attacks U.S. fleet based at Pearl Harbor, Hawaii (1941)	72	84
North Korea invades South Korea (1950)	37	46
Cuban missile crisis (1962)	67	74
U.S. ships attacked by North Vietnam in the Gulf of Tonkin (1964)	42	72
Mayaguez merchant ship captured by Cambodia (1975)	40	51
Rescue attempt of Americans held hostage by Iran (1980)	39	43
United States invades Grenada to prevent communist takeover (1983)	45	53
United States bombs Libya (1986)	63	69
United States lands troops in Panama to arrest its dictator on drug charges (1989)	71	80
Persian Gulf War (1990)	58	89
United States launches cruise missile attack on Iraqi intelligences headquarters (1993)	39	50
United States troops invade Haiti to restore a democratically elected government (1994)	34	45

Source: Data on 1941, 1950, 1962, and 1975 episodes from Jong R. Lee, "Rallying around the Flag: Foreign Policy Events and Presidential Popularity," *Presidential Studies Quarterly* 7 (Fall 1977), pp. 254–255; data on 1980, 1986, 1993, and 1994 episodes from Theodore J. Lowi and Benjamin Ginsberg, *American Government*, 4th ed. (New York: Norton, 1996), p. 258; the 1964 data comes from Larry Berman, "Gulf of Tonkin Resolution," in Leonard W. Levy and Louis Fisher, eds., *Encyclopedia of the American Presidency*, vol. 2 (New York: Simon & Schuster, 1994), p. 714. Data from 1983, 1989 and 1990 comes from *The Gallup Report*, no. 219, p. 18; no. 291, p. 3, and from no. 292, p. 17.

mer president George Bush by firing twenty-three Tomahawk computer-guided missiles aimed at the headquarters of Iraqi intelligence (Mukhabarat) in Baghdad. Although three missed their designated target and killed eight civilians, Clinton's action was considered a success by the media and his popularity increased 11 percent the day after the incident.[48]

George Bush was involved in several of these short wars. After the Panama invasion in 1989 to arrest the Panamanian dictator on drug charges, 73 percent approved of Bush's handling of foreign policy and 74 percent thought the invasion was justified.[49] But the best was yet to come: 89 percent of Americans gave President Bush a record high approval rating after the Allied victory in the Persian Gulf War.

EXPERTISE

Although the president cannot totally dominate national security policy, he has major advantages and expertise is one.[50] The commander in chief has privileged access to information and the ability to monopolize it.

CIA

The Central Intelligence Agency (CIA) is probably the most important agency that funnels information to the commander in chief. Created by the National Security Act of 1947, it has responsibility to advise the NSC on intelligence and espionage activities. Operating from embassies in foreign capitals, the CIA keeps in constant contact with Washington. It is involved in covert and many overt actions, including the marine landing in Lebanon in 1982, planning for military actions against Grenada, El Salvador, and Angola, and espionage work in the Soviet Union and China.

The CIA's effectiveness depends on its relationship with the president, particularly the political skill of its director. President Kennedy was confronted by a CIA under the leadership of Allen Dulles (brother of the secretary of state under Eisenhower), that was strongly committed to the Bay of Pigs invasion of Cuba even before JFK assumed office. Kennedy was unable to resist the CIA's strength and pressure within his own administration. Ronald Reagan, in contrast, delegated to CIA Director William Casey great leeway to tailor operations in foreign policy. During the Reagan years the United States experienced "the biggest peacetime buildup in the American intelligence community since the early 1950's,"[51] including an expansion of the CIA's own authority. An executive order gave the CIA permission to "conduct special activities approved by the President." No other agency except the military in time of war has the authority to do this.[52]

A president's attitude about the legitimacy of intelligence gathering is also relevant. William Casey claimed that President Jimmy Carter's attitudes had "crushed the spirit of the CIA"[53] because Carter had stopped the CIA's distribution of funds to Jordan and limited the number of its agents abroad. President Reagan had quite a different attitude and, as a result, the funds budgeted for intelligence operations were increased from $55.3 million in 1981 to $84.6 million in 1982.[54]

One potential danger posed by the CIA is its tendency to advocate covert operations. Congress is the primary check on an overzealous CIA, and before 1980 several standing committees had oversight responsibilities including the House and Senate Appropriations Committees, both Intelligence Committees, the House International Relations Committee, and the Senate Foreign Relations Committee. The Accountability for Intelligence Activities Act of 1980 limited oversight responsibilities (partly to avoid leaks of intelligence information) to the House Intelligence Committee and the Senate Intelligence Committee.

FBI

The Federal Bureau of Investigation (FBI) for years has supplied presidents with information on various suspect activities. For example, President Franklin Roosevelt asked the FBI to record the names of all persons who sent telegrams opposing the government's national defense policies and to monitor those supporting the "isolationist" policies of aviation pioneer Charles Lindbergh.[55] Ronald Reagan in 1981 gave both the FBI and the CIA the authority to "infiltrate" domestic groups that were under investigation and suspected by the administration of acting on behalf of a foreign nation;[56] whereas Bill Clinton, either deliberately or accidentally, used the FBI to create information files on more than four hundred Republicans, most of whom had served in the Bush administration. The White House claimed the "Filegate" controversy was little more than a "monumental snafu" and that FBI files were not ill used.[57]

Wartime Censorship

During wartime a commander in chief has access to emergency statutes, such as the espionage and internal security acts, that allow him to manipulate information which affects national defense and to impose controls over the news media. The Eisenhower administration drafted perhaps the first systematic censorship codes to prevent newspapers and wire services from giving information to the enemy forces.[58] This tradition of information control carried over to the 1991 Persian Gulf War, as described by Michael Getler:

> The Pentagon and the U.S. Army Central Command conducted what is probably the most thorough and sophisticated wartime control of American reporters in modern times—what they could see, who they could talk to, where they could go, what they could tell the public and when they could tell it—a collection of restrictions that in its totality and mindset seems to go beyond World War II, Korea and Vietnam.[59]

Presidents also have been able to persuade the news media to delay printing information. In the 1950s reporters from the *Washington Post* and the *New York Times* knew American U-2 spy planes were gathering photographic information over the Soviet Union even before one of the pilots, Gary Powers, was brought down in 1960. The Gary Powers U-2 incident exposed this covert activity, but President Eisenhower convinced reporters that publishing such a story might jeopardize future flights over the Soviet Union.[60]

Iran-contra Affair

Presidents also try to control public opinion through distortion or false information. The Iran-contra affair began in 1985 when the Reagan administration thought it could make some progress with Iran if U.S. allies would sell military arms to Iran.[61] Those directly involved were individuals in the NSC and CIA, but the State Department was excluded because of Secretary George Shultz's opposition.

Israel was first asked by National Security Council staffer Michael Ledeen in July 1985 to be the transfer country for facilitating the sale. Israel appeared interested. The president, according to National Security Advisor Robert McFarlane, gave his approval for the sale, hoping U.S. hostages held by pro-Iranian groups in Beirut might be released as a consequence of the U.S. shipment of arms from Israel. By September 1985, 508 TOW missiles were shipped from Israel to Iran through a third country, and later that month one hostage (Benjamin Weir) was released. By November the CIA furnished Israel an aircraft to ship 18 Hawk missiles to Iran.

In December 1985 Robert McFarlane, who had recently resigned as national security advisor, and Lieutenant Colonel Oliver North, an NSC aide, met with Iranian representatives. They indicate that the United States would end arms shipments unless more hostages were released. North urged Iran to acquiesce to additional hostage releases in exchange for Hawk missile parts. In a White House memorandum of April 4, 1986, allegedly written by North, $12 million from the sale of the Hawk missile parts was to be used to purchase supplies for the Nicaraguan Democratic Resistance (the "contras"). In May, McFarlane and North, with the president's approval, secretly met for four days with Iranian arms dealers concerning the shipments and possible release of other hostages. The meeting ended in failure, but McFarlane learned from North that a portion of the money from the Iranians would be diverted to the Nicaraguan contras.

Congress on June 26, 1986, approved the president's request for military aid for the contras. The next month a hostage (Lawrence Jenco) was released after Iran made certain that Hawk missile parts would be arriving. By November of that year Israel sent five hundred more TOW missiles to Iran, which allowed the release of David Jacobson as a hostage. November 6 was also the first time the press received information about the shipment of arms to Iran and confronted President Reagan.

The revelation led to a series of investigations carried out by Congress and the president. Congress began its investigations on November 21,

1986, and five days later President Reagan named the three-member Tower Commission to investigate the NSC's role in the matter. In December an independent prosecutor, Lawrence Walsh, was appointed by the courts to begin a separate investigation; the House Intelligence Committee and the Senate Intelligence Committee continued with their investigations.

The Tower Commission was comprised of former senator John Tower (R–Tex.), its chair, Edmund Muskie (D–Me.) and Brent Scowcroft, retired air force general, who had served in several Republican administrations. The Tower Commission Report was critical of two national security advisors, Robert McFarlane and John Poindexter, for their role in the Iran-contra affair. The Tower Commission Report also cited Donald Regan, Reagan's chief of staff, as sharing blame because he allowed the NSC to get out of control. It also concluded that the CIA should have been in charge of the operation instead of the NSC.[62] In the final analysis, however, the Tower Commission said little about Reagan's role in the affair.

In November 1987 the House Select Committee to Investigate Covert Arms Transactions with Iran and the Senate Select Committee on Secret Military Assistance to Iran and the Nicaraguan Opposition submitted their two reports. There was a majority report from fifteen Democrats and a minority report filed by eight Republicans. The majority report was more critical of President Reagan than the Tower Commission had been, charging him with the "ultimate responsibility" for the scandal. The majority charged that the Iran-contra affair occurred because the persons involved disobeyed the law. The report argued that President Reagan did not take his constitutional responsibility seriously in "taking care" that the laws are faithfully executed.[63] The Democratic majority was also concerned that the role of Congress in foreign policy be respected and urged the president to report all future covert operations to Congress before they take place. It further recommended that the NSC cease participating in covert operations and the president report regularly to Congress on NSC activities.

Classification Systems

During peacetime the commander in chief can maintain his control over information by using classification systems to deny widespread public access. The first extensive security classification system under President Eisenhower remained in effect for some twenty years. It limited the number of agencies that could restrict information and succeeded in classifying approximately 470 million pages of documents covering the years 1939 to 1954.[64] The trend to classify information has continued to increase since that time, and the reasons given for classification have often had very little to do with the nation's security. As James C. Thomson, Jr., observes,

> Most of what is concealed through classification is anything whose revelation might be politically embarrassing to the Administration in power, or to individual officials, in terms of The Enemy at home the opposition party, the Congress, the press and thereby the wider voting public.[65]

In a few cases the Supreme Court has limited presidential control over information. In *U.S. v. District Court for the Eastern District of Michigan* (1972), President Nixon defended wiretapping done without search warrants in the name of national security,[66] but the high court rejected Nixon's justification and ruled that warrants are essential to the process of justice. In the more important case of *U.S. v. Nixon* (1974), the Supreme Court required Nixon to release the infamous Watergate tapes and transcripts of his discussions in the White House.[67] Nixon had refused to supply the materials requested by the Congress, invoking executive privilege and claiming their release would hurt national security. The Court was not sympathetic to his arguments, although it admitted that "executive privilege" and "confidentiality" could extend to legitimate matters of national security. So although this decision appeared to limit presidential power, under other circumstances the *U.S. v. Nixon* decision might well extend a president's power because the Court indicated that no longer was executive privilege and confidentiality based on mere tradition; it now had a constitutional basis.

CRISIS

Today we live in an age when "total war" is always a possibility. World War I and World War II required a total commitment of the nation's human and material resources. Total war also may require the suppression of such civil liberties as free speech, press, and due process in order to maintain a united front against the enemy and national morale.

Japanese American Internment

A shocking episode during World War II was the violation of civil liberties suffered by Japanese American citizens on the mainland. Their trying experience shows how the Congress, the president, and even the Supreme Court can rationalize serious abuses of civil liberties in the face of war.

On February 19, 1942, Franklin D. Roosevelt issued Executive Order 9066 to respond to the potential danger of Japanese sabotage on the West Coast. The president established military zones along the coast to protect military installations. He ordered the forceful removal of some 120,000 Japanese Americans from their homes, who were then sent to "relocation centers" in California, Arizona, Idaho, Utah, Colorado, Wyoming, and Arkansas. Congress supported the president's action on March 21, 1942, by passing a resolution making it a misdemeanor against the United States to leave or enter another military zone without permission from the secretary of war and the commanding military officers.

Those violations of constitutional rights were reviewed by the Supreme Court in the cases of *Hirabayashi v. United States* (1943) and *Korematsu v. United States* (1944). The more important case of *Korematsu* concerned presidential authority to implement the exclusionary order that housed the Japanese Americans in internment camps. In a 6 to 3 decision, the majority of justices upheld the commander in chief's order arguing that the exclusionary order was a legitimate outgrowth of both presidential and congressional authority.[68]

Truman's Steel Seizure

One major exception to the tendency of the Supreme Court to allow the commander in chief extraordinary powers was President Harry Truman's seizure of the steel mills during the Korean War. In 1951 the United Steel Workers (USW) union called a strike to shut the steel mills in April, but President Truman saw a possible disaster affecting not only workers in the steel industry but the whole economy, jeopardizing his war effort. Steel was essential to produce war armaments and equipment. As one option Truman could have used the Taft-Hartley Act of 1947[69] that was passed over his veto and provided for an eighty-day cooling-off period during management-labor disputes that seriously impact the national well-being. But Truman already had used the law on other occasions and did not want to offend the unions, which characterized the hated Taft-Hartley Act as "slave-labor" legislation. After several failed attempts to work out a settlement, President Truman saw no choice except to issue Executive Order 10340 directing Secretary of Commerce Charles Sawyer to seize the mills and keep them operating. The mill owners would now work for the U.S. government.

The executive order was not based on any statute that covered labor disputes, but President Truman did not believe he needed additional power other than commander in chief authority to seize the mills. The steel companies went to court seeking an injunction to prevent the takeover. On May 3, 1952, the Supreme Court heard the case and rendered a decision on June 12. In *Youngstown Sheet and Tube Company v. Sawyer* (1952) the justices (dividing 6–3) ruled against the president.[70] For the court majority, Justice Black took a narrow view of presidential power by arguing that, for the president to have power to issue such an executive order, he would have to trace that authority back to the Constitution or a law of Congress. Black found no such power in the commander in chief clause of Article II nor in the "take care" clause that laws be faithfully executed.

Emergency Powers

Presidents also have expanded their powers through emergency grants of authority from Congress, but rarely do they dissolve those powers once the emergency ceases. In 1973 a Special Senate Committee on the Termination of the National Emergency discovered that pursuant to four executive proclamations (Roosevelt's in 1933, Truman's in 1950, and Nixon's in 1970 and 1971) 470 emergency statutes were involved that granted extraordinary powers to the president. These statutes allowed a president "the right to seize property, organize and control the means of production, seize commodities, assign military forces abroad, call reserve forces amounting to 2.5 million men to duty, institute martial law, seize and control all means of transportation, regulate all private enterprise, and restrict travel."[71] Even though those emergencies had all long passed, the president retained those extraordinary powers. Thus Congress enacted the National Emergencies Act to rescind those extraordinary powers and that law was signed by President Gerald Ford in 1976.

SUMMARY

Although the case has been made by some respected conservative observers that the presidency today appears ineffective and weak and should be further strengthened and "energized,"[72] a president in the role of commander in chief seems difficult if not impossible for Congress, the Supreme Court, or the public to limit in power. In the early years no president claimed an inherent right or plenary authority to justify warmaking, nor did any president seek extraconstitutional grounds for using force. Contemporary presidents have not been so constrained. As historian Arthur Schlesinger, Jr., observed of Richard Nixon's powers,

> Today President Nixon has equipped himself with so expansive a theory of the powers of the Commander in Chief, and so elastic a theory of defensive war, that he can freely, on his own initiative, without a national emergency, as a routine employment of Presidential power, go to war against any country containing any troops that might in any conceivable circumstances be used in an attack on American forces.[73]

What is disturbing is that Schlesinger's observation could apply to any contemporary president. Congress could check the commander in chief powers by virtue of its constitutional right to declare war and to appropriate funds, but rarely has Congress exerted its authority and only in a few instances has it been effective.

Passage of the War Powers Resolution of 1973 was designed to assure executive-congressional debate and consultation over war-making, but it has not limited war initiatives by the president and has failed to include congressional leaders in crucial wartime decisions. Every president since has sidestepped the resolution in whole or in part, and Congress has been unwilling to call him to account for violating the law. Instead, Congress seems more willing to expand the presidential commander in chief authority. Enactment of the 1964 Gulf of Tonkin Resolution was more typical than not of the tendency for Congress to support a wartime president. Nor has the Supreme Court restrained the commander in chief. With the one exception of the *Youngstown* decision, the Court has never interfered with the president's interpretation of his war powers.

No easy solution has been found to the problem of restraining a commander in chief during wartime. Care in selecting presidents who are self-restrained would seem to be a weak response to the problem at hand. Historian Arthur Schlesinger, Jr., accuses modern presidents of having "neglected the collection of consent, removed significant executive decisions from the political process, and departed considerably from the principles, if somewhat less from the practice, of the early republic."[74]

NOTES

1. Sidney Hyman, *The American Presidency* (New York: Harper and Brothers, 1954), p. 10.

2. Warren W. Hassler, Jr., *The President as Commander in Chief* (Menlo Park, CA: Addison-Wesley, 1971), p. 11.

3. See *Youngstown Sheet and Tube Co. v. Sawyer*, 343 U.S. 643 (1952).

4. See J. Terry Emerson, "The War Powers Resolution Tested: The President's Independent Defense Power," 51 *Notre Dame Lawyer* 187,209 (1975); A. Sofaer, *War, Foreign Affairs and Constitutional Power: The Origins* (Cambridge, MA: Ballinger, 1976), pp. 31–32; and David G. Alder, "The Constitution and Presidential Warmaking: The Enduring Debate," *Political Science Quarterly* 103(1) (1988), p. 4.

5. See Louis Fisher, *Presidential War Power* (Lawrence: University Press of Kansas, 1995).

6. Ruth Marcus and Helen Dewar, "Clinton Tells Congress to Back Off," *Washington Post* (Oct. 19, 1993), pp. A1, A18.

7. Helen Dewar, "Move to Curb Clinton on Troops Is Rejected," *Washington Post* (Oct. 20, 1939), p. A32.

8. Helen Dewar, "Senators Approve Troop Compromise," *Washington Post* (Oct. 21, 1993), p. A1

9. See Richard Rose, *The Post-Modern President: George Bush Meets the World*, 2nd ed. (Chatham, NJ: Chatham House, 1991), p. 306.

10. Michael R. Gordon, "Modest Air Operation in Bosnia Crosses a Major Political Frontier," *New York Times* (April 11, 1994), p. A1.

11. A.M. Rosenthal, "Clinton in Wartime," *New York Times* (April 12, 1994), p. A15.

12. "Bankruptcy Amendments Act of 1993," *Congressional Record—Senate*, 103rd Congress, 2nd session, April 21, 1994, p. S4642.

13. See Larry Berman and Emily O. Goldman, "Clinton's Foreign Policy at Midterm," in Colin Campbell and Bert A. Rockman, eds., *The Clinton Presidency: First Appraisals* (Chatham, NJ: Chatham House, 1996), p. 314.

14. It won't negate criticism from persons like Representative Matt Salmon (R–Ariz.) who was horrified at the thought that one of his staff could only purchase toy soldiers labeled "U.N. Troops" in the market and not the "American" toy soldiers he was accustomed to. His response: "How far has this madness gone? It used to be, when I was a little boy, I would play with my G.I. Joe. They were American soldiers we used to play with. They were not United Nations troops." "Foreign Command of U.S. Troops," *Congressional Record—House*, 104th Congress, 1st session, February 16, 1995, H1895.

15. Thomas G. Weiss, "When the U.S. Washes Its Hands of the World," *Christian Science Monitor* (May 25, 1994), p. 23.

16. U.S. Congress, Senate, "The War Power after 200 Years: Congress and the President at a Constitutional Impasse," Hearings before the Special Subcommittee on War Powers of the Committee on Foreign Relations, 100th Congress, 1st Session, September 29, 1988, p. 567.

17. See Donald L. Robinson, *"To the Best of My Ability": The Presidency and the Constitution* (New York: Norton, 1987), p. 13.

18. See Papers Relating to the Foreign Relations of the United States, Doc. l, 58th Congress, 3rd Session 244 (1905); and 54 Department of State Bulletin, 474, 485 (1966).

19. See a complete listing of 192 U.S. military engagements that took place from 1798 to 1970 without a formal declaration of war in J. Terry Everson, "War Powers Legislation," *West Virginia Law Review* (August/November 1971), pp. 53–119.

20. See chapter 15 in Clinton Rossiter, *Constitutional Dictatorship* (New York: Harcourt, Brace & World, 1963).

21. *Luther v. Borden*, 48 U.S. (7 How.) 44 (1849).

22. U.S., "Neutrality Act of 1935," August 31, 1935. *Statutes at Large*, vol. 49, pt. 1, pp. 1081–1085.

23. See Robert Dallek, *Franklin D. Roosevelt and American Foreign Policy, 1932–1945* (New York: Oxford, 1979), for a treatment of Roosevelt's prewar involvement, especially pp. 172, 252.

24. See U.S. Congress, "Acquiring Certain Naval and Air Bases in Exchange for Certain Over-Age Destroyers," September 3, 1940, Document no. 943, 76th Congress, 3rd session.

25. "Viet Nam Resolution," *1964 Congressional Quarterly Almanac* (Washington, DC: Congressional Quarterly, 1965), p. 332.

26. Arthur Schlesinger, Jr., *The Imperial Presidency* (Boston: Houghton Mifflin, 1973), p. 193.

27. See War Powers Resolution, *Statutes at Large*, vol. 87 (1973), pp. 555–560.

28. See Christopher Madison, "Despite His Complaints, Reagan Going Along with Spirit of War Powers Law," *National Journal* (May 19, 1984), p. 990.

29. Robert A. Katzmann, "War Powers: Toward a New Accommodation," in Thomas E. Mann, ed., *A Question of Balance: The President, The Congress and Foreign Policy* (Washington, DC: The Brookings Institution, 1990), p. 58.

30. Ibid.

31. See Michael L. Mezey, *Congress, the President, and Public Policy* (Boulder, CO: Westview Press, 1989), p. 165.

32. Carroll J. Doherty, "New Scene, Familiar Script,"*Congressional Quarterly Weekly Report* 51(42) (Oct. 23, 1993), p. 2897. This position did represent a change for Clinton from May 1993. When a reporter asked him about the constitutionality of the War Powers Act regarding the incident in Somalia, he indicated the law had worked "reasonably well." See Carroll J. Doherty, "Skirmishing over Somalia," *Congressional Quarterly Weekly Report* 51(11) (May 8, 1993), p. 1171.

33. See U.S. House, HR 4730, Department of Defense Reorganization Act of 1986, 99th Congress, 2nd session (1986), (Washington, DC: U.S. Government Printing Office), and Pat Towell,"Major Pentagon Reorganization Bill Is Cleared," *Congressional Quarterly Weekly Report* 44 (Sept. 20, 1986), pp. 2207–2208.

34. This discussion of the Korean war is based on Glenn D. Paige, *The Korean Decision* (New York: Free Press, 1968).

35. This discussion of the Cuban missile crisis is based on Graham T. Allison, *Essence of Decision: Explaining the Cuban Missile Crisis* (Boston: Little, Brown, 1971).

36. See Charles G. Cogan,"Not to Offend: Observations on Iran, the Hostages and the Hostage Rescue Mission—Ten Years Later," *Comparative Strategy* 9 (1990), pp. 415–432, for an interesting reflection on the hostage mission.

37. The source of those steps leading up to the hostage rescue can be found in "Chronology of the U.S.-Iranian Relations . . . throughout the American Hostage Crisis," *Congress and the Nation,* vol. 5. (Washington, DC: Congressional Quarterly, 1981), p. 116.

38. See Carter's statement to Congress in "Iran Rescue Mission," *1980 Congressional Quarterly Almanac* (Washington, DC: Congressional Quarterly, 1981), p. 49E.

39. Ibid., p. 50E

40. Examination of the Grenada war comes from the following studies: Richard D. Hooker, Jr., "Presidential Decisionmaking and Use of Force: Case Study of Grenada," *Parameters: U.S. Army War College Quarterly* 21(2) (1991), pp. 61–72; Ralph Kinney Bennett, "Grenada: Anatomy of a 'Go' Decision," *Reader's Digest,* (Feb. 1984), pp. 72–77; H.W. Brands, Jr., "Decisions on American Armed Intervention: Lebanon, Dominican Republic, and Grenada," *Political Science Quarterly* 102(4) (1987), pp. 607–624; and Michael Rubner, "The Reagan Administration, the 1973 War Powers Resolution, and the Invasion of Grenada," *Political Science Quarterly,* 100(4) (Winter 1985–1986), pp. 627–647.

41. See "The Role of the Senate in Foreign Policy," U.S. Congress, Senate, *Congressional Record* 129, 98th Congress, 1st session, October 29, 1983, pp. 29900–29901.

42. "Poll Shows Support for Presence of U.S. Troops in Lebanon and Grenada," *New York Times* (October 29, 1983), p. 9.

43. Theodore Draper argues that the actual decision to become involved in the war seems to have been a decision of President Bush encouraged by Secretary Cheney, Vice President Quayle, and National Security Advisor Scowcroft. As a result, he concludes it was basically a "presidential war." Theodore Draper, "The True History of the Gulf War," *New York Review of Books,* 39(3) (January 30, 1992), p. 39.

44. Data on U.S. involvement in Korea and Vietnam comes from John E. Mueller, "Trends in Popular Support for the Wars in Korea and Vietnam," *The American Political Science Review* 65 (1971), pp. 358–375; and Philip E. Converse and Howard Schuman, "'Silent Majorities' and the Vietnam War," *Scientific American* (June 1970), pp. 17–25.

45. See "The Trend," and "Nixon's Handling of Vietnam," *Gallup Poll Index* 54, (Dec. 1969), pp. 1–2.

46. Rita James Simon, *Public Opinion in America: 1936–1970* (Chicago: Rand McNally, 1974), p. 150. Our discussion of public opinion during World War II is based on Simon's analysis on p. 123–147. In three surveys asking Americans whether U.S. entry into World War II had been a mistake, overwhelming majorities said "no" in 1946 (77 percent), in 1947 (66 percent), and in 1948 (78 percent).

47. The American Institute of Public Opinion (Gallup) surveys taken in 1937 and in 1939 showed that 60 percent of the respondents viewed U.S. involvement in World War I as a mistake. Some 79 percent surveyed in five polls between the years 1939 and 1941 felt the United States should stay out of the coming war between the Allies and the Axis powers. Ibid.

48. Seymour M. Hersh, "A Reporter at Large: A Case Not Closed," *The New Yorker* (Nov. 1, 1993), p. 80.

49. Michael Oreskes, "Approval of Bush, Bolstered by Panama, Soars in Poll," *New York Times* (Jan. 19, 1990), p. A20.

50. Thomas E. Mann, ed., *A Question of Balance: The President, the Congress and Foreign Policy* (Washington, DC: The Brookings Institution, 1990), p. 29.

51. See Phillip Taubman, "Casey and His CIA," *New York Times Magazine* (Jan. 16, 1983), pp. 20–62.

52. See "Executive Order 1233 of December 4, 1981" in Title 3—The President, *Federal Register* 46(235), December 8, 1981, pp. 59945–59946.

53. Bob Woodward, *Veil: The Secret Wars of the CIA, 1981–1987* (New York: Simon & Schuster, 1987) p. 380. In our examination of the Reagan period, we have relied on Bob Woodward's account of the activity of William Casey as CIA director.

54. There has been a steady increase in budget funds for the CIA since that significant increase in the first years of the Reagan administration. The following figures (all in millions of dollars) come from the U.S. Office of Management and Budget, *Budget of the U.S. Government, 1984–1993* (Washington, DC: U.S. Government Printing Office, 1992).

1983—91.3
1984—86.3
1985—99.3
1986—101.4
1987—125.8
1988—134.7
1989—144.5
1990—154.9
1991—165.0
1992—164.0 est.
1993—169.0 est.

55. To some, Lindbergh's policies showed more of a pro-German orientation and not an isolationist one at all.

56. See John Orman, *Presidential Accountability: New and Recurring Problems* (New York: Greenwood Press, 1990), p. 61.

57. "A Snafu, and More," *Christian Science Monitor* (June 13, 1996) @http://www.csmonitor.com/plweb-cqi . . . hives++Clinton%26 and %26FBI% 26files; and Linda Feldmann, "What's behind Latest White House Scandal?" *Christian Science Monitor* (June 21, 1996) @http://www.csmonitor.com/plweb-cqi . . . hives++Clinton%26 and %26FBI%26files.

58. David Wise, *The Politics of Lying: Government Deception, Secrecy and Power* (New York: Vintage Books, 1973), p. 203.

59. Michael Getler, " . . . The Gulf War 'Good News' Policy Is a Dangerous Precedent," *The Washington Post National Weekly Edition* (March 25–31, 1991), p. 24.

60. See Arthur S. Miller, *Presidential Power in a Nutshell* (St. Paul: West, 1977), pp. 281–284.

61. Most of this information on Iran-contra comes from the U.S. Congress. U.S. House Select Committee to Investigate Covert Arms Transactions with Iran, and the U.S. Senate Select Committee on Secret Military Assistance to Iran and the Nicaraguan Opposition, *Report of the Congressional Committees Investigating the Iran-Contra Affair*, H. Report No. 100–433, and

S. Report No. 100–216, 100th Congress, 1st session, November 1987 (hereafter referred to as *Report*).

62. See U.S. Congress, House, Investigations Subcommittee and the Defense Policy Panel of the Committee on Armed Services, *Tower Board—NSC Function Hearing*, 100th Congress, 1st session, April 30, 1987; and *The Report of the President's Special Review Board* (The Tower Commission Report) (New York: Bantam Books, 1987), pp. xvii–xix.

63. *Report*, p. 423.

64. Norman Dorsen and Stephen Gillers, *None of Your Business: Government Secrecy in America* (New York: Penguin, 1975), p. 71.

65. James C. Thomson, Jr., "Government and Press: Good News about a Bad Marriage," *New York Times Magazine* (Nov. 25, 1973), p. 56.

66. *U.S. v. District Court of the Eastern District of Michigan*, 407 U.S. 297 (1972).

67. See *U.S. v. Nixon*, 418 U.S. 683 (1974).

68. *Korematsu v. United States*, 323 U.S. 214 (1944).

69. See U.S. House, 80th Congress, 2nd session, HR. 3020, "Labor Management Relations Act," Washington, DC: U.S. Government Printing Office, 1947.

70. *Youngstown Sheet and Tube Company v. Sawyer*, 343 U.S. 579 (1952).

71. "Committee Lists 'Unlimited' Presidential Powers," *Congressional Quarterly Weekly Report* (Oct. 13, 1973), p. 2732.

72. As an example of this approach see Terry Eastland, *Energy in the Executive: The Case for the Strong Presidency* (New York: Free Press, 1992).

73. Arthur Schlesinger, Jr., "Presidential War: 'See If You Can Fix Any Limit to His Power,'" *New York Times Magazine* (Jan. 7, 1973), p. 26.

74. Arthur M. Schlesinger, Jr., "Who Makes War—and How," *American Bar Association Journal* (Jan. 1977), p. 79.

14

Insight on Commander in Chief: George Bush and the Persian Gulf War

In his inaugural address George Bush told Americans that his presidency would put the legacy of Vietnam behind them. Nearly two years to the day after taking over the Oval Office, the Persian Gulf War began, and less than three months later Bush declared, "By God we've killed the Vietnam syndrome once and for all."[1] This Insight looks at President Bush as commander in chief during the Persian Gulf crisis following Iraq's invasion of Kuwait in early August 1990, the period of Desert Shield. It continues through the Persian Gulf War, referred to as Desert Storm, from January 16 to February 27, 1991. In those forty-three days from the beginning to its close—a period during which Saddam Hussein guaranteed that George Bush would not be ignored by history—a president considered by his critics to be a "wimp" became the leader of a new post–Cold War coalition and demonstrated "a commanding vision of a new world order."[2]

Prior to the summer of 1990, Iraq and its leader Saddam Hussein were generally recognized in a limited sense as American allies in the Middle East, although the relationship had proved tenuous at times given the delicate balance of power in the region. Iraq had proved important in curbing Iran during the 1980s, largely because of massive defense expenditures throughout the decade. At the same time Saddam Hussein had brought an unprecedented degree of stability to Iraq and was described as having a "canny understanding of the political dynamics of his society" and as being "a consummate politician at the height of his power."[3]

On August 2, 1990, after weeks of posturing and diplomatic miscues, the equation abruptly changed. Iraqi troops invaded and occupied neighboring Kuwait despite nearly unanimous global opinion that the Iraqi invasion was an unjustified use of force. At the request of Kuwait and Iraq's neighboring state, Saudi Arabia, George Bush committed American air, naval, and ground forces to the Gulf region. His commitment not only demonstrated U.S. opposition to the invasion of Kuwait by Iraq, but it also demonstrated U.S. concern for other Arab nations and Israel. This was done in conjunction with UN Security Council resolutions condemning Iraq's actions and Bush's plea that the "international community act together to ensure that Iraqi forces leave Kuwait immediately."[4]

Early critics of the U.S. role in the Gulf crisis immediately raised the haunting memories of Vietnam and the profound negative effect of that particular war on the whole nation. Recollections of massive U.S. troop commitments without a military or political victory in the end did not bode well for the American public's mindset. For example, midway through the crisis in the fall of 1990, 51 percent of those Americans polled felt that President Bush had not clearly explained why so many troops had been dispatched to a desert halfway around the world. As one *New York Times*/CBS News Poll respondent commented, "It reminds me of Vietnam, and that's everyone else's opinion I talk to . . . they keep sending people over there. And it's just kind of scary, so many of our people over there."[5] Others claimed that the economic value of the Gulf's vast oil reserves would merely lead to "a modern day spice war" in defense of crucial economic interests rather than a defense of Kuwait's freedom as argued by President Bush.[6]

The military build-up in the Middle East continued through the fall of 1990, including an announcement by Bush two days after the midterm elections in November 1990 that he would increase troop commitments in the region. There were clear political overtones in this decision, especially because the presidential order to do so had actually been given a week before the election. Meanwhile the fall of 1990 saw economic sanctions being levied against Iraq in an effort to force Saddam Hussein to reconsider the consequences of his invasion. The United States and the 28-nation five-continent allied force that would eventually act together in the Gulf War recognized early on that economic sanctions and an international trade embargo against Iraq were ineffective. In this regard, CIA director William H. Webster noted that economic sanctions imposed by the United Nations had little effect on the Iraqi military effort, providing Bush with an additional rationale to continue the buildup of the American military presence in the Gulf.[7]

Previous high-level administrative positions both inside and outside of the White House prepared George Bush for his role as commander in chief. Bush was no stranger to the stress and consequences of international conflict, and he understood well the actions to be taken, the support required, and the maneuvering necessary to military objectives. As a past U.S. ambassador to the United Nations (1971–1972), CIA director (1976–77), and vice president (1981–1989) during the Lebanon and Grenada military engagements under President Reagan, as well as a former World War II fighter pilot, Bush brought to the Oval Office considerable experience and strong feelings about the role of commander in chief.

Moreover, he understood better than many of his predecessors both the advantages and consequences of using the resources of political power available to an incumbent president during an international crisis.[8] Just how effectively these power resources were utilized may be debated, especially in retrospect as observers on both sides of the political spectrum reexamine the war crisis.[9] Yet these resources are relevant for our understanding of how the interplay of forces create momentum and energy in the presidential role as commander in chief.

Bush, like most of his forty predecessors in the Oval Office, believed his "inherent" *authority* as commander in chief was derived from Article II of the Constitution and superseded the powers granted to Congress.[10] Although very much aware of this authority, Congress argued it held the power to declare war during the entire prewar period. Bush made his position quite clear, suggesting that regardless of the powers of Congress, as he emphatically stated, "I'm the commander in chief."[11]

Overall, the Bush presidency was successful in deflecting some of the early congressional concern about the military commitment in the Gulf by pointing out that the United States was acting in response to an invitation from its ally Saudi Arabia for protection from Iraqi aggression. Second, by gaining UN support, which condemned the actions of Iraq through a series of Security Council resolutions, Bush sidestepped some of the questions about his presidential authority early in the crisis despite the largest deployment of military forces since Vietnam.[12] Up through the last week before the war commenced, Bush proclaimed his unlimited power by noting, "I have the constitutional authority."[13]

The United Nations and allied support for this U.S. troop buildup in the Gulf area represented the first united front for an American military involvement since the Korean War was waged by President Truman. UN approval was viewed as a turning point for the Bush administration,[14] yet the Congress and President Bush remained at odds over the role of the commander in chief until the legislative branch gave sanction to the armed conflict (although no declaration of war was approved) in January 1991—5½ months after the beginning of the crisis.

In November 1990, as Bush declared his commander in chief predominance, Senate Armed Services Committee chairman Sam Nunn (D–Ga.) became the first political leader to criticize Bush publicly for acting too quickly in committing U.S. forces in a military buildup.[15] In a similar vein, Senate Majority Leader George Mitchell (D–Me.) pointed out forcefully that the Constitution specifically granted war powers to Congress.[16] In response, the president contended that "history is replete with examples where the President had to take action" without congressional approval and that he had "no hesitancy at all to do so."[17] Moreover, Secretary of State Jim Baker hinted that the president could launch an attack without any consultation with Congress.[18]

Bush tried to maneuver around Congress by discouraging a special legislative session to debate the issue of war in the Gulf before the upcoming Christmas holidays. By avoiding a premature vote and showdown with the president before the holidays, members of Congress on both sides of the aisle were able to go home and ascertain the feelings of their constituents. One of the first orders of business in the 102nd Congress was action on January 12, 1991, on a congressional resolution authorizing the use of force in the Persian Gulf. The resolution was drawn up "pursuant to United Nations Security Council Resolution" and subject to the exhaustion of diplomatic means to reach a peaceful settlement, as well as requiring compliance with the War Powers Act of 1973.[19] It passed narrowly on a 52 to 47 vote in the Senate but with votes to spare in the House of Representatives (250–183).

As events unfolded, legislative support for the president proved to be important from several standpoints even allowing President Bush to avoid close scrutiny in terms of the intricacies of the 1973 War Powers Resolution, which even liberals like Senate Foreign Relations chairman Claiborne Pell (D–R.I.) felt would "upset the applecart."[20] For the future, it meant that President Bush would be recorded in the history books as having obtained explicit congressional approval prior to engaging U.S. forces in military actions in Iran.

It is important to understand how Bush gained congressional approval to use military force in light of the War Powers Resolution. Senator Daniel Moynihan (D–N.Y.) suggested, in the midst of the crisis, that legislation was "a dead-letter" leading to "a fruitless standoff between Congress and the President."[21] This was particularly true inasmuch as the judiciary has been reluctant to address the legalities of the resolution on either procedural or constitutional grounds. Bush's opinion of the War Powers Resolution and the relationship between the executive and legislative branches that it established was echoed in the views of such key White House staffers as Assistant for National Security Affairs Brent Scowcroft. Long before the events of 1991 Scowcroft had argued the following:

> Congress has become too minutely involved in the day-by-day operation of foreign policy. . . . Moreover, I do question the constitutionality of any legislation authorizing the Congress, by joint resolution, to direct the withdrawal of the armed forces of the United States while engaged in combat or to terminate a declaration of national emergency.[22]

Scowcroft, President Bush, and other high-level officials were aware of judicial precedents in the area of national security policy.

Historically the courts avoid foreign policy disputes between the two branches of government, and they did so in this case, judging it to be too political. When Bush was challenged by certain members of Congress in federal district court in December 1990, the judge first noted that it was premature to seek an injunction restraining the commander in chief and, furthermore, that any resolution supporting presidential actions would require a majority vote in Congress. That ruling had the effect of weakening opposition on the basis of the War Powers Resolution.[23] We may assume that the Bush team of advisors also was aware of the position taken by Chief Justice William Rehnquist when he was assistant attorney general during the Nixon administration and defended Nixon's bombing of

Cambodia in 1970.[24] Finally, the UN resolutions in support of allied actions further bolstered Bush's legal position vis-à-vis Congress.

During the Gulf crisis, George Bush intimately controlled the *decision-making* process from the Oval Office. Bush's strong control was evident even as the crisis began to unfold in the summer of 1990. One of the well-recognized factors in the decision-making process was Bush's personalization of the war. His individual feelings against Saddam Hussein were quite visible throughout the months leading to the invasion, so much that even his closest advisors were at times amazed at the president's moral personalization and the extent to which it directed decision making. Bush appeared to many to be doing what he could to shed his "wimp" image,[25] yet although he clearly exhibited personal animosity for Hussein, he seemed to be able to keep his equilibrium, put the events in the Gulf within his worldview of a "new world order," and remain calm. Although Bush was a pragmatist, here it appeared to be a matter of "black and white, good versus evil."[26]

President Bush remained steadfast to a hard-line position and kept his promise regarding the U.S. role, even with respect to the setting of deadlines given to Iraq.[27] It was evident that Bush was the most hawkish member of his inner circle, which included Brent Scowcroft, Secretary of State James Baker, Joint Chief of Staff chairman General Colin Powell, and Defense Secretary Richard Cheney.[28] The decision to humiliate Hussein politically and push for a military rout of the Iraqi troops was equally important in Bush's calculus. He was successful regarding the latter because of the massive military buildup, but was less successful in achieving his first objective: Saddam Hussein still remains in power.[29]

Once Congress gave Bush its support, the decision-making group was narrowed to Bush, Powell, and Cheney, and Secretary of State Baker was relegated to making diplomatic overtures in the Middle East and to gathering support from Western European allies. In addition, Scowcroft and Robert M. Gates moved from the periphery of the decision-making process to the center. They were the ones who filled Baker's peacetime role as Bush's key advisors during the war.[30] Scowcroft had advocated military action from the outset of the crisis.[31]

The decision-making group surrounding the president was marked by two characteristics: first was its considerable loyalty to the president; and second was its similarity to a closed system with all the elements of group think. As one analyst noted, "Bush wants twins around him and that can be dangerous."[32] No devil's advocate against the use of force appeared, except Secretary of State Baker who promoted diplomatic options more than the other advisors did, but in the end, Baker too deferred to his close friend the president. Carter's former national security advisor, Zbigniew Brzezinski, suggested of the Bush situation that the decision-making was too narrow and that presidents need "alternate strategic perspectives" including "an in-house dissident." His concern about the limited group focused on the "situation in which views are reinforced rather than examined," as well as the failure to discuss openly the really important decisions.[33]

The inner circle unquestionably provided most of the *expertise* to the president. Secretary Baker and Chief of Staff John Sununu tested the political waters for a more moderate approach in early November.[34] Cheney and Powell were sent to the Middle East to assess the readiness of the American and allied effort. In these ways the president was supplied with information from personal advisors in whom he bestowed considerable confidence, instead of the normal intelligence sources available to the commander in chief. The use of personal emissaries allowed Bush to develop his own timetable for the escalation of hostilities without the distraction from competing bureaucracies, a point overlooked by many political analysts.

Once the timetable for military action was put into effect, Cheney, Powell, and the U.S. commanders in the Gulf were left to operate as they saw fit. Once Bush committed American and allied forces, the operation was depoliticized and delegated to the military. Bush found himself in a situation to determine the terms for peace in the Middle East at the same time he was preparing for war. Total withdrawal from Kuwait was demanded, thereby linking the presidential role as commander in chief with the follow-up role of chief diplomat. So the decision-making process became a package that included Bush's desire to humiliate Saddam Hussein.[35] The issue of the "liberation of Kuwait" was not, in Bush's opinion or that of his closest advisors, a legislative question. Thus Congress, once it gave approval through its vote of January 12, 1991, was excluded from the military phase of the decision-making process.

President Bush also was able to secure political backing as well as financial aid from other countries and international political agencies. Over $50 billion in aid for the war effort was obtained from foreign governments, enabling him to act more decisively rather than have to lobby Congress for vast sums of money.[36] Even a sometimes unreliable ally, President François Mitterand of France, committed troops and aircraft to the war and voiced support for Bush's agenda, albeit his own.[37] Soviet president Mikhail Gorbachev supported Bush through the UN Security Council resolutions even when Bush rebuked a Soviet peace proposal before the start of the ground phase of the war in late February.[38] Bush used Secretary of State Jim Baker to line up foreign support through trade agreements and loans, illustrating his use of presidential powers unavailable to other branches of government.[39] With such extensive backing from traditional allies and leaders in the Communist bloc, Bush was not only U.S. commander in chief but the de facto commander in chief of the combined international force in the allied Gulf effort.[40]

Mobilization of public opinion during times of military crisis has always been a valuable *public input*, and President Bush maximized public support for his role as commander in chief throughout the Gulf crisis. The nation went to the war supporting the president, despite the fact that Americans did not necessarily expect a short war and still had concerned recollections of Vietnam.[41] Bush made two convincing arguments to the American public: first, he maintained that aggression against a friendly nation could not be tolerated; second, he downplayed narrow strategic concerns such as Middle East oil. Bush's support among Americans rose in August when the crisis started, but then fell by November and through the year-end holiday period as many people began to ponder the consequences of a prolonged war (Figure 14-1). By early January 1991 public opinion was divided over the issue, with 46 percent supporting military action and 47 percent favoring further diplomatic and economic actions.[42]

One day after the start of the war on January 16, 1991, Bush's approval rating increased to an all-time high of 89 percent—above the previous high of President Kennedy's 83 percent approval after the unsuccessful Bay of Pigs military operation in 1961.[43] The 89 percent level of support provided Bush with political leverage to convert any doubters in Congress into supporters and made it very difficult for the Democratic majority to second-guess the objectives and strategy of the commander in chief.

There were pockets of opposition to the war, however, from remnants of the anti-Vietnam movement. But opponents of the war were a distinct minority, weakly organized and, in fact, never openly acknowledged by the White House, even though protesters literally beat drums across the street. Even later, when George Bush tried to come from behind in the 1992 campaign, little if any criticism of his handling of the Gulf War was echoed by the Democrats or Bill Clinton. Victory in the Persian Gulf War was, indeed, the high-water mark of the Bush administration.[44]

The *expertise* Bush exhibited as commander in chief finds its roots in the military establishment. The president did not rush the war once the timetable was established but, instead, relied on the input of his inner circle. He waited for the military to implement its logistics and allowed military expertise to prevail over political and public pressure. The technical

Figure 14–1. Percentage of the American Public in Support of Bush's Handling of the Gulf Crisis, August 1990 to January 1991

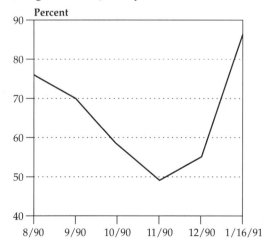

Sources: Compiled from the *New York Times*/CBS Poll, Gallup for *Newsweek*, and ABC/*Washington Post* Poll.

sophistication of the American weapons systems proved vastly superior to those of the Iraqi forces, especially the Patriot anti-missile missile, even though the value of the Patriot has been scrutinized since its success in a number of investigations.[45] At the time, however, the apparent success of American military hardware was exploited by White House public relations as evidence of the ability of President Bush to act effectively, especially in his call for a continuation of the air war before the commitment of ground forces. Although this no doubt was a military-initiated decision, it was used by Bush and his staff to demonstrate that the president was in charge. For example, while commending the expert advice from Secretary Cheney and General Powell, Bush, in announcing the decision to continue an air war, noted that in the next phase, the commitment of ground troops, it would be a decision "I will make . . . because that is a decision for the President of the United States."[46]

Bush's role was complemented by the previous experiences in Vietnam of Chairman Powell and General H. Norman Schwarzkopf, the field commander in the Gulf. Schwarzkopf's knowledge of the Middle East also enhanced the president's expertise. These two military leaders, along with their staffs, had learned from their earlier experiences that secrecy was the key to developing an effective battle plan, especially where the press was concerned. Their suggestion to the media that a naval invasion would spearhead the war against Iraq—when no such thing was contemplated—shows how information can be used for purposes of manipulation, which, in this instance, strengthened the allied military strategy against Iraq. These veterans of the Vietnam War had seen the failure of gradualism in conducting a modern war, and therefore they were determined to mount a modern blitzkrieg against Saddam Hussein. Because Iraq had one of the largest armies in the world, the advice from General Powell and the military establishment was "If you do it, do it real and do it right."[47]

Bush, as commander in chief, relied on military expertise and was able to shift the question of news coverage restrictions to the military. From the perspective of the media, it was the military that violated the First Amendment freedom of the press, and lawsuits thus followed.[48] The major networks and press correspondents bitterly complained, especially in light of their distrust of the military that was rooted in the misinformation it provided during the Vietnam War, but President Bush and his military advisors held the political advantage.[49] In essence, the Bush administration monopolized information on the war effort so effectively that the president escaped any real criticisms, and the military establishment resisted pressure under the guise of national security.

War is *crisis*, although President Bush was able to exploit the Persian Gulf diplomatic crisis from the early days when there was considerable anxiety among some Americans and the Congress about whether sanctions and diplomatic means should be exhausted before military force was used. Only a week before the allied offensive, 46 percent of those surveyed expressed a preference for giving sanctions more time.[50] The advent of warfare, however, brought about a situation in which Bush enjoyed unified public and political support. The use of force that began on January 16 and ended on February 27—eventuating in a war that lasted a mere one hundred hours—forged such a widespread sense of a military crisis that not only did the public rally around the commander in chief but now Congress shifted its attention from legalistic questions about war powers to a desire to receive its share of the recognition as a supporter of Americans fighting abroad and a partner in the war effort.

Although in some quarters it has been suggested that the crisis was misread and diplomatic miscues took place,[51] President Bush was able to define the issues on his terms and rally the nation behind his leadership. Once the war actually began, arguably he was more effective than he was during the planning stages of the offensive. During the Gulf crisis Bush exercised power in such a way that the initial war plans were never altered, despite distracting proposals coming from Baghdad and Moscow.[52] He was, by one description, wearing Caesar's purple mantle, in reference to a cloak symbolic of supreme powers. During the Persian Gulf War, Bush, perhaps like no other president since Franklin Roosevelt during the Second World War, was able to use military force to generate the needed public and political support both within and outside the United States and to monopolize expertise and information. Throughout the crisis, President Bush held the position that there would be no long-term commitment of American troops, brushing aside the long shadows of the Vietnam era. The final result—a 43-day war, a 100-hour ground assault, and the destruction of Iraq's army—was one of the major one-sided victories in military history.[53]

NOTES

1. "The Reward of Leadership," *Newsweek* (March 11, 1991), p. 30.
2. "Men of the Year," *Time* (Jan. 7, 1991).
3. Jean Edward Smith, *George Bush's War* (New York: Henry Holt, 1992), pp. 31–32.
4. Ibid., 67.
5. Maureen Dowd, "Americans More Wary of Gulf Policy, Poll Finds," *New York Times* (Nov. 20, 1990), p. A8.
6. Michael Oreskes, "A Debate Unfolds Whether the U.S. Should Go to War," *New York Times* (Nov. 12, 1990), pp. A1, A8.
7. Michael R. Gordon, "U.S. Decides to Add as Many as 100,000 to Its Gulf Forces," *New York Times* (Oct. 26, 1990), pp. A1, A6.
8. Maureen Dowd, "Bush Intensifies a War of Words against the Iraqis," *New York Times* (Nov. 11, 1990), pp. A1, A6.
9. Elaine Sciolino, "Gore Says Bush's Efforts to Befriend Iraqi Leader Led to Gulf War," *New York Times* (Sept. 30, 1992), p. A11.
10. John T. Rourke and Russell Farnen, "War, Presidents, and the Constitution," *Political Studies Quarterly* 18 (1988), p. 3.
11. Maureen Dowd, "President Seems to Blunt Calls for Gulf Session," *New York Times* (Nov. 15, 1990), pp. A1, A8.
12. Gordon, "U.S. Decides to Add as Many as 100,000 to Its Gulf Forces," pp. A1, A6; Dowd, "Bush Intensifies a War of Words, pp. A1, A6.
13. Smith, *George Bush's War*, p. 4.
14. Bob Woodward, *The Commanders* (New York: Simon & Schuster, 1991), p. 341.
15. Michael Oreskes, "A Debate Unfolds Whether the U.S. Should Go to War," pp. A1,

A8; Michael R. Gordon, "Nunn Assailing a 'Rush' to War, Criticizes Troop Rotation Decision," *New York Times* (Nov. 12, 1990), p. A9; James David Barber, "Empire of the Son," *The Washington Monthly* (October 1991), p. 27.

16. Neil A. Lewis, "Sorting Out Legal War Concerning Real War," *New York Times* (Nov. 15, 1990), p. A8.

17. Ibid.

18. Barber, "Empire of the Son," p. 27.

19. United States Congress, "Text of Congressional Resolution on the Gulf," *New York Times* (Jan. 14, 1991), p. A11.

20. Larry Berman and Bruce W. Jentleson, "Bush and the Post-Cold War World: New Challenges for American Leadership," in Colin Campbell and Bert A. Rockman, eds., *The Bush Presidency: First Appraisals* (Chatham, NJ: Chatham House, 1991), p. 106.

21. Lewis, "Sorting Out Legal War Concerning Real War," p. A8.

22. R. Gordon Hoxie et al., *The Presidency and National Security Policy*. Center for the Study of the Presidency, Proceedings 5(1), p. 27.

23. Neil A. Lewis, "Lawmakers Lose War Powers Suit," *New York Times* (Dec. 14, 1990), p. A9.

24. See William H. Rehnquist, "The Constitutional Issues—Administration Positions," *New York University Law Review* (June 1970), pp. 628–639.

25. Smith, *George Bush's War*, pp. 233–234.

26. Berman and Jentleson, "Bush and the Post-Cold War World," p. 98.

27. Nelson, "Bush Wagering Personal War, Associates Reveal," pp. A1, A20, A26.

28. Charles W. Kegley, "The Bush Administration and the Future of American Foreign Policy: Pragmatism, or Procrastination?", *Presidential Studies Quarterly* 19 (1989), p. 727.

29. Thomas L. Friedman, "For Bush, Half a Loaf," *New York Times* (Feb. 20, 1991), p. A1; George D. Moffett, III, "Bush Claim to Foreign-Policy Skills Doubted," *Christian Science Monitor*, (Aug. 17, 1992), p. 8.

30. Andrew Rosenthal, "Scowcroft and Gates: A Team Rivals Baker," *New York Times* (Feb. 21, 1991), p. A6.

31. Smith, *George Bush's War*, pp. 68–73.

32. Cited in Berman and Jentleson, "Bush and the Post–Cold War World," p. 103.

33. R.W. Apple, Jr., "Bush Told to Heed Voices of Dissent," *New York Times* (Dec. 7, 1990), p. A10.

34. Thomas L. Friedman, "Baker Seen as a Balance to Bush on Crisis in Gulf," *New York Times* (Nov. 3, 1990), pp. A1, A4; Maureen Dowd, "Bush Intensifies a War of Words against the Iraqis," pp. A1, A6.

35. Thomas L. Friedman, "The Rout Bush Wants," *New York Times* (Feb. 27, 1991), pp. A1, A9.

36. David E. Rosenbaum, "U.S. Has Received $50 Billion in Pledges for War," *New York Times* (Feb. 11, 1991), p. A7.

37. Alan Riding, "Mitterand Calls Iraqi's Choice Fatal," *New York Times* (Feb. 25, 1991), p. A16.

38. Daniel Sneider, "Moscow Regrets Fighting, but Stands with Coalition," *Christian Science Monitor* (Feb. 25, 1991), p. 3.

39. Barber, "Empire of the Son," p. 28.

40. George D. Moffett, III, "Bush Opening of Ground War Ensures a Weakened Saddam," *Christian Science Monitor* (Feb. 25, 1991), p. 1.

41. Andrew Rosenthal, "Americans Don't Expect Short War," *New York Times* (Feb. 15, 1991), pp. A1, A7.

42. *New York Times/CBS News Poll*, "Views on the Gulf," *New York Times* (Jan. 9, 1991), p. A6.

43. Michael R. Kagay, "Approval of Bush Soars," *New York Times* (Jan. 19, 1991), p. A7.

44. George D. Moffett, III, "Bush's Tough Choices in Facing Down Saddam," *Christian Science Monitor* (July 27, 1992), pp. 1, 4.

45. George Lardner, Jr., "Did the Patriot Missile Obey the Hippocratic Oath?," *Washington Post National Weekly Edition* (April 20–26, 1992), p. 34; Ben Sherwood, "The Bulls-Eye That Never Happened," *Washington Post National Weekly Edition* (Sept. 28–Oct. 4, 1992), p. 24.

46. Andrew Rosenthal, "President Asserts He Is Putting Off Land-War Decision," *New York Times* (Feb. 12, 1991), pp. A1, A6.

47. Woodward, *The Commanders*, p. 251.

48. R.W. Apple, Jr., "Correspondents Pool System," *New York Times* (Feb. 12, 1991), p. A8; R.W. Apple, Jr., "Pentagon Moves to Widen Reporters Access to Gulf Ground Units," *New York Times* (Feb. 13, 1991), p. A9.

49. R.W. Apple, Jr., "Press and the Military: Old Suspicions," *New York Times* (Feb. 4, 1991), p. A6.

50. Kagay, "Approval of Bush Soars," p. A7.

51. Lamis Andoni, "Iraqi Insider Says Misperception of US 'Partnership' Led to War," *Christian Science Monitor* (Aug. 3, 1992), pp. 1, 4.

52. Marshall Ingwerson, "Next Bush Decision: How Far into Iraq?" *Christian Science Monitor* (Feb. 26, 1991), pp. 1–2.

53. Smith, *George Bush's War*, p. 9.

15

Managing the Economy: The Interplay of Four Presidential Roles

It is said that peace and prosperity are the twin pillars of presidential popularity because Americans would like to enjoy a good economy and international stability in the absence of war. Worldwide events force presidents to deal with foreign policy and presidents may enjoy a degree of discretion in shaping their domestic priorities, but the economy is an ongoing responsibility of the national government. Economic prosperity makes the president's job easy, but recessions pose a challenge to presidential leadership because the public holds him accountable whether or not he has adequate resources to bring about economic recovery.

Because the economy is one constant in the policy agenda of every president, this chapter analyzes presidential leadership and the economy. For the most part, this area of public policy involves four presidential roles. In making and implementing economic policy the president acts mainly as chief executive and legislative leader, but opinion/party leadership is obviously relevant, although the degree to which he can lead public opinion is questionable. Because the U.S. domestic economy today is so intimately related to world trade, international finance, and events abroad that may disrupt the flow of raw materials to America, economic policymaking may require presidential leadership as chief diplomat. However rarely does the commander in chief role become associated with economic policy, although it can happen. One reason behind President Bush's decision to intervene in the Persian Gulf War was the threat posed by Iraq to the flow of crude oil from the Middle East to the United States, even though the president did not publicly justify war-making on these grounds.

RESPONSIBILITY WITHOUT POWER

In the late 1950s Clinton Rossiter, a well-known presidency scholar, observed that the president had undertaken a new responsibility—"manager of prosperity"[1]—which begs the questions of what responsibility is implied by that phrase and what legal authority is available to the president to pursue that grand objective.

Legal authority is power legitimized by the Constitution, statutes, judicial precedents, and customary practice. No constitutional mandate exists for overseeing the economy, and the customary practice—until the Great Depression of the 1930s—was for presidents of both major parties to praise the ideal of balancing the federal budget[2] and to keep presidential hands off the economy. The Supreme Court similarly was a nonplayer in the domain of macroeconomic policy, and high court decisions in the early 1900s even restricted efforts by some states to regulate capitalism. Thus the key to understanding this new responsibility lies with a fundamental change in public expectations and key enactments of the twentieth century including the Federal Reserve Act of 1913, the Budget and Accounting Act of 1921, the Employment Act of 1946, the Congressional Budget and Impoundment Control Act of 1974, and the Full Employment and Balanced Growth Act of 1978.

By coining the phrase "manager of prosperity," Rossiter claimed that the Employment Act of 1946 heralded in a new era in economic policymaking. Section 2 of that act was stated as follows:

> The Congress hereby declares that it is the continuing policy and responsibility of the Federal Government to use all practicable means consistent with its needs and obligations and other essential considerations of national policy, with the assistance and cooperation of industry, agriculture, labor, and State and local governments to coordinate and utilize all its plans, functions, and resources for the purpose of creating and maintaining, in a manner calculated to foster and promote free competitive enterprise and the general welfare, conditions under which there will be afforded useful employment opportunities, including self-employment, for those able, willing, and seeking to work, and to promote maximum employment, production, and purchasing power.

There are, of course, several qualifications in this declaration of public policy. The statute, for one, gives the federal government the management responsibility but not much authority over macroeconomic policy (broad spheres of the national economy such as business investment and consumer spending). The 1946 act, popularly known as the "Full" Employment Act is a misnomer because it dedicates the federal government to a variety of (and sometimes contradictory) economic goals, that is, to promote free competitive enterprise, to establish "conditions" which facilitate "useful employment" for those able, willing, and seeking employment, and to facilitate maximum employment as well as production and purchasing power (meaning stable prices without inflation).

It simply created the Council of Economic Advisors (CEA), a Joint Economic Committee—comprised of both senators and representatives—and requires an *Economic Report of the President* be submitted to Congress each year. The *Economic Report* presents the administration's assessment of the national economy, pinpointing strengths and weaknesses and offering a forecast of economic activity for the coming year; it also signals what kind of macroeconomic policies the administration endorses.

The 1946 law was also a political symbol, suggesting the Great Depression had permanently altered the relationship between the federal government and the national economy. One in four Americans was unemployed during that 1930s economic collapse, and in 1938 a "recession within the depression" occurred. This decade-long experience with high unemployment caused leading economists to develop a stagnation thesis, suggesting that U.S. capitalism may be incapable of generating sufficient jobs for all able-bodied Americans. Thus the economic anxiety that led Congress to enact the 1946 Act was unemployment, not rising prices. Americans' collective memory of the Great Depression served as the backdrop for enacting this new legislation, but for future generations it symbolized new expectations that the national government should pursue economic policies to ensure there would be no repeat of the 1930s.

Even though the nation turned away from strict laissez-faire capitalism—government plays almost no role—to embrace mixed capitalism—government and private enterprise cooperate to achieve economic goals—there were limits to how far Congress would tolerate an activist federal role. For example, the sponsors of the original employment bill would have allowed the federal government to utilize the budget, even deficits, to pump enough money into the economy to guarantee full employment in those years when private investment was inadequate to assure employment opportunities for everyone. But that controversial provision was stripped from the final legislation by a congressional coalition of Republicans and (southern) Democrats who were opposed to transplanting so-called European socialism in America and who feared executive tyranny. Indeed, establishing a three-person Council of Economic Advisors was intended to prevent the president from being influenced by officials inside the executive branch who favored economic planning as well as providing the White House with expert advice from professional economists.

Three decades later, the 1946 legislation was presumably strengthened by the (Humphrey-Hawkins) Full Employment and Balanced Growth Act of 1978, but this enactment was more symbolic than real. Despite its stipulation that a 4 percent unemployment rate and a 3 percent inflation rate be achieved in five years, President Carter delayed those objectives until the mid-1980s. Both have yet to be attained at the same time. The act did require that the Federal Reserve Board testify before Congress about its long-term plans for monetary policy, which is probably the act's most significant development.

If he so desires, the president can set the economic agenda for the Congress because of his constitutional duty to give an annual State of the Union Address and, from time to time, deliver special messages. Most observers judged that Bill Clinton earned a mandate in 1992 to improve the national economy, and in the early weeks of the 103rd Congress he proposed an economic stimulus plan, but it was defeated by Republicans who filibustered in the Senate, arguing it was laden with pork barrel projects and betrayed Clinton's campaign rhetoric to reduce federal deficits. Deficits occur because the federal government spends more than its revenues, and President Clinton subsequently offered a budget that sought to reduce the federal deficit mainly by raising tax revenues (which prompted every Republican in the House and Senate to vote against the plan; in the Senate a tie vote had to be broken by Vice President Gore). Once the GOP gained control of the 104th Congress, Clinton first resisted and then accepted the Republican goal of reaching a balanced budget in seven years. However he abdicated his legislative leadership role by not submitting a realistic budget proposal for fiscal year FY96 or FY97 to attain that seven-year goal. Rather he crusaded against the congressional Republicans for making drastic cuts in popular programs like Medicare.

By countercyclical policy, economists mean the objective of public policy should be to reverse the course of the business cycle—periods of prosperity followed by periods of recession—by restraining the inflation that accompanies prosperity and by preventing downturns from deteriorating into depressions. The overall objective of countercyclical policy, therefore, is to moderate the ups and down of the business cycle, and policymakers try to achieve that objective by manipulating the money supply (monetary policy) as well as taxing and spending (fiscal policy).

Monetary policy is not directly controlled by the White House but by an independent Federal Reserve Board (the "Fed"), although its members are appointed by the president. The Fed was established by the Federal Reserve Act of 1913 to supervise the federal reserve banks located in various regions of the country. The 1913 act never contemplated using monetary policy to correct the business cycle, but in the 1930s the chairman of the Federal Reserve Board was a New Deal appointee who cooperated with Roosevelt's efforts to bring about economic recovery. However today, fiscal policy, rather than monetary policy, has been the preferred approach to manipulating the macroeconomy, which means the federal budget can be used to achieve economic objectives in addition to simply paying government's bills and providing federal services.

The budgeting process is complex (see chapter 16), and the use of fiscal policy to achieve economic objectives, therefore, depends on how much the budgetary authority is delegated by Congress to the president. Two landmark statutes are particularly relevant. The 1921 Budget and Accounting Act authorized the president to formulate a complete federal budget for submission to Congress at the beginning of each calendar year. The Congressional Budget and Impoundment Control Act of 1974 restored budgetary prerogatives to Congress by adding a congressional budget process that begins once the executive budget has arrived on Capitol Hill.

The Republican-controlled 104th Congress crafted a statute designed to give the president, beginning in 1997, authority to disapprove single appropriations accounts in spending bills. Congress could restore those cuts by passing new legislation, which the president presumably would veto, thereby requiring an override by a two-thirds vote in the House and Senate for final passage. In effect, this procedure puts the burden on Congress to prevent line-item vetoes by having to rally supermajorities in order to disallow a presidential rejection of spending for specific purposes.

The president also could choose to veto entire appropriations bills, as Gerald Ford did during 1976 when he faced reelection. Ford had more vetoes relative to his time in office than recent presidents, and he used that power in an unsuccessful effort to stop excessive spending by the Democratic-controlled Congress. But observers generally agree that the veto is more a defensive than offensive weapon because it means the president has almost no other political leverage over the Congress. A veto *threat* is a more effective strategy to persuade Congress to shape legislation more to the president's liking. Ronald Reagan used this leverage against the Democrats in the House when his party held the majority in the Senate from 1981 to 1986.

In summary, little formal authority is available to the president to implement the 1946 Employment Act or the more ambitious "Humphrey-Hawkins" Law of 1978. Presidents formulate a federal budget, present their economic program to Congress, and threaten to veto or actually veto bills they deem damaging to the nation's economic well-being. As of 1997 a president has use of a statutory item veto to cut pork barrel projects from the federal budget.

ECONOMIC SUB-PRESIDENCY PLUS

Although the federal government has been given the responsibility to safeguard the nation's economic well-being, this duty has *not* been delegated to the president alone. He must collaborate with Congress and many other decision-makers who shape the course of America's economic future. Here we can conceptualize four circles moving outward from the president who is in the center. Closest to him in the first circle are the White House staffers including the CEA chairman and the OMB director who along with the secretary of the treasury comprise the troika that dominates economic policy within the executive branch. The second circle represents whatever specialized agencies may be created to focus on particular economic problems, such as Clinton's National Economic Council or the Council on Wage and Price Stability under President Carter, as well as those cabinet departments (Labor, Commerce, Agriculture) that focus on microeconomic policies affecting the interests of their clientele groups (respectively, labor, business, and farmers). As chief executive, the president appoints all these advisors and organizes their relationships within the Executive Office of the President.

In the third circle stands Congress, which controls the power over the purse. In the fourth circle, the most removed from direct presidential control, is the Federal Reserve Board. Although members of the Fed are appointed by the chief executive, they serve fourteen-year staggered terms, which means that normally the majority would not be appointed to office by the sitting president. When the Fed chairman participates in economic consultations with the OMB director, CEA chairman, and secretary of the treasury, this informal group is known as the quadriad. The Supreme Court is not usually an economic decision-maker, although it holds the potential to be crucially important whenever a law aimed at the economy is declared unconstitutional.

Early in this century the high court disallowed state child and women's labor laws as well as minimum wage statutes; even during the calamity of the Great Depression, the justices struck down FDR's bold effort to resurrect prosperity. A crucial section of the National Industrial Recovery Act of 1933 was held to be unconstitutional in *Schechter Poultry Corp. v. United States* (1935) on the grounds of excessive delegation of legislative authority to the president; other aspects of the law were invalidated in *Panama Refining Co. v. Ryan* (1935). The Agricultural Adjustment Act of 1933 was struck down one year later in *United States v. Butler* (1936). By the next year, however, the Supreme Court had reversed itself (one pivotal justice began voting to support FDR), paving the way for the "Roosevelt Revolution"—aggressive federal regulation of the private economy, equipping the Congress with substantial authority to regulate economic activities and redistribute wealth.

Rarely do the justices block congressional or presidential efforts to manage the economy, although exceptions still occur. Abuses by President Nixon of his impoundment authority was curbed by the high court in *Train v. City of New York* (1975) and, more recently, in *Bowsher v. Synar* (1986) in which the Supreme Court nullified part of the original (1985) Gramm-Rudman-Hollings law because it gave a deficit-reduction role to the comptroller general (the watchdog of Congress). Congress had to revise that law in 1987, delegating authority entirely to the OMB to order those automatic spending cuts (see chapter 16).

MAKING ECONOMIC POLICY

Formulating domestic policy involves a fluid decision-making arena because policy entrepreneurs can surface anywhere to advocate programmatic initiatives. Obviously members of Congress have political incentives to advocate new domestic programs. For years, before it became fashionable, Senator Edward Kennedy (D–Mass.) championed universal health care coverage. Interest group lobbyists are continually making appeals to Congress or the White House to expand programs or create new ones. Although a domestic policy staff in the White House exists, those aides do not necessarily monopolize the domestic policy agenda because departmental secretaries or agency heads may themselves become policy advocates rather than silent administrators.

In other words, domestic policymaking is not highly structured like foreign policy is, which is dominated by the NSC, the national security advisor, the secretaries of state and defense, and White House aides. Macro-economic policymaking is more analogous to national security policy-making, because the direction of countercyclical policy is largely formu-lated by decision-makers within the presidential orbit. It was Kennedy's CEA chairman, Walter Heller, who originally advocated an income tax cut to stimulate economic growth, just as CEA chairman Gardner Ackley tried (unsuccessfully) to persuade President Johnson to impose an income tax surcharge to head off inflationary pressures from massive federal spend-ing on the Vietnam War and the Great Society.

An unusual case of economic policy innovation was the decision by President Nixon to fight inflation by imposing the first peacetime use of wage and price controls. Nixon's CEA was opposed to that policy, but Nixon was persuaded by his newly appointed treasury secretary, former governor (D–Tex.) John Connally, declaring that existing anti-inflation policies were inadequate and that wage-price controls were needed.

Macroeconomic policymaking requires a degree of coordination among agencies and consensus on goals that occur more often by chance than by design.[3] Competition among White House advisors results from personal rivalries, the jurisdictional claims of their agencies, and legiti-mate disagreements over macroeconomic policy. Each participant in eco-nomic policy has its own mindset and priorities. The Department of the Treasury worries about revenues because it has the responsibility of fund-ing the national debt. Generally the CEA and its chair are more liberal than the treasury secretary and would favor a more aggressive policy to stim-ulate economic growth.

Yet across administrations are real differences in how the CEA pur-sues its macroeconomic objectives depending on whether members work for a Republican or a Democrat. Interviews with CEA chairmen led two political scientists to conclude the following:

> Except for Truman, the Democrats tried too hard to fine-tune remedies for in-flation. Understandably they wanted the smallest possible recession. As a re-sult, they opted for the least restraint that their models told them would slow down the economy. . . . The Republicans, on the other hand, because they seem to abhor inflation more and unemployment somewhat less, tended to adopt stabilization strategies which, if anything, erred on the side of overkill. Under all three Republican administrations [Eisenhower, Nixon, Ford], they tended to hit the economy hard with restraint and then bring the patient back to life with stimulus if that was needed, as it always was.[4]

Policy disagreements between the secretary of the treasury and the chair of the Council of Economic Advisors are not uncommon. Under President Kennedy, for example, CEA chair Walter Heller urged JFK that an immediate tax cut was needed to prevent an oncoming recession, but his advice to Kennedy was countered by Treasury Secretary Douglas Dil-lon, who instead favored tax reforms. In this high-level policy debate Kennedy initially sided with Dillon and only after Heller made his case to Congress and through the media did President Kennedy finally agree that cuts in individual and corporate income taxes were warranted.

Unlike Treasury or the CEA, the OMB has the responsibility of formulating the executive budget every year and thus is most concerned about estimating the rate of spending, whereas the Fed historically has focused mainly on price stability and thereby applies monetary brakes to prevent inflation. The Fed was meant to be independent of both the executive and legislative branches of government[5] and, although monetary policy is roughly compatible with fiscal policy, there have been instances when Fed policy clashed with the short-term macroeconomic objectives of the popular branches. President Kennedy was worried that Fed chairman William McChesney Martin might raise interest rates just at the time when the president was ready to propose tax cuts, fearing that restricting money supply would contradict lowering taxes in order to stimulate business investment and household consumption. But Martin was concerned about inflationary pressures, whereas Kennedy was troubled with slowed economic growth. Indeed, the Federal Reserve Board has frequently been made the scapegoat whenever the economy turned sour. The Congress blamed the Fed for economic slowdowns in 1966–1967, 1969–1970, and 1974–1975, and the Reagan administration resorted to Fed bashing during the 1982 recession.

Although Reagan staffers may have complained at the time, in retrospect knowledgeable observers credit Paul Volcker—whom President Carter appointed Fed chairman—for orchestrating the cold turkey approach of keeping the money supply tight during the 1981–1982 recession and driving up unemployment (which reached 10 percent one month, a post-Depression high) in order to undermine the inflationary spiral that had plagued the country since the 1970s. The inflation rate peaked at 13.5 percent in 1980 but fell to 3.2 percent by 1983; the country has since experienced relatively low and stable rates of prices increases (well under 5 percent into the mid-1990s).

STRUCTURAL DEFICITS AND BALANCED BUDGETS

For their part, Congress and presidents make budgets that seem more attuned to electoral needs—cutting taxes or raising expenditures—than to the requirements of modern economic policy. Cutting taxes and raising expenditures may be the proper budgetary response when faced with recession but not when inflationary pressures threaten the economy. When rising prices become excessive, the appropriate budgeting response would be to curb governmental expenditures and raise taxes, but those options are politically unappealing—especially during election years—which is why many economists believe fiscal policy has been neutralized with respect to the problem of inflation. Only the Federal Reserve Board can restrict the money supply and raise interest rates as anti-inflation policies without having to worry about disgruntled voters.

In fact, the political calculations that encourage tax cuts and expenditure increases is made worse by a policy bias that has reduced congressional budgetary discretion in the modern era. Between 45 and 50 percent of federal expenditures are entitlements that cannot be cut without statutory amendments. The best known example are Social Security pensions. People who qualify are legally entitled to receive those pensions, and Congress cannot refuse to appropriate those funds; moreover, Social Security pensions are increased along with the rate of inflation (such COLAs are "cost-of-living adjustments"). When other entitlements such as veterans' benefits, Medicare, and federal employee and military pensions are added up as well as the interest on the national debt and the relatively fixed cost of paying the salaries of three million federal employees, roughly three-fourths of the federal budget is uncontrollable in the short term, meaning Congress cannot make substantial reductions in its size.

There has been increased momentum in recent years to attach a balanced budget amendment to the Constitution, even though most economists are opposed to it. An amendment garnered the necessary two-thirds vote in the House but fell two votes short in the Senate during the 104th Congress. Early indications were that the 105th Congress would have no trouble passing a constitutional amendment because the Republicans increased their margin in the Senate to 55 to 45. But President Clinton remained opposed as did the Democratic leadership of Congress, so prospects of an early vote were dim. What has caused the Republicans, some Democrats, conservatives, and a few economists to embrace the balanced budget amendment is the perpetual failure of the federal government to balance its budget even during periods of prosperity.

Most economists have defended unbalanced budgets and deficit spending during recessionary periods because the added government expenditures would help ease the nation back to prosperity, but those cyclical deficits would presumably become surpluses after economic recovery began, leading economists to argue that yearly balanced budgets were less important than balancing budgets over the course of a business cycle. But the last balanced budget was in 1969 and today the deficit is a structural component of the federal budget, meaning deficits are routine even during times of economic prosperity simply because the federal government spends more money than it receives as revenues.

One concern is that these structural deficits would balloon ever larger as the cyclical deficit is added if the nation slips into an economic downturn. The wide but shallow recession under President Bush pushed the federal deficit to over $300 billion and, at that level, not much room was left for policymakers to cut taxes and increase spending as countercyclical policies. In a sense, therefore, high structural deficits have straightjacketed the ability to utilize fiscal policy, yet the same worries generate opposition to a balanced budget amendment from economists, Clinton's treasury secretary Robert Rubin, and Democrats.

The balanced budget amendment now being considered would require an annual balanced budget unless three-fifths of the House and Senate vote to unbalance it. Deficits could be allowed during wartime and economic recessions, but the opponents fear that a recalcitrant minority of representatives and senators could prevent the budget from being utilized as a countercyclical policy during hard economic times. A purely political ploy by some Democrats in Congress is that they would vote for a balanced budget if Social Security was not included in those calculations. However, because the Social Security Trust Fund has been utilized to fund the national debt, and thus reduce the actual size of the annual budget deficit, to exclude Social Security from estimating the size of the deficit would serve to increase markedly the existing structural deficit, making it virtually impossible to ever balance the budget without deep spending cuts or higher taxes.

POLICY LAGS

The problems of policy coordination and outright political conflicts among economic decision-makers explain why internal lags affect macroeconomic policymaking. The first internal lag is a *recognition* lag from the time an economic problem begins until decision-makers acknowledge the need for corrective action. The Truman administration was so preoccupied with inflation that the 1949 recession was diagnosed only after it had begun, and the nation slipped into a recession just as newly elected Dwight D. Eisenhower was reorganizing his Council of Economic Advisors. When President Kennedy recommended an income tax cut in early 1963 to head off a recession, this closing of the recognition gap was highly unusual. What was especially perplexing to President Bush, who was facing an uphill battle for reelection in 1992, was that the economic forecasters were unable to chronicle the exact turning point when the economy shifted from its recessionary phase to a renewed expansion. It was not until December 22, 1992 (after Bush lost the election to Clinton) that the National Bureau of Economic Research (NBER) announced that the recession had hit bottom (the "trough" of the business cycle) in March 1991.

The second internal lag is the policy *formulation* lag—the period of time necessary to prepare a corrective policy response. Monetary policy has shorter internal lags than fiscal policy because the Fed can act unilaterally; changes in taxes and spending, however, often require extensive negotiations to cultivate majority support in the House and the Senate. Although President Kennedy recommended a tax cut to head off an anticipated recession, it took Congress fourteen months to enact that measure— passed after Kennedy's death, when Lyndon Johnson assumed the presidency. Although it was becoming obvious to most economists that Johnson's guns and butter policies of increased domestic spending for his Great Society and escalating defense expenditures for the Vietnam War had fueled inflationary pressures in the economy, ten months passed before Johnson's income tax surcharge was approved by Congress. Indeed, research shows that discretionary countercyclical policy during the recessions of 1948–1949, 1953–1954, 1957–1958, and 1960–1961 had its greatest economic impact *after* the economic recoveries had already begun.[6]

Although fiscal policy hastened the economic recoveries, the length of those recessions from peaks to troughs was largely unaffected by governmental policy.

Decision-makers also must reckon with three external lags as policies spread throughout the American economy. Monetary policy generally has longer external lags than fiscal policy because the economic impacts from tax and expenditure changes are more immediate. The first external lag, which may be called a policy *implementation* lag, is the time involved in carrying out any corrective action. Regulations must be issued to federal agencies, notices sent to businesses or households, and compliance procedures established, after which there is a second external lag: the policy *effectiveness* lag. This is the period that elapses before the effects of a corrective policy are manifested. Only after people begin to pay more taxes, for example, do they understand that taxes are higher and they must make adjustments in their consumption or savings patterns.

The third external lag is most long term: the *reversal* lag. Given the time involved in the previous four lags, it is very likely that the effects of a policy designed to correct a specific economic problem will continue into the next phase of the business cycle and thus exacerbate the next round of economic problems. For example, a countercyclical policy to stimulate the economy during a recession may not take hold until the recovery phase, at which time the resulting increased aggregate demand works to intensify future inflationary pressures.

In this kind of scenario, future decision-makers would have to consider more drastic actions to bring down the high inflation caused by present-day macroeconomic policies. The situation after 1968 illustrates this dilemma. Because President Johnson's income tax surcharge was not large enough to curb inflationary pressures resulting from massive federal spending for the Vietnam War and the Great Society domestic programs, inflation continued unabated and Nixon had to resort to wage-price controls.

External lags are inevitable as macroeconomic policy works its way through America's competitive, private, and capitalistic economy. The macroeconomy is so enormous, diversified, and interdependent that decisions on whether to consume or save and whether to expand or cut back production are made by millions of households and thousands of businesses in the United States and worldwide. Moreover, from 8 to 10 percent of the U.S. gross national product (GNP) is generated by state and local governments whose budgetary decisions may not coincide with the macroeconomic goals of the national government. Budgets of fifty states and more than eighty thousand localities actually may exert a procyclical effect insofar as state constitutions may require balanced budgets or impose debt limits on school districts and municipalities.

The difficulties in taking into account the external lags are multiplied as a national economy becomes intertwined with international economic markets and decision-makers on a global scale. More and more the domestic economy is affected by the decisions of multinational corporations, bankers around the world, foreign governments, and the workings of the international financial markets. Wars, natural disasters, revolutions, population changes, and technological innovation hold profound economic consequences, and their impact on the United States is summarized by U.S. international economic accounts.

As chief diplomat, Presidents Johnson, Nixon, Reagan, and Clinton had to contend with serious imbalances in U.S. economic relationships abroad. President Clinton charged in the 1992 campaign that the Bush administration had not been forceful enough in trying to open Japanese markets to American business, and in mid-1994 (another election year) the Clinton administration and China were hinting at a full-blown trade war, with each country poised to impose new duties on each other's exported goods.

The share of American GNP depending on exports has doubled over the past five decades, so the United States is tied more closely than ever to world economic conditions. Because of the trade imbalance with Japan, military forces overseas, and other capital outflows, the United States is now the largest debtor nation, representing a dramatic turn-around since World War II. The odds are worse today—compared to fifty years ago—that Bush or Clinton could dictate terms to European and Japanese governments to reduce their exports while adding to their purchases of U.S. government securities. Richard Rose argues that presidential leadership in the postmodern era means the White House will have to negotiate with other world leaders one on one as equals because unified Germany and Japan are now economic superpowers.[7] At base, presidents cannot impose solutions but must achieve their economic goals by influencing the self-serving economic choices that private consumers and businesses and autonomous foreign governments make.

WHOSE ECONOMIC WISDOM?

Does the president have the requisite knowledge to achieve macroeconomic goals? John F. Kennedy was interested in economics and eager to learn from his economic advisors, but even he was not an expert in the field. As chief executive, the president makes the key appointments to the Office of Management and Budget, the Council of Economic Advisers, and the cabinet including the very influential secretary of the treasury. Those appointees are the conduit by which economic advice reaches the White House.

Before the 1974 budgetary reforms were enacted, the president overwhelmed Congress with revenue estimates, projections of economic activity, and details of budget expenditures. The Congressional Budget Office was created in 1974 to provide Congress with an independent source of data about the economy and the budget to counter the OMB. But this expertise means little when Congress refuses to follow its advice. Research indicates that the CBO has been far more accurate than the OMB in its predictions of future economic activity.[8] Yet, even though the CBO had forecasted correctly that the 1981 income tax cut would lead to excessive deficits, Congress seemed eager to be persuaded by the optimistic predictions of OMB director David Stockman.

Government studies, the federal budget, and the *Economic Report of the President* can be scrutinized by experts beyond the reach of the White House including economists associated with banks, financial institutions, and universities, who are in possession of their own methods of tracking the economy. One illustration is the widely publicized consumer confidence measure devised by the University of Michigan to survey people about how they feel regarding their economic future. The economics profession is an invaluable source of technical knowledge about macroeconomic policy. Indeed, the Council of Economic Advisors has been the preserve of academic economists. One advantage to this inside-outside mode of recruitment is that the CEA is beholden to no clientele groups or bureaucratic interests when assessing economic problems and policies.

CHANGING ECONOMIC THEORY

Although economists may agree on economic principles, they can and do disagree about economic policy. Because presidents are not experts, they must rely on professional economists and financiers for guidance, and within any group of professionals there will be enough variability in viewpoints for a president to choose between liberals and conservatives or Republicans and Democrats, or ideological shades in between.

The first chairman of the CEA, Edwin Nourse, was a highly respected professional who had been president of the American Economic Association, but his brand of economic advice was not to President Truman's liking. As a nonpartisan who was not sympathetic to the New Deal, Nourse saw his role as advising Truman on various economic alternatives and their consequences rather than endorsing any specific policy. The story is told that, after reading a report in which Nourse pondered the alternatives "on the one hand" and "on the other hand," President Truman expressed an anguished cry for a one-armed economist."[9] When Nourse resigned in 1949, Truman elevated CEA member Leon H. Keyserling (who was a fervent New Dealer) to be the CEA chairman, and his policy preferences were more in line with Truman's.

Today, economics is probably the most scientific of the social sciences (certainly more so than political science), yet the state of economic knowledge is not analogous to the hard sciences or to medicine. Moreover, state-of-the-art economics constantly changes as older theories are abandoned or refined to accommodate new economic realities and unanticipated economic problems, so what might be economic orthodoxy to one generation of economists may be economic heresy to the next generation. Over the course of recent economic history we can identify four schools of thought that have had a profound impact on macroeconomic policymaking (there are other viewpoints, for example, those who subscribe to a neo-Marxian perspective, but neo-Marxists are a distinct minority among academics and they have not had a decisive impact on any recent administration).

Classical economics dates back to the laissez-faire arguments of Adam Smith in the eighteenth century but remains a very influential force.[10] Keynesian economics began in the 1930s and came to dominate the economics profession during the 1960s. Then monetarism emerged in the mid-1960s as the leading intellectual challenge to Keynesian economics, to be followed in the early 1980s by so-called supply-side economics.

It was not so long ago that governmental involvement in the economy was viewed with suspicion. Since the late eighteenth century, thinkers who subscribed to laissez-faire or classical economics believed that national prosperity was linked to the forces of supply and demand operating within a competitive marketplace limiting the state to a role of umpire. The idea that government should—and could—utilize fiscal policy (taxes and spending) and monetary policy (money supply and interest rates) to moderate the ups and downs of the business cycle was not accepted wisdom. As President Warren G. Harding declared in 1921, "There has been vast unemployment before and there will be again. There will be depression and inflation just as surely as the tides ebb and flow."[11]

These assumptions were challenged by British economist John Maynard Keynes, who authored a new theory[12] during the 1930s that later became known as Keynesian economics. Viewing the macroeconomy as composed of four enormous sectors—business, consumers, foreign, and government—he argued that economic collapse occurs because businesses do not invest during a depression; increased joblessness means that consumers have less money to spend on goods and services, and international markets diminish as the worldwide effects of a depression are felt. Under those conditions only the government can spend money to spur industrial production, increase employment, and eventually begin the process of economic recovery.

For government to spend money during a period when tax revenues are falling means that deficits will result, and Keynes therefore believed that deficits were not a problem. Keynesian economics not only urged the federal government to undertake tax-and-spend policies to bring about economic recovery (and to counter the business cycle, or countercyclical policies) but encouraged the federal government to intervene continually with public policies designed to keep production high, joblessness low, and economic growth sustained. As such, Keynesian economics rejected the limited view of government held by laissez-faire advocates and, moreover, discounted the value of balanced budgets, one of the cardinal virtues of classical economics.

Keynes did not have much influence on how President Roosevelt waged his economic fight against the Great Depression. In seeking the presidency in 1932, Roosevelt had campaigned on the need for a balanced budget and, with a couple of exceptions, his most trusted advisors were not sympathetic to Keynes's argument that the U.S. government had to spend on the order of $400 million a month in order to end the economic collapse. As Keynes remarked, "I don't think your President Roosevelt knows anything about economics."[13] But by the 1940s Keynesian economics was the new orthodoxy within the economics profession, and its philosophy influenced the drafting of the Employment Act of 1946, although conservatives in Congress refused to sanction deficit spending as an appropriate goal of fiscal policy.

Nor did President Truman embrace any activist countercyclical policies, although he appreciated the fact that economic recessions could be moderated by the so-called automatic stabilizers (such as unemployment compensation and welfare checks) which assure people without jobs that they will have some income to provide for necessities. But Truman did try to balance the budget. President Dwight D. Eisenhower was too conservative to embrace Keynesianism, and his major concession to modern countercyclical policymaking was his willingness to tolerate unbalanced budgets during recessions. It was not until the 1960s that Keynesian economics reached its zenith of political influence during the Kennedy administration, but at that very time, an opposition school of thought (monetarism) was gaining prominence among a minority of professional economists.

The founder of monetarism was economist Milton Friedman at the University of Chicago. Essentially, he and his disciples argued that a stable rate of growth in the money supply (hence monetary policy) offers the best approach for achieving economic growth without inflationary pressures. They further claimed that trying to fine-tune the economy by fiscal policy is, at best, problematic if not entirely unproductive. Monetarism was embodied in the gradualist game plan at the start of the Nixon administration; its goal was to restrict the supply of money and credit slowly in order to bring down the inflation rate (caused by massive spending for the Vietnam War and Great Society domestic programs under President Johnson) without prompting too high an increase in the unemployment rate.

By 1981 supply-side economics shaped the policy agenda of President Reagan. Supply-siders argued forcefully that large cuts in the income tax would encourage Americans to work harder and produce more goods and services (increasing the "supply" of goods and services would increase production but not force prices up), save more money for use as business investment, and ultimately would yield such economic growth that federal revenues would rise despite the original income tax cut. Mainstream economists were critical of this pie-in-the-sky theory as F. Thomas Juster observed: "Seldom has an economic experiment been put in place with less conventional credentialing by professional economists."[14] But Reagan surrounded himself with advisors who believed in that approach and this groupthink—the tendency among groups of decision-makers to find quick agreement rather than explore a wide range of policy alternatives—grew worse by the end of Reagan's first term. With the appointment of Beryl Sprinkel as CEA chair (a business economist associated with Harris Bank in Chicago) and the elevation of Treasury Secretary Donald

Regan to White House chief of staff in 1985, there were few voices in the White House to urge moderation and to raise objections about the huge deficits.

President Reagan's experience is symptomatic of a more generalized problem. Presidents want economic advisors whose theories are compatible with their political views and ideology. As the departure of Murray Weidenbaum and Martin Feldstein (the first and second CEA chairs under Reagan) showed, any economic advisor who preaches what the president does not want to hear will not be invited to the White House very often. Laissez-faire principles mixed well with the antigovernment philosophy of Dwight Eisenhower; Keynesianism was perfect for John Kennedy's brand of domestic liberalism; and supply-side economics reinforced Reagan's ardent conservatism. This pattern continued with Bill Clinton when he assumed the presidency. Liberalism returned insofar as all three of Clinton's original appointments to the CEA were economists who received their doctorates from Massachusetts Institute of Technology, a bastion of Keynesianism.

During the 1970s the failure of Keynesian economics to predict, or adequately explain, the stagflation (rising prices but slowed economic growth) that gripped the nation badly undermined its legitimacy within public opinion. Experts lose credibility when so-called objective macroeconomic indicators send conflicting messages or when economic forecasts prove to be highly inaccurate. Professionalism and expert knowledge also suffer when economists disagree publicly over macroeconomic theory and public policies. In this situation of uncertainty, policymakers have the discretion to choose among contending approaches until they find one that best suits their political purposes. This explains why Richard Nixon experimented with monetarism and Reagan embraced supply-side economics.

In reality, Reaganomics was probably a validation of the Keynesian model because the post-1982 economic expansion has been fueled by massive deficits, the demand side of the equation, whereas the economy failed to generate the increased savings, revenue gains, and balanced budgets that the supply-siders had predicted would result from a 23 percent income tax cut. The dangers that loom in the future from triple-digit deficits are the legacy of a public policy based on misconceived economic principles. Nonetheless, the Reagan administration had proclaimed its economic game plan a success and apparently most Americans felt reassured. The success of any macroeconomic policy ultimately is judged by public acceptance, not by expert opinion. The trouble is that public opinion can be fickle.

A FICKLE PUBLIC

How supportive is public opinion of presidential leadership of the economy? The answer depends on what perceptions of the macroeconomy the public holds and whether people defer to the president's game plan. On the one hand, the kind of macroeconomic goals an administration pursues has class implications because Republicans have electoral incentives to cater to middle- and upper-class voters, who fear inflation, whereas Democrats draw disproportionate support from the working class, who are more likely to fear unemployment. Thus there is a partisan cast to macroeconomic policymaking argue political scientist Douglas Hibbs[15] and liberal economist Paul Samuelson. According to Samuelson,

> The difference between the Democrats and the Republicans is the difference in their constituencies. It is a class difference . . . the Democrats constitute the people, by and large, who are around the median incomes or below. These are the ones whom the Republicans want to pay the price and burden of fighting inflation. The Democrats [are] willing to run with some inflation [to increase employment]; the Republicans are not.[16]

On the other hand, the public may react uniformly to objective economic conditions, whether high unemployment or rising prices. Reagan's performance ratings plunged to a new low for the first fourteen months in office, and the Republicans lost twenty-six House seats in the midterm elections. The decline in approval for President Reagan was correlated with the coming of the 1982 recession, just as his immense popularity in 1983 and 1984 was bolstered by a strong economic recovery. Economic conditions do affect presidential popularity, so the incumbent is held accountable—at least retrospectively—by the voters.

Should an incumbent seek reelection during an economic downturn, as did Nixon in 1960, Ford in 1976, Carter in 1980, and Bush in 1992, then the odds will be against him. Those who are fortunate enough to face the electorate during an economic upturn, Nixon in 1972, Reagan in 1984, Bush in 1988, and Clinton in 1996, have a real advantage over the opposition. This pattern has led some academics to hypothesize that a "political business cycle" exists, meaning that presidents have political incentives to manipulate macroeconomic policy to help their reelection campaigns.[17]

Nixon's 1972 reelection bid is a possible example of this thesis, but the weight of scholarly opinion argues against that interpretation. Given the internal and external policy lags it is unlikely that a president can fine-tune macroeconomic policy to assure maximum expansionary impact at some precise moment prior to the November election.

The public makes impossible demands on government. Bad economic times hurt the incumbent more than good times help him, and specific actions by a president may antagonize voter blocs or special interests. As opinion/party leader, President Kennedy attacked the leading steel companies because they announced price increases in their products, and the price of steel affects prices of many goods including automobiles. But a backlash by the business community after JFK's confrontation with "Big Steel" companies[18] caused a mini "Kennedy Recession" on Wall Street, so then Kennedy had to find ways to reassure corporations he was not antibusiness.

This episode partly explains why Kennedy moved ahead with his proposal to reduce personal and corporate income tax rates. During the 1960s a mainstay of anti-inflation policy by Kennedy and Johnson were efforts to show opinion/party leadership by jawboning unions not to negotiate huge wage raises and pressuring corporations to restrain price increases. Under President Johnson, his CEA devised wage and price guideposts to support its public rhetoric. The CEA guidepost for noninflationary wage raises was pegged at 3.2 percent, and the hope was that companies and their workers voluntarily would abide by that widely publicized target to help restrain inflationary pressures (it did not happen; the guideposts collapsed in 1966 when airline machinists won a wage increase of 4.9 percent).

Today, corporate and union leaders have joined hands in lobbying Congress for protectionist legislation against Japanese imports while, at the same time, American business wants expanded markets for its products throughout the world. On these issues presidents act in various roles to show their opposition to foreign imports that cost Americans their jobs. President Bush as chief diplomat made state visits to Japan, as did members of his administration, to convince the Japanese to open their markets to American products and to curb their exports to the United States. Bill Clinton elevated Japan bashing to an art form during the 1992 presidential campaign, alleging that the Bush administration was not tough enough on Japan, and in 1995 President Clinton, in his chief executive role, authorized the U.S. trade representative to announce trade sanctions, imposing high excise taxes on imported luxury Japanese automobiles. Secretary of Commerce Ronald Brown became a globe-trotting ambassador for American business, trying to win foreign contracts for U.S. companies.

The work begun by President Bush as chief diplomat in gaining agreement with the president of Mexico and the prime minister of Canada for NAFTA (North America Free Trade Agreement) was completed by President Clinton, as legislative leader, when he personally (and successfully) lobbied the Congress in 1993 to approve that trading arrangement. In the process of winning congressional approval, moreover, Bill Clinton assumed the role of opinion leader by going public to convince the American people that NAFTA would gain more jobs for Americans than would be lost. Probably a turning point in the public debate came when Vice President Al Gore agreed to a televised debate with Ross Perot, who had been campaigning along with labor leaders against the pact. By all accounts Gore made a more persuasive argument than Perot did.

In trying to win the hearts of Americans for his economic program, a president faces a no-win situation. On abstract economic values there is a degree of consistency in public opinion. The majority supports capitalism, rejects socialism, and endorses a mixed public-private economy rather than a purely laissez-faire system. Americans want positive action by the federal government, but there is no easy way to reconcile the contradictory policy preferences Americans express. People want the federal government to balance its budget, and a lopsided majority now favors a balanced budget amendment to the Constitution. But when the public is asked to support cutbacks in government programs, its hostility to big government evaporates.

Opinion leadership is quite problematic when presidents try to convince the public to take strong medicine to help the economy. Although President Reagan made sizable cutbacks in programs targeted to the needy, his attempt in 1985 to reduce middle-class entitlements (so-called sacred cows) quickly stalled as legions of senior citizen groups, veterans, and home owners protested those cutbacks. From this perspective, the so-called Reagan Revolution has been a failure; Americans seem no more willing today to accept smaller government when programs giving them benefits are jeopardized. The outcome of the 1994 midterm and the 1996 presidential elections may be interpreted as a test of the public's resolve in the trade-off between ideological conservatism and operational liberalism, a political threshold that may signal the degree of public commitment to ending the spiral of red ink (the national debt stands at over $5 trillion).

By winning control of both houses of Congress in 1994, the congressional Republicans read into the election returns a policy mandate to balance the budget in seven years, devolve federal programs to the states, and curb excessive regulations on business. Congress and the White House became locked in a budget battle, which led to shutdowns of federal agencies on two occasions during 1995. President Clinton blamed GOP extremists in the House of Representatives for harsh cuts in social programs—notably Medicare—and opinion polls showed that most Americans blamed the Republicans for the government shutdowns.

Fighting back, the GOP argued that Clinton's budgets projected fake savings and overestimated future economic growth (and thus federal revenues), meaning he was not remotely serious about slowing down the growth in federal expenditures. In 1996, an election year, the Republicans tried to regroup around their presidential nominee Senator Robert Dole (R–Kans.), and Clinton moved to paint himself as a centrist who held the line against excessive budget cuts by the congressional Republicans. The way this political scenario was developing, clearly President Clinton was banking on more voters supporting of his proposals for continued social expenditures.

There is little public outcry about tax cuts and increased spending when the purpose is to stimulate the economy, but policymakers must contemplate the political risks whenever they seek to raise taxes or cut expenditures to curb inflation and reduce deficits. President Johnson delayed recommending his income tax surcharge because he sensed a hostile public opinion. Among the Democrats contending for the 1988 presidential nomination, only ex-governor of Arizona Bruce Babbitt called for new taxes, and he ranked last in the standings among Democratic voters. Fiscal policy has been neutralized by public opinion, which is why monetary policy by the Federal Reserve Board may be the only viable anti-inflation strategy left.

Many opinions are not grounded in factual information about the economy.[19] Support for balanced budgets means that Americans understand little about Keynesian economics. Another consequence of this misinformation is that the majority supports programs which most economists oppose. The public, to illustrate, continually endorses protectionist trade legislation and favors wage-price controls. At the time, the wage-price freeze in Nixon's "New Economic Program" of 1971 won wholehearted support from public opinion, but the disastrous results of that policy either were forgotten by most people or perhaps never fully recognized. It is probable that few citizens really understood what Nixon planned to do or the economic implications of his actions. What influenced the public was decisive action by the chief executive in the face of a genuine economic crisis.

DEPRESSION AND CRISIS

Will the nation rally around presidential leadership during economic crises? A crisis transforms the usual executive-legislative conflict relationships into an urgent need to formulate a policy response. These dynamics are best shown during the Great Depression. With one-fourth of the work force unemployed and the GNP plummeting, the severity of the 1930s economic collapse was apparent to all. The United States was desperate for strong leadership. In 1932 Franklin D. Roosevelt offered the American people a New Deal and proceeded, after being elected, to bombard the Congress with new programs. The legislative output of the first 100 days of the New Deal has been unmatched by any of Roosevelt's successors. The unemployed got relief, the financial system was reformed, and efforts were begun to spur economic recovery.

Almost immediately FDR acted to prevent any more bank defaults because people with checking and savings accounts, who observed that banks across the nation were going broke, were lining up at their banks to withdraw their money, which, of course, only worsened the situation and led even more banks to declare bankruptcy. No federal insurance protected depositors' money (that reform came later in the New Deal), so Roosevelt declared bank holidays to prevent any more runs on the banks and to calm the public panic.

To confront the Depression, President Roosevelt wanted direct controls over the economy in order to spur recovery, and the Congress quickly obliged him by enacting the National Industrial Recovery Act (NIRA) and the Agriculture Adjustment Act (AAA) in 1933. FDR did not understand countercyclical policy and so relied on regulatory powers. His objective was to arrange government and private cartels (essentially state-sponsored monopolies) through which prices, wages, and output could be stabilized in each major industry.

The theories of John Maynard Keynes, first published in 1936, had not received widespread acceptance among economists at the time so they had little impact on Roosevelt's thinking and, looking back, economists universally agree that the NIRA policy was the wrong thing to do. NIRA tried to restrict the supply of goods when, in fact, what government should do during a depression is stimulate industrial production by encouraging public spending, private investment, and household consumption. Nonetheless, the crisis conditions of the 1930s enabled President Roosevelt to take bold and untried steps to cope with the economic calamity, and not until the Supreme Court ruled against NIRA in 1935 and AAA in 1936 did those experiments with a planned economy come to an end.

What actually ended the Great Depression was World War II, but the Roosevelt Revolution marked a decisive turning point in American history. Laissez-faire economics was repudiated and, by enacting the Employment Act of 1946, the people now looked to their political leadership to guard against any new economic catastrophe. This fundamental transformation in economic thinking and public policy might not have come about without the shock of the 1930s Depression.

The president is uniquely equipped to act quickly and decisively during an emergency and thus, even today, he tries to exploit such conditions for political purposes. As William Mullen explains, "In 'doing what needs doing for the people,' our chief executives have come to operate a crisis presidency as almost a routine way of doing business. Even relatively minor issues are now encased in terms of emergency."[20] But it is not quite so easy. Crisis cannot be routinely employed as an everyday occurrence because Congress and the public may not agree an emergency situation really exists.

President Carter referred to the energy problem as the "moral equivalent of war," but the public simply ignored it and Congress made a shambles of his energy program. A crisis mobilizes political power within the White House only when there is widespread agreement that urgent and drastic action is required. Nothing since the 1930s matches the Depression, but there have been acute economic problems that have galvanized political action. What forced President Nixon to announce his New Economic Program was a badly deteriorating international balance sheet. Nixon's decision was triggered by a supposedly international monetary crisis that began when Great Britain wanted assurances that the United States would redeem its holdings of U.S. dollars in gold.[21]

INTERNATIONAL MONETARY CRISIS

From the end of World War II until 1973, when Nixon acted, most currencies had fixed exchange rates with respect to the U.S. dollar (the U.S. dollar had a certain value when compared to the British pound or the Japanese yen), and only the United States could settle its international transactions (deficits or surpluses with other countries because of trade, military bases, foreign travel, and the like) by buying and selling gold—the so-called open gold window—at the rate of $35 per ounce. The gold standard guaranteed the stability of the U.S. dollar exchange rate against other currencies.

So when President Nixon—by executive action—closed the gold window (ending the policy of converting U.S. dollars held by foreigners into gold) and allowed the value of the U.S. dollar to float and be determined by international marketplace forces, the U.S. dollar became devalued (worth less against other currencies). Nixon hoped a devaluated dollar would raise the price of foreign goods (thus discouraging imports) while making U.S. goods cheaper worldwide (thus encouraging exports) so the U.S. deficit in the international balance sheets would be converted to a surplus. Nixon's bold reform of the world's monetary system was applauded by economists, financiers, Congress, and the public, although it did not solve America's international monetary position for long. Virtually every year since, Americans have spent more U.S. dollars abroad—traveling and buying imports—as compared to how much foreign currencies are spent by citizens of other countries for U.S. goods and services.

SUMMARY

For the president to uphold the expectations (if not the reality) of acting as manager of prosperity means the White House is constrained by the limitations inherent in the roles of opinion/party leader, legislative leader, and chief executive because those roles are primarily involved when a president seeks to shape the macroeconomy. In recent decades the perennial problems of trade imbalances and balance of payments crises with other nations have brought the chief diplomat role to the forefront of economic policymaking, but the commander-in-chief role normally would not become activated, although President Bush justified U.S. intervention in the Persian Gulf War on the grounds that Americans rely heavily on imports of crude petroleum from Saudi Arabia as well as the threat posed by Iraq to the Middle East and Israel in particular.

Whether the president seeks to educate the American people about the dangers of deficits, lobby Congress to enact a higher minimum wage, or formulate an executive budget with the optimal balance between taxes and expenditures, the entire process is shaped more by his persuasive abilities than by his authority to command and control. After all, the public and Congress, and to a lesser extent a president's subordinates within the executive agencies, are decision-makers who are independent of the White House or who have sufficient political resources to frustrate the presidential economic game plan.

Yet America has had no repeat of the Great Depression and, in the postwar era, periods of economic expansion have been longer than periods of recession. Between 1854 and 1945 the United States experienced 454 months of contraction or recession (42 percent) and 636 months of economic expansion (58 percent), but since 1945 through March 1993 there have been 97 months of contraction (17 percent) versus 470 months of expansion (82 percent).[22]

Something must be working right, but what? Frendreis and Tatalovich posed the question "Does it make a difference who is president, or is the performance of the economy largely a function of forces beyond the president's control?" They gave a guarded response: "The correct answer to these questions is probably yes and no. No in the sense that much of the performance of the U.S. economy is due to structural features of the economy and to market forces that are beyond the reach of U.S. policymakers." Yet "the question of presidential control can also be answered in the affirmative, since the president and other policymakers do play a role in some significant areas affecting the macroeconomy," namely fiscal policy, monetary policy, and budgeting.[23]

The key variable, however, may be America's mixed public-private economy. Spending by all governments is now 35 percent of GNP and because of automatic stabilizers the federal share rises during contractions. Although political commentators may lambast big government as an assault on liberty and the free market, its growth since the New Deal is doubtless the single most important reason why the economy has performed reasonably well over the past five decades. This record of success continues despite the political rhetoric, ideological turns, and policy tinkerings associated with presidential politics. In the final analysis, therefore, the notion that any president can be manager of prosperity is, at best, a misnomer or, at worst, hyperbole.

NOTES

1. Clinton Rossiter, *The American Presidency* (New York: Harcourt Brace and World, 1960), p. 37.

2. Lewis H. Kimmel, *Federal Budget and Fiscal Policy, 1789–1958* (Washington, DC: The Brookings Institution, 1959).

3. See Michael A. Genovese, "The Presidency and Styles of Economic Management," *Congress and the Presidency* 14 (Autumn 1987).

4. Erwin C. Hargrove and Samuel A. Morley, *The President and the Council of Economic Advisers* (Boulder, CO: Westview Press, 1984), p. 33.

5. See Donald F. Kettl, *Leadership at the Fed* (New Haven, CT: Yale University Press, 1986); John T. Woolley, *Monetary Politics: The Federal Reserve and The Politics of Monetary Policy* (Cambridge, England: Cambridge University Press, 1984).

6. John P. Frendreis and Raymond Tatalovich, *The Modern Presidency and Economic Policy* (Itasca, IL: F.E. Peacock, 1994), pp. 176–177.

7. Richard Rose, *The Postmodern President: George Bush Meets the World*, 2nd ed. (Chatham, NJ: Chatham House, 1991).

8. John Frendreis and Raymond Tatalovich, "The Use (and Abuse) of Macroeconomic Forecasting by Presidential Administrations: A Comparative Analysis," Paper delivered to the 1991 annual meeting of the American Political Science Association, San Francisco, CA.

9. Reported in Crauford D. Goodwin and R. Stanley Herren, "The Truman Administration: Problems and Policies Unfold," in Crauford D. Goodwin, ed., *Exhortation and Controls: The Search for a Wage-Price Policy 1945–1971* (Washington, DC: The Brookings Institution, 1975), p. 37.

10. See Steven E. Rhoads, *The Economist' View of the World* (Cambridge, England: Cambridge University Press, 1985). Specifically, Rhoads offers a critique of microeconomics and its application to problem solving.

11. Quoted in Stephen K. Bailey, *Congress Makes a Law* (New York: Columbia University Press, 1950), p. 6.

12. John Maynard Keynes, *The General Theory of Employment, Interest, and Money* (New York: Harcourt, Brace and Company, 1936).

13. Quoted in Arthur M. Schlesinger, Jr., *The Politics of Upheaval* (Boston: Houghton Mifflin, 1960), p. 406.

14. F. Thomas Juster, "The Economics and Politics of the Supply-Side View," *Economic Outlook USA* (Autumn 1981), University of Michigan, Survey Research Center, p. 81.

15. Douglas A. Hibbs, Jr., *The American Political Economy: Macroeconomics and Electoral Politics in the United States* (Cambridge, MA: Harvard University Press, 1987), pp. 183–184.

16. Paul A. Samuelson, "Some Dilemmas of Economic Policy," *Challenge* 20 (1977), pp. 30–31.

17. Edward R. Tufte, *Political Control of the Economy* (Princeton, NJ: Princeton University Press, 1978).

18. Grant McConnell, *Steel and the Presidency, 1962* (New York, Norton, 1963).

19. See the results of one set of polling questions in Frendreis and Tatalovich, *The Modern Presidency and Economic Policy*, p. 227.

20. William F. Mullen, *Presidential Power and Politics* (New York: St. Martin's Press, 1976), p. 95.

21. Joanne Gowa, *Closing the Gold Window: Domestic Politics and the End of Bretton Woods* (Ithaca, NY: Cornell University Press, 1983).

22. Frendreis and Tatalovich, *The Modern Presidency and Economic Policy*, p. 170.

23. Ibid., pp. 312, 313.

16

Insight on Executive and Legislative Leadership Roles: Budgetary Reforms and Deficit Politics

This Insight discusses the budgetary process from the perspective of the chief executive and legislative leader roles because both are intimately involved in getting the federal budget prepared and approved for each fiscal year. Today there are essentially two budgets—an executive budget and a congressional budget—which must be reconciled into one budget document, but this scenario has developed only since 1974. In fact, there have been three broad eras in budgeting and modifications in the most recent period since 1974. Budgeting is arguably the most important ongoing responsibility that mandates interaction between the executive and legislative branches. To fully understand this process and the political tug of war between the president and Congress, our discussion focuses on authority, decision making, expertise, public inputs, and crisis.

The *authority* to formulate a budget for the federal government has shifted from the legislature to the executive over the course of the three eras of budgeting. The first era runs from the Founding until 1921. The Framers intended Congress to have jurisdiction over public finances. Article I grants to Congress the power to "To lay and collect Taxes, Duties, Imposts and Excises, to pay the Debts and provide for the common Defense and general Welfare of the United States, . . . To borrow Money on the credit of the United States, . . . To coin Money [and] regulate the Value thereof." Article I also stipulates that "No Money shall be drawn from the Treasury, but in Consequence of Appropriations made by Law." Together these clauses mandate congressional control over both taxing and spending.

During the Federalist era, Secretary of the Treasury Alexander Hamilton dominated financial affairs by recommending to Congress his proposals to establish a mint and Bank of the United States, assume state Revolutionary War debts and monetize the national debt, levy tariffs on imports, and aid the commercial development of the nation. The House eventually balked at Hamilton's leadership, and Congress asserted its prerogatives over public finances. With the exception of those early years, prior to 1921 Congress predominated in budgetary matters.

A string of deficits during the 1890s and the first decade of the twentieth century led President Taft to urge Congress to create a Commission on Economy and Efficiency to review the budget process. Its report recommended that the president collect agency spending estimates into a budget for Congress to approve, but the Congress rejected that advice. Taft tried to avoid congressional consideration by directing his agency heads to prepare a national budget in addition to the traditional "Book of Estimates" that was submitted to Congress, but again Congress reacted by ordering the agencies not to formulate any such document. The reform momentum was not successful until Congress enacted the Budget and Accounting Act of 1921. Under this law the chief executive was delegated the authority to prepare an "executive budget" for presentation to Congress, which had final authority to amend the budget before enacting the regular appropriations bills by the start of the new fiscal year. His control over the agenda-setting process probably caused the balance of power over budgeting to shift toward the executive branch in the years that followed. The act created a Bureau of the Budget and, at the very beginning, President Harding appointed Charles G. Dawes as the first Bureau of the Budget (BOB) director who, in turn, issued Budget Circular No. 40, requiring all federal agencies to submit their budget estimates to the BOB before any would be forwarded to Congress for its consideration.

By 1974 the relationship between the president and Congress had badly deteriorated, mainly because a Democratic Congress now faced a Republican in the White House. The annual ritual of partisan conflict over spending priorities—the "Seven-Year Budget War"[1]—culminated in enactment of the Congressional Budget and Impoundment Control Act of 1974. The specific incident that triggered its passage was a constitutional crisis in which President Nixon asserted he had the power to refuse to spend monies appropriated by Congress for water pollution projects and also that he had the power to spend funds not appropriated by Congress to expand the Vietnam War into neutral Cambodia.[2] Congress responded by passing bills designed to redress the imbalance between the executive and the legislature, namely, the Impoundment Control Act, which severely restricted presidential impoundment authority both temporarily (deferrals) and permanently (rescissions); and the Congressional Budget Act that established an entirely new congressional budget process. According to budget expert Howard Shuman, "The Congress passed the 'Impoundment Control Act' to discipline the president. It passed the 'Congressional Budget Act' to discipline itself."[3] By the latter, Shuman means that the 1974 Act designed an entirely new budgetary process that added other decision-makers to the traditionally fragmented system by which Congress raises revenues and makes appropriations.

By the early 1800s Congress had routinized its budgetary procedures and that early *decision-making* process actually was more rational and coherent than what ultimately would evolve. The Ways and Means Committee, which the House established as its first standing committee in 1802, scrutinized appropriations bills and the Senate followed suit when its Committee on Finance was created in 1816. At this point, both these committees had jurisdiction over revenue and appropriations bills, although this unified control over finances did not survive the Civil War.

In 1865 the House limited the jurisdiction of Ways and Means to revenue bills only and shifted funding bills to new committees including Appropriations. A highly fragmented committee system was fully operational by the turn of the twentieth century, with tax bills assigned to the Ways and Means and Finance Committees, spending bills going to the House and Senate Appropriations Committees, and some funding bills for particular purposes (public works projects such as rivers and harbors) still under the jurisdiction of the standing committee with legislative authority over them. This fragmentary system continued after 1921 and persists, in a modified form, even today. What the 1974 Act did was establish an additional layer of two more standing committees (the House and Senate Budget Committees) that were charged with formulating a coherent "congressional budget" resolution with estimated total spending, total revenue, and the deficit following presentation of the "executive budget" (now due) by the first Monday in February. There is now an established decision-making process within the executive branch as well as a decision-making process within Congress.

EXECUTIVE BUDGET

The combined executive and congressional budget process spans nearly two years prior to the start of the new fiscal year. For example, the FY98 budget (October 1, 1997 to September 31, 1998) was submitted to Congress in February 1997 based on preliminary estimates the agencies began gathering in February and March 1996.

During February-March the agencies try to estimate their budgetary needs for the next year based on the higher costs of implementing existing programs and any anticipated new programs. The president consults with the Council of Economic Advisors about trends affecting unemployment, economic growth, and inflation and with the OMB regarding its estimate of total expenditures. In May and June the president and the OMB make tentative decisions on levels of spending that are communicated to the departments, and the various federal agencies submit their budget requests to the OMB by September.

Throughout September the OMB examiners scrutinize agency budgets so that by October and early November the OMB director and other

White House staffers can meet in their budget review sessions. Once again the president checks with the CEA, Department of Treasury (on anticipated revenues), and the OMB about economic and budgetary developments. It is during this period when the OMB examiners review agency budget requests that interest groups, state and local agencies, and other affected parties try to lobby the White House to defend their favorite programs from cuts. In the negotiations between the OMB and the agencies, unresolved disputes are invariably appealed to the president in late November and early December for a final decision. Once those decisions are finalized, the agencies must comply with the White House directives and the OMB proceeds to prepare the budget document and budget message, which the president presents to Congress at the start of the new calendar year.

CONGRESSIONAL BUDGET

After Congress receives the presidential budget that OMB prepared, the congressional budget process begins. The original timetable was established by the Congressional Budget Act of 1974 but was modified when Congress enacted the Balanced Budget and Emergency Deficit Control Act of 1985 (popularly known as Gramm-Rudman-Hollings after its Senate cosponsors). The procedures under the 1974 Act also were streamlined, although the essential logic of the process has survived. First, the 1974 Act changed the fiscal year (or budget year)—taking effect in 1976—to run from October 1 to September 31, thereby giving Congress about three more months to approve a federal budget. From 1844 until 1976 the fiscal calendar had extended from July 1 to June 30, meaning Congress had less than six months after the president submitted his executive budget in January to process it. Under this arrangement, Congress was unable to complete action on its spending bills until after July 1. The new fiscal year gives Congress three more months for its deliberations.

Second, at the heart of the 1974 Act was the requirement that Congress pass two concurrent resolutions on the budget, but now only one is used. Originally, all standing committees were supposed to give their spending estimates to the Budget Committees by March 15, and the Budget Committees were required to formulate their first concurrent resolution on the budget no later than April 15. Both the House and Senate had to approve one version of that resolution by May 15, which originally laid out targets for expenditures and taxes and the deficit. After Congress fully debated its taxing and spending priorities, the 1974 Act provided that a second concurrent resolution with binding maximums on total spending and minimums on total revenue be approved by September 15, two weeks before the start of the fiscal year. However the 1985 Act accelerated this timetable by one month and now the first—and only—concurrent budget resolution has to be approved by April 15.

Third, a concurrent resolution is binding on the House and Senate but is not signed by the president, and thus is not legislation. To implement the congressional budget, therefore, the 1974 Act provided for a "reconciliation" bill to be enacted into law and this feature survived the 1985 revision. Originally the reconciliation bill—which implemented the second concurrent resolution on the budget—had to be passed by September 25, but Gramm-Rudman-Hollings mandated that reconciliation legislation be approved by June 15, based on the concurrent budget resolution that was passed two months earlier.

What was radical about Gramm-Rudman-Hollings was its timetable to reduce the federal deficit to zero by FY91 coupled with a new delegation of authority to the White House. Once OMB estimated the size of the deficit, the president was armed with a sequestering order to impose spending cuts to prevent the deficit from growing larger than what was allowed in the legislated targets for deficit reduction. Obviously 1991 came and went, and triple-digit federal deficits are projected to continued into the late 1990s.

Further changes were legislated by the Budget Enforcement Act of 1990, which resulted from high-level negotiations between the congressional Democrats and the Bush White House. The 1990 Act effectively repealed Gramm-Rudman-Hollings because no goal for attaining a balanced budget was created; instead, the law simply reduced the federal deficit to $83 billion by FY95. Pursuant to the latest revisions (Table 16–1), if everything goes according to schedule, Congress would complete its work on the budget resolution by April 15. If no budget resolution is adopted by then, the Budget Committees can report their preferred spending limits to the Appropriations Committee. After May 15 appropriations bills may be considered in the House and by June 10 the House Appropriations Committee should have reported all thirteen regular appropriation bills. Any supplementary appropriations bills that allowed discretionary spending to exceed the targeted expenditures limits, unless corrected by Congress, could be reduced by a presidential sequester order. However, Congress provided for exempting any automatic cuts in discretionary funding for military personnel. By August 20 the OMB is supposed to release its forecast of how large the deficit will be.

Raw partisan politics and near deadlock between the two branches led to the enactment of the 1990 Act. In the current era of heightened awareness of the national debt and the failure of Congress to enact a balanced budget (not since 1969), the budgeting process every year generates partisan conflict and institutional rivalry between the two ends of Pennsylvania Avenue. Budgeting was a much more peaceful enterprise during the post–World War II years when federal revenues roughly kept pace with federal expenditures.

Budgetary policy prior to 1974 was a classic example of "incremental" decision making, according to well-known political scientist Aaron Wildavsky.[4] In this strategic game, agencies would ask for larger budgetary increases for the next fiscal year, knowing the House of Representatives would make cuts and some monies would be restored by the Sen-

Table 16–1. Congressional Budget Timetable for Fiscal Year 1996

Date	Action to Be Completed
February 6	President Clinton submits his FY96 budget to Congress.
April 15	Deadline for adoption of a House and Senate conference report on the *congressional budget resolution* for FY96. If a budget resolution is not approved by this date, the House Appropriations Committee can begin work on spending bills.
May 15	Appropriations bills may be considered in the House starting on this date even if a budget resolution has not been agreed to.
June 10	Deadline for the House Appropriations Committee to report all thirteen regular appropriations bills to the House floor.
July 1	Supplemental (extra) appropriations for FY95 exceeding the agreed upon spending "targets" that are enacted before this date will trigger a fifteen-day postenactment *sequester* order.
August 10	Notice of optional sequester order exemption for military personnel.
August 20	Deficit forecast update is released by the Office of Management and Budget (OMB).
October 1	FY96 begins. This date is the deadline for enactment of all appropriations bills. If they are not enacted by this date, then a *continuing resolution* must be enacted to continue the flow of funds to agencies; otherwise, unfunded government operations will have to cease.

Source: "President's Fiscal 1996 Budget," *Congressional Quarterly Weekly Report* (Feb. 11, 1995), p. 408.

ate, with the consequence that agencies typically got more funding than they had the previous year. In this scenario the House Appropriations Committee served as a "guardian of the federal treasury," trimming presidential requests, and the Senate Appropriations Committee played the role of "court of appeals" where affected agencies could seek redress.[5] The polite workings of the budgetary process was supported by a policy consensus among the participants that stressed balanced or nearly balanced budgets while accepting a gradual rise in federal spending plus a preference for "hidden" taxes rather than any across-the-board changes in the tax code.[6]

In today's battle over the budget, both ends of Pennsylvania Avenue are armed with *expertise* and specialists in public finance and economics, but between 1921 and 1974 the executive branch held a decisive advantage. The Bureau of the Budget and its successor—the Office of Management and Budget (OMB)—monopolized the preparation of the executive budget. With the establishment of the Council of Economic Advisers in 1946, the White House also had the expertise of highly respected economists from academia to offer their forecasts of future economic activity.

Congress could debate and challenge the president's budgetary priorities—whether too much or too little was spent for domestic policies or national defense—but members of Congress were constrained by the data supplied by the White House.

This imbalance was corrected after the 1974 Congressional Budget Act established a Congressional Budget Office (CBO) to be its counterweight to the OMB for predicting future economic trends and validating the economic assumptions on which the executive budget was based. The CBO has developed into a nonpartisan and highly respected agency whose directors have avoided the kind of partisan advocacy so typical of OMB directors. By law the CBO director is authorized to obtain information and data estimates directly from federal agencies if necessary, and the CBO is free to respond to requests for budgetary information from the Budget Committees or any other standing committee or member of Congress.

Generating statistics on expected revenues and projected outlays that contradict administration estimates has proven to be the CBO's primary asset. CBO's reputation soared following the disclosure that Reagan's OMB director had distorted the numbers during the crucial 1981 budget debate. Too optimistic economic projections influenced Congress to enact the Reagan economic program. A columnist reported that OMB director David Stockman originally did a computer forecast, based on President Reagan's tax cuts and increased defense spending, which predicted deficits of unprecedented size. What Stockman did was simply change all the economic assumptions in his model to produce a more optimistic outcome.[7] Stockman recollected his "rosy scenario" this way:

> The error in the 1981 fiscal plan was thus staggering [because of the] Rosy Scenario's contribution to the mistake. It shows that money GNP in 1986 ended up *$660 billion* lower than what [CEA Chairman] Murray Weidenbaum slapped out of his computer. The money GNP number turned out so much lower after five years because both of its two component parts, real GNP and inflation, increased far less than we had projected. Since the revenue share of GNP is driven up by both real growth and inflation . . . we began our revolution with almost no margin to cut taxes at all.

In fact, the CBO economic forecasts have been more accurate than OMB economic forecasts, according to CBO research[8] and scholarly analysis,[9] so today budgetary conflicts are essentially conflicts over economic assumptions. According to Donald Kettl,

> During most of the 1980s, Republicans used their projections of high deficits to restrain Democrats' plans for domestic programs. Democrats did likewise to reduce President Reagan's defense buildup. Both sides have searched for optimistic economic projections when ducking the issue during presidential election years was attractive. In 1990, OMB's projections showed that the president's capital gains tax reduction would bring more money in, while congressional Democrats produced numbers that showed a long-term reduction in revenues. Whose projections are used heavily shapes the nature of the battle. The computers, programs, and databases have become so widely

available that most of the key players can now produce their own projections. Budget negotiations therefore have become battles not only over programs but also over competing economic forecasts.[10]

This technical debate continued into the Bush administration when, in March 1992, the CBO predicted a deficit in fiscal 1996 of nearly $200 billion despite the fact that administration economists the year before had predicted a budgetary surplus by the mid-1990s.[11] Later that same year CBO estimates for an antimissile defense system showed a potential cost of $37 billion over a five-year period, whereas the Bush administration figures showed the estimate to be $10 billion less.[12]

In fundamental ways the annual budget debate is framed by *public inputs*—public opinion, but especially the clientele who receive benefits from federal programs. Americans want fiscal restraint and lower taxes and a balanced budget—in the abstract. Polls show that large majorities favor a constitutional amendment to balance the budget—more than three-fourths of the respondents in the late 1970s and early 1980s[13]—and the 104th Congress came very close to sending an amendment to the states for ratification. It received the required two-thirds vote in the House but fell two votes short in the Senate when crucial "no" votes were cast by Senators Mark Hatfield (R–Oreg.) and Majority Party Leader Robert Dole (R–Kans.). (In fact, the "no" vote cast by Dole was simply a parliamentary tactic to allow him to reschedule a later vote on the amendment because he fully supported the amendment had the support of two-thirds of the senators been assured.)

When Americans are queried about whether spending ought to be increased or decreased for a variety of federal programs, however, public opinion generally supports more funding. In 1990, for example, most Americans believed the government was spending "too little" money on health care (72 percent said so), the environment and education (71 percent), crime (70 percent), drug addiction (64 percent), and big cities (50 percent).[14] Three decades ago this same contradiction in public opinion led two researchers to conclude that most Americans were "ideological conservatives" but "operational liberals" because they are conservative on spending and taxes but liberal on domestic programs that may benefit them.[15]

A major reason for runaway federal spending are entitlement programs such as Medicare and pensions under Social Security tied to COLAs (cost-of-living adjustments) that increase with rising prices. Any effort to extract savings from Social Security is attacked by the American Association of Retired Persons (AARP) and opinion polls shows that Social Security has become so enshrined as a sacred cow that no politician would dare threaten it.

The primary reason that President Reagan failed to reduce domestic spending was his inability to cut the growth in domestic entitlement programs. Unlike his first term, in which budget cuts fell disproportionately on discretionary spending for the poor, following his landslide win over Walter Mondale, his 1985 State of the Union Address proclaimed a "Second American Revolution" and promised severe retrenchment. Now the budget axe would fall on those sacred cow programs for the middle class and special interests. Reagan proposed a one-year freeze on total spending, although he told Congress there would be political opposition because every dollar "benefits someone, and that person has a vested self-interest in seeing those benefits perpetuated and expanded." Then he asked, "Where is the political log rolling going to stop?" His answer was a budget that proposed a 5 percent pay cut for civilian federal employees, a one-year elimination of the COLA on civilian (including Social Security) and military pensions, cuts in farm price supports, a freeze on Medicaid payments to hospitals and physicians, and the abolishment of twelve domestic programs. In toto, the FY86 budget represented the largest spending cutback in the nation's history and was intended to reduce the deficit by $56 billion in 1986 and $300 billion over the following three years.[16]

The battle lines were drawn when the Senate Budget Committee approved a budget resolution that included a one-year cost-of-living freeze on Social Security. Immediately there was talk among House Democrats that they would resist any cuts in Social Security, and the Democratic-controlled Budget Committee in the House reported a budget resolution with no Social Security freeze. Other major differences between the Senate and House versions of the budget resolution caused the House-Senate conference committee to deadlock in late June. The stalemate over Social Security led President Reagan to hold meetings with the House Democrats, and the upshot was his decision to abandon the Senate GOP and side with the House Democrats. As Speaker O'Neill (D–Mass.) declared after a meeting with the White House, "We agreed that Social Security, in every phase, is not on the table anymore. No COLAs slippage, no taxes on Social Security, nothing happens to Social Security."[17]

The protracted conflict over the FY86 budget continued past the October 1 start of the fiscal year. No regular appropriations bills had been enacted and continuing resolutions were needed to fund agencies through mid-November in order to avoid a partial shutdown of the federal government. Eventually the stalemated budgetary process caused enough anxiety on Wall Street and among opinion leaders that political conditions were ripe for Congress to consider radical steps to bring down the mounting deficits. The consequence (see later discussion) was Gramm-Rudman-Hollings.

In 1985 President Reagan betrayed the Senate Republicans who were politically vulnerable when they voted a one-year freeze in Social Security increases. A decade later the Republican majority in the House of Representatives took a similar political beating from congressional Democrats and President Clinton when they proposed to slow the growth in Medicare (the health care program for senior citizens tied to Social Security). The "Mediscare" tactics by congressional Democrats allied with organized labor during the 1996 election campaign failed to defeat enough freshman Republicans for Democrats to assume control of the House, but those political advertisements had an impact on the presidential contest because Clinton carried retiree-rich Florida and Arizona (Arizona had not voted for a Democratic presidential candidate since 1948).

When divided government characterizes the relationship between the White House and Congress, the budget battle is fundamentally a conflict over different policy priorities. Republicans want tax cuts, generally more defense spending, and less social welfare. Democrats promote a more aggressive domestic agenda even though they may not publicly call for tax increases to pay for those additional programs. Budgeting is never easy, but the choices become more difficult when Republicans and Democrats control different branches of government.

The 1974 budgetary reforms did not cause any legislative roadblocks when the Democrats controlled Congress and the White House occupant was Jimmy Carter. For FY79, to illustrate, there was less than a 1 percent difference between Carter's executive budget and the congressional budget as reflected in the second concurrent budget resolution. James Thurber affirmed that "[a]lthough President Carter and his advisers . . . lost several major policy battles to Congress, the budget committees seem to be taking their major cues from the President."[18]

There was a different political scenario in 1981 when President Reagan and his newly elected Republican Senate faced a Democratic House. A president who rallies public opinion around his leadership can exert political leverage over Congress, and it is more difficult for critics to attack a popular president. Backing from public opinion was crucial to President Reagan's radical departures in budgetary and tax policy. Because of Reagan's victory over Jimmy Carter, the Republican Party took control of the Senate for the first time in three decades, and Reagan proclaimed he had a mandate to cut back domestic spending, increase military expenditures, and reduce income taxes drastically.

The Democratic Party was in disarray, unable to formulate any policy alternative to Reaganomics, and conservative southern Democrats (or "Boll Weevils") abandoned their party's leadership to give Reagan the winning edge in the House of Representatives after President Reagan spoke to a nationwide TV audience before a joint session of Congress to rally his supporters to pressure their representatives and senators. Activists within the congressional districts, in making their support for Reagan's budget and tax proposals known to their representatives, were critically important to the legislative outcome. One analysis showed the following:

> [T]he influence of [district] activist opinion and members' perceptions of issues and popular views about them emerged as critical components of the decision. The case study of decision making on the tax cut illustrates the role played by activist opinion. For late deciders [in the House], that critical swing group of legislators who made up their minds at the last minute (and which also included most of the Boll Weevils), activists having intense preferences were an especially important consideration. This factor far outdistanced the influence of the members' own conservatism and appears to have been the critical component of the decision.[19]

By this stroke of political genius, Reagan won his first budget battle, and later Congress enacted the 23 percent income tax cut that he also had promised the American people. It is generally agreed that Reagan's legislative leadership in 1981 was unmatched in recent decades.[20]

When Congress failed to approve a budget on October 1, 1985, Senators Phil Gramm (R–Tex.), Warren Rudman (R–N.H.), and Ernest Hollings (D–S.C.) proposed legislation mandating a step-by-step reduction in federal deficits until 1991, when a balanced budget would be achieved. Any deficit that exceeded the targets established in the bill would be subjected to automatic cuts by a presidential sequester order. House Democrats tried to stall, but President Reagan immediately endorsed the bill, saying, "The United States government is not only going to pay its bills, but we're also going to take away the credit cards. From now on it'll be cash and carry."[21] The Democratic leadership of the House and Senate wanted more time to study the legislation, but the Senate moved quickly.

On October 6 the Senate held an unusual Sunday session (only its fourth in twelve years). Majority Leader Robert Dole (R–Kans.) and President Reagan wanted to put pressure on the Democrats because the federal government was approaching the ceiling in the statutory debt limit (Congress must pass legislation specifying how large the national debt can be). House Democrats alleged that the White House was orchestrating a fake emergency but, nonetheless, on October 9 the Senate voted 75 to 24 to pass Gramm-Rudman-Hollings. Even liberal senator Edward Kennedy (D–Mass.) joined the bipartisan coalition that approved the bill.

The fact that 1986 was an election year put its opponents on the defensive. In mid-October a conference committee of members from the House and Senate tried to resolve their differences, but still more legislative deadlock ensued, prompting another financial crisis. The Treasury Department announced on November 1, 1985, that it would have to borrow funds from the Social Security Trust Fund unless Congress agreed to raise the ceiling on the national debt. The new OMB director James Miller, III, warned, "If nothing is done before the 14th, and the Congress has not acted, then there would be the orderly shutting down of the entire government and stopping of checks going to almost everyone."[22]

On November 1 the House approved the Democratic version along strictly partisan lines, and four days later the Senate passed its Gramm-Rudman-Hollings bill. Now personal negotiations involved Senator Dole, Speaker O'Neill, and President Reagan, and there was greater urgency because the president was supposed to meet with the Soviet premier later in November. To prevent default, two more stopgap spending bills were enacted into law, but so far only four of the thirteen regular appropriations bills had been approved by Congress. Finally the conference committee impasse ended in early December, both houses approved Gramm-Rudman-Hollings by wide margins, and on December 13 President Reagan signed into law the Balanced Budget and Emergency Deficit Control Act of 1985 as well as new legislation raising the debt ceiling above $2 trillion.

The following July the Supreme Court nullified that part of Gramm-Rudman-Hollings which allowed the General Accounting Office (GAO) to participate in decision making. The high court in *Bowsher v. Synar* (1986) argued that, by giving a deficit-reduction role to an agency of Congress (the GAO, headed by the comptroller general), the statute denied the president direct control over the automatic across-the-board spending cuts. The entire deficit-reduction timetable was put in jeopardy. Democrats feared giving any more authority to the Reagan administration, and this legislative stalemate continued into the next year. Not until late September 1987 did Congress enact and President Reagan sign revised legislation (known as Gramm-Rudman II), which delegated authority entirely to the OMB to order those automatic spending cuts. The date for a balanced budget was postponed two years, until 1993.

The deficit-reduction targets under Gramm-Rudman I (1985) and Gramm-Rudman II were never met, and no balanced budget was achieved by the time Bill Clinton was inaugurated president. Gramm-Rudman-Hollings was a noble experiment in forced government austerity which, although its objective was not accomplished, helped to slow the growth of federal spending over this period. The passage of such a radically new approach to federal budgeting was due in large measure to the sense of political *crisis* attributable to the ongoing deadlock over the FY86 budget, the approaching debt ceiling, plus the threat of a government shutdown.

Yet another political calculus affected budgetary politics under President Clinton after the Republicans took control of both houses of the 104th Congress. The legislative-executive budget confrontations in 1995–1996 resulted in Clinton's first use of the veto since taking office. In June 1995 he vetoed a Republican spending cut measure[23] that began months of gridlock between the Republican Congress and the Democratic administration where neither would relent.[24] Federal workers in so-called nonessential governmental services were furloughed as 1995 ended and 1996 began,[25] and the federal government operated many months on temporary spending bills.

Opinion polls showed, however, that the public did not blame President Clinton as much as the congressional Republicans for the budget stalemate, which emboldened Clinton to warn the GOP leadership not to send him appropriations bills with "poison pills" riders—amendments that would force him to reverse his policy priorities, such as ending Medicaid coverage for poor children.[26] Finally, by April 1996—in the midst of an election year when both sides were becoming worried about a voter backlash—the president and Congress ended their seven-month budget confrontation. In that period there had been fourteen partial spending bills and two shutdowns of the federal government—the longest shutdowns in history—that affected not only the furloughed federal workers but also the programs administered by those employees.[27]

Budgeting is an annual ritual between Congress and the president and, although there may be intense partisan conflict during periods of divided government, most observers would assess those episodes as politics as usual rather than any political crisis. To have the crisis factor impact the budgeting process is rare, but the prolonged deadlock between the Senate and White House GOP versus the House Democrats over the FY86 budget indicated to many people that a dangerous impasse had gripped the political system, and there was a window of opportunity for policy entrepreneurs in the Senate to propose radical reforms of the budgeting process.

SUMMARY

Today the OMB formulates an executive budget because Congress granted the president that authority in the Budget and Accounting Act of 1921, but the Constitution requires all funds to be appropriated by an act of Congress. Because both branches have budgeting authority, there is a decision-making process within and between the executive and legislative branches. Preparing the executive budget is a relatively straightforward affair, but the "congressional budget" process that the 1974 Congressional Budget and Impoundment Control Act created was amended by the 1985 Gramm-Rudman-Hollings legislation and by the 1990 Budget Enforcement Act.

The institutional rivalries are exaggerated when divided government exists because public inputs send mixed messages to our political leadership. Americans want government frugality in the abstract but resist cutbacks in domestic programs, particularly such sacred cows as Social Security and Medicare. By electing Republicans and Democrats, American voters assure partisan conflict because fundamentally the parties represent different political constituencies. Democrats want to defend social-welfare programs for their less affluent supporters and Republicans champion tax cuts and less spending, goals their middle-class constituents appreciate. The White House and Congress can marshal expertise via the OMB and CBO to defend their economic assumptions and budgetary priorities. No longer can the president—as Reagan did in 1981—dominate the technical debate by manipulating the economic and budgetary statistics because the CBO has become a highly regarded rival to the OMB. Finally, *crisis* is not relevant to most budget conflicts, although we argue that passage of Gramm-Rudman-Hollings in 1985 resulted from a legislative impasse that seemed worse than most and threatened to shut down the entire federal government.

NOTES

1. Alan Schick, *Congress and Money* (Washington, DC: The Urban Institute, 1980), p. 17.
2. Howard E. Shuman, *Politics and the Budget: The Struggle between the President and Congress*, 3rd ed. (Englewood Cliffs, NJ: Prentice-Hall, 1992), pp. 212–214.
3. Ibid., p. 214.
4. See Aaron Wildavsky, *The New Politics of the Budgetary Process* (Glenview, IL: Scott, Foresman, 1988).

5. Richard F. Fenno, Jr., *The Power of the Purse* (Boston: Little, Brown, 1966), pp. 162–163.

6. Wildavsky, *The New Politics of the Budgetary Process*, pp. 136–138.

7. William Greider, "The Education of David Stockman," *Atlantic Monthly* (December, 1981), p. 27.

8. Congressional Budget Office, Appendix A, "Evaluating CBO's Record of Economic Forecasts," *The Economic and Budget Outlook: An Update* (Washington, DC: Congressional Budget Office, 1993).

9. John Frendreis and Raymond Tatalovich, "The Use (and Abuse) of Macroeconomic Forecasting by Presidential Administrations: A Comparative Analysis," paper presented to the 1996 annual meeting of the American Political Science Association, San Francisco, CA.

10. Donald F. Kettl, *Deficit Politics: Public Budgeting in Its Institutional and Historical Context* (New York: Macmillan, 1992), pp. 111–112.

11. See Steven Greenhouse, "Wider U.S. Deficits Are Now Forecast for the Mid-1990's," *New York Times* (March 23, 1992), p. A1.

12. See "Congress Report Says Antimissile Defense Would Cost $37B," *Boston Globe* (May 28, 1992), p. 4.

13. Frendreis and Tatalovich, *The Modern Presidency and Economic Policy*, p. 231.

14. Ibid., p. 233.

15. Lloyd A. Free and Hadley Cantril, *The Political Beliefs of Americans* (New York: Simon & Schuster, 1968), chap. 3.

16. See Francis X. Clines, "Reagan Has His Eye on Congress and the Calendar," *New York Times* (May 12, 1985), p. E1; Jonathan Fuerbringer, "Reagan to Submit Budget for 1986 to Congress Today," *New York Times* (Feb. 4, 1985), pp. 1, 10–11.

17. See David Rogers and Jane Mayer, "Plan to End Social Security Rises for '86 Dropped by Reagan, Leaders of Congress," *Wall Street Journal* (July 10, 1985), p. 2.

18. James A. Thurber, "New Powers of the Purse: An Assessment of Congressional Budget Reform," in Leroy N. Rieselbach, ed., *Legislative Reform* (Lexington, MA: Lexington Books, 1978), p. 168.

19. Darrell M. West, *Congress and Economic Policy Making* (Pittsburgh: University of Pittsburgh Press, 1987), pp. 80–81.

20. See the excellent essays by Norman J. Ornstein; Allen Schick; Stephen J. Wayne; and I.M. Destler in Norman J. Ornstein, ed., *President and Congress: Assessing Reagan's First Year* (Washington, DC: American Enterprise Institute for Public Policy Research, 1982).

21. See Jonathan Fuerbringer, "Plan to Balance U.S. Budget by '91 Delayed in Senate," *New York Times* (Oct. 5, 1985), pp. 1, 7. Quote on p. 1.

22. See Gerald M. Boyd, "Reagan Aides Prod Congress on Debt," *New York Times* (Oct. 31, 1985), p. 16.

23. "Clinton Exercises His First Veto on Spending-Cuts Bill," *Salt Lake Tribune* (June 8, 1995), p. A1.

24. See "For Congress and Clinton Dead Ends at Every Turn," *New York Times* (Dec. 22, 1995), pp. A1, A36.

25. Helen Dewar and Stephen Barr, "Congress Still Split on Furlough Plans; Budget Negotiations to Resume," *Washington Post* (Jan. 1, 1996), p. A1.

26. See "Remarks on the Legislative Agenda and an Exchange with Reporters," *Public Papers of the President* (May 8, 1996).

27. George Hager, "Budget: Congress, Clinton Yield Enough to Close the Book on Fiscal '96," *Congressional Quarterly Weekly Report* (April 27, 1996), p. 1155.

17

Conclusion

The best insights on presidential leadership, we have argued, are gained by asking these five specific questions about five presidential roles:

- How much *legal authority* is available to the president in this role?

- How many other *decision-makers* participate with the president in this role?

- Are *public inputs*—popular opinion and organized interests—deferential to presidential leadership or mobilized against him in this role?

- Can the president monopolize policy *expertise* and prevent outsiders from getting access to that information in this role?

- What is the likelihood that *crisis* will rally the nation around presidential leadership in this role?

Unlike most other textbooks on the presidency that approach it by topics, we have discussed presidential leadership systematically, in terms of one analytical model or framework. By asking these questions about each presidential role, our objective has been to explain the legal and political resources that shaped the prospects for presidential leadership and success.

Our approach also resolves the intellectual debate between two famous presidency scholars, the late Edward Corwin[1], who emphasized legal authority, and Richard Neustadt[2], whose legendary work stressed personal influence (see especially chapter 3). Each was correct regarding certain of the presidential roles, but each failed to explain power in all the roles.

The power of the commander in chief and chief diplomat is best understood by looking at the formal, legal authority that is available to the president. The subtle uses of political persuasion are essential to exerting presidential leadership in the roles of chief executive, legislative leader, and opinion/party leader. As the formal authority available to a president is lessened, presidents must necessarily draw on informal and personal resources to achieve policy objectives. In the executive, legislative, and opinion/party arenas, the Constitution, statutes, judicial precedent, and customary practice have only marginally routinized power in those roles, which is why each incumbent must begin anew to create his power base.

Thus presidential power is a complex and elusive phenomenon, not amenable to simple or one-dimensional explanations. By thinking about the existence or absence of legal authority, the decision-makers who are participants with the president, the deferential nature of public inputs whether popular opinion or organized interests, the extent to which expertise is monopolized by the White House and secrecy assured, and the likelihood that genuine crisis may occur, analysis of presidential power using our approach is more inclusive of the range of factors that support or undermine presidential leadership. Simply put, we have argued that presidential leadership depends on the role(s) in which the president is operating: war-making, diplomacy, administration and policy implementation, legislation, or opinion and party leadership.

It was once commonplace to conclude a text on the presidency with a wish list of reform recommendations. We do not because these so-called reforms typically reflected the normative bias of scholars who had an ideological agenda to promote (chapter 2), notably from the era of the idealized, or heroic presidency. Consider three kinds of reforms that influenced presidency watchers in the past and why they are irrelevant in today's era of the inflated presidency. First, some reforms argued the *electoral college* is an historical anachronism that denies the president a true democratic mandate. Second, other reforms urged the people and the media to be more alert to aberrant personality types and thus look to *character* when making their electoral choice for president. Third, yet another set of reforms that remains attractive to certain observers was aimed at subverting the separation of powers system by strengthening *party* and changing the U.S. election process into a kind of parliamentary regime. Implicit in all three reform packages was the assumption that the only progressive and enlightened force in American politics emanated from the White House.

There is an age-old proverb: if it isn't broken, don't fix it. As already indicated (chapter 4), there was a time when an academic college industry developed around the goal of improving on the electoral college by somehow making sure the winning presidential candidate has a mandate to govern. The electoral college has not failed since 1824 (the mishap in 1876 occurred because there was political infighting among certain states of the South that were readmitted to the Union). Once scholars worried about the remote possibility that the electoral college loser could be the popular vote winner, but 1888 was the last time that happened. The more common occurrence in the post–World War II era has been the election of presidents with only a plurality of the popular vote, although they won the majority—and usually a large majority—of the electoral votes.

In other words, the electoral college seems to have made legitimate the election of presidents with no popular vote mandates. Consider Clinton's double victories in 1992 and 1996, Kennedy in 1960, Nixon in 1968, and Carter in 1976. Indeed, newspaper headlines in 1996 proclaimed that Clinton won an electoral college "landslide" over Robert Dole even though Clinton wanted to get a majority of the popular vote and campaigned vigorously in the campaign's final weeks. Simply no evidence indicates that the size of the popular vote or the size of the electoral college vote has any bearing on presidential leadership. What matters is how the election is interpreted on Election Day by the media elites and political pundits. The tendency is to showcase the election as a legitimate exercise in democracy. Whatever shows majority support—either electoral votes or popular votes—is emphasized when the postelection analysis takes place. Thus it would appear that until the electoral college fails to deliver such a "winner"—in the event that minor presidential candidates or third parties become serious contenders—it will no longer be of much interest to us, having lost its earlier fascination.

No student of the presidency can be entirely sanguine about voters *not* electing the wrong person at the wrong time to be president. Even now textbook writers are concerned about the misuse or abuse of presidential power. Those who are struck by how the right man emerged to assume the White House during periods of crisis—Washington at the Founding, Lincoln during the Civil War, Franklin Roosevelt in the midst of Depression and World War II—have yet to explain exactly how the political system "knew" enough to elect those giants among politicians. Similarly, those who raised the alarm about "character" and the need to find "democratic" or "healthy" personality types[3] were overreacting to Lyndon Johnson and Richard Nixon when, in point of fact, President Johnson, in assuming office after Kennedy's assassination, was deemed a consensus leader who pointed the nation in the right direction.

Even though textbook authors feel obliged to talk about the healthy "active positive" and the dangerous "active negative" presidents, the Barber typology (see chapter 2) has not promoted many other scholars to pursue psychoanalytical research on presidents, nor has it encouraged the media elites to shift their attention to character concerns. Although the character of Bill Clinton, who has been typed as another active-positive[4] (along with Ford, Carter, and Bush), became a campaign issue, the journalistic accounts hardly focused on his upbringing to predict his level of self-confidence and ego esteem. Rather, Clinton's character was judged by commonsense standards of marital fidelity, truthfulness, and integrity, and his character has remained a viable issue judged by these same criteria despite his election and reelection.

Even assuming the active-negative personality might be dangerous during times of crisis, it is not so much the incumbent as the transformation within the political system that allows any president, healthy or otherwise, too much discretion. Crisis, we have shown, expands the scope of presidential power because Congress capitulates, the public becomes deferential, and the news media, for lack of information, is unable to hold the White House accountable. In other words, despite the separation of powers principle designed by Madison and the Framers to preclude executive tyranny, the constitutional and political dangers posed by crises—mainly those involving armed forces—result because the *external* institutional checks on presidential authority break down. Nobody then or now presumes that a crisis would seriously undermine the executive-legislative relationship in lawmaking or that the president could dangerously politicize the federal bureaucracy. What worried the commentators was a commander in chief too quick to act in an era of rapid-response warfare and the threat of nuclear destruction.

Perhaps we should breathe easier today, with the end of the Cold War and the advent of the postmodern presidency.[5] If future presidents are not burdened with having to assure military parity if not superiority in a world with two superpowers, the collapse of the Soviet Union as a military threat promises a measure of security from the danger of nuclear conflict. At the same time the United States is no longer the dominant economic power it was at the end of World War II, and presidents now must contend with the heads of a reunified Germany and Japan as coequals in the international marketplace. The rise of the postmodern presidency does not negate his constitutional and political advantages within the U.S. political system to formulate national security policy, although those domestic advantages do not extend to a president's negotiating position with other nations.

Political scientists are beginning to accept the presidency in a separated system as virtuous because of an appreciation of what the Framers intended to accomplish, and why they did so, which may serve to heighten the awareness that checks and balances ought not to be so easily abandoned during times of crisis. Thus the cure for a President Clinton—or any president who threatens an imperial action—who argues that he alone has the power to commit U.S. troops to an international peacekeeping force in Bosnia, is not to dissect the inner meaning of personality at the expense of character or integrity, but to bolster the workings of the separation of powers system so the entire process is not subverted every time a president claims a crisis and threatens military action for whatever reason.

It was (and remains in some quarters) standard fare to argue that the electoral system should be reformed to ensure that the president could act as the leader of his party. Together with his congressional allies, according to this viewpoint, presidents ought to campaign on the party platform in order to win office with an explicit mandate for legislative action. These reforms would have strengthened the national party organization at the expense of state parties and, most importantly, changed the two-year congressional term to run concurrently with the presidential four-year term. This package of reforms was predicated on two assumptions that are now considered suspect: unified party control of both branches is essential to governing, and the presidential mandate ought to guide congressional deliberations.

Both of these suppositions are throwbacks to the idealized or heroic presidency (chapter 2) that mainly liberal Democratic scholars had promoted during the era of Roosevelt, Truman, and Kennedy. Its high point came when such so-called party reforms were endorsed in 1950 by a committee of the American Political Science Association.[6] Although that report provoked dissent within the profession which has since diminished, its argument resurfaced during the bicentennial commemoration of the Constitution.[7] Likely its foremost advocate today is James L. Sundquist, who believes that "[t]he midterm election cannot result in a clearly defined change in governmental direction. . . . All it can do is deadlock the government."[8]

Underlying all three reform packages was an article of faith among scholars who upheld the idealized presidency, namely that the president (certainly Democratic presidents) would promote a liberal domestic agenda and an enlightened internationalist foreign policy. Therefore the White House had to be strengthened against the forces of conservatism, localism, and ethnocentrism that dominated the Congress. Presidency scholar Robert J. Spitzer agrees that this argument "springs more from ideology and partisanship" because "[l]iberals advocated a stronger presidency during the Roosevelt-Truman-Kennedy-Johnson era in large measure because these liberal Democratic presidents were attempting to enact a progressive agenda through Congresses that were often resistant."[9]

Obviously that interpretation made no sense after 1986 when a liberal Democratic Congress resisted the avowedly conservative policy agenda of Presidents Reagan and Bush. Indeed, once the conservatives took over the White House in 1981, a curious about-face in this intellectual debate occurred. Now it was the political right, not the political left, that argued the presidency was under siege by an "imperial" Congress.[10] The irony of this role reversal did not affect those liberals who remain enamored with the idealized presidency, but the obvious contradiction prompted Robert Spitzer to chide his ideologically committed colleagues for playing fast and loose with constitutional principles:

> Liberal-conservative clashes over politics and policy are the legitimate stuff of American politics, but when that debate is cast in abstract, institutional terms involving the possibility of structural shifts between the branches of government, partisan motives must be identified and reconciled with the consequences of proposed changes. (After all, only a fool changes the rules of the game because of losing a contest or two.)[11]

In summary, presidential scholarship has passed through six normative eras: the intended, imperiled, idealized, imperial, impotent, and now the inflated presidency (chapter 2). The precepts of an inflated presidency obviously influence us just as the aspirations for an idealized presidency mobilized an earlier generation of political scientists.

Serious students of the presidency have now come full circle: the inflated presidency has renewed our respect for the intended presidency as crafted by the Framers of the Constitution. What caused this latest normative shift among intellectuals? Most important was the recognition that divided government is the normal political condition of the national government.

The institutional separation of powers now is coupled with an ideological and partisan divide between the executive and legislative branches. Divided government has characterized all but six years in the three decades since Nixon was elected in 1968. It seems a bit utopian if not surrealistic to keep focusing on the benefits of unified government when the voters think otherwise.[12] Because Congress exists and cannot be ignored or dominated by the White House, a wiser course of action would be for presidents to find ways of governing through a system of divided and separated powers.

In the abstract, this challenge may seem formidable; in reality, the revisionists have verified empirically that divided government can be productive government.[13] Total deadlock or stalemate is still the exception—the confrontation between Clinton and the Republican 104th Congress over the FY96 budget is the most recent example at this writing. Yet that dispute, when viewed from a longer perspective, undoubtedly helped moderate both sides and encouraged President Clinton and the Republican leadership of the 105th Congress to attempt a bipartisan approach to the problem of balancing the budget by the year 2002.

Having laid to rest any fears of divided government, the inflated presidency thesis is more concerned that presidential rhetoric is the cause for the malaise, disillusionment, and mistrust felt by many Americans for their institutions of government. Presidents simply oversell their ability to solve problems—whether Reagan's false hope to balance the budget in four years or Clinton's empty plea—because he asked for no federal funding—for uniforms for all elementary school students. The "rhetorical presidency"[14] is a fundamental departure from what the Framers intended. Although Americans cannot return to the eighteenth century, they can begin to reeducate themselves and downsize their expectations about presidential leadership.

Rhetorical overkill can have dysfunctional if not dangerous consequences for democratic governance. Theodore Lowi warned that presidents are now judged by the services they deliver rather than by traditional standards of accountability or representation.[15] Because service delivery is a more precise criteria for political judgment, presidents who fail to match performance with their promises—as they inevitably do—cannot help but promote a self-fulfilling prophecy which affirms to citizens that their suspicions about politicians are not unfounded.

The spirit of this conclusion is our collective hope that presidency scholars can keep separate their empirical analyses and their normative judgments. Using the analytical model of this book, we feel, is one way to focus our energies on understanding the modern presidency and the hopes and limitations of presidential leadership rather than clamoring for constitutional reforms to achieve political perfection.

NOTES

1. Edward S. Corwin,*The President: Office and Powers* (New York: New York University Press, 1957).

2. Richard E. Neustadt, *Presidential Power: The Politics of Leadership* (New York: New American Libary (Signet), 1964).

3. See Erwin C. Hargrove, *Presidential Leadership* (New York: Macmillan, 1966); James David Barber, *The Presidential Character* (Englewood Cliffs, NJ: Prentice-Hall, 1973); Erwin C. Hargrove, *The Power of the Modern Presidency* (New York: Knopf, 1974).

4. Norman C. Thomas and Joseph A. Pika, *The Politics of the Presidency*, 4th ed. (Washington, DC: CQ Press, 1996), p. 164.

5. Richard Rose, *The Postmodern President: The White House Meets the World* (Chatham, NJ: Chatham House, 1991).

6. Committee on Responsible Parties; American Political Science Association, *Toward a More Responsible Two-Party System* (New York: Rinehart, 1950).

7. Committee on the Constitutional System, *A Bicentennial Analysis of the American Political Structure* (Washington, DC: January 1987), pp. 10–11.

8. James L. Sundquist, *Constitutional Reform and Effective Government* (Washington, D.C.: The Brookings Institution, 1986), p. 115; also see James L. Sundquist, "Needed: A Political Theory for the New Era of Coalition Government in the United States," *Political Science Quarterly*, 103 (Winter 1988), pp. 613–635.

9. Robert J. Spitzer, *President & Congress: Executive Hegemony at the Crossroads of American Government* (New York: McGraw-Hill, 1993), pp. 251–252.

10. See L. Gordon Grovitz and Jeremy A. Rabkin, eds., *The Fettered Presidency* (Washington, DC: American Enterprise Institute, 1989); Gordon S. Jones and John A. Marini, eds., *The Imperial Congress* (New York: Pharos, 1988).

11. Spitzer, *President & Congress*, p. 252.

12. Morris Fiorina, *Divided Government*, 2nd ed. (Boston: Allyn & Bacon, 1996).

13. See David R. Mayhew, *Divided We Govern* (New Haven, CT: Yale University Press, 1991); Charles O. Jones, *The Presidency in a Separated System* (Washington, DC: The Brookings Institution, 1994).

14. Jeffrey Tulis, *The Rhetorical Presidency* (Princeton, NJ: Princeton University Press, 1987).

15. See Theodore J. Lowi, *The Personal President* (Ithaca, NY: Cornell University Press, 1985).

Appendix 1: Congressional/Executive Interaction on Major Foreign Military Decision, 1962–1996

Decision	Congressional Involvement	Initiator	Predominant Influence	Resolution/ Legislation	Violence or Threat of Violence	Decision Time
Cuban missile crisis, 1962	low	Exec.	Exec.	yes	yes	short
Limited test-ban treaty, 1963	high	Exec.	Exec.	yes	no	long
Gulf of Tonkin Resolution, 1964	high	Exec.	Exec.	yes	yes	short
Dominican intervention, 1965	none	Exec.	Exec.	no	yes	short
First Hanoi bombing, 1966	none	Exec.	Exec.	no	yes	long
Vietnam peace talks begin, 1968	high	Exec.	Exec.	no	yes	long
U.S. troops into Cambodia, 1970	none	Exec.	Exec.	no	yes	long
SALT I, 1972	high	Exec.	Exec.	yes	no	long
U.S.-USSR wheat sale, 1972	low	Exec.	Exec.	no	no	long
Vietnam involvement ended, 1973	high	Cong.	Cong.	yes	yes	long
Military aid cutoff to Turkey, 1974	high	Cong.	Cong.	yes	no	long
Vladivostok Accord, 1974	none	Exec.	Exec.	no	no	short
Mayaguez incident, 1975	none	Exec.	Exec.	no	yes	short
Panama Canal Treaty, 1978	high	Exec.	Exec.	yes	no	long
Camp David Accord, 1978	none	Exec.	Exec.	no	no	long
SALT II, 1980	high	Exec.	Cong.	no	no	long
Iran hostage rescue, 1980	none	Exec.	Exec.	no	yes	long
U.S. AWAC sale to Saudi Arabia, 1981	high	Exec.	Exec.	no	no	long
U.S. marines enter Lebanon, 1982	high	Exec.	Exec.	yes	yes	long
U.S. invades Grenada, 1983	low	Exec.	Exec.	no	yes	short
Aid to Afghanistan rebels, 1984	high	Cong.	Cong.	yes	no	long
United States shells Syrian strongholds from Beirut, 1984	low	Exec.	Exec.	no	yes	long
Marines withdrawn from Lebanon, 1984	high	Exec.	Cong.	no	no	long
Sanctions imposed against South Africa, 1985	high	Cong.	Cong.	yes	no	long

(continued)

Appendix 1 (*continued*)

Decision	Congressional Involvement	Initiator	Predominant Influence	Resolution/ Legislation	Violence or Threat of Violence	Decision Time
Sanctions imposed against Phillippines, 1985	high	Exec.	Exec.	no	no	short
U.S. planes bomb Lybia, 1986	low	Exec.	Exec.	no	yes	long
Sanctions imposed against Angola, 1986	high	Exec.	Cong.	yes	no	short
NARCO conflict, 1986	high	Cong.	Cong.	yes	yes	long
Sanctions imposed against Haiti, 1986	high	Cong.	Cong.	yes	no	long
U.S. Navy escorts tankers in Persian Gulf, 1987	high	Exec.	Exec.	yes	yes	short
Marines invade Panama, 1989	high	Exec.	Exec.	yes	yes	long
U.S. Troops enter Kuwait, 1990	high	Exec.	Exec.	yes	yes	long
U.S. Troops enter Somalia, 1992	low	Exec.	Exec.	yes	yes	short
Sanctions imposed against Haiti, 1993	low	Exec.	Exec.	yes	yes	short
U.S. Troops withdrawn from Somalia, 1993	high	Exec.	Exec.	yes	yes	long
United States shells Iraqi intelligence building, 1993	low	Exec.	Exec.	no	yes	short
U.S. planes down Serbian planes over Bosnia, 1994	low	Exec.	Exec.	no	yes	short
Military intervention Rwanda, 1994	high	Exec.	Exec.	yes	yes	long
Military intervention Haiti, 1994	high	Exec.	Exec.	yes	yes	long
U.S. marines Return to Somalia, 1995	low	Exec.	Exec.	no	yes	long
Ground troops in Bosnia, 1995–1996	high	Exec.	Exec.	yes	yes	long

Appendix 2: Undeclared Hostilities in Which U.S. Troops Have Been Committed Abroad to Conflict or Potential Conflict, by President, 1789–1994

President	Conflicts	Number
Washington (1789–1797)	None	0
Adams, J. (1797–1801)	• Naval conflicts with France—1798	1
Jefferson (1801–1809)	• Tripoli—1801 • Mexico (Spanish Territory)—1806 • Gulf of Mexico—1806	3
Madison* (1809–1817)	• W. Florida—1810 • Amelia Isl. and E. Florida—1812 • W. Florida—1813 • Marquesas Isl.—1813 • Caribbean—1814 • Spanish Florida—1814 • Second Barbary War—1815 • Tripoli—1815 • Spanish Florida—1816 • First Seminole War—1816	10
Monroe (1817–1825)	• Amelia Isl.—1817 • Oregon—1818 • West Africa—1820 • Cuba—1822 • Cuba—1823 • Cuba—1824 • Puerto Rico—1824	7
Adams, J.Q. (1825–1829)	• Cuba—1825 • Greece—1827 • W. Indies—1828	3
Jackson (1829–1837)	• Haiti—1830 • Falkland Isl.—1831 • Sumatra—1832 • Argentina—1833 • Peru—1835 • Samoa—1835 • Mexico—1836	7
Van Buren (1837–1841)	• Mexico—1837 • Sumatra—1838 • Fiji—1840	3

Appendix 2 *(continued)*

President	Conflicts	Number
Harrison, W. H.[†] (1841)	None	0
Tyler, J. (1841–1845)	• Drummond Isl.—1841 • Samoa—1841 • Mexico—1842 • China—1843 • Africa—1843 • Mexico—1844 • China—1844	7
Polk* (1845–1849)	• African Coast—1845	1
Taylor[†] (1849–1850)	• Smyrna—1849 • Africa—1850	2
Fillmore (1850–1853)	• Turkey—1851 • Johanns Isl—1851 • Argentina—1852	3
Pierce (1853–1857)	• Nicaragua—1853 • Japan—1853 • Ryukyu and Bonin Isl.—1853 • Smyrna—1853 • China—1854 • Nicaragua—1854 • W. Coast Africa—1854 • Okinawa—1854 • China—1855 • Fiji—1855 • Uruguay—1855 • Panama—1856 • China—1856	13
Buchanan (1857–1861)	• Nicaragua—1857 • Uruguay—1858 • Turkey—1858 • Fiji—1858 • African Coast—1858 • Cuban Waters—1858 • Mexico—1859 • China—1859 • African Coast—1859 • Paraguay—1859 • Angola—1860 • Columbia—1860 • Kissembo—1860	13

Appendix 2 *(continued)*

President	Conflicts	Number
Lincoln† (1861–1865)	• Japan—1863 • Japan—1864 • Japan—1864	3
Johnson, A. (1865–1869)	• Panama—1865 • Mexico—1866 • China—1866 • Nicaragua—1867 • Formosa—1867 • Japan—1868 • Uruguay—1868 • Columbia—1868	8
Grant (1869–1877)	• Dominican Republic—1869 • Mexico—1870 • Hawaiian Isl.—1870 • Korea—1871 • Columbia—1873 • Cuban waters—1873 • Mexico—1873 • Hawaiian Isl.—1874 • Mexico—1876	9
Hayes (1877–1881)	None	0
Garfield† (1881)	None	0
Arthur (1881–1885)	• Egypt—1882 • Panama—1885 (Jan.)	2
Cleveland (1885–1889)	• Panama—1885 (March, May) • Korea—1888 • Samoa—1888 • Haiti—1888	4
Harrison, B. (1889–1893)	• Hawaiian Isl.—1889 • Argentina—1890 • Haiti—1891 • Bering Straits—1891 • Chile—1891 • Hawaiian Isl.—1893	6
Cleveland (1893–1897)	• Brazil—1894 • Nicaragua—1894 • Korea—1894 • China—1894	8

Appendix 2 (*continued*)

President	Conflicts	Number
	• China—1895	
	• Korea—1895	
	• Columbia—1895	
	• Nicaragua—1896	
McKinley[†] (1897–1901)		
	• Nicaragua—1898	
	• China—1898	
	• Nicaragua—1899	
	• Samoa—1899	7
	• Philippine Isl.—1899	
	• Boxer Rebellion—1900	
	• China—1900	
Roosevelt, T. (1901–1909)		
	• Panama—1901	
	• Columbia—1902	
	• Panama—1902	
	• Honduras—1903	
	• Dominican Republic—1903	
	• Syria—1903	
	• Panama—1903	
	• Abyssinia—1903	16
	• Dominican Republic—1904	
	• Morocco—1904	
	• Panama—1904	
	• Korea—1904	
	• Korea—1904	
	• Dominican Republic—1905	
	• Cuba—1906	
	• Honduras—1907	
Taft (1909–1913)		
	• Nicaragua—1910	
	• Honduras—1911	
	• China—1911	
	• Honduras—1912	
	• Panama—1912	9
	• Cuba—1912	
	• China—1912	
	• Turkey—1912	
	• Nicaragua—1912	
Wilson* (1913–1921)		
	• Mexico—1913	
	• China—1913	
	• Haiti—1914	
	• Dominican Republic—1914	21
	• Mexico—1914	
	• Haiti—1915	
	• Dominican Republic—1915	
	• China—1916	
	• Dominican Republic—1916	

Appendix 2 *(continued)*

President	Conflicts	Number
	• China—1917	
	• Cuba—1917	
	• Armed Atlantic merchant ships—1917	
	• Mexico—1918	
	• Panama—1918	
	• Soviet Russia—1918	
	• Dalmatia—1919	
	• Turkey—1919	
	• Honduras—1919	
	• China—1920	
	• Guatemala—1920	
	• Siberia—1920	
Harding[†] (1921–1923)	• Panama-Costa Rica—1921 • Turkey—1922 • China—1922	3
Coolidge (1923–1929)	• Honduras—1924 • China—1924 • Panama—1925 • China—1925 • Honduras—1925 • China—1926 • Nicaragua—1926 • China—1927	8
Hoover (1929–1933)	• China—1932	1
F.D. Roosevelt[*†] (1933–1945)	• Cuba—1933 • China—1934 • Spain—1936 • China—1937–1938 • British possessions in Western Atlantic—1940 • Greenland—1941 • Dutch Guiana—1941 • Iceland—1941 • Germany—1941	9
Truman (1945–1953)	• China—1945 • Vietnam—1945 • Trieste—1946 • Turkey—1946 • Greece—1946 • Palestine—1948 • Mediterranean—1948 • China—1948–1949 • Korea—1950 • Formosa (Taiwan)—1950	10

Appendix 2 *(continued)*

President	Conflicts	Number
Eisenhower (1953–1961)	• Korea—1953 • Tachen Islands (China)—1954–1955 • Vietnam—1955–1960 • Egypt—1956 • Indonesia—1956 • Taiwan—1957 • Venezuela—1958 • Indonesia—1958 • Lebanon—1958 • The Caribbean—1959–1960	10
Kennedy† (1961–1963)	• Dominican Republic—1961 • Vietnam—1961–1963 • Cuba—1962 • Thailand—1962 • Laos—1962 • Haiti—1963	6
Johnson, L. (1963–1969)	• Vietnam—1963–1968 • Congo—1964 • Laos—1964 • Dominican Republic—1965 • Syrian Coast—1967 • Congo—1967	6
R. Nixon‡ (1969–1974)	• Vietnam—1969–1973 • Jordanian-Syrian crisis—1970 • Cambodia—1970	3
Ford (1974–1977)	• Cyprus (evacuation)—1974 • Vietnam (evacuation)—1975 • Cambodia (evacuation)—1975 • South Vietnam—1975 • *Mayaquez* incident—1975 • Lebanon—1976 • Korea—1976	7
Carter (1977–1981)	• Zaire—1978 • Iran—1980	2
R. Reagan (1981–1989)	• El Salvador—1981 • Libya—1981 • Sinai—1982 • Lebanon—1982 • Egypt—1983 • Honduras—1983–1989 • Chad—1983 • Grenada—1983	17

Appendix 2 *(continued)*

President	Conflicts	Number
	• Lebanon—1983	
	• Persian Gulf—1984	
	• Italy—1985	
	• Libya—1986	
	• Gulf of Sidra—1986	
	• Bolivia—1986	
	• Persian Gulf—1987–1988	
	• Panama—1988	
	• Libya—1989	
Bush (1988–1992)	• Panama—1989	
	• Andean initiatives—1989	
	• Philippians—1989	5
	• Persian Gulf—1991	
	• Somalia—1992	
Clinton (1993–1995)	• Somalia—1993	
	• Haiti—1993	6
	• Iraq—1993	
	• Bosnia—1994	
	• Rwanda—1994	
	• Bosnia—1995	

Total Number: 249

*These presidents were also involved in "declared wars."

†These presidents died while in office.

‡Resigned from office.

Sources: "Instances of Use of United States Armed Forces Abroad, 1798–1989," *Congressional Record—Senate* 137(1), 102nd Congress, 1st Session (Jan. 3, 1991), pp. S14–S19; "War without Declaration," *Congressional Record-Senate* 119, part 20, 93rd Congress, 1st Session (July 20, 1973), pp. 25066–25077; and the Reagan conflicts came from Amicus Brief of Cong. Howard Berman, for *Lowry v. Reagan*, U.S. District Court (DC), civil action no. 87–2196, in "The War Power after 200 Years: Congress and the President at a Constitutional Impasse," *Hearings before the Special Subcommittee on War Powers of the Committee on Foreign Relations*, U.S. Senate, 100th Congress, 1st Session (July 13, 14, August 5, September 7, 15, 16, 20, 23, and 29, 1988), pp. 1004–1005; "Chronology of the Year's Events," *World Almanac and Book of Facts 1994*, (NJ: Funk and Wagnalls), pp. 44–64 and 73–76.

Author Index

Subject Index

DATE DUE

Demco, Inc. 38-293